COMMUNITY AND CONSENSUS
IN ISLAM

A list of the books in the series will be found at the end of the volume.

COMMUNITY AND CONSENSUS IN ISLAM

Muslim Representation in Colonial India, 1860–1947

FARZANA SHAIKH

Clare Hall, Cambridge

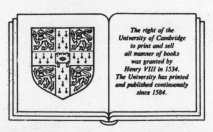

The right of the
University of Cambridge
to print and sell
all manner of books
was granted by
Henry VIII in 1534.
The University has printed
and published continuously
since 1584.

CAMBRIDGE UNIVERSITY PRESS

CAMBRIDGE

NEW YORK   NEW ROCHELLE   MELBOURNE   SYDNEY

In association with
Orient Longman

ORIENT LONGMAN LIMITED

Registered Office
3-6-272 Himayatnagar, Hyderabad 500 029

Other Offices
Kamani Marg, Ballard Estate, Bombay 400 038
17 Chittaranjan Avenue, Calcutta 700 072
160 Anna Salai, Madras 600 002
1/24 Asaf Ali Road, New Delhi 110 002
80/1 Mahatma Gandhi Road, Bangalore 560 001
3-6-272 Himayatnagar, Hyderabad 500 029
Birla Mandir Road, Patna 800 004
Patiala House, 16-A Ashok Marg, Lucknow 226 001
S.C. Goswami Road, Panbazar, Guwahati 781 001

© Cambridge University Press 1989
ISBN 0 521 36328 4
First Published 1989

First published in India 1991
OLBN 0 00210 025 8

Published by Orient Longman Limited
Kamani Marg, Ballard Estate, Bombay 400 038

Printed in India at Bindu Art, Bombay 400 013

To the memory of my father

CONTENTS

ACKNOWLEDGEMENTS

One question, above all, dominated my approach to this study. How could I, a Muslim by birth, confront the contradictions of a faith the perfection of which is deemed by its followers to be self-evident and the historical vindication of which they are rarely inclined to question.

The endeavour was considerable. Without the confidence and exceptional support of some, despair might well have led me to abandon the project. My greatest intellectual debt is to Francis Robinson whose kindness was matched only by the breadth of his understanding and grasp of the issues that concerned me. To Philip Oldenburg, friend and teacher, I owe my determination to flout the rigid (and often senseless) boundaries between political science and history in the certainty that neither could survive without the other.

To Patrick I owe, quite simply, the essentials. His belief in me and in the worth of this study, have been fundamental. Beyond this, I can only say that without his intellectual companionship and judgement, the fruit of my efforts would have been much the poorer.

Amongst the others who have lent both their support and professional help, I wish particularly to thank Bill Roff whose interest in my work was a great source of encouragement, and John Dunn, whose comments on parts of the manuscript account for the care with which some of the larger, more conceptual, issues have been addressed. I wish also to acknowledge the support of Ainslee Embree, Howard Wriggins, Stan Heginbotham, and Leonard Gordon.

No study of this kind can be attempted without substantial institutional help. I wish, in particular, to thank the Presidents (past and present) and Fellows of Clare Hall, Cambridge, for electing me into a Research Fellowship and for providing me with financial assistance.

I wish also to thank the staff of the India Office Library and Records in London, especially Mr Salim Quraishi, whose assistance with Urdu sources and their occasional translation was invaluable. The staff of the library of the Centre of South Asian Studies in Cambridge, as well as of the University Library, were at all times, most helpful. The Cambridge Smuts Fund enabled me to undertake additional research into Urdu sources.

My little boy, Emile, made much of this possible simply by being so good.

Finally, it remains for me to acknowledge the wisdom and the foresight of my father whose trust in me and my scholarship I could not, perhaps, wholly reward in his lifetime. In dedicating this study to his memory, I wish to pay tribute to his courage and to the tenacity with which he held by his convictions.

GLOSSARY

ahl al-kitāb	'People of the Book', especially Jews and Christians who are deemed by Muslims to have received revelation from God.
'ālim	(pl. *'ulamā'*), a person learned in Islamic law; sometimes used interchangeably with the word *muftī.*
amīr	a Muslim secular leader or military commander, see also *imārat.*
anjuman	a society or gathering.
ashrāf	(sing. *sharīf*), a term used to connote gentility among Indian Muslims who trace their ancestry to the prophet, Muhammad, his Companions or the historic Muslim ruling classes.
Baboo	originally a title of respect more common in Bengal that came later to be used by officials to describe and denigrate Western-educated Indians.
bay'a	a public acclamation of, and swearing allegiance to, a Muslim leader.
bid'a	innovation or deviation from traditional Muslim thinking and practice.
birādarī	lit. brotherhood, but used in the Indian context to suggest groups bound by lineage and kinship ties.
Burra Sāhib	lit. master; commonly used as an honorific affix for Europeans in British India.
dār al-harb	'abode of war', usually refers to a non-Islamic country.
dār al-Islām	the sphere of Islam or lands under Muslim rule.
dhimmī	non-Muslim citizen entitled to *dhimma,* or protection under a Pax Islamica instituted by ruling Muslims.
dīn	faith or religion.
durbār	a royal court or public levee.
faqīh	(pl. *fuqūhā'*), a Muslim jurist.
fatwā	(pl. *fatāwā*), a legal opinion delivered by a Muslim qualified to interpret Islamic law, namely, an *'ālim* or *muftī.*
fiqh	Islamic jurisprudence.
fitna	civil strife.
ghair muqallid	non-conformist, or one who does not abide by the *taqlīd,* or tradition, developed by one of the four established schools of Islamic law, namely, the Hanīfite, the Hanbalite, the Mālikite and the Shāfi'ite.

hadīth   the words of the prophet, Muhammad, as transmitted through a chain of verbal, authorised reports.

ʿibāda   (pl. *ʿibādāt*), worship, but more specifically, the code of conduct governing Muslim religious observance, including, prayer, pilgrimage, fasting and almsgiving.

ijmāʿ   the consensus of the community, but more often that of its learned men.

ijtihād   individual judgement exercised by one qualified to establish a legal opinion, namely a *mujtahid*.

imārat   (also amīrate), the province or sub-province over which the *amīr* administers authority, either partial or absolute.

jāhilīyya   the condition of ignorance usually applied by Muslims to refer to pre-Islamic Arabia.

jihād   struggle; used by Muslims to refer both to individual moral endeavour in the way of God as well as to collective warfare against non-Muslims.

jizya   a poll tax payable by protected non-Muslim minorities under Muslim rule.

kāfir   unbeliever.

khalīfa   (Eng. *caliph*), successor or deputy charged with representing God on earth through the institution of the *khilāfat* (Eng. *Caliphate*).

madrasa   a Muslim religious seminary.

maulānā   a title of respect reserved for Muslims reputed for their religious learning.

maulvī   a learned man.

millat   (Turkish, *millet*), a religious community which became synonymous under the Ottomans with autonomous non-Muslim groups.

mujtahid   a Muslim qualified to practise *ijtihād* or ascertain a rule of *Sharīʿa*.

mullah   Muslim religious preacher.

murīd   the disciple of a spiritual mentor or *pīr*.

panchāyat   a court of arbitration; usually a council of five.

pīr   spiritual mentor or guide having a number of followers.

purda   the practice of veiling women that has traditionally been more common to Muslims than non-Muslims on the Indian subcontinent.

qaum   lit. nation; a term used by *sharīf* Indian Muslims in the late nineteenth and twentieth centuries to suggest their distinct religious, racial and social ancestry.

qiyās   a mode of analogical reasoning used by Muslim jurists as an additional source of law after the Qurʾān, the *sunna* and *ijmāʿ*.

Quāʾid-i-Aʿzam   great leader, a title bestowed upon Muhammad ʿAlī Jinnah by his followers.

sajjadā nashīn   the successor to a *pīr*.

sayyid	descendant of the prophet, Muhammad.
Sharī'a	the totality of revealed Islamic law.
sharīf	(pl. *ashrāf*), a person distinguished by high birth.
Shī'as	Muslims belonging to a minority sect who believe that the right to succession and leadership of the Muslim community should rest with the descendants of 'Alī, the son-in-law of the prophet Muhammad.
shūrā	the practice of consultation in a Muslim polity.
siyāsa	politics, but used more generally to connote secular affairs.
sunna	the normative conduct of the prophet Muhammad and his early Companions.
Sunnīs	the majority of Muslims who recognise the authority of the prophet Muhammad's immediate successors, in particular the first four caliphs.
tablīgh	conversion, proselytisation, missionary activity.
tālukdār	the holder of a proprietary estate.
tanzīm	organisation or consolidation of a movement.
tauhīd	a Muslim concept to express the unity of God.
'ulamā'	(sing. *'ālim*), the body of Muslim learned men.
umma	the Islamic community.
waqf	(pl. *auqāf*), an endowment of property held in trust for the welfare of the Muslim community.
zamīndār	a landholder who pays revenue directly to the government.

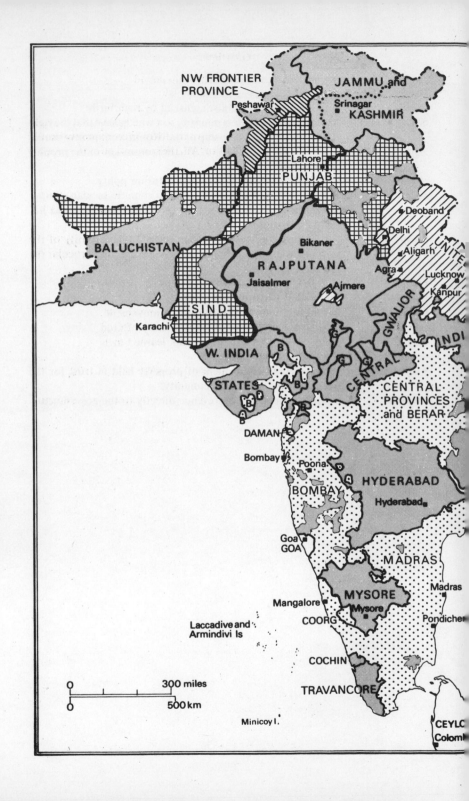

NW FRONTIER
PROVINCE

Peshawar

JAMMU and

Srinagar
KASHMIR

Lahore

PUNJAB

Deoband

Delhi

Aligarh

BALUCHISTAN

Bikaner

RAJPUTANA

Agra

Jaisalmer

Ajmere

Lucknow

Kanpur

Karachi

SIND

W. INDIA

STATES

B

B

D

B

A

C

G

G

GWALIOR

CENTRAL

CENTRAL
PROVINCES
and BERAR

INDI

DAMAN

Bombay

Poona

BOMBAY

HYDERABAD

Hyderabad

Goa
GOA

MADRAS

Madras

MYSORE

Mangalore

COORG

Mysore

Pondicher

Laccadive and
Armindivi Is

COCHIN

0   300 miles

0   500 km

TRAVANCORE

Minicoy I.

CEYLO

Colom

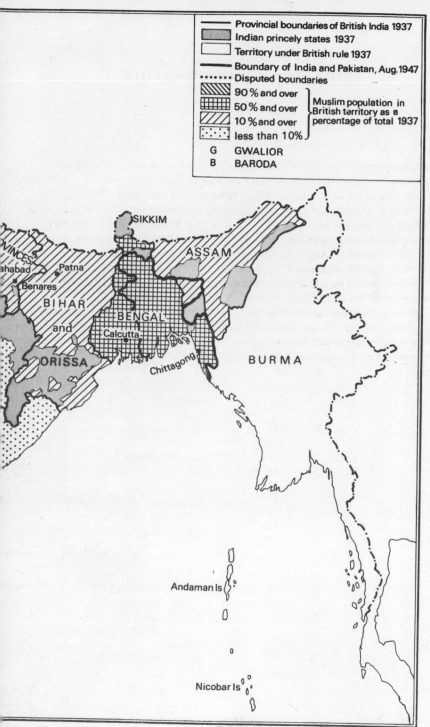

Legend:

- —— Provincial boundaries of British India 1937
- ▨ Indian princely states 1937
- ☐ Territory under British rule 1937
- —— Boundary of India and Pakistan, Aug. 1947
- ····· Disputed boundaries
- ◩ 90 % and over
- ⊞ 50 % and over
- ⊘ 10 % and over } Muslim population in British territory as a percentage of total 1937
- ⋰ less than 10 %
- G GWALIOR
- B BARODA

SIKKIM

...VINCES

ahabad · Patna

Benares

B I H A R ASSAM

and BENGAL

ORISSA · Calcutta

BURMA

Chittagong

Andaman Is

Nicobar Is

British India, c. 1937

NOTE ON TRANSLITERATION

The problem with any system of transliteration, as I see it, is one of too much or too little. Whatever the formula, it is unlikely to please everyone.

For my part, I have sought only to be consistent and simple. The need for consistency was dictated in large part by the confusion which surrounds the spelling of common Muslim proper names like 'Muhammad' and 'Ahmad'. Where inconsistencies appear, as in the 'National Mahommedan Association' or 'Mohammedan Anglo-Oriental College', these have been retained in deference to their established usage. Similarly, Indo-Muslim names appear in the form in which they are locally preferred and recognised, e.g. "Abdu'r Rahīm' instead of the more artificial, Arabicised 'Abd ar Rahīm'.

As far as Arabic personal names and nouns are concerned, I have chosen only to indicate the 'ayn' ('), the hamza (') and long vowels (–), except in cases where their use may contribute to confusion or be uncommon in practice. All other diacritical marks have been omitted in the interests of simplicity.

Introduction
Islam and Muslim politics in colonial India concepts in community and representation

There are today strong arguments to suggest that Muslims in India are 'integrated', both anthropologically and historically speaking. Studies inspired by the seminal works of Imtiaz Ahmad[1] and Muhammad Mujeeb[2] have concluded that Islam's historical and cultural accommodations with its local environment in India have wrought profound changes in its substance and fundamentally altered the practices and modes of thinking of its local adherents. Indian Muslims, it is argued quite simply, are more Indian than Muslim.[3]

This claim has not been without its critics. Of these, clearly the most distinguished was the historian Aziz Ahmad who, in a series of classic expositions in the 1960s, sought to demonstrate that separatist trends were far more characteristic of Indian Islam than had hitherto been acknowledged.[4] A generation of younger scholars, most notably, Rafiuddin Ahmed,[5] Barbara Metcalf[6] and Gail Minault,[7] have done much to establish the value of Ahmad's intellectual contribution. Whilst

[1] See especially, Imtiaz Ahmad (ed.), *Caste and Social Stratification among the Muslims* (Delhi, Manohar, 1973); *Family, Marriage and Kinship among Muslims in India* (Delhi, Manohar, 1976); *Ritual and Religion among Muslims in India* (Delhi, Manohar, 1981) and *Modernization and Social Change among Muslims in India* (Delhi, Manohar, 1983).
[2] Muhammad Mujeeb, *The Indian Muslims* (London, George Allen and Unwin, 1967).
[3] For the anthropologists' statement of this view as applied to Bengali and Tamil Muslims see the essays by Lina Fruzzetti, 'Muslim rituals: The household rites vs. the public festivals in rural India' and Mattison Mines, 'Islamization and Muslim Ethnicity in South India' in Imtiaz Ahmad, (ed.), *Ritual and Religion among Muslims in India* (Delhi, Manohar, 1981), pp. 91–112 and 65–89. For an example of a historical study which shares the general thrust of this assumption, although somewhat more stridently, see Ayesha Jalal and Anil Seal, 'Alternative to Partition: Muslim Politics Between the Wars', *Modern Asian Studies*, 15, 3 (1981), p. 416.
[4] Aziz Ahmad, *Studies in Islamic Culture in the Indian Environment* (Oxford, Clarendon Press, 1964); *Islamic Modernism in India and Pakistan, 1857–1964* (London, Oxford University Press, 1967) and *An Intellectual History of Islam in India* (Edinburgh University Press, 1969).
[5] Rafiuddin Ahmed, *The Bengal Muslims 1871–1906: A Quest for Identity* (Delhi, Oxford University Press, 1981).
[6] Barbara Daly Metcalf, *Islamic Revival in British India: Deoband, 1860–1900* (Princeton University Press, 1982).
[7] Gail Minault, *The Khilafat Movement: Religious Symbolism and Political Mobilization in India* (New York, Columbia University Press, 1982).

1

their studies can by no means be read simply as evidence of the separatist direction of Indian Islam, they suggest, by their emphasis upon movements of reform and revival, that the resilience of Muslim tradition as a code of conduct, both moral and political, cannot be easily discounted.

However, one of the most trenchant critiques in recent years of the assimilationist thesis and its limitations as a basis for the study of Indian Islam, has come from Francis Robinson.[8] While some have deemed his approach to suffer from an unwarranted stress upon textual or 'high' Islam at the expense of a living Muslim 'folk-theology',[9] and others expressed concern about its in-built teleology,[10] its real value must be seen to lie in its emphasis upon historical change in Muslim societies as 'the dynamic relationship' between 'visions of the ideal Muslim life and the lives Muslims lead'.[11]

The question of change in the context of Muslim moral discourse has recently been more broadly investigated. In a perceptive essay on how Islam, as understood by the believer, may actually constitute social relations in a variety of Muslim societies, William Roff suggests that while the 'real world...impinges on all human actors, not excepting Muslims... we may observe [them] acting in ways for which they derive, and to which they give force and meaning through a wide range of common, Islamically supplied (or enjoined) wellsprings of behaviour and response'.[12] It is to such an 'Islamically supplied' political discourse, shaped within the world of colonial India, that this study will address itself. It will seek to impart to Muslim action and, in particular, to Muslim political action, something of that 'intelligibility' which Jacques Berque regards as 'conceived in the same mode as the subject itself'.[13]

[8] Francis Robinson, 'Islam and Muslim Society in South Asia', *Contributions to Indian Sociology* (n.s.) 17, 2 (1983), pp. 185–203.
[9] Veena Das, 'For a folk-theology and theological anthropology of Islam', *Contributions to Indian Sociology* (n.s.) 18, 2 (1984), pp. 293–300.
[10] Gail Minault, 'Some reflections on Islamic revivalism vs. assimilation among Muslims in India', *Contributions to Indian Sociology* (n.s.) 18, 2 (1984), pp. 301–5. For Robinson's defence of his case see Francis Robinson, 'Islam and Muslim Society in South Asia: a reply to Veena Das and Gail Minault', *Contributions to Indian Sociology* (n.s.) 20, 1 (1986), pp. 97–104.
[11] Robinson, 'Islam and Muslim Society' (1983), p. 196.
[12] William Roff, 'Islamic Movements: One or Many?', in William Roff (ed.), *Islam and the Political Economy of Meaning: Comparative Studies of Muslim Discourse* (London, Croom Helm, 1987), p. 31.
[13] Jacques Berque, 'The popular and the purified', *Times Literary Supplement*, 11 December 1981, p. 1433.

However this concern with Muslim political discourse is not to deny that wide gaps exist, as indeed they do, between the formal letter of Islamic law and the actual practice of Muslims in India,[14] or that modern Indian history is not replete, as it is, with instances of inter-communal solidarity.[15] It is rather to raise the question of whether Indian Muslims have not, as Muslims, tended to make certain assumptions about the nature of social and political relations that lend themselves to the definition of an 'Islamic' world-view which demands attention as such.

Yet, it is the case that some of the most influential historical interpretations of political change among Muslims in colonial India have tended either to deny its relevance or underestimate its significance. These interpretations tend to fall into three separate categories. There are, firstly, those which are grounded firmly in the view that whatever assumptions existed among Muslims concerning the nature of politics and political identity were dictated by the course of colonial policy and the order of its priorities. Such an approach is typified by the early studies of Hardy, Robinson, Page[16] and, more recently, by the work of Jalal.[17] The second body of historical interpretation holds that while Muslim separatist politics may well have stemmed from sources that were internal to the evaluative framework of Muslims in India, their selection was manipulated and determined by an elite whose interests such politics were designed to serve. The most committed exponent of this view is the political scientist, Paul Brass.[18] Finally,

---

[14] A point persuasively demonstrated with reference to Bengal by Asim Roy, *The Islamic Syncretist Tradition in Bengal* (Princeton University Press, 1983).

[15] The underlying emphasis of much modern Indo-Muslim historiography, notably studies by Zia ul Hasan Faruqi, *The Deoband School and the Demand for Pakistan* (Bombay, Asia Publishing House, 1963); Mushirul Haq, *Muslim Politics in Modern India 1857–1947* (Meerut, Meenakshi Pradashaw, 1970) and more recently, Mushirul Hasan, 'Religion and Politics in India: The *'Ulamā'* and the Khilāfat Movement' in Mushirul Hasan (ed.), *Communal and pan-Islamic trends in Colonial India* (Delhi, Manohar, 1981), pp. 1–26, as well as his *Mohamed Ali: Ideology and Politics*, (Delhi, Manohar, 1981).

[16] Peter Hardy, *The Muslims of British India* (Cambridge University Press, 1972) and Francis Robinson, *Separatism Among Indian Muslims: The Politics of the United Provinces' Muslims 1860–1923* (Cambridge University Press, 1974). David Page, *Prelude to Partition: The Indian Muslims and the Imperial System of Control 1920–1932* (Delhi, Oxford University Press, 1982).

[17] Ayesha Jalal, *The Sole Spokesman: Jinnah, the Muslim League and the Demand for Pakistan* (Cambridge University Press, 1985).

[18] Paul Brass, *Language, Religion and Politics in North India* (Cambridge University Press, 1974). See also his 'Elite Groups, Symbol Manipulation and Ethnic Identity among the Muslims of South Asia' in David Taylor and Malcolm Yapp (eds.), *Political Identity in South Asia* (London, School of Oriental and African Studies, 1979), pp. 35–77.

there are studies that attempt to explain the development of Muslim separatism in colonial India not so much in terms of colonial policy or the cynical misuse of religious values, but by the instinct for self-preservation of a minority fearsome at the prospects of majority rule and permanent subjection. This is implicit in studies by some Muslim scholars in India and Pakistan, most notably Rafiq Zakaria and Khalid bin Sayeed.[19]

What is lacking in these approaches is not so much reasonably well-grounded explanations of political change, but a more sustained regard for the normative prescriptions of a religious and political tradition which shaped and constrained the conduct of colonial Muslim politics. To account for the force of these prescriptions, as they were understood and acted upon by Muslims at the time is not to suggest, as much established Pakistani historiography is wont to do,[20] that 'Islam' somehow determined the course of Muslim politics in the late nineteenth and twentieth centuries. It is, however, to draw attention to the influence of a prevailing discourse whose understanding of the proper ends of political action were deeply embedded in Indo-Muslim religious tradition. The fact that this discourse, tended also to reflect the preoccupations of a dominant class of well-born Muslim, *ashrāf,*[21] cannot, in itself, either exhaust its usefulness as a mode of analysis for the conduct of Indo-Muslim politics, or deny that its assumptions were shared more widely by non-*ashrāf* Muslims.[22]

[19] Rafiq Zakaria, *Rise of Muslims in Indian Politics: An Analysis of Developments from 1885 to 1906* (Bombay, Somaiya Publications, 1970) and Khalid bin Sayeed, *Pakistan: The Formative Phase 1857–1948* (London, Oxford University Press, 1968).

[20] Chiefly Hafeez Malik, *Moslem Nationalism in India and Pakistan* (Washington, Public Affairs Press, 1963); Waheed-uz-Zaman, *Towards Pakistan* (Lahore, Publishers United, 1963) and I.H. Qureshi, *The Struggle for Pakistan* (University of Karachi Publications, 1965).

[21] For a superb discussion of the social and cultural milieu of the north Indian Muslim *ashrāf* see David Lelyveld, *Aligarh's First Generation: Muslim Solidarity in British India* (Princeton University Press, 1978), chapter II. For another discussion, particularly with reference to the Bengali *ashrāf,* see Rafiuddin Ahmed, *The Bengāl Muslims,* chapter I, especially pp. 7–27.

[22] The process of 'ashrāfisation', which might be compared to Srinivas's understanding of 'sanskritisation', was essentially a means of social mobility among Muslims concerned to improve their social status in periods of rapid change. It involved the adoption not only of modes of social behaviour such as *purda,* but also an adherence to what was believed to be 'high' Islam and the social and political values that derived from its prescriptions. On 'ashrāfisation' see Imtiaz Ahmad, 'The Ashrāf-Ajlāf Distinction in Muslim Social Structure in India', *Indian Economic and Social History Review* 3 (September 1966), pp. 268–78; on 'sanskritisation' see M.N. Srinivas, *Social Change in Modern India* (Berkeley and Los Angeles, University of California Press, 1966). See also Cora Vreed-de Steurs, *Parda* (Assen, Netherlands, Van Gorcum, 1968). For a discussion of the adoption of 'high' Islam as a basis for 'ashrāfisation' among Muslims

At a more general level, and with an eye to recent developments in the Muslim world, it might be said that any suggestion that their culture's religious base has little to do with the politics of Muslims, is best treated with caution. There has been very little indeed to sustain the claim, either historically or in present times, that political theories and practices which are fundamentally at odds with Muslim assumptions survive, let alone thrive.[23] To pretend therefore that the ideological contextual dimension was irrelevant to, or somehow independent of, the conduct of colonial Muslim politics may well prove to be both misguided and naive.

A glance at some of the existing literature on Indo-Muslim colonial politics shows how a disregard for the significance of Muslim moral discourse has contributed to studies that tend either to be excessively rigid or lacking in depth. It has been argued by Jalal, for example, that the Muslim League, and more particularly its leader Muhammad Ali Jinnah, cared little or nothing at all for Pakistan as a cultural or religious ideal, and that what really impelled Muslim separatist politics in the 1940s was the quest for Congress-League parity and power at the centre of a federal India.[24] To claim that Jinnah was neither inspired by, nor aspired to, a separate state for Muslims is a bold thesis and one that is likely to disturb many well established ideas about the Quā'id-e-A'zam.

in North India and Bengal in the later nineteenth century see Barbara Metcalf, *Islamic Revival in British India* and Rafiuddin Ahmed, *The Bengal Muslims*. There were of course other means by which the political and cultural pre-occupations of the class of *ashrāf* Muslims were transmitted in India, most notably through Urdu poetry which, particularly after the Mutiny of 1857, tended to assume distinctly political overtones. See Aziz Ahmad, *Islamic Modernism in India and Pakistan*, pp. 97–102 and Gail Minault, 'Urdu Political Poetry during the Khilafat Movement', *Modern Asian Studies* 8, 4 (1974), pp. 459–71.

[23] Contemporary literature in the 1980s abounds with discussions of Islam's relation to modern politics. Some of the better studies which deal sensitively with the issue of Islam's constraining influence upon the political and social vision espoused by Muslims in the Middle East, Asia and Africa include John Esposito (ed.), *Islam and Development Religion and Sociopolitical Change* (New York, Syracuse University Press, 1980); *Voices of Resurgent Islam* (Oxford University Press, 1983); James Piscatori (ed.), *Islam in the Political Process* (Cambridge University Press, 1983); Mohammad Ayoob (ed.), *The Politics of Islamic Re-Assertion* (New York, St. Martin's Press, 1982); Oliver Carré (ed.), *L'Islam et L'Etat dans le Monde d'Aujourdhui* (Paris, Presses Universitaires de France, 1982) and A.S. Cudsi and Ali E. Dessouki (eds.), *Islam and Power* (Baltimore, Johns Hopkins University Press, 1981).

[24] For Jalal, Jinnah's purpose was primarily 'to unite for a nationalist cause on equal terms...This had been the heart and centre of his strategy...Jinnah's "Pakistan" did not entail the partition of India; rather it meant its regeneration into an union where Pakistan and Hindustan would join to stand together proudly against the hostile world without. This was no clarion call of pan-Islam; this was not pitting Muslim India against Hindustan; rather it was a secular vision of a polity where there was real political choice and safeguards, the India of Jinnah's dreams...' Jalal, *The Sole Spokesman*, p. 122.

However, the fundamental question of why Jinnah finally opted for a course which, we are told, went against both his and, presumably, Muslim interests[25] leads Jalal to plump for a more conventional explanation. Jinnah's acceptance of a 'moth-eaten' Pakistan, she concludes, was forced upon him by the combined intransigence of Congress and Attlee's Labour Party both of which were determined to resist the League's exclusive right to nominate Muslims at the centre.

Whilst the chicanery of high politics may well have contributed substantially to the final shape of Pakistan, the quest for a locus of Muslim dominance in India was far less subject to the 'rational' pursuits of Jinnah and his party than Jalal would have us believe. For what constrained the choices of these 'rational' political actors were not only the studied moves conducted in the boardroom of high politics, but a set of normative considerations by which their actions assumed legitimacy in the eyes of those whom they claimed to represent.[26] If Jinnah stressed the compelling importance of the Muslim League's exclusive right to represent Muslims at the centre, it was not only because therein lay the political secret of his and his party's undisputed claim to power, but also because he could not do otherwise if he was not to reject the very sources of his own and his party's legitimation.[27]

An understanding of these sources and their significance for Muslim politics lies, therefore, not within the confines of a poker game of politics, but in the vision of societal and political organisation espoused by Muslims as part of an active tradition. It is a vision that has tended to stress the dichotomy between Muslims and non-Muslims, and to reject the 'dualism' obtained by subjecting Muslims to non-Muslim law. It is a vision that has assumed, sometimes against historical odds of considerable magnitude, a united political community bound by a substantive, if

[25] *Ibid.* pp. 2–4.
[26] The problems inherent in the approach commonly known as the 'Cambridge School' of history, which underlies studies such as those of Jalal and Page, were examined in some depth in the mid-1970s by Eugene Irschick in his review of J. Gallagher, G. Johnson, A. Seal (eds.), *Locality, Province and Nation: Essays on Indian Politics, 1870–1947* (Cambridge University Press, 1973) in *Journal of Asian Studies* 34, 2 (1975), pp. 461–72; by G. Pandey in a review article which included a discussion of the same volume as well as of Anil Seal's *The Emergence of Indian Nationalism* (Cambridge University Press, 1968) and G. Johnson's *Provincial Politics and Indian Nationalism* (Cambridge University Press, 1973), in *Indian Economic and Social History Review*, 11, 1–2 (1974), pp. 326–40 and by Gail Minault in a review of Francis Robinson, *Separatism Among Indian Muslims: The Politics of the United Provinces' Muslims 1860–1923* (Cambridge University Press, 1974) in *Indian Economic and Social History Review*, 14, 3 (1977), pp. 417–20.
[27] An idea more fully discussed in Quentin Skinner, 'Some Problems in the Analysis of Political Thought and Action', *Political Theory*, 2, 3, (1974), pp. 277–303.

not procedural, consensus. Jinnah was bound by these assumptions. For him, as for his Muslim followers, it mattered little whether Muslims in India were in fact an indivisible community: what was imperative was that all politics should be conducted as if they were.

Arguments which purport to explain Indo-Muslim separatism in terms of the manipulation of cultural symbols by politically interested elites must also be approached with equal care. For while the gist of the claim which demonstrates the mobilising potential of Islam is undoubtedly compelling, it relies too heavily on a view of political elites as essentially independent of their own and their community's normative context and too little if at all, on the constraining influence of Muslim religious ideology. To believe that political elites always manipulate symbols while remaining themselves independent of these symbols and the preferences they dictate is, as Robinson has shown, extremely problematic in relation to Muslim politics whether in India or elsewhere.[28]

Two examples, which appear to testify to the strengths of the Brass thesis, show just what the limitations of such an approach are likely to be. The first is that of Sir Sayyid Ahmad Khān, an Indian Muslim whose politics are commonly believed to have been shaped more by his concern for the economic and political welfare of his community than by the need to preserve a religious tradition as such. The second is that of Muhammad 'Alī Jinnah, whose secular demeanour has led to the impression that his campaign for a centre of Muslim power in India was little else but a cynical manipulation of Islamic symbols.

But, in both cases, the application of Brass's thesis can only be sustained by ignoring the cultural and normative context within which these men had to carve out what they believed would be a worthy place for their community. In the case of Sir Sayyid it implies a disregard for his 'whole life and work' and the spirit that pervaded them.[29] It means dismissing as disingenuous Sayyid Ahmad's political conviction that 'the more worldly progress we make, the more glory Islam gains'.[30] It suggests, above all, an arrogant disregard for those closest to Sir Sayyid in his daily and professional life who were in no doubt about the

[28] Francis Robinson, 'Islam and Muslim Separatism' in David Taylor and Malcolm Yapp (eds.), *Political Identity*, pp. 78–112. See also his 'Nation-Formation: The Brass Thesis and Muslim Separatism', *Journal of Commonwealth and Comparative Politics*, 15, 3 (1977), pp. 215–30.

[29] Robinson, 'Islam and Muslim Separatism', p. 92.

[30] Quoted in J.M.S. Baljon, *The Reforms and Religious Ideas of Sir Sayyid Ahmad Khan* (Leiden, E.J. Brill, 1949), p. 88.

relationship between this Muslim's faith and his political action.[31]

The case of Jinnah is obviously more complex.[32] A man not known for his devotion to religion and yet leader of the movement for the first self-consciously Islamic state in modern history, he appears by all accounts to fit neatly into the Brass mould. Here, it would seem, was the shrewd political operator given to manipulating his community's most cherished values. And yet what is important is not whether Jinnah himself believed Islam to be the 'right' ideology for whatever India it was that he wanted, but whether or not in the process of organising Muslim politics and demanding for Muslims a position equal to that of non-Muslims he was led, forced or inspired to ground his programme of political action in ideological foundations – which, not coincidentally, derived from traditional Muslim assumptions. To say this is not to say that Jinnah embodied an Islamic *jihād* – it is to say, however, that he could not devise and organise a unitary Muslim political movement outside Muslim principles, admittedly open to interpretation, and that these principles constrained his political practice.

The elements of Indo-Muslim moral discourse and the assumptions that flowed therefrom, are also crucial if we are to understand more fully the significance of Muslim separatism as the triumph of 'minority politics'. For what is noteworthy about Muslim separatism is not so much its evolution as a movement designed to protect the interests of a minority, although this was unquestionably important, but its affirmation of the claim that being Muslim demanded special considerations in excess of those commonly granted to political minorities. The demands for separate Muslim electorates, 'weightage' and Hindu-Muslim parity were, admittedly in part, the responses of a minority uncertain of its political future,[33] but they were also, fundamentally, the manifestations of a profound belief that Muslims in India 'bore no analogy to . . . the

[31] His biographer and contemporary, the poet Altāf Husain Hālī wrote 'Sir Sayyid's belief in the reality of Islam and a passion for the community of Muslims was ingrained in him from the very outset'. Altāf Husain Hālī. *Hayāt-i-Jāwed* (Lahore, Ishrat Publishing House, 1965), p. 293.

[32] Some insights into the complexities of Jinnah's personality may be found in K.B. Sayeed. 'The Personality of Jinnah and his Political Strategy' in C.H. Philips and M.D. Wainwright (eds.), *The Partition of India: Policies and Perspectives, 1913–1947* (London, George Allen and Unwin, 1970), pp. 276–93; Saleem Qureshi, 'Iqbal and Jinnah: Personalities, Perceptions and Politics' in C.M. Naim (ed.), *Iqbal, Jinnah and Pakistan* (Delhi, Jinnah Publishing House, 1982), pp. 11–39 and more recently in Stanley Wolpert, *Jinnah of Pakistan* (New York, Oxford University Press, 1984).

[33] For some comparisons in the Asian context see Robert Kearney, *Communalism and Language in the Politics of Ceylon* (Durham, North Carolina, Duke University Press, 1967); Jeyaratnam Wilson, *Electoral Politics in an Emergent State: The Ceylon General Election of May 1970* (Cambridge University Press, 1975); P.B. Harris, 'Representative

minor communities'.[34] What is important is to recognise that these
concerns had as much to do with the status of Muslims as a minority as
with the espousal of a view that presupposed this minority's pre-eminent
claim to power. Such a view was shaped not only by the ingredients of a
Mughal political culture nurtured in the context of Muslim political
domination in India, but by a religious tradition whose relationship to
power was deemed to be both necessary and divinely endorsed.[35]

To recognise the influence of such normative concerns upon the
conduct of Muslim politics in colonial India is not to maintain that there
was no serious debate about 'right' Muslim conduct.[36] Indeed, any
understanding of the problem of Muslim representation in colonial
India must proceed from some discussion of the variety and diversity of
Muslim counsels in the late nineteenth and early twentieth centuries. It is
the purpose of this study to make a contribution towards that end.

Politics in a British Dependency: Some Reflections on Problems of Representation in
Hong Kong', *Parliamentary Affairs*, 28, 2 (1975), pp. 180–91 and Karl von Vorys,
Democracy without Consensus: Communalism and Political Stability in Malaysia
(Princeton University Press, 1977).
[34] See Deputation to the Secretary of State for India: 27 January 1909, in K.K. Aziz (ed.),
Ameer Ali: His Life and Work, Part 2 (Lahore, Publishers United, 1968), p. 319.
[35] The politics of separate Muslim representation and the concerns which underlay them
are more fully discussed in chapter 4.
[36] See Barbara Daly Metcalf, *Moral Conduct and Authority: The Place of Adab in South
Asian Islam* (Berkeley, University of California Press, 1984).

1

The model of Muslim political action

To talk in terms of the assumptions Muslims make about politics leads inexorably to questions about the way in which they conceive of the ends of political action and the purpose of collective endeavour. It need not of course follow that these ends and purposes have always either been easily discernible to, or consciously pursued by, Muslims. Nor does it imply that these may not, from time to time, whether among Muslims in colonial India or elsewhere, have been displaced by other more exigent if less elevated concerns that happen, at the time, to shape Muslim politics.

However, neither its often intangible quality nor its vulnerability to existing political pressures have diminished the power or the reality of what Muslims have traditionally regarded as the 'model' of their individual and collective behaviour, whether religious, social or political. For while it may be true that the components of this 'model' have not always been consistent with one another, nor free from radically different evaluations by Muslims throughout history, they remain unquestionably relevant to the practice of Muslim politics.

The basis of this 'model' of political action and indeed its significance is, for many Muslims, most comprehensively contained in the Qur'ān. The purpose of God's revealed word has been characteristically summarised by Fazlur Rahman as being essentially concerned with 'producing the right moral attitude for human action' as well as the framework for the release of man's 'creative moral energy'.[1] This, Muslims believe, the Qur'ān teaches them by showing men the way to both righteousness and creativity through 'ibāda, or the service of God.

It is precisely Man's submission to Divine will that constitutes for many Muslims both the central imperative of their lives and the desired end of their association with their fellow men. Individually, it signifies a Muslim's commitment to God's Law as this was revealed, directly and finally, to his Prophet, Muhammad. Collectively, it signifies the extension and elaboration of that Law by the Community as a whole, either by reference to the exemplary life of the Prophet and his

---

[1] Fazlur Rahman, *Islam* (University of Chicago Press, 2nd edition, 1979), p. 241.

companions (the *sunna*), or by means of communal deliberation and concurrence, (*ijmāʿ*) or, finally, by applying the modes of systematic analogical reasoning in the light of the Community's own historical precedents (*qiyās*).[2] The body of this Law, known as the *Sharīʿa*, expresses at once, both the principal objective of the social and political life of the Community as well as the supreme 'good' to which all Muslims, as individuals, aspire.

As an organising principle of Muslim collective life then, the importance of the *Sharīʿa* and what it signifies, cannot be overemphasised. It has been compared by the poet Muhammad Iqbāl to 'an inner core' without which the Community is like 'scattered dust'.[3] Certainly any understanding of what Muslims conceive of as the 'good', whether moral or political (and the distinction is unreal for Muslims for whom the very purpose of all human activity is moral) depends upon our ability to grasp something of the nature of the *Sharīʿa* itself.

A common approach to the *Sharīʿa* is one adopted by Fazlur Rahman who regards it as a body of legal enactments as well as a set of moral imperatives. It comprises, in his view, to quote al-Shāṭibī, 'acts of the heart as well as overt acts' and, as such, represents both the structure and the essence of the faith. Rahman argues that later developments in Islam which tended to stress the legal, at the expense of the 'mystic', aspects of the *Sharīʿa* were a serious deviation which violated its significance as both law and morality.[4]

But there is yet another critical dimension to the complex nature of the *Sharīʿa*. For while like law it is seen to lead men to realise, purposefully, the object of their individual and collective endeavours, it is also the object itself. It is, in Rahman's succinct phrase, 'coterminous with the "good"'. It embodies, for Muslims, the supreme moral law that must be discovered, provide guidance and be lived. It is both the 'highway to the good life' and the 'good life' itself.[5]

That God devised and ordained a moral law for Man and his welfare forms an essential part of the Muslim's faith. What does not is the premise that Man rather than God is at the centre of this moral law.[6] For

---

[2] Joseph Schacht, *The Origins of Islamic Jurisprudence* (Oxford, Clarendon Press, 1950); *An Introduction to Islamic Law* (Oxford, Clarendon Press, 1964); A.A.A. Fyzee, *Outlines of Muhammedan Law* (Oxford University Press, 1964).

[3] Muhammad Iqbal, *Rumuz-i-Bekhudi, The Mysteries of Selflessness*, R.A. Nicholson (trans.) (London, J. Murray, 1953), p. 37.

[4] Rahman, *Islam*, pp. 100–16.

[5] *Ibid.* p. 115.

[6] Aziz Ahmad, however, believed that Iqbāl's thought could reasonably be seen to have been an exception. He writes 'In classical Islam, in the totality of the traditionalist and fundamentalist current attitudes and in all Indo-Muslim modernist thought except in

the very purpose of this law, as Muslims see it, is to *each Man obedience to God. The ends of Muslim social and political action have tended therefore to be quite distinct. They assume that society is a venue that exists not so much to realise individual human wants but to pursue most actively Man's service to God. This is not to say that the ideal Muslim social order is not concerned with providing itself with a livelihood sufficient both to bear the cost of its own defence and to keep its members alive and active. It is to emphasise however that these are undertaken primarily with a view to the practice of the true faith and of devotion to God.[7]

The ends of Muslim social organisation are not then, as it were, properly humanist in that they do not aspire to 'the creation of a man-conceived utopia on earth'.[8] Nor is the purpose of conscious human association seen to lie in the pursuit of a humanly defined 'common good'.[9] Human history, according to that most eminent of modern Muslim visionaries, Muhammad Iqbāl, was designed to bring Man closer to God. Islam, he claimed 'as the most historical of all faiths' had achieved this objective by persuading men to reject the false individualism propagated by the West which had led to its moral decline.[10] For Iqbāl as for Muslims like him, the dawn of 'civilised' human history began not with a 'social contract' conducted between equal parties, each with its own interests guaranteed in some common pursuit, but with a 'Divine Constitution' ordained for Man by God for ends known only to Him.

The rules that govern the politics of Muslims and the choices that are expected of them are amongst the principal concerns of this 'Consti-

that of Iqbāl, God and not man remains the key figure of the universe dominating man's political, social, economic, and cultural life. Iqbāl alone takes the position which is not very different from Jacques Maritain's concept of "humanisme integrale" ...'. Aziz Ahmad, *Islamic Modernism in India and Pakistan, 1857–1964* (London, Oxford University Press, 1967), p. 271.
[7] Peter Hardy, 'The Ideal Social Order' in William de Bary (ed.), *Sources of Indian Tradition*, volume I (New York, Columbia University Press, 1964), pp. 501–2.
[8] *Ibid.* p. 315.
[9] Indeed, 'the common interests, rights and obligations of the members of the Islamic community are as defined by God in his Holy Law, not as determined by that community's choices and decisions'. Peter Hardy, *Partners in Freedom – and True Muslims: The Political Thought of Some Muslim Scholars in British India, 1912–1947* (Lund, Scandinavian Institute of Asian Studies, 1971), p. 11.
[10] He wrote: 'The idealism of Europe never became a living factor in her life, and the result is a perverted ego seeking itself through mutually intolerant democracies ... The Muslim, on the other hand, is in possession of these ultimate ideas on the basis of a revelation, which, [can produce] ... that spiritual democracy which is the ultimate aim of Islam'. Muhammad Iqbal, *Reconstruction of Religious Thought in Islam* (London, Oxford University Press, 1934), p. 170.

tution'. That this should be so stemmed from the Prophet Muhammad's conviction that political activity and the creation of effective political institutions were the necessary preconditions for the propagation of God's law.[11] Indeed, the political organisation of this community, its processes of political deliberation and its political relations with groups founded on bases other than its own, formed integral features of this 'Constitution'.

It has by no means been conclusively demonstrated that the passage of time has succeeded in eroding the fundamental contribution of these features to the conduct of modern Muslim politics. On the contrary, it seems certain that any study of Muslim approaches to politics, including those concerned with an understanding of the meaning and purpose of political representation, must begin with a serious consideration of values that are 'Islamically derived'. These would necessarily include the meaning of the political community as an extension of religious fellowship; its claim to total allegiance and its ceaseless preoccupation with the 'Islamic' dispensation of power.

The Umma: the unit of social and political organisation

The communal group or *umma* is, undoubtedly, the basis of all social and political life in Islam.[12] Although like other revelatory religions it seeks what Nieuwenhuijze has termed 'the maximisation of the religious aspect of human... life', its most enduring feature rests clearly in its political activity.[13]

---

[11] Montgomery Watt, *Muhammad at Medina* (Oxford, Clarendon Press, 1956), pp. 221–60, *Islamic Political Thought*, (Edinburgh University Press, 1980), pp. 3–30, Maxime Rodinson, Mohammad (Middlesex, Penguin Books, 1983), pp. 215–92 (Cook), Michael Cook, *Muhammad* (Oxford University Press, 1983), pp. 51–60.

[12] On the importance and historical development of the *umma* see *The Encyclopaedia of Islam* (Leiden, E.J. Brill, 1971), pp. 1015–16; C.A.O. Nieuwenhuijze, 'The Ummah – An Analytical Approach', *Studia Islamica*, 10 (1959), pp. 5–22; Louis Massignon, 'L'Umma et ses synonymes: notion de communaute sociale', *Revue des Etudes Islamiques* (Cahier unique, 1941–1946), pp. 150–7; Watt, *Muhammad at Medina*, pp. 238–49; *Islamic Political Thought*, pp. 9–14; Rodinson, *Mohammed*, pp. 152–4.

[13] Nieuwenhuijze, '*The Ummah*', p. 9. The importance of the political community in Islam, writes Grunebaum, hinges upon the idea that 'the service (*ibada*) of God requires of the faithful... an organized community of believers. Such a community cannot exist without government'. Gustave von Grunebaum, *Modern Islam: The Search for Cultural Identity* (Berkeley, University of California Press, 1962), p. 61. For Smith, Islam's preoccupation with political organisation is a reflection of its 'central conviction that the true Muslim life includes the carrying out in this world of the divine injunction as to how mankind, individually and corporately, should live'. Wilfred Cantwell Smith, *Islam in Modern History* (Princeton University Press, 1957), p. 39.

The importance of what might be called the quest for power amongst Muslims stems both from the actual historical roots of Islam as an emerging sect forced to deal politically with a hostile environment, as well as from its traditional image as a code of action rather than as a speculative philosophy.

It is now widely accepted by scholars of Islamic history that the opposition of local tribesmen in Mecca, including his own tribe of Quraysh, led Muhammad to conclude that the political supremacy of his followers remained the only real guarantee of the new faith he sought to propagate.[14] It has even been suggested that the effective consolidation of Muhammad's *umma* began only after he had succeeded in winning the co-operation of local tribes in Medina who accepted his political, if not religious, authority in his campaigns against the pagan Qurayshites.[15]

These interpretations suggest that the original *umma* instituted by Muhammad at Medina may have been more political than consciously religious in outlook.[16] However, as Serjeant observes, given the prevalence of 'sacred enclaves' centred around local gods in seventh-century Arabia, Muhammad tended naturally also to organise his community around a religious nucleus.[17] Though his long term objective was therefore, unquestionably, the creation of a religious order under his leadership, his immediate concerns evidently revolved around a political confederation organised for specifically political purposes and characterised by the noticeable inclusion of non-Muslim, particularly Jewish, communities.[18]

What is then clearly significant about the nature of Muhammad's early community is that it appeared to bear little resemblance to the much later, more exclusive, Muslim *umma*. One obvious reason for the *umma*'s subsequent development along these lines lay in the refusal of non-Muslim communities to accept Muhammad's prophetic message

[14] Montgomery Watt, *Muhammad at Mecca* (Oxford, Clarendon Press, 1953), pp. 100–37, 151–250, and Marshall Hodgson, *The Venture of Islam: Conscience and History in a World Civilization*, I (The University of Chicago Press, 1974), pp. 146–96.

[15] Watt, *Muhammad at Medina*, pp. 151–91 and Rodinson, *Mohammed*, pp. 215–92.

[16] R.B. Serjeant, 'The "Constitution of Medina"', *Islamic Quarterly*, 8, 1 (1964), pp. 3–16.

[17] R.B. Serjeant, 'Haram and Hawtah and the sacred enclave in Arabia' in A.R. Badawi (ed.), *Mélanges Taha Husain* (Cairo, Dar el Ma'aref, 1962), pp. 50–1.

[18] 'In other words the religious factor was present in the motives leading Muhammad and the men of Medina to seek an agreement, but the details of the agreement were in terms of pre-Islamic political concepts.' Watt, *Islamic Political Thought*, p. 14. See also R.B. Serjeant, 'The Sunnah Jāmia'h, Pacts with the Yathrib Jews, and the Tahrīm of Yathrib: Analysis and Translation of the Documents Comprised in the so-called "Constitution of Medina"' in *Bulletin of the School of Oriental and African Studies*, XVI (1978), pp. 1–42.

or, for that matter, the legitimacy of his Prophethood.[19] It is likely that once Muhammad realised that political control alone could not secure the total allegiance of those who had come to form his community, he found it necessary to conduct his politics and organise his community on overtly different lines. The religious factor which had always been important may now have assumed a much more crucial role. It led to Muhammad's more insistent assertion that there was an alternative and superior centre of power that was Divine and that the true *umma* consisted of those prepared to accept him as the chosen bearer of this Divine authority.[20] In doing so he ushered in the more familiar features of the *civitas Islamica*.

But the immediate historical exigencies of his time were not the only reasons for Muhammad's resort to and reliance upon the machinations and modalities of power. For if that were the case the spectacular military victories and the steady expansion of Islam in his lifetime ought to have been sufficiently reassuring to encourage him to return to the business of conventional religious proselytisation. To have done so however would be to negate 'the inevitable fulfilment of Muhammad's Prophethood'.[21] For politics was not some temporary compromise in the face of adverse conditions but integral to the very ends that Islam was designed to represent. For Muhammad's disciples these ends needed continuously to be worked out through a political order where Muslims would yield power as the sole repositories of God's will.[22]

The Muslim understanding of the role and pursuit of power is best summarised by the medieval jurist, Ibn Taymiya. He wrote, 'the exercise of authority is a religious function and a good work which brings near to God, and drawing near to God means obeying God and his Prophet'.[23] Much later, in his *Muqaddima*, Ibn Khaldūn was to reaffirm the supreme importance of military and political power for the successful propagation of religion. Relying on a prophetic tradition, he maintained, 'God sent no prophet who did not enjoy the protection of his people'.[24] In the twentieth century, Islam's relation to politics and power was more

---

[19] S.D. Goitein, 'The Four Faces of Islam' in *Studies in Islamic History and Institutions* (Leiden, E.J. Brill, 1966), pp. 30–8.
[20] For a discussion of what he calls this 'ideology' see Rodinson, *Mohammed*, pp. 234–41.
[21] Rahman, *Islam*, p. 22.
[22] Its theoretical dimensions – medieval and modern – are worked out in E.I.J. Rosenthal, *Political Thought in Medieval Islam* (Cambridge University Press, 1958) and Hamid Enayet, *Modern Islamic Political Thought* (London, Macmillan, 1982).
[23] Quoted in Rosenthal, *Political Thought*, p. 54.
[24] Ibn Khaldun, *The Muqaddimah*, I, E.I.J. Rosenthal (trans.) (London, Routledge and Kegan Paul, 1958), p. 322.

philosophically cast by Muhammad Iqbāl. 'Is it possible' he asked, 'to retain Islam as an ethical ideal and to reject it as a polity...?' He answered categorically: 'the religious order of Islam is organically related to the social order which it has created. The rejection of the one will eventually involve the rejection of the other.'[25]

No doubt these interpretations owe much to the absence of any formal distinction in Muslim law between power and authority.[26] Traditionally, the institution of the Caliphate was seen to embody both aspects and even when in practice they were separated, as in the eleventh century with the emergence of powerful Muslim *amīrs* independent of the Caliph, their fusion remained an ideal norm.[27]

In modern times, Muslims as different from one another as Maulānā Abū'l Kalām Āzād and Sayyid Qutb have approached the notion of power not as a quantity that is intrinsically corrupting, apropos say of Christian doctrine, but as God's most eminent instrument for Man in the service of Divine justice. For Maulānā Āzād, Islam's greatest contribution lay in the restoration of power as a legitimate pursuit without forfeiting morality. Judaism, he argued, had taught men to invoke power to escape enslavement while Christianity had stressed morality as necessary to resist the temptations of the temporal world. Islam alone, he claimed, had sought to reunite power and morality by instituting a social order that was both fundamentally power-oriented as well as righteous.[28]

For Sayyid Qutb, the importance of power stemmed incontrovertibly from the mandate handed to the Muslim community. This, he maintained, consisted in assuming 'the role of leadership of humanity'. For him 'Islam [was] not a theological system that is realised when appropriated as an ideology', but 'a pragmatic activistic system of life'.[29] As a political radical, Qutb was not naturally inclined to be

---

[25] Iqbal's presidential address to the All India Muslim League in December 1930 quoted in S.S. Pirzada (ed.), *Foundations of Pakistan*, II (Karachi, National Publishing House, 1970), pp. 156–7.
[26] Indeed, it has recently been argued that the authority of the early Caliphate extended also to religious authority which has otherwise been presumed by conventional scholarship to have been the preserve of the *'ulamā'*. Patricia Crone and Martin Hinds, *God's Caliph: Religious Authority in the first Centuries of Islam* (Cambridge University Press, 1986).
[27] Rosenthal, *Political Thought*, pp. 23–4. See also H.A.R. Gibb, 'Some Considerations on the Sunni Theory of the Caliphate', *Archives d'histoire du droit Oriental*, 3 (1948), pp. 401–10.
[28] Abū'l Kalām Āzād, 'Al-dīn w-al siyāsat' in Mahmūdul Hasan Siddīquī (ed.), *Mazāmīn-i-al-Balāgh* (Lahore, Ainah-e-Adab, 1981), pp. 11–36.
[29] Yvonne Haddad, 'Sayyid Qutb: Ideologue of Islamic Revival' in John L. Esposito (ed.), *Voices of Resurgent Islam* (New York, Oxford University Press, 1983), pp. 80–2.

embarrassed by the pursuit of power. However, what is particularly revealing is that so much of what he wrote and said should have been acknowledged by him and others to be a truthful exposition of his faith and its relationship to power.[30]

For Muslims like Āzād and Qutb, the purpose of power was clearly to obtain salvation by the extension of Divine Justice through worldly conquest; but power has also been seen by other Muslims to constitute the indispensable means of guaranteeing the solidarity of the community. The steady disintegration of the Muslim community, particularly after the eleventh century, had led Muslim thinkers, like Ibn Taymiya and al-Baghdādī, to conclude that it was primarily the loss of power that had contributed to the erosion of communal solidarity.[31] The urgent appeal of this idea manifested itself in the eighteenth and nineteenth centuries particularly in India and the Middle East where men like Shāh Walīullāh and Jamāl al-Dīn al Afghānī battled relentlessly for the return of Muslim power in the name of Muslim solidarity.[32]

Like their forebears, Āzād and Qutb found the implications of the loss of Muslim power and unity to be profoundly disturbing and fundamentally inadmissible. Without power, wrote Āzād, the community was disunited and disunity signified *jāhilīyya* (barbarism).[33] For Qutb power was the means to a universal, civilised society – a society guided and united by God's Law, the *Sharīʿa*. The absence of power led to inhumanity and the very negation of all that Islam was seen to signify.[34]

If it is true that communal solidarity, or the lack of it, can evoke profound sentiments among Muslims, what precisely are the forms of ideal conduct, political or otherwise, that are actually demanded by such solidarity? It has been suggested by Montgomery Watt that the notion of communal solidarity in Islam proceeds naturally from a view which encourages men to act primarily as members of a community, rather than as individual persons.[35] Others see the preoccupation with communal solidarity to stem from the absence in traditional Muslim

---

[30] The influence of Qutb's ideas upon contemporary politics in the Middle East is examined in Emmanuel Sivan, *Radical Islam: Medieval Theology and Modern Politics* (New Haven, Yale University Press, 1985).

[31] Rosenthal, *Political Thought*, pp. 32–3, 51–61.

[32] Fazlur Rahman, 'The Thinker of Crisis: Shah Waliy-ullah'. *Pakistan Quarterly*, 6, 2 (1956), pp. 44–8; S.A.A. Rizvi, *A History of Sufism in India*, II (Delhi, Munshiram Manoharlal, 1983), pp. 374–86; Nikki Keddie, *Sayyid Jamal al Din al Afghani; a political biography* (Berkeley, University of California Press, 1972).

[33] Āzād, 'Al-dīn w-al siyāsat', p. 35.

[34] For a detailed treatment of Qutb's notion of *jāhilīyya*, see Sivàn, *Radical Islam*, pp. 16–49.

[35] Watt, *Islamic Political Thought*, pp. 96–8.

thinking of an ontological understanding of Man as an isolated reality.[36]

Whatever the reasons for their communal bias, it is abundantly clear that Muslims tend, more often than not, to evaluate individuals strictly within their communal framework. It is however worth noting that the way in which Muslims conceive of the communal 'whole' and its relationship with the individuals that constitute it, is in fact, quite distinct from other familiar parallels. Roger Garaudy has observed that the Islamic 'whole' and the place of the individual within it is comparable neither to Hegel's notion of state and society as an 'organic reality', nor akin to the totalitarianism postulated by Fascism. He argues that the relationship of whole to part, in the Muslim world-view, shares little with parallels drawn either from the biology of living matter or functional theory. For these, he declares, rest incontrovertibly on an assumption notably absent in Muslim theory: that society, or the social organisation, is itself its own end.[37]

Muslims themselves would be inclined to agree with Garaudy. Few would deny the holistic bias in their thinking, though many would, like him, question its likeness to contemporary forms of Western holism. They would assert fundamental differences between systems wherein men pursue ends that are ultimately of their own making and those where they endeavour to fulfil God's transcendent scheme.[38]

Perhaps no aspect of traditional Muslim thinking so lends itself, potentially, to the charge of holism as its approach to the question of individual rights. Some, like Montgomery Watt, have cast doubt on the very existence of any such approach and point to the notable absence of 'any mention of the rights of man'.[39] Others, like Gardet and Grunebaum, have drawn attention to the distinct understanding of rights amongst Muslims not so much in terms of the secondary importance accorded to them, but in terms of their accepted source. Gardet, for example, has suggested that the specificity of the Muslim notion of individual rights stems primarily from its rejection of the premise that these inhere in the individual or derive from any 'Natural Law'. On the contrary, Muslims, he argues, see the source of all rights to

[36] See in particular Louis Gardet, *La Cité Musulmane: vie sociale et politique* (Paris, Librarie Philosophique J. Vrin, 1961) and Franz Rosenthal, *The Muslim Concept of Freedom* (Leiden, E.J. Brill, 1960).

[37] Roger Garaudy, *Promesses de l'Islam* (Paris, Editions du Seuil, 1981), pp. 64–7.

[38] Fazlur Rahman, *Major Themes of the Quran* (Mineapolis and Chicago, Bibliotheca Islamica, 1980), pp. 17–64.

[39] Watt, *Islamic Political Thought*, p. 96.

lie in 'the common law of the believer accorded by God to those who adhere to his pact'.[40]

Grunebaum too has been concerned to show the existence of a 'theory' of rights amongst Muslims. Like Gardet, he acknowledges their dissociation from any ontological understanding of Man and stresses that 'rights come to life' only for the believer. It is primarily the Muslim's religious tie, he concludes, that 'fixes for each member and for all members together the conditions and rules of life'.[41]

No doubt the complexity that attaches to the question of rights in Muslim thinking owes much to the fact that Muslims themselves tend to be aware much less of rights than of their obligations to God. Muslims, as Watt has emphasised, 'act, or refrain from acting' because God has commanded it rather than because society expects it.[42] This is both consistent with, and integral to the Muslim's faith.

Muslim notions of individual equality and freedom support the view that these are seen to derive pre-eminently from the believer's communal existence rather than his human attributes. While it is true therefore that many Muslims remain deeply committed to the idea of egalitarianism, they do so on the understanding that true 'equality does not effectively establish itself except amongst the believers' – that is members of Muhammad's *umma*.[43] Juridical equality, which alone can confer rights, remains therefore squarely within the organised community of believers.

No less distinct in meaning and problematic in content are Muslim approaches to individual freedom and liberty. In part this stems from the very paradox, wherein the Muslim links true freedom to his submission to God, His Prophet and His Community. But this metaphysical understanding of freedom inevitably raises difficult questions at the level of social and political action. Franz Rosenthal in his study of *The Muslim Concept of Freedom*, has acknowledged that the idea of freedom did in fact command the attention of medieval jurists. Nevertheless, he doubts whether it was ever considered a 'basic human attribute' or 'of any real value for the individual if the individual was properly adjusted to the permanent metaphysical establishment'.[44] Because of this, Rosenthal argues, freedom as a political force never occupied 'a central position within the [Muslim] political organism and

[40] Gardet, *La Cité Musulmane*, p. 102.
[41] von Grunebaum, *Modern Islam*, p. 49.
[42] Watt, *Islamic Political Thought*, p. 96.
[43] Gardet, *La Cité Musulmane*, p. 57.
[44] Franz Rosenthal, *The Muslim Concept of Freedom*, pp. 34, 121.

system of thought'.[45] Rosenthal does, of course, acknowledge the pre-eminent need to preserve Muslim society 'as a completely integrated structure' as an important contributing factor but, he emphasises, this absence of a consistent theory of freedom and the pressure to conform were, nevertheless, to produce profound consequences. It led quite simply to the failure 'to produce rebels against societal restraint who might have fought such restraint openly in the name of individual liberty'.[46]

The nature of the community as Muslims have seen it over generations, as one that is Divine in origin and integrated in purpose, has determined their attitude to both the significance and the scope of individual conduct. The primacy and solidarity of the community was sought by positing, on the one hand, an active communal existence as the only legitimate source of individual rights and, on the other, a rigid monotheism that demanded a unified, if not always, united community. Even if it is increasingly the case that individual Muslims today no longer, consciously, associate their allegiance to the communal group with their obligations to submit to Divine commandments, they are nevertheless aware that a show of individual political dissent is likely to appear dangerously like *bid'a* or innovation, which traditionally bred heresy.[47]

However powerful the tendency amongst Muslims to think primarily in terms of their community as an integrated social and political structure, bound by its monotheistic doctrine, it would be naive to pretend that this community signifies today what it did to Muhammad's early disciples. The political realities which followed the decline of the Muslim Caliphate in the eleventh century led many Muslims to concentrate increasingly upon religious solidarity as the only real bond that drew Muslims together.[48] Without quite abandoning the ideal of the religio-political community, therefore, jurists sought to adjust the theory of the Caliphate by investing it with symbolic powers that would

---

[45] *Ibid.*, p. 122.
[46] *Ibid.*
[47] The evils of *bid'a* tended especially to preoccupy Sunni thinking. The idea of what does and does not constitute legitimate dissent in Islam has of course been challenged, most notably by the Shīʻa's but also by other lesser known sectarian groups, including the Khāwarij. See Henri Laoust, *Les Schismes dans l'Islam* (Paris, Payot, 1965) and Rahman, *Islam*, pp. 167–80. For one study of the revolutionary implications of Shīʻa dissent see Nikki Keddie, *Roots of Revolution: An Interpretive History of Modern Iran* (New Haven, Yale University Press, 1981).
[48] Its effects upon Indo-Muslim thinking have been examined in some depth in Hardy, *Partners in Freedom*.

continue to reflect a universal Muslim community, albeit bereft of political unity.[49]

In this century, drastic changes have entailed an even deeper shift in the original meaning of the Muslim community as a universal religio-political entity. The emergence of territorial nationalism in the nineteenth century and its subsequent consolidation appears to have decisively checked (at least for the time being) the momentum in the direction of a universal Muslim community more popularly known as 'pan-Islamism'.[50] Where attempts have been made to incorporate larger numbers of Muslims of diverse nationalities into a common federation, as, for example, in the 1950s under the garb of 'pan-Arabism', these have been vociferously denounced by Muslim fundamentalists.[51] Their opposition stems from their antagonism to the inherently secular orientations of 'pan-Arabism' which, they argue, by including non-Muslims who do not adhere to Islamic tenets, undermine the very ends of the universal Islamic community.[52] For them, better the pain of Muslim political disunity and the bitter pill of territorial Muslim nationalism than any compromise with a Godless universalism.

The dilemmas expressed in this debate had already become familiar to Muslims elsewhere earlier in this century. In India, Muslims had been debating amongst themselves at least since the 1930s on the merits of a Muslim territorial state which, though incompatible with Islamic universalism, still promised a measure of real protection for their faith against the composite, secular nationalism propounded by Congress which threatened their political existence but left intact the notion of an integrated community.

There were of course differences that shaped Muslim approaches to this question in the Middle East and India. Not least important was the fact that while in the Middle East Muslims did in fact constitute the majority and were therefore neither politically nor culturally threatened (except indirectly by the ubiquitous presence of 'Westernism'), it was quite the reverse in the Indian subcontinent. Here Muslims were a minority and many believed that both their cultural autonomy and their political future were in danger of being displaced by the demands of a predominantly non-Muslim secular nationalism. For some the solution appeared to lie in a separate Muslim state, but for others this option

[49] A.K.S. Lambton, *State and Government in medieval Islam: the jurists* (Oxford University Press, 1981).
[50] James Piscatori (ed.), *Islam in a world of Nation-States* (Cambridge University Press, 1986).
[51] Sivan, *Radical Islam*, pp. 28–47.
[52] *Ibid.*, p. 45.

signified a tacit and inadmissible compromise with the idea of territorial nationalism that would further divide an already widely dispersed Muslim population.[53]

There is little doubt that Muslim nationalism in the twentieth century constitutes a significant break with the principles of a universal Islamic community. Summarising the intellectual mood that pervaded the Muslim world in the 1920s, Sir Hamilton Gibb wrote of a new spirit which advocated 'a family of Islamic nations independently organised under civil governments' without compromising the idea of a common Islamic heritage or the value of an Islamic Commonwealth.[54] Iqbāl was among those who came to express the re-orientations in Muslim thinking. In 1934 he wrote

For the present every Muslim nation must sink into her own deeper self, temporarily focus her vision on herself alone, until all are strong and powerful to form a living family of republics. A true and living unity .... is truly manifested in a multiplicity of free independent units whose racial rivalries are adjusted and harmonized by the unifying bond of a common spiritual aspiration.[55]

The place of the community as a central organising principle in Muslim social and political life suggests some important consequences for political representation. If we accept that a useful starting point consists in defining who or what is represented, then it is reasonable to assume that Muslims will tend more often than not to presuppose a form of communal rather than individual representation. The emphasis upon Man as an irredeemable part of a cosmic and social 'whole' leads inexorably away from the preoccupation with the claims, political or otherwise, of the individual.[56] Insofar as Muslims have tended to define themselves in relation to the 'community of believers', the interests they espouse are seen, whether or not this is in fact the case, to pertain not to themselves as individuals but to their community as a whole.

If, on the other hand, the question of communal representation amongst Muslims is approached by way of traditional Muslim theories

---

[53] For a discussion of the quite different attitudes to nationalism expressed by modern-day Muslims, depending on whether or not they happen to constitute minorities or majorities, see J.O. Voll, *Islam: Continuity and Change, in the Modern World.* (Boulder, Colorado, Westview Press, 1982), chapters 5 and 6.

[54] H.A.R. Gibb, *Whither Islam?* (London, Victor Gollancz, 1932), p. 364.

[55] Muhammad Iqbal, 'The Principle of Movement in the Structure of Islam' in *The Reconstruction of Religious Thought in Islam* (London, Oxford University Press, 1934), p. 151.

[56] Nieuwenhuijze, 'The Ummah', p. 21. For rather more legalistic interpretations of the place of the individual in Muslim thinking see N.J. Coulson, 'The State and the Individual in Islamic Law', *International and Comparative Law Quarterly*, 6, part I (January 1957), pp. 49–60 and Henry Siegman, 'The State and the Individual in Sunni Islam', *The Muslim World*, LIV, 1 (1964), pp. 14–26.

of the Caliphate, it is plain that there the *vox populi* is clearly assumed to be corporately rather than individually vested.[57] Medieval Muslim theorists of the Caliphate from al-Māwardī to Ibn-Jāmaʿā all took as their starting point the assumption that the Caliph represented the *body* of Muslims before God.[58] As the vice-regent to whom Muhammad was believed to have delegated his powers in order to ensure that Muslims lived their lives in obedience to God's law, the Caliph's role was pre-eminently that of the intermediary between God and his community.

What is distinctive about Muslim views up to the nineteenth century is not that they regarded the Caliph's powers as divine in origin nor that they believed he acted on behalf of an integrated society rather than of the individuals composing that society. Both themes had already found echoes in medieval Jewish and Christian political theory which saw the institution of kingship as divine and its role as one of mediation between God and a human, primarily religious, society.[59] What *is* peculiar to traditional Muslim political thought is its understanding of its own society as pre-eminently engaged in the service of some higher end beyond those devised by individual human interest. What this implies politically, as Hardy has so powerfully argued, is that Muslims who act on behalf of other Muslims do so not in relation to what might be described as 'a self-governing collectivity' but 'in the name of Islam'.[60] This is embodied most essentially in the process of *ijmāʿ* or communal consensus which has frequently been compared by Muslims to representative or public opinion.

Ijmāʿ: the basis of political consensus

The unifying and self-preserving impulses of the traditional Muslim community were perhaps best expressed through one of its most complex and subtle processes – *ijmāʿ*.[61] As a term that has traditionally signified both procedure and outcome, its translation has generally been

[57] Some of the problems posed by this view of representation in the evolution of a constitution for Pakistan immediately after independence are discussed in Lini May, *The Evolution of Indo-Muslim Thought after 1857* (Lahore, Shaikh Muhammad Ashraf, 1970), pp. 307–23.

[58] Rosenthal, *Political Thought*, pp. 21–61. See also H.A.R. Gibb, 'Al-Māwardī's Theory of the Khalīfah', *Islamic Culture*, 11 (1937), pp. 291–302.

[59] Rosenthal, *Political Thought*, pp. 13–20.

[60] Peter Hardy, 'Force and Violence in Indo-Persian Writing on History and Government in Medieval South Asia', in Milton Israel (ed.), *Islamic Society and Culture: Essays in Honour of Professor Aziz Ahmad* (New Delhi, Manohar, 1983), pp. 199–200.

[61] *The Encyclopaedia of Islam*, III (Leiden, E.J. Brill, 1971), pp. 1023–6. See also G.F. Hourani, 'The Basis of Authority of Consensus in Sunnite Islam', *Studia Islamica*, 21 (1964), pp. 13–60.

rendered as the 'agreed practice' of the community.[62] The actual variety of interpretations accorded to its meaning however, has led some scholars to suggest that the notion of *ijmā'* in Muslim discourse is characterised by 'an absence of complete conceptualization'.[63] Muslims themselves have ruefully conceded that there is, in fact, little agreement about 'agreed practice'![64]

Kenneth Cragg has observed that the continuing debate about *ijmā'* stems primarily from disagreement about its scope and purpose.[65] Those who claim that the application of *ijmā'* is to be confined to matters of exegesis have tended, on the whole, to regard the body of technically trained religious scholars to be its main exponents.[66] Those, on the other hand, who believe the function of *ijmā'* to lie in providing practical guidance on all matters relating to the past and present life of the Community are inclined to see it as the prerogative of the Community.[67]

It is the second of these interpretations, expressed more generally by modern Muslims, that is of specific concern here. For it is one that has tended to see in *ijmā'* either the potential for a popular democratic assembly,[68] or the signs of a burgeoning Muslim 'public interest'[69] and even evidence of 'an enlightened [Muslim] public opinion'.[70] In short, they all assume that *ijmā'* approximates, what modern political parlance deems, representative opinion. It is necessary therefore that any study of

---

[62] Rahman, *Islam*, pp. 72–5.
[63] Watt, *Islamic Political Thought*, p. 98.
[64] Rahman, *Islam*, p. 262.
[65] Kenneth Cragg, *Counsels in Contemporary Islam* (Edinburgh University Press, 1965), pp. 74–83.
[66] Some typical expositions of this view, helf chiefly by the *'ulamā'*, in Pakistan may be found in *The Report of the Court of Inquiry – Munir Report . . . (to enquire into the Punjab Disturbances of 1953)* (Lahore, Government Printing, 1954), pp. 208–11.
[67] The 'modernist' stance on *ijmā'* is perhaps most cogently expressed by Fazlur Rahman who concludes 'The question, then, as to who is competent or "authorized" to interpret divine law turns out to be not a serious question at all, since the physical source of all authority and power is the Muslim Community'. Rahman, *Islam*, p. 263.
[68] A view espoused by Rashīd Ridā and Muhammad Iqbāl. For some modern assessments of Rashīd Ridā's view of *ijmā'*, see Malcolm Kerr, *Islamic Reforms: The Political and Legal theories of Muhammad Abduh and Rashid Rida* (Berkeley, University of California Press, 1966), pp. 197–204; A.H. Hourani, *Arabic Thought in the Liberal Age (1798–1939)* (London, Oxford University Press, 1962), pp. 230–44 and E.I.J. Rosenthal, 'Religion and Politics in Islam', *Islam and the Modern Age*, I, 1 (1970), pp. 50–64. For discussions of Iqbāl's theory of *ijmā'* see Aziz Ahmad, *Islamic Modernism*, pp. 153–5; and Parveen Feroze Hassan, *The Political Philosophy of Iqbal* (Lahore, Publishers United, n.d.), pp. 143–50.
[69] On 'Abduh see Kerr, *Islamic Reforms*, pp. 143–5; Hourani, *Arabic Thought*, pp. 130–60 and Cragg, *Counsels*, pp. 33–41.
[70] Rahman, *Islam*, p. 75.

Muslim attitudes to representation and representative opinion should include some attention to the idea of *ijmā'* both in its traditional sense and its more modern expressions.

Whatever the disagreements among Muslims, both past and present, as to who, or what, constitutes the consensus of their community, there appears always to have been some common understanding of its role as an instrument of social cohesion. Thus, the value of *ijmā'* has traditionally been seen to rest pre-eminently in its capacity to counteract individual activity and thereby to ensure the solidarity of the community.[71] This emphasis upon its homogenising power has, however, in the eyes of some Muslims like Fazlur Rahman contributed substantially to *ijmā'*'s later development as a bastion of conservatism and a 'static tool of oppression'.[72] Instead of developing into a dynamic force embodying a creative public opinion that would initiate and demand change, *ijmā'* degenerated into 'a mere recognizer of the brute force of circumstances'.[73]

One reason for the development of *ijmā'* as an agent of conformity rather than creative change may have stemmed from the absence of any real debate about the scope of individual dissent in relation to the communal consensus.[74] Where such possibilities were explored, as for example in the works of the eighteenth-century, Indo-Muslim scholar, Shāh Walīullāh, the approach has been distinctly conservative.[75] His underlying assumption (understandable in the light of his principal concern to restore the religious solidarity of a deeply divided Muslim community in India) was that there were no individual (or sectarian) concerns such as were not open to incorporation into the body of the dominant consensus – namely Sunnī orthodox tradition.[76] Being essentially catholic in temperament, Shāh Walīullāh was unable to ignore the significance or the value of individual differences; as a Muslim, committed to the restoration of his community's traditional solidarity, however, he remained deeply sceptical of their value as sources of innovation. Nor surprisingly, therefore, his appreciation of the positive contribution of individual speculative reasoning, *ijtihād* was substanti-

---

[71] Nieuwenhuijze, 'The Ummah', p. 21.
[72] Rahman, *Islam*, p. 72.
[73] *Ibid.*
[74] On the ambiguities surrounding the question of dissent in Islam see *The Encyclopaedia of Islam* III, p. 1024.
[75] Rizvi, *A History of Sufism*, pp. 374–8.
[76] I.H. Qureshi, *Ulema in Politics: A Study Relating to the political activities of the Ulema in the South Asian Subcontinent from 1556 to 1947* (Karachi, Ma'aref, 1972), pp. 107–26.

ally qualified by calling for its subordination to the consensus of other *'ulamā'*.[77]

The object of *ijmā'*, as medieval Muslim scholars understood it, was to ensure the absolute unity of the *umma*. At the same time, however, they also believed that in order to be truly effective, *ijmā'* needed to be based upon a recognisable degree of unanimity.[78] Traditionally, such unanimity was sought within the body of religious scholars, the *'ulamā'*, who actually made the decisions that were subsequently accepted as the *ijmā'* of the community.[79] Although such unanimity was rarely assumed to imply the complete absence of dissenting views it did clearly reject *ikhtilāf* or 'the dissemination of... different ideologies', the protagonists of which would attempt 'to seek the support of a majority'.[80] Indeed, what has always been at stake in the definition of *ijmā'* is its radical distinction from forms of consensus which relied upon 'the law of numbers' for their final sanction.

The reluctance to equate *ijmā'* with notions of representative opinion derived from the rules of 'arithmetical democracy', has contributed substantially to the ambiguities that surround its modern interpretations. For while considerable efforts have been made, most notably in the works of Muhammad Iqbāl and Rashīd Ridā, to question the exclusive right of a minority such as the *'ulamā'* to constitute *ijmā'*, they remain characteristically averse to any easy co-relation between *ijmā'* and the norms of Western popular democracy. One reason for this appears to have been the absence of any notion within Muslim discourse of *ijmā'* as a consensus directly founded on the *vox populi*. No doubt, this in turn contributed substantially to its rather limited traditional definition as a process concerned with the discovery and resolution of the Law for which task only the technically competent were seen to be fit. At the same time, it is important to stress the point that, even traditionally, the decisions of the Doctors did not formally constitute *ijmā'* without the general assent of the Muslim community;[81] and,

---

[77] Aziz Ahmad, *Studies in Islamic Culture in the Indian Environment* (Oxford, Clarendon Press, 1964). pp. 204–5.

[78] *The Encyclopaedia of Islam*, III, p. 1023.

[79] *Ijmā'*, argues one contemporary Muslim scholar, was never deemed to be the prerogative of the people. 'The view of Muslims over centuries has been that giving opinion on the problems of Law should be the function of the *'ulamā'* ... The concept of *ijmā'* has always implied the consensus of those qualified in matters of Law...'. Seyyed Hossein Nasr, *Ideals and Realities of Islam* (Boston, Beacon Press, 1972), p. 100. Gardet points out that the only means by which *ijmā'* could ensure the unity of the *umma* lay in the quest for unanimity among a small body of religious scholars. Gardet, *La Cité Musulmane*, p. 123.

[80] Rizvi, *A History of Sufism*, p. 378.

[81] Ignaz Goldziher, *Le Dogme et la Loi de l'Islam* (Paris, Edition Geuthner, 1920), p. 45.

although such assent could, more often than not, be taken for granted, its importance as a necessary condition has been by modernists to suggest a measure of popular participation.

Nevertheless, the idea of *ijmā'* as the result of a consciously formulated popular voice is notably absent even in modern Muslim political discourse. Nor, for that matter, does it lend itself easily to comparisons with an 'unconscious' General Will, such as Rousseau was to make familiar to Western political theory.[82] The problem lies of course in the distinction between forms of representative opinion that recognise the claims of the majority as decisive and one whose very legitimacy is seen to depend upon a broader consensus. But the problem of equating *ijmā'* with notions of popular public opinion, whether in the context of representative or direct democracies, is obviously more complex and needs greater attention.[83]

Firstly, and perhaps most importantly, the institution of *ijmā'* is founded upon the assumption that it reflects a profoundly integrated society that bears little or no relation to the social and political pluralism common to Western representative democracies. This is not to say that the process of *ijmā'* actually represents a society bound by a substantive consensus. What it does suggest is that the role of dissent as a form of legitimate political activity is far less central to Muslim discourse than to Western democratic theory.[84]

The second difficulty, and one that is encountered most frequently in superficial comparisons drawn between *ijmā'* and Rousseau's General Will, stems from ignoring *ijmā'*'s intrinsic relation to a body of transcendent rules. Admittedly both approaches share much in common. Both tend to mystify the voice of the social aggregate and both are inclined to treat its expression as an unconscious if not imperceptible

---

[82] This is not to say that comparisons have not in fact been attempted. See Sami G. Hajjar, 'The Jamahiriya Experiment in Libya: Qadhafi and Rousseau', *The Journal of Modern African Studies*, 18, 2 (1980), pp. 181–200.

[83] For one recent attempt to explore the 'democratic dimension' inherent in the institutional forms peculiar to West African Islam see Donal B. Cruise O'Brien, 'Wails and Whispers: the people's voice in West African Muslim politics' in Patrick Chabal (ed.), *Political Domination in Africa: Reflections on the Limits of Power* (Cambridge University Press, 1986), pp. 71–83.

[84] The practice of *ijtihād* or individual judgement has, however, been exploited differently by Muslim 'reformists' on the one hand, and 'modernists' on the other. The former have used it to express their opposition to the established political order in nominally Muslim societies, while the latter have sought to direct it against the hold of religious orthodoxy. See John Voll, 'Renewal and Reform in Islamic History: *Tajdid* and *Islah*' in John L. Esposito (ed.), *Voices of Resurgent Islam* (Oxford University Press, 1983), pp. 32–47 and Rahman, *Islam*, pp. 77–9, 214–26. On the concept of *ijtihād*, see *The Encyclopaedia of Islam*, III, pp. 1026–7.

process.[85] On the other hand, their differences on the precise modes by which the 'communal consensus' and the 'General Will' are to be finally obtained, set them radically apart. Here, Gardet reminds us that 'whereas in Rousseau consensus results from the sum of votes, a norm unto itself, in Islam this consensus is subjected to a supreme positive law that is held to be Divinely revealed.'[86] The one has no sanction beyond the force of popular numerical configurations; the other rests clearly on the principle that transcendent rules not numbers determine its authenticity.

It is precisely in this difference that the antipathy of the two approaches is most fully contained. For while Rousseau's *vox populi* is self-evidently supreme and provides the grounds, theoretically at least, for the rejection of any representation, the very nature of *ijmāʿ* as essentially the quest for Divine rules has been seen by Muslims to necessitate some mediation, though by whom remains admittedly open to question. Muslim scholars like Abū'l Aʿlā Maudūdī, for whom the Islamic state is a 'popular vicegerency', nevertheless believed that 'Islamic knowledge' must constitute a prerequisite for those who exercised *ijmāʿ*.[87] Even those Muslim modernists, like Muhammad Iqbāl and Muhammad ʿAbduh in Egypt, who were concerned to introduce a more popular dimension to *ijmāʿ*, saw it primarily as a process of deliberation involving a degree of expertise rather than an exercise in direct democracy.[88]

However, if there are real problems in attempting to understand *ijmāʿ* in terms of Western notions of representation and consensus, is its usefulness as an analytical tool for the study of Muslim attitudes to representation substantially diminished? Is it possible, or indeed realistic, to refer to the *ijmāʿ* of a modern Muslim community such as was present in colonial India when its sheer political diversity, to say nothing of its social and political differentiation, appeared to be the very antithesis of consensus, let alone, unanimity? Is it reasonable to suppose that those who claimed to represent this community, and who were for the most part not members of the class of '*ulamā*', were qualified as such to formulate the *ijmāʿ* of their community? What, if anything, can the

---

[85] For Goldziher, 'le sentiment général de la communauté (*ijma*) [s'exprime] 'non dans des synodes et des conciles, mais par une vox populi presque inconscient, qui dans sa collectivité est censée ne pas pouvoir se tromper'. Goldziher, *Le Dogme*, p. 45. See also Jean Jacques Rousseau, *Du Contrat Social* (Paris, Garnier-Flammarion, 1966).

[86] Gardet, *La Cité Musulmane*, p. 122.

[87] Charles J. Adams, 'Mawdudi and the Islamic State', in Esposito (ed.), *Voices of Resurgent Islam*, pp. 116, 124.

[88] Hourani, 'The Basis of Authority', pp. 42–3 and Aziz Ahmad, *Islamic Modernism*, p. 155.

institution and the practice of *ijmā'* really tell us about who and what actually represented the wishes of Indian Muslims or how these wishes were, in fact, ascertained?

The tenor of modern Muslim thinking suggests that the institution of *ijmā'* is deemed not only to be wholly relevant to the life of modern Muslim political communities but also that its adaptation and application are important priorities in the process of Muslim intellectual reconstruction. It suggests that Muslims in the twentieth century believe that the growing complexity of Muslim communities and their tremendous regional differences do not, in themselves, invalidate the consensus of a common culture and civilisation.[89] Nor would they, in the light of contemporary Muslim concern with the right of the community as a whole to constitute *ijmā'*, be inclined to associate it exclusively with the *'ulamā'*.[90]

Finally, the view that *ijmā'* can and does provide an accurate reflection of Muslim public opinion, even if such opinion is not expressed through the formal apparatus of election, is tenaciously held by Muslims today. Indeed to some, like the distinguished Indo-Muslim scholar Aziz Ahmad, the great strength of *ijmā'* lies precisely in its ability to convey gradually and *over time* and without the pressures of transient popular demands, the 'true' interests of the community.[91]

It is necessary now to consider in somewhat greater detail the way in which modern Muslims have treated these issues. One of the most dangerous consequences of Western imperialism for many Muslims has quite obviously been the steady fragmentation of their community. Political disunity, the emergence of nationalism and the insidious presence of secular values are seen as fundamental threats to the ideals of Muhammad's universal community.[92] In the absence of any structural homogeneity, what has preoccupied Muslim thinkers was whether or not there still remained a *substantive consensus* that could render *ijmā'* meaningful even in the radically changed circumstances provoked by Western imperial domination.

The pan-Islamic movement and the campaign for a universal Muslim Caliphate which gained momentum in the 1890s, largely under the influence of Jamāl al-Dīn al Afghānī, were expressions of this new

[89] Altaf Gauhar (ed.), *The Challenge of Islam* (London, Islamic Council of Europe, 1978).

[90] John J. Donahue and John L. Esposito (eds.), *Islam in Transition: Muslim Perspectives* (New York, Oxford University Press, 1982).

[91] Aziz Ahmad, *Studies in Islamic Culture*, p. 75. Similarly, Seyyed Hossein Nasr believes that *ijmā'* is a process 'whose results are only gradually felt'. Seyyed Hossein Nasr, *Ideals and Realities*, p. 100.

[92] Mohammad Ayoob (ed.), *The Politics of Islamic Reassertion* (New York, St. Martin's Press, 1982).

concern.[93] Although the demand for a universal Caliphate was subsequently abandoned, no doubt because of its historical inappropriateness, the authenticity of 'pan-Islamism' as a principle, if not as a political movement, was never directly challenged. Even those like the Turkish sociologist and ideologue, Ziya Gökalp, who remained sceptical of its value in the service of a universal Muslim consensus, were unwilling to reject it altogether.[94] Likewise in India, Muhammad Iqbāl fought relentlessly for a 'national' Muslim 'homeland' without ever abandoning his commitment to a worldwide Muslim community bound by its sense of high destiny.[95] For both men, neither Turanian nationalism nor Muslim separatism could abate their insistent vision of a faith founded on brotherhood and consensus.

But there was yet another kind of rupture that threatened the traditional consensus of Muslims by the turn of the last century.[96] This was the increasingly fragile relationship between the community and its religious leaders, the *'ulamā'*, who had once been almost exclusively responsible for the formulation of *ijmā'*. Across the Muslim world, the *'ulamā'* appeared estranged from those whom they regarded as their natural constituency. Their role as conservative guardians and agents of continuity was out of place in a community which, like most others, demanded change.

The problem was one that preoccupied the minds of Muslim scholars in this century, most notably the Syrian, Rashīd Ridā, and, to a somewhat lesser extent, Muhammad Iqbāl. Of the two, Rashīd Ridā was clearly more conscious of the need to restore the traditional consensus which had existed between the *'ulamā'* and members of the Muslim community at large. Through his important treatise, *al-Khalīfah aw al-Imamah al-'Uzma* (translated by Henri Laoust under the title *Le Califat dans la Doctrine de Rasīd Ridā*),[97] and the pages of his influential journal, *al-Manār*, he propounded the view that in order to constitute the *ijmā'* of thier community, the *'ulamā'* must act in conformity with the demands of the present age. This, he argued, they

[93] Nikki Keddie (ed.), *An Islamic Response to Imperialism: Political and Religious Writtings of Sayyid Jamal al-Din al Afghani* (Berkeley and Los Angeles, University of California Press, 1968).

[94] Niyazi Berkes (ed. and trnas.), *Turkish Nationalism and Western Civilization: Selected Essays by Ziya Gökalp* (London, George Allen and Unwin, 1959), pp. 223–7.

[85] Muhammad Iqbal, *Reconstruction of Religious Thought*, pp. 151–2.

[96] Some aspects of this process are illuminated in comparative perspective in Nikki R. Keddie (ed.), *Scholars, Saints and Sufis: Muslim Religious Institutions since 1500* (Berkeley, University of California Press, 1972).

[97] Rashīd Ridā, *Le Califat dans la Doctrine de Rasīd Ridā*, Henri Laoust (trans.) (Beirut, L'Institut Français de Damas, 1938).

could only do by restoring *ijtihād*. Without it the *'ulamā'* would be incapable of initiating reform, which was what, in his view, Muslims needed most urgently.[98] The issue was unquestionably crucial for Rashīd Ridā. For while he was persuaded that the process of *ijmā'* required the participation of the *'ulamā'*, he was enough of a modernist to realise that without a substantial reorientation in their approach to modern legislation, the consensus of the Doctors would cease to constitute the *consensus universalis*.[99]

The status of the *'ulamā'* and its implications for the development of *ijmā'* in the context of the modern Muslim community was of equal concern to Muhammad Iqbāl. Although he was himself persuaded that the only contemporary form *ijmā'* could assume was that of the modern legislative assembly, he remained sceptical of any radical reform. He clearly doubted whether any process of *ijmā'* could benefit from dispensing altogether with the deliberations and counsels of the *'ulamā'*.[100] Aziz Ahmad has suggested that some of Iqbāl's difficulties on the issue of *ijmā'* stemmed precisely from his attempt to formulate a 'modern' theory which would, at the same time, include the *'ulamā'*. It was, he argues, ultimately Iqbāl's 'moderating conservatism' on the question of *ijmā'* that led him to reject 'the unrestrained transfer of the right of constituting *ijmā'* to the masses of the people'.[101]

It is important to bear in mind that however conservative their approaches to *ijmā'* (and the role or the *'ulamā'* therein), both Rashīd Ridā and Iqbāl were part of a wider modernist movement, set in motion in the nineteenth century, which sought to deny any intrinsic relationship between a knowledge of Divine Law and the perception of communal interest. It rested on the claim that *ijmā'* was originally designed to reflect a community that was an integrated spiritual and temporal whole. It argued that the *'ulamā'*, who had traditionally constituted *ijmā'*, did so not as the members of a synod whose authority derived from an established, uniquely spiritual Church 'but as delegates of a freely constituted community'.[102] Their ability to pronounce decisions in the common interest was accessible, even if only in theory, to

---

[98] E.I.J. Rosenthal, 'Some Reflections on the Separation of Religion and Politics in Modern Islam', reprinted separately from *Islamic Studies* (Karachi), Autumn 1964, pp. 254–5.

[99] But much of his commitment to the participation of the *'ulamā'* in the process of law-making and representation stemmed from his conviction that they should be 'free and not mercenaries of the powers that be'. *Ibid.*, p. 258

[100] Muhammad Iqbal, *Reconstruction of Religious Thought in Islam*, pp. 164–7.

[101] Aziz Ahmad, *Islamic Modernism*, p. 155.

[102] A view shared by present day modernists like Fazlur Rahman. See his *Islam* (University of Chicago Press, 1979, 2nd edition), p. 260.

all members of the 'community'. Proponents of this view did of course acknowledge that not all Muslims were capable of exercising considered judgements that would render them *mujtahids*; but those who were, were entitled to participate fully and equally as representatives of their community.

The gist of these ideas was widely elaborated in the nineteenth century by eminent Indo-Muslim reformers, including Sir Sayyid Ahmad Khān and Chirāgh ʿAlī. Sir Sayyid categorically rejected the *ijmāʿ* of the *'ulamāʾ* as a source of law and denied their exclusive right to formulate *ijmāʿ*.[103] He argued that *ijtihād* was the inalienable right of all individual Muslims and fought strenuously for a more liberal interpretation of *ijmāʿ*.[104]

Chirāgh ʿAlī, a close associate of Sir Sayyid and a forerunner of Muslim modernism in the subcontinent, also rejected the classical *ijmāʿ* of the *'ulamāʾ* and denied that such *ijmāʿ* was binding on future generations as traditionalists had claimed.[105] Although both Sir Sayyid and Chirāgh ʿAlī were concerned primarily with the status of *ijmāʿ* as a source of law rather than as an expression of popular consensus, they were nevertheless instrumental in effecting a significant break with traditional notions which confined *ijmāʿ* to the deliberations of the *'ulamāʾ*.

By the early twentieth century, the debate on *ijmāʿ* had come to incorporate a much greater concern for its political significance as a form of popular public opinion. The Indo-Muslim scholar and political activist, Amīr ʿAlī, campaigned vigorously for the function of *ijmāʿ* to be delegated to a modernised Muslim intelligentsia, instead of the *'ulamāʾ*.[106] He argued that *ijmāʿ* could no longer be seen as the decisions of the *'ulamāʾ* but rather as the interaction between the people and a modern elite.

In Egypt, Muhammad ʿAbduh, founder of the influential *al-Manār* group and a prominent figure in the movement for Islamic reform, stressed the possibilities of re-interpreting and extending the concept of *ijmāʿ* as a political principle. He did so by defining the Muslim community as the source of power (albeit delegated by God) and by asserting that it was collectively equipped to arrive at decisions,

---

[103] Aziz Ahmad, *Islamic Modernism*, pp. 53–4.
[104] Altāf Husain Hālī, *Hayāt-i-Jāwed* (Lahore, Ishrat Publishing House, 1965), pp. 499–508.
[105] Chiragh Ali, *The Proposed Political, Legal and Social Reforms in the Ottoman Empire and Other Mohammedan States* (Bombay, 1883), pp. xxi–xxiii.
[106] Syed Ameer Ali, *The Spirit of Islam: A History of the Evolution and Ideals of Islam* (London, Christopher's, 1961), pp. 251, 278–9.

preferably within the institution of a political assembly.[107] Aziz Ahmad has maintained that 'Abduh remained convinced that the concept of *ijmā'* was 'applicable to all Muslims.' In it, he sought the vindication of his claim that 'government and legislation by the chosen representatives of the people was entirely in harmony with the spirit of Islam'.[108]

The influence of these perspectives has not failed to leave its mark on more recent assessments of the theory and practice of Muslim politics, whether in colonial India or elsewhere. Aziz Ahmad's seminal studies on Indian Islam refer constantly to the position adopted by Indian Muslims in educational institutions, legislative councils, the press and political parties as either consistent, or out of tune, with 'the Muslim *ijmā'*'. In his view *ijmā'* is quite clearly synonymous with Muslim public opinion as a whole and has little or nothing to do with the consensus of the *'ulamā'*, except, of course, as one important part of the communal consensus.[109]

From two very different vantage points, representing scholarly modernism and religious fundamentalism respectively, Professor Fazlur Rahman and Hassan al-Turābī, focus attention on the political and popular dimension of *ijmā'*. For the former, *ijmā'* is indistinguishable from democratic public opinion as this is expressed in an assembly of Muslim elected representatives.[110] For the latter, *ijmā'* was always intended to signify 'a popular concept' and, as such, endorses the claims of 'other formal delegates [besides the *'ulamā'* to] lawfully represent the ummah'.[111]

What emerges from these approaches is firstly, that they are agreed, if not equally and to the same degree, on the validity of applying the notion of *ijmā'* independently of the participation of the *'ulamā'*. Secondly, they suggest that the concept can be understood not only as a process that authenticates legal decisions, but also as one that reflects Muslim public opinion on a variety of political and other issues. Finally, they imply that it is possible to treat as legitimate representatives and bearers of the communal *ijmā'* Muslims who are not members of the class of *'ulamā'*.

However if, as modernist discourse would have us believe, it *is* possible to conceive of a Muslim political consensus, how in fact is such consensus to be established? What are the precise criteria that signify *ijmā'* on specific issues? Does *ijmā'*, or its absence, depend upon the

---

[107] Hourani, *Arabic Thought*, pp. 130–60 and Kerr, *Islamic Reform*, pp. 143–5.
[108] Aziz Ahmad, *Islamic Modernism*, p. 270.
[109] See in particular Aziz Ahmad, *Studies in Islamic Culture*, pp. 68, 69, 265, 269, 276.
[110] Rahman, *Islam*, pp. 260–3.
[111] Hassan al-Turabi, 'The Islamic State' in Esposito (ed.), *Voices of Resurgent Islam*, pp. 243–4.

opinion of a majority of Muslims or does it also depend on some notion of what is deemed to be 'Islamically' just? The question is of central importance if one is to make any sense of the claim, propounded by scholars as distinguished as Aziz Ahmad, that Muslim separatism in colonial India represented the *ijmāʿ* of Indian Muslims even though, at least until the 1940s, only a minority of Muslims appeared to share this view.

One way of approaching the question may lie in turning our attention to the ways in which Muslims have attempted to distinguish *ijmāʿ* from the practices of Western democracy, particularly its emphasis on 'the law of numbers'. In Egypt, Rashīd Ridā, who hailed the Turkish National Assembly in the 1920s as an example of Islamic democracy and the legislative power of the community, did not hesitate to underline its differences from Western democracy.[112] Although he acknowledged its introduction of political practices derived from Western democratic traditions, he did not believe these to be susceptible to the same weaknesses. Western parliamentary institutions, he argued, because of their emphasis on 'rule by majority', had failed 'to impose on those who constitute them the intellectual and moral qualities' demanded by the Islamic community of its own representatives. The shortcomings of Western democracy, he claimed, had been decisively avoided by Muslim communities where the pursuit of a just law had remained independent from the superior to the force of numbers.[113]

In India, Amīr ʿAlī cautioned against direct, popular participation by the community in the formulation of *ijmāʿ* on the grounds that this could deflect the original purpose of *ijmāʿ* as primarily the quest for God's just law.[114] For him the practice of *ijmāʿ* was pre-eminently the business of a Muslim elite, both modern and informed in Islamic law, rather than of the people as a whole. Almost a generation later, Muhammad Iqbāl was to champion a more republican spirit within the Muslim body politic but not without distinguishing it sharply from Western democracy where, he contended, 'people are counted not weighted'.[115] His idea of a 'democratic' consensus consisted of a modern legislative assembly which was prepared to subject itself to the deliberations of 'more of less unique individuals, presided over by the most unique individual

---

[112] Rosenthal, 'Some Reflections', p. 257.
[113] Rashīd Ridā, *Le Califat dans la Doctrine de Rashīd Ridā*, Henri Laoust (trans.) (Beyrouth, Institute Français de Damas, 1938), p. 100.
[114] Ameer Ali, *The Spirit of Islam*, p. 251.
[115] A statement attributed to Muhammad Iqbāl in Fazlur Rahman, 'Some Aspects of Iqbāl's Political Theory', *Studies in Islam* (New Delhi), Vol. 5, 1968, p. 165.

possible'.[116] This was ideally what he wanted modern forms of *ijmāʿ* to embody.

It has been suggested by Louis Gardet that when modern Muslims refer to the desirability of democracy they tend to confuse notions which in Western political theory stem from two quite distinct traditions. The one, which he describes as the 'Aristotelian Thomist', is concerned primarily with democratic government as the means of obtaining a just constitution wherein God alone is sovereign. The other, which he terms 'Rousseauist', is founded on the premise that the social aggregate (or General Will) is sovereign, and that consensus is determined not by reference to some abstract yardstick of justice but by the number of votes cast.[117]

Gardet's argument is that while at the level of values modern Muslims espouse the norms of 'Aristotelian-Thomist' doctrine, at the level of practical application they tend towards Rousseauist principles. What appear to be two antithetical forms in Western political theory are adopted as complementary features in the political law of Islam.[118] Whether or not Gardet's claims are legitimate, and whether or not they are tenable is best left as a moot point. What is important is whether or not they shed some light on the way in which Muslims themselves conceive of and establish the existence of *ijmāʿ* under the complex circumstances that prevailed in colonial India.

The attempts made by modern Muslim scholars to render *ijmāʿ* as a meaningful expression of popular consensus, suggests that Gardet's understanding is not altogether ill judged. One is struck both by Muslim awareness of the difficulties inherent in reducing *ijmāʿ* to a mere quantitative measure of consensus, as well as by the resolve to demonstrate the usefulness of this concept as the only real means of determining what the body of Muslims demand at any given time.

In his study on *Islamic Culture in the Indian Environment*, Aziz Ahmad defines *ijmāʿ* as 'the consensus of the community, which is not a counting of votes, but either a "slowly accumulating pressure of opinion over a long period of time", or in hostile surroundings and moments of crisis a spontaneous group decision, such as Muslim India has taken on several occasions in its chequered history'. In the course of his analysis, Ahmad points emphatically to key events in Indo-Muslim history as evidence of the *ijmāʿ* of the Indian Muslim community. He singles out

---

[116] Quoted in Iqbal Singh, *The Ardent Pilgrim* (London, Longmans, Green, 1951), p. 243.
[117] Gardet, *La Cité Musulmane*, pp. 331–40.
[118]. *Ibid.* , p. 343.

'pan-Islamism' and Muslim separatism as issues which represented the Muslim *ijmā*.[119]

It is of course inconceivable that Ahmad was unaware that neither issue commanded any degree of mass following until quite late in their respective developments: the 1920s for the former and the 1940s for the latter. But it is clear that what concerns Ahmad, and indeed what he means by *ijmā* in relation to these issues, is not some instantly produced public opinion such as one might expect from electoral results, but a self-vindicating process 'whose effects are only gradually felt'.[120] Something of the sense of what Ahmad may have wanted to convey is captured by Hardy who describes *ijmā* as a steady progression towards consensus and whose 'existence is perceived only on looking back'.[121]

One could of course argue cynically that *ijmā* is nothing but an exercise in *ex post facto* reasoning – mere tacit acceptance of a *fait accompli* generated by specific political and material interests but justified as the expression of a Divinely informed communal consensus. It is here that other Muslim modernists like Fazlur Rahman have stepped in to demystify *ijmā*. *Ijmā*, according to Fazlur Rahman, is primarily a human instrument which is endowed 'with a strong practical bent' in which 'there is no talk of the absolute truth value of its contents'.[122] At the level of practical application Rahman emphasises *ijmā*'s immense flexibility, if not pragmatism. It is, he asserts, capable of change as for example when, in the process of debate, the numerical balance of consensus is likely to shift.[123] The content of *ijmā*, he concludes, is neither infallible nor unerring; neither right nor wrong, but 'insofar as it reflects the will of the community, it will be both Islamic and democratic'.[124]

For Fazlur Rahman then, the concept of *ijmā* signifies something close to Rousseau's doctrine of the General Will, although he is clearly unwilling to see sovereignty as the prerogative of the people. Nevertheless, his notion of *ijmā* appears to depend, for its final sanction, not so much upon some abstract idea of justice as upon popular assent, because he acknowledges 'there is no other way in a democratic society'.[125]

[119] Aziz Ahmad, *Studies in Islamic Culture*, p. 75.
[120] *Ibid.*, p. 75.
[121] Peter Hardy, 'The Foundations of Medieval Islam' in William de Bary (ed.), *Sources of Indian Tradition*, I, p. 397.
[122] Rahman, *Islam*, pp. 74–5.
[123] *Ibid.*, p. 262.
[124] *Ibid.*
[125] *Ibid.* See also Javid Iqbal, 'Democracy and the Modern Islamic State' in Esposito (ed.), *Voices of Resurgent Islam*, p. 257 for a corroboration of this view.

It is clear that neither the increasingly fragmented nature of modern Muslim society, nor the steady decline of the *'ulamā'* as a source of political influence nor, finally, the uneasy relationship between *ijmā'* and the forms of modern liberal-democratic consensus, have really persuaded Muslims of the demise of *ijmā'* as a significant concept for the conduct of politics. Certainly few Muslims would deny the extreme complexity of the notion of *ijmā'* or refuse to acknowledge the difficulties inherent in applying it to Muslim political action. At the same time, there appears to be a profound belief that *ijmā'* can and does suggest, in arguably the most meaningful sense, ways of establishing what Muslims really want.[126]

This has depended on a view of *ijmā'* that no longer regards it as the extraneously demanded, inherently 'right' consensus of a community immune to the vicissitudes of change and errors of judgement. At the same time, it is a view that is clearly unwilling to dissociate *ijmā'* altogether from its relation to certain invariant norms. Above all, it suggests that while *ijmā'* can most decisively and perhaps desirably be expressed through democratic means, its authenticity cannot be seen to depend exclusively upon these means.

The ahl adh dhimmī: Muslims and non-Muslims

In a cogent and thoughtful exposition of the elements that constitute Muslim tradition, Francis Robinson has emphasised the crucial importance of Muslim attitudes to non-Muslims. 'More flows from [this]', he suggests, than the Muslims' 'desire to assert and maintain their distinctiveness'.[127] It is certainly likely that any real insight into the conduct of Muslim politics would have to depend as much upon the assumptions Muslims make about the nature of their own community and its cohesive basis, as about their assumptions concerning other groups. The question is undeniably important if one is to grasp what it is precisely that has so dicisively constrained Muslims in accepting a political order founded on the notion of a common political 'good'

---

[126] For reformers as diverse as Sir Sayyid Ahmad Khān and Muhammad Iqbāl then, '... the community itself, as long as it was faithful to its origins, and as it improved its education, would be able to work out a reasonable consensus, and decide for the better and against the less good in matters of human behaviour'. Sheila McDonough, *The Authority of the Past: A Study of Three Muslim Modernists* (Chambersberg, Pennsylvania, American Academy of Religion, 1970), p. 52.

[127] Francis Robinson, 'Islam and Muslim Separatism' in David Taylor and Peter Robb (eds.), *Political Identity in South Asia* (London, School of Oriental and African Studies, 1979), p. 85.

whose definition would extend (even if in fact it does not always do so) equally to all groups prepared to partake of it.

Like all world religions that preceded it, Islam was confronted from the outset with intense theological opposition whose sources lay in the already well established Christian and Jewish communities that flourished in seventh century Arabia. Such opposition was most vehemently expressed in Medina where Muhammad had migrated in 622 A.D. following repeated attacks upon him at the hands of his Meccan tribesmen. In Medina, Christian and Jewish denunciation of Muhammad's new religion did not however preclude the conclusion of political agreements between the fledgling group of Muslims and resident tribes. Bitter, internecine warfare led many of these to accept Muhammad's offer to guarantee the peace in return for their acceptance of his political authority and co-operation in raids organised against the pagan Meccans.[128]

By the time Muhammad and his followers had gained victory over the Meccans in 629 A.D. however, it became clear that the political arrangements between the Muslims and their non-Muslim allies were under considerable strain. The reasons offered by scholars for this hostility have varied widely. There are those who believe that it stemmed from deliberate Jewish treachery during Muhammad's campaigns against the Meccans;[129] others who assert that it was provoked by Muslims disappointed with Jewish and Christian resistance to Muhammad's teachings;[130] and yet others who suggest that as Muhammad's political strength grew so did pressure to conform to his religious message.[131]

There were of course real matters of religious difference that separated the existing communities. Marshall Hodgson has pointed to the unwillingness of 'serious Christians...[to]... accept a timeless monotheism stripped of the Incarnation' and to Jewish reluctance to 'accept a universalism in which their history as a chosen people lost its unique significance'.[132]

However plausible each individual argument, it is clear that a combination of both political and religious factors encouraged Muhammad to redefine the relations between Muslims and non-Muslims. No doubt, as political overlord, Muhammad still continued to

---

[128] Montgomery Watt, *Muhammad in Medina* (Oxford, Clarendon Press, 1956), pp. 151–91.
[129] Rahman, *Islam*, pp. 20–9.
[130] Goitein, 'Four Faces of Islam', pp. 30–42.
[131] Watt, *Islamic Political Thought*, pp. 12–14.
[132] Hodgson, *The Venture of Islam*, I, p. 177.

offer protection to non-Muslims but, where once his *umma* had encompassed groups drawn from a variety of religious denominations, it now excluded all who did not accept his message. Accompanying this fundamental shift, was the emergence of the view that hitherto there were only two criteria of political grouping, Muslims and non-Muslims.

This discovery, which was subsequently to dominate Muslim political thinking, arose from the steady disappearance of a third category known to early Muslims only as 'unbelievers' or polytheists.[133] It was their physical elimination, or conversion, that contributed gradually to the consolidation of Muslims on the one hand, and *dhimmīs*, the protected minorities who belonged to one of the many confessional communities recognised by Muhammad, on the other.[134]

The *dhimmīs*, who came later also to be known as the *ahl al-kitāb*, 'people of the book' or those in possession of written scriptures, were guaranteed both religious autonomy and their own internal structure of government.[135] This policy of coexistence was however exacted at a certain price. *Dhimmīs* were required to pay a poll tax or *jizya* which, during Muhammad's lifetime, often tended to take the form of a share of the date crop harvested by prosperous Jewish communities in the northern Arabian oases.[136]

Muhammad's policy of coexistence in relation to the major confessional communities has been seen by Marshall Hodgson to stem from the absence of any real interest on the part of the early Muslims to convert those who already belonged to one of the established religions. The only real exception, he argues, was the Arabian peninsula where it was believed that all ought to be Muslims. Elsewhere, beyond these frontiers, he claims, 'the object was not conversion but rule' grounded in the hope that 'the superiority of Islam as a religion... would justify [it].[137]

---

[133] 'The worst curses of the Kuran are directed against the latter, (polytheists and unbelievers), with whom the people of the Scripture are contrasted. Hence the Sacred Law eventually laid it down that... on the conquest of new territory by Muslim armies polytheists must accept Islam or die...'. H.A.R. Gibb and Harold Bowen, *Islamic Society and the West: A Study of the Impact of Western civilization on Muslim Culture in the Near East*, I (Oxford University Press, 1957), pp. 207–8.

[134] Watt, *Islamic Political Thought*, pp. 11, 13.

[135] S.D. Goitein, 'Minority Self-Rule and Government Control in Islam', *Studia Islamica*, 31 (1970), pp. 101–16.

[136] Watt, *Islamic Political Thought*, p. 49. See also A.S. Triton, *The Caliphs and their non-Muslim Subjects* (Oxford University Press, 1930), pp. 5–17; Gibb and Bowen, *Islamic Society and the West*, I, pp. 251– 61 and Lambton, *State and Government in medieval Islam*, pp. 201–18.

[137] Hodgson, *The Venture of Islam*, I, p. 199.

A somewhat less charitable view is offered by Goitein. Coexistence, he argues, had less to do with Muslim large-mindedness on the issue of conversion than with a supremely pragmatic orientation. 'The very numbers of the subjected peoples', he writes, '... their economic importance for the Muslim state and their comparatively high technical and educational standards made religious persecution an impracticable proposition... Thus the universalistic bent in Muhammad's message got the upper hand'.[138]

Whatever the real reasons for the pursuit of coexistence by the early community of Muslims, they generated a set of assumptions that were to become characteristic of later Muslim political thinking and even if the system of alliances forged by Muhammad in the early part of his Medinan career were more political than religious, the lines of differentiation came later to be unquestionably denominational. It was assumed, whatever the actual political complexity of individual groups, that they were homogenous in religion and that their religious traditions moulded and defined their personal and social life.[139]

It is of course more than likely that early Muslims shared these assumptions with prevailing social and religious groups. The rigidly organised and tightly knit Jewish and Christian communities probably persuaded Muhammad of their fundamental homogeneity. At the same time, he may also have been deeply impressed with the strenuous efforts made by rabbinical Jews and the high priests of Mazdaism to bring every detail of individual and social life in line with religious principles.[140]

It is important to emphasise however that these assumptions were derived from more than merely the local context. They also signified characteristic elements of the Qur'ān's own intellectual outlook which stressed the primacy of religious categories and the undifferentiated nature of religious groups. There is, for example, little to suggest that early Muslims recognised individual *dhimmīs*. The primary unit was clearly the *dhimmī* community whose leading representatives were invariably ecclesiastical figures who were either patriarchs or rabbis.[141] This is hardly surprising when one considers, as Watt reminds us, that the Qur'ān itself never ceases to declare that God's messengers are always sent to a tribe or community.[142]

The legal position of the *dhimmīs* or the religious communities

138 Goitein, 'Four Faces of Islam', p. 37.
139 Watt, *Islamic Political Thought*, pp. 50–1 and Hodgson, *The Venture of Islam*, I, pp. 315–16.
140 Hodgson, *The Venture of Islam*, I, p. 316 and Rodinson, *Mohammed*, p. 159.
141 Gibb and Bowen, *Islamic Society and the West*, I, p. 212.
142 Watt, *Islamic Political Thought*, p. 50.

(*millats*) to which they belonged has been subjected to close analysis by Louis Gardet. He maintains that the status of non-Muslim *dhimmīs* under Islamic law is comparable to that of permanent guests. He is careful to emphasise however that they are not second-class citizens, for such a notion is applicable only where the dominant norm is Western democratic pluralism. It presupposes, as Muslims do not, a common temporal welfare and recognises (or at least ought to recognise) the equality of civil rights. Muslim society, he contends, is a 'lay theocracy' which is much less concerned with the rights of non-Muslims than with their claim to 'a form of generosity on the part of the *umma*'. Gardet believes that the underlying rationale of this system of protective tutelage lies in the extraordinary belief espoused by Muslims who assert that *dhimmīs* are endowed with fewer rights because they bear fewer obligations (towards the community).[143]

The thrust of conservative Muslim political thinking in the nineteenth and twentieth centuries on the status of non-Muslims in early and medieval Islam would appear to confirm Gardet's general hypothesis. In a series of essays published early this century, the Indian Muslim scholar and political activist, Shiblī No'mānī, drew attention to the principles of justice that shaped early Muslim attitudes to non-Muslims. In a vein that is distinctly apologetic, Shiblī takes as his starting point the self-evident fact that no imperial system ever granted equality to those over whom it ruled.[144] As one among many imperial systems, however, Islam, he maintains, proved itself to be exceptional. This, he argues, was nowhere as manifest as in its treatment of subject peoples where it demonstrated its profound commitment to the respect of their lives, property and religion.[145]

The object of Shiblī's essays is clearly to emphasise his faith's inherent qualities not only as a superior world-view but also as a world power whose magnanimity was unequalled. One is left with the impression however that if the absence of civil and political rights for non-Muslims is distinctly unproblematic for Shiblī, it appears to have less to do with his acceptance of the established practices of imperialism, whether Islamic or other, than with an altogether distinct set of assumptions grounded in his understanding of his faith. This entailed the view that the obligations and the responsibilities imposed by God upon his

[143] Gardet, *La Cité Musulmane*, p. 58.
[144] Shiblī No'mānī, 'Huqūq al-zhimmī' in his *Rasā 'īl i Shiblī* (Amritsar, Vakil Trading Company, 1911), pp. 3–28. See also his *Islāmī Hukūmat* (Amritsar, Vakil Trading Company, 1910), for an extension of this argument as it applied to Mughal rule in India.
[145] *Ibid.*, pp. 27–39.

community were of such exaltedness as to entitle it alone to rights that were commensurate with that position.

Shiblī's reflections on *jizya*, the poll tax imposed on non-Muslims, and *jihād*, support these conclusions. In his essay, *Al-Jizya*,[146] he dismisses the claim that the poll tax was a disabling measure imposed on non-Muslims by their Muslim masters. On the contrary, he argues that it was part of a reciprocal arrangement designed for the benefit of both parties. *Jizya*, he claims, was not a penalty but a gesture of recognition required of non-Muslims for those who risked their lives in defence of the *pax Islamica* of which they were a part. As an obligation, *jizya*, he maintains, was considerably less onerous than the business of *jihād* which was compulsory for all Muslims. True justice required that those who were subjected to the greatest demands be rewarded with the greatest privileges.

It is clear that Shiblī's whole approach to the unequal relations between Muslims and non-Muslims is altogether beyond any notion of second-class citizenship which necessarily presupposes norms of common citizenship and a common political 'good'. Neither is relevant to Muslim political thinking. As Gardet has emphasised, even to attempt to apply the notions of rights and obligations would be inappropriate. For what is signified, to use one metaphor, is no more than what any guest could legitimately expect at the hands of a benevolent host.

More recent Muslim expositions on the subject of non-Muslims share some of Shiblī's underlying assumptions. Though most postulate Muslim dominance in the context of a modern Islamic state, they are nevertheless significant as expressions, more generally, of the assumptions which sustain Muslim attitudes to non-Muslims. The works of the contemporary Pakistani scholar, Muhammad Asad (Leopold Weiss), who was to have a profound influence on Sayyid Qutb, the chief ideologue of the Muslim Brotherhood in Egypt, testify to the continuing influence of traditional perspectives.[147]

Asad stresses the importance of approaching the question of non-Muslims within the context of the 'ideological' polity that is Islam. He argues that the difficulties of according the same position to Muslims and non-Muslims stem principally from a very particular understanding of 'concepts of "right" and "wrong"' espoused by

---

146 Shiblī No'mānī, 'Al-Jizya' in *Rasā'īl*, pp. 6–15.
147 Yvonne Haddad, 'Sayyid Qutb: Ideologue of Islamic Revival' in Esposito (ed.), *Voices of Resurgent Islam*, p. 70.

Muslims which allows for no political compromise.[148] The separate measures applied to non-Muslims, he maintains, are as much forms of discrimination as reflections of a superior justice. Asad justifies his otherwise unusual claim by drawing attention to the absurdity of imposing on non-Muslims the kinds of demands that 'in all fairness could not be made of them'. Yet, he asserts, this is precisely what would obtain were non-Muslims to participate as full members of the community.[149]

What is particularly striking about Asad's approach is the manner in which it appears to reverse the argument about non-Muslim participation as equal members of the community. The stress is not so much upon the constraints imposed on non-Muslims as upon the magnitude of responsibilities borne by Muslims. But what is even more revealing is his conviction that the relations between men, and for that matter, between Muslims and non-Muslims, are not intended to conform to some humanly-devised system of democratic pluralism. Rather they reflect, or ought to reflect, general principles of Divine justice.

To understand this is to grasp a fundamental dimension of the issue as it appears to Muslims. For what those who are intent on pursuing the subject are concerned to show is not whether the treatment of and attitude to non-Muslims comes up to the standards of Western liberal democracy, but whether or not it is in keeping with 'the limits that have been prescribed by God'.[150] In his *Islamic Law and Constitution*, Abū'l A'lā Maudūdī stresses the Muslims' commitment to ensure the equitable treatment of non-Muslims.[151] But what Maudūdī is referring to are not the norms of political equality but the limits of tolerance. The question, as he sees it, is not one of demonstrating his faith's commitment to the equality of Muslims and non-Muslims for that would erode the very basis of his community's claim to be the best among all communities. It is rather one of establishing its credentials as a bearer of Divine compassion and fulfilling its promise to God to ensure a humane social order.[152]

---

[148] Muhammad Asad, *The Principles of State and Government in Islam* (Los Angeles, University of California Press, 1961), p. 50.
[149] *Ibid.*, pp. 40–1.
[150] Ishtiaq Husain Qureshi quoted in May, *The Evolution of Indo-Muslim Through*, p. 320.
[151] Abul Ala Maududi, *The Islamic law and Constitution* (Lahore, Islamic Publications, 1967), pp. 263–5.
[152] Abul Ala Maududi, *The Nature and Contents of Islamic Constitution*, Khurshid Ahmad (ed.) (Karachi, Jamaat-i-Islami Publications, n.d.) p. 50. For one assessment

Many of the assumptions that underlie the works of Shiblī, Asad and Maudūdī appear to have remained intact among modernist Muslims. Even when they acknowledge the need for some adjustment in the traditional modalities of Muslim – non-Muslim relations, they are unwilling to dispense altogether with the categories of 'Muslim' and 'non-Muslim' as governing principles of social and political life. This is not to say that they do not positively endorse a more open and liberal Muslim society. It is to emphasise however, their aversion to any form of secularism that would explicitly question the validity of these distinctions.

The ideas of Ghulām Ahmad Parwez, Khalīfa 'Abdu'l Hakīm and Kemāl Fārūkī, prominent figures associated with the modernist movement in Pakistan, illustrate the continuing vitality of traditional Muslim political values as they seek a more contemporary expression. In the case of Parwez, his unorthodox position on theological and social issues was tempered considerably by his conventional stance on the question of non-Muslims.[153] Although his concern for fundamental human rights has been seen to be more 'unequivocal' than that of Maudūdī's it is doubtful whether he ever envisaged the unqualified right of non-Muslims to participate politically in the administration of an Islamic State.[154] His theory of a 'Quranic democracy' is, potentially, more radical in its implications for its Muslim than its non-Muslim members.[155] Indeed, it is more than likely that for a Muslim like Parwez, who refuses to admit the rules of modern political parties into his 'Quranic democracy', the evolution of a common polity based on other than explicitly Islamic principles, as he sees them, would be inadmissible.[156]

Parwez's modernism, because of its religious and social implications, tended to attract widespread publicity. The same was hardly true of Khalīfa 'Abdu'l Hakīm who, as Director of the semi-official Pakistan Islamic Research Institute in the 1950s, was charged with the task of expounding a more cautious variety of religious modernism. In his *Islamic Ideology*, Hakīm undertakes to examine, amongst other issues, the basis of the modern Islamic state.[157] He concludes that such a state

of Maulānā Maudūdi in the context of his party and its political orientations see Mumtāz 'Alī Āsī, *Maulānā Maudūdī aur Jama'at-i-Islāmi: ek jāeza* (Lahore, Maktaba'-i Jadīd, 1964).

[153] See Ghulam Ahmad Parwez, *Islam: A Challenge to Religion* (Lahore, Idara-i-Tule-e-Islam, 1968), p. 276. For a discussion of Parwēz's theological concerns see Sheila McDonough, *The Authority of the Past: A Study of Three Muslim Modernists* (Chambersberg, Pennsylvania, American Academy of Religion, 1970), pp. 35–49.

[154] Aziz Ahmad, *Islamic Modernism*, p. 233.

[155] On Parwez's Qur'ānic system see *ibid.*, pp. 228–33.

[156] Parwez, *Islam*, pp. 277–8.

[157] Khalifa Abdul Hakim, *Islamic Ideology: The Fundamental Beliefs and Principles of*

would have to extend civil liberties to all its members regardless of their religious affiliations. On the question of political participation, however, Hakīm is persuaded that even the modern Islamic state would have to treat *dhimmīs* as a special category.[158] Like Asad, he remains convinced of the 'ideological imperatives' of such a state. His commitment to commonly understood principles of economic and social justice remain firmly subordinated to the pursuit of a specifically Muslim communal 'good', accessible to Muslims alone.

One of the most extensive treatments by a Muslim modernist of the relations between Muslims and non-Muslims has been undertaken by Kemāl Fārūkī, a Pakistani barrister and scholar of Islam. In his study, entitled *Islamic Constitution*, Fārūkī describes a system of representation which he regards as a true reflection of the priorities of a Muslim society. He writes

... Islam stresses belief as more important than deeds, in the sense that deeds are essentially derived from one's beliefs, or should be. Islam itself is primarily a loyalty or belief from which action should follow.[159]

It is clear that when Fārūkī refers to 'faith' he means religious faith. His blueprint for a system of representation includes the rejection of territorial constituencies in favour of 'communal' constituencies that would enable voters 'to act according to their religious beliefs.'[160] This measure, he argues, would make a substantial contribution towards Muslim political reform for it would no longer oblige an individual to vote 'with people of totally different outlooks' because 'he resides within a certain territorial section'.[161]

Fārūkī's entire system is postulated on the premise that society is broadly divided into Muslim and non-Muslim components. For him, the object of representation is seen to lie not in the development of a commonly defined, self-governing political entity, but in the espousal of certain universal norms of tolerance which endorse the autonomy of non-Muslim constituents. At the same time, such autonomy is clearly predicated on the understanding that non-Muslims can make little or no contribution towards a common political society, which, in the context of a Muslim state, would remain a Muslim prerogative.

Two things emerge from this brief survey of modernist approaches.

Islam and their Application to Practical Life (Lahore, The Institute of Islamic Culture, 1965), pp. 189–243.
[158] *Ibid.*, p. 206.
[159] Kemal Faruki, *Islamic Constitution* (Karachi, Khokrapur Gateway Publication, 1952), p. 66.
[160] *Ibid.*, pp. 56–8.
[161] *Ibid.*, p. 58.

The first suggests that however committed to an 'open society' these interpretations may be they do not admit a common political society equally accessible to Muslims and non-Muslims. Secondly, their understanding of 'a just and equitable role' for non-Muslims is firmly grounded in a Qur'ānic conception wherein their status stems not from their claims as members of one society, but from a set of separate rules reserved for those as yet unwilling to partake of God's compact for all men.

One interesting question that arises from these interpretations is how Muslims themselves reconcile the exclusivism clearly inherent in these positions with the universalist pretensions of their faith. A persuasive explanation has been offered by Marsall Hodgson. He acknowledges that like the other great confessional communities, Islam adopted the practice of defining itself as 'an autonomous social organism with its own law for its own members'.[162] The organisation of its early empire, and later the *millet* system of the Ottoman empire, reflected the essentials of this practice by extending to other religious communities a remarkable degree of autonomy and freedom to regulate the lives of their members. At the same time however, Hodgson maintains, Muhammad had always envisaged his religion as one endowed with universal implications.[163] But it was a universalism that was quite unlike anything associated with the other great world religions, namely Judaism and Christianity. Hodgson's contention is that Islamic universalism was founded neither upon the moral appeal of Christianity with its stress upon the brotherhood of man nor upon the Jewish promise of a 'chosen people' forced to live in a world bereft of divine guidance. What was distinctive about Islam, Hodgson claims, is that while it pursued its own definition as an exclusive social organism, it never lost sight of its cosmopolitan mission – 'to rule over and then to supersede all other [communities] ... to bring the true and uncorrupted divine guidance to all mankind'.[164]

Hodgson's reflections on the tensions between the exclusivist and universalist impulses had already been more poetically expressed by Iqbāl in 1921. In a letter to his English translator, R.A. Nicholson, Iqbāl attempted to explain the seeming contradiction between the Muslim's loyalty to his community, on the one hand, and his commitment to a universal social order, on the other. He wrote

---

[162] Hodgson, *The Venture of Islam*, I, p. 317.
[163] *Ibid.*, pp. 187–96. There is, however, clearly some debate about whether or not Islam started out, originally, as something of a 'national' religion for the Arabs. See Rahman, *Islam.* pp. 19–28 and Rodinson, pp. 237–41.
[164] Hodgson, *The Venture of Islam*, I, p. 317.

...if you want to make it [universalism] an effective ideal and work it out in actual social life, you must start... with a society exclusive in the sense of having a creed and a well defined outline but ever enlarging its limits by example and persuasion. Such a society, according to my belief, is Islam.[165]

Iqbāl's notion of universalism appears to have been predicated neither on a humanism based on what Gardet has termed 'anthropocentrism réfléchi',[166] nor on the principles of imperial conquest which he condemned as 'the re-paganisation of Islam's political ideas'.[167] It did however, as Iqbāl himself acknowledges, aim at absorption – an absorption achieved 'by the simplicity of its teaching'.[168] It was, above all, a universalism that postulated the superiority of Islamic principles and a world integrated on these principles.

The combination of religious exclusivism with a much broader ecumenical approach that has characterised traditional Muslim thinking is crucial to our understanding of contemporary Muslim political responses. It suggests not only how Muslims envisage the organisation of political institutions in a heterogeneous society, but also under what circumstances they would be prepared to coexist with non-Muslims. It is often assumed, not without reason, that their religious exclusivism, or 'communalism' as some have preferred to call it, has encouraged some Muslims to pursue political separatism. At the same time, few would deny that the cosmopolitan ingredients of their faith have been equally decisive in leading other Muslims to seek different options, whether in Maulana Āzād's theory of composite nationalism or Liāquat 'Alī Khān's 'Objectives Resolution' for a Pakistan founded on the political equality of all religious groups.[169]

Wha᷄ is important however is not whether these quite significant (though possibly only apparent) differences exist, but whether or not they succeed in displacing traditional assumptions about the relation of Muslims to non-Muslims. One could of course argue that the concern to maintain differences between Muslims and non-Muslims was never more than a disguise to maintain the political dominance of one group by the other. This would certainly appear to be the case where Muslims formed a majority. What is more interesting though (and also much less

[165] Iqbāl to R.A. Nicholson, 24 January 1921 in Bashir Ahmad Dar (ed.), *Letters of Iqbal* (Lahore, Iqbal Academy, 1978), p. 144.
[166] Louis Gardet, 'Humanisme musulmane d'hier et aujourdhui: éléments culturels de base', quoted in Aziz Ahmad, *Islamic Modernism in India and Pakistan*, p. 271.
[167] Iqbāl to R.A. Nicholson, 24 January 1921, in Dar, *Letters of Iqbal*, p. 146.
[168] *Ibid.*
[169] On Āzād see Aziz Ahmad, *Islamic Modernism*, pp. 187–90; on Liāquat 'Alī Khān's proposal see May, *The Evolution of Indo-Muslim Thought*, pp. 317–18, 322.

easily dismissed), is the commitment of Muslims to what Hodgson calls
'the Shar'ī vision' of non-Muslims in those societies where Muslims
constitute a minority *and* face the prospect of non-Muslim rule as in
colonial India.[170]

In his study of the Indian Muslim '*ulamā*' in the first half of this
century, Peter Hardy has shown how they adjusted their orthodox
understanding of Muslim – non-Muslim relations with an ostensibly
'progressive' political stance which endorsed the claims of composite
Indian nationalism.[171] He emphasises the otherwise little known fact
that the political organisation representing the '*ulamā*', the Jam'īyyat al-
'ulamā'-i-Hind pursued its political preferences without really compromising either its vision of society as a confederation of religious
communities or its pursuit of an 'autonomous Muslim society'. Nor, for
that matter, did the Jam'īyyat's politics deter it from 'rejecting a unitary
democratic state in India with authority over all persons and causes'.[172]

Hardy's study demonstrates, it would appear conclusively, how
despite very different policies, the 'nationalist' '*ulamā*' and separatist
Muslims shared essentially the same set of assumptions. The only
obvious difficulty confronting the '*ulamā*' stemmed from the prospect of
large numbers of non-Muslims who would be independent of Muslim
overlordship and therefore, entitled to equal treatment. This, Hardy
suggests, was dealt with by regarding the prospect as temporary; to hold
on so long as Islam could once more rule the world or until non-Muslims
would themselves 'freely [choose] to come to Islam'.[173]

The tenacity with which Muslims continue to adhere to these
assumptions has been more recently expounded by another Muslim
scholar, Tahir Mahmood.[174] He highlights the difficulties encountered
by successive Indian governments which have attempted to reform
Muslim personal law with a view to creating a common civil code
applicable to Muslims and non-Muslims. Although he is critical of
Muslim traditional opposition to reform, he is nevertheless sensitive to
the feelings of the vast majority of Muslims on the question of personal
law. Thus, while he clearly recognises that Muslim personal law is not
properly constitutive of the Shari'ā, it represents for many Muslims 'a
symbol of their cultural identity'. The 'war against a common civil code'
is, he concedes, in 'the eyes of such Muslims a jihād, a holy agitation for
the protection of Islam in India'.[175]

---

[170] Hodgson, *The Venture of Islam*, I, p. 322.
[171] Hardy, *Partners in Freedom*.
[172] *Ibid.*, p. 34.
[173] *Ibid.*
[174] Tahir Mahmood, *Muslim Personal Law: Role of the State in the Sub-Continent* (New
Delhi, Vikas Publishing House, 1977).
[175] *Ibid.*, pp. 135–6.

2

Participation or representation?
The colonial model for India,
1860–1900

The application after 1858, of a 'colonial' model of representation which would extend some features of 'western' democratic representation to Indians, provoked growing anxiety among Indian Muslims. Their concerns stemmed however not only from considerations of interest which they, as a minority, believed were imperilled, but also from the values which they, as Muslims, had learnt to cherish. Many saw the 'colonial' model to be merely a variation of existing Western models of representation which were deemed to be contradictory to Muslim assumptions about the proper focus of men's allegiance, the nature of political consensus and the correct organisation of power in society. But in order to grasp precisely the thrust of these objections, it is necessary to obtain, in the first instance, some idea of the preoccupations of those who were entrusted with the task of defining the limits of 'Indian representation'.

The pattern of representation envisaged by Britain for her Indian subjects was not, at least at the outset, intended to imitate Western models. The tenor of official debates on Indian representation suggests that there was a widely held belief that the practices common to Western systems of representation, particularly popular elections, were unsuited to India. The argument was that the creation of Western representative institutions assumed a homogeneous society and that, as such, it was unlikely to succeed where, as in India, considerations of caste and creed set men radically apart and determined their political choices. Notwithstanding the force of these reservations which were to dominate official thinking for much of the later nineteenth and early twentieth centuries, it would be wrong to suggest that there was no appreciation whatever of the need to secure greater Indian participation. Indeed, the concern to obtain Indian representation was especially marked after the Mutiny of 1857, which was seen widely to have stemmed from a simmering discontent at the exclusion of Indians from law-making bodies. The Council reforms of 1861, for example, were intended precisely to recognise some of these inadequacies. Their purpose was to involve greater numbers of Indians in the process of government even if such participation was clearly designed to be

49

advisory rather than representative, that is to say, implying a degree of accountability.

However the Mutiny was not the only incentive for change; the pressure for Indian political reform grew from other sources as well. The return of the Liberals in Britain under Gladstone in 1880 lent a measure of urgency to the question of Indian representation.[1] More importantly perhaps, there appeared to be a new order of emphasis. Where hitherto officials had tended to stress Indian representation primarily as a means to ensure a more efficient government less likely to suffer the strain of Indian political discontent, the concern now lay in extending Indian representation as a means of preparing Indians for the greatest political 'good' – self-government. Growing contacts between Indians and the colonial metropolis during the 1880s and 1890s also contributed substantially to the demand for representative institutions for India. Western-educated Indians, at home and abroad, came increasingly to question the assumption that the influence of religion, caste and language constrained their capacity for democratic institutions; and some pointed to the newly founded Indian National Congress as evidence of a burgeoning Indian political consensus that transcended traditional social barriers.[2]

Indian participation in the aftermath of the mutiny

One important consequence of the Mutiny was a much more sustained concern among British officials for the need to obtain greater Indian co-operation. For this they turned to two separate, and incompatible, groups of Indians. The first consisted of Western-educated Indians drawn mostly from the presidency towns of Calcutta, Madras and Bombay; the second of the established, predominantly landed, gentry based in parts of northern India who had tended habitually to command social and political deference from those over whom they exercised control. The participation of these two groups of Indians

[1] For some discussions of the interaction between British Liberalism and the question of Indian representation during this period see R.J. Moore, *Liberalism and Indian Politics, 1872–1922* (London, Edward Arnold, 1966) and S. Gopal, *British Policy in India, 1858–1905* (Cambridge University Press, 1965). See also Stephen Koss, *John Morley at the India Office, 1905–1910* (New Haven, Yale University Press, 1969).

[2] B.B. Majumdar, *Indian Political Associations and Reform of Legislature, 1818–1917* (Calcutta, Firma L. Mukhopadhyay, 1965); Sankar Ghose, *The Western Impact on Indian Politics, 1885–1919* (Bombay, Allied Publishers, 1967): S.R. Mehrotra, *The Emergence of the Indian National Congress* (New York, Barnes and Noble, 1971) and Anil Seal. *The Emergence of Indian Nationalism* (Cambridge University Press, 1971).

stemmed in part from 'a new and improved model' of political change that had begun to permeate official policy as far back as the 1830s,[3], and partly from the lessons learned from the uprising of 1857. This led officials to underline the advantages of English education for Indians, as a means to create a class of 'collaborators' whose representation could secure the kinds of links between rulers and ruled that were presumed to be missing on the eve of the Mutiny.[4] It also strengthened the view that the co-operation of India's 'natural leaders', drawn from the class of *zamindārs* and *tālukdārs* whose hostility had provoked the Mutiny, was indispensable in order to secure Indian political stability.[5]

However, whilst the Mutiny was undeniably crucial in intensifying pressure for greater Indian representation, other developments also demanded changes in the organisation of government. Of these the most obvious was the growth of a massive administrative and military system that had to be paid for from Indian revenues. This entailed a much greater administrative intervention in Indian society than had hitherto been witnessed. But, as Seal has emphasised, such intervention 'was exposed to the perennial dilemma of the Raj. If the administrative cost of intervening was not to overtake the returns and the security of the state not to be put at risk, Indian collaboration would have to be much extended. So the Raj mitigated its administrative drive by devising new methods of winning the co-operation of a larger number of Indians. Systems of nomination, representation and election were all means of enlisting Indians to work for imperial ends.'[6]

Whatever the real driving force that led officials to recognise the need for more Indians in consultative positions in government, it is clear that few believed the purpose of Indian representation at the time to lie either in political education or in the preparation for self-government. The considerations at hand tended, on the whole, to be more properly utilitarian insofar as they were dictated by questions of the political costs of attempting to govern India with the aid of a handful of officials. This is not to say that the merits of instituting a more benevolent empire were wholly absent from official thinking;[7] but the concerns of administrators

[3] Mehrotra, *The Emergence of Indian National Congress*, pp. 51–106.
[4] For one of the most comprehensive accounts of the rise of this class and its contribution to Indian nationalism see Seal, *The Emergence of Indian Nationalism*.
[5] Thomas, R. Metcalf, *The Aftermath of the Revolt* (Princeton University Press, 1965), pp. 134 ff.
[6] Anil Seal, 'Imperialism and Nationalism in India', *Modern Asian Studies*, 7, 3 (1973), p. 328.
[7] Reginald Coupland, *The Indian Problem, 1833–1935* (London, Oxford University Press, 1942), pp. 18–20.

like Thomas Munro and Henry Lawrence, who campaigned for a humane application of British rule in India, appeared to have been inspired more by their belief in the inherent magnanimity of British imperialism than by their faith in the capacity of Britain's Indian subjects to govern themselves.[8] Although it is true that some officials like Thomas Macaulay were inclined to adopt a more radical view of Britain's role in India which deemed her task to lie in the education of Indians for 'European institutions', theirs tended to be lone voices pitted against established opinion.[9]

There were essentially three principal considerations that impinged upon colonial policy on Indian representation in the years between the end of the Mutiny and the consolidation of a Liberal government in Britain. The first stressed the importance of India's indigenous political institutions which, many officials believed, were suited more to the practice of political consultation than of political control. The second drew attention to India's social diversity which was deemed to preclude the emergence of a coherent 'public opinion' that could effectively sustain Western representative institutions. Finally, there was the notion that the ends of British rule in India demanded that the object of Indian participation be conceived pre-eminently as a quest for good government, rather than for self-government.

The most urgent problem which confronted British officials immediately after the Mutiny was how best to secure a more responsive government without incurring the political risks inherent in representative government. Many sought a solution in what they believed constituted the 'traditional' modes of Indian political practice. Here they hoped to distinguish a notion of representation that would legitimise the kind of participation they envisaged for Indians. Such participation involved the recognition of formal, consultative arrangements between the ruler and his subjects without seeking to conceive of them as, in any way, suggestive of the ruler's political responsibility towards those over whom he ruled. Of all India's 'native' political institutions, none was so

---

8 See Munro's Minute of 31 December 1824, quoted in R. Muir (ed.), *The Making of British India* (Manchester University Press, 1917), pp. 283–4 and Sir Henry Lawrence, *Essays – Military and Political written in India* I (London, W.H. Allen, 1859). pp. 59–60.
9 Macaulay told the House of Commons: 'It may be that the public mind of India may expand under our system till it has outgrown that system; that by good government we may educate our subjects into a capacity for better government; that, having become instructed in European knowledge, they may in some future age demand European institutions... whenever it comes, it will be the proudest day in English history'. See Macaulay's speech in the House of Commons on 10 July 1833, *Hansard's Parliamentary Debates* (Commons) (1833), volume 19, column 536.

readily invoked by officials as a model for Indian representation as the *durbār*, or the public audience, held at the behest of princely potentates.[10] One pointed reference to the *durbār* as a basis for the reformed Indian Councils came from Sir Bartle Frere. Frere, who was a member of the Viceroy's Council from 1859 to 1862 with something of a scholarly interest in Indian institutions, recommended that the proposed legislative council could be best construed as 'the durbar of a native Prince', designed not so much to establish political accountability as to serve as a 'channel from which the ruler learns how his measures are likely to affect his subjects'.[11]

In the discussions leading up to the reforms of 1861 it became clear that what officials envisaged for India was a strictly consultative body with none of the features of a 'constitutional parliament'.[12] In his speech to the Commons during the second reading of the Bill on Indian Council reform the Secretary of State for India, Sir Charles Wood, confessed that his officials tended overwhelmingly to favour a Council that would resemble the *durbār* of a native chief and enable the governor to 'assemble from time to time a considerable number of persons whose opinions he should hear and by whose opinions he should not be bound'.[13] There was little that separated this vision from one that presumed an assembly of hand-picked notables whose task was merely to endorse royal decrees. Indeed, when the Bill came finally to be law it demonstrated just how far officials had sought to emulate the Indian *durbār*, or at least their conception of it. The composition of the new Council was restricted to Indians nominated by the Governor-General, their powers were restricted to deliberation, and they were denied the right of interpellation.[14] Political deference rather than political control defined the scope of the new Councils and the overall emphasis lay unquestionably 'upon associating influential Indians with the process of

---

[10] For one account of how British officials tended to conceive of the *durbār* and the 'pomp and show' that went with it see Veena Talwar Oldenburg, *The Making of Colonial Lucknow, 1856–1877* (Princeton University Press, 1984), pp. 246–60.

[11] Frere's Official Minute of 16 March 1860, quoted in *Indian Constitutional Reforms, Parliamentary Papers* (1918), Cmd. 9109, paragraph 60.

[12] Wood to Dalhousie, 23 December 1854, *Wood Papers* MSS EUR F 78, quoted in R.J. Moore, *Sir Charles Wood's Indian Policy* (Manchester University Press, 1966), p. 51. See also Cecil Cross, *The Development of Self-Government in India, 1858–1914* (Chicago University Press, 1922), pp. 31–48.

[13] Charles Wood's speech in the House of Commons, 6 June 1861, *Hansard's Parliamentary Debates* (Commons) (1861), volume 163, column 640.

[14] Durga Das Basu, *Indian Constitutional Documents*, I (Calcutta, S.C. Sarkar, 1969), p. 43.

legislation rather than upon sounding representatives of popular opinion'.[15]

It is important to bear in mind, however, that although official interest in indigenous political institutions like the *durbār* was prompted in part by the concern to withhold real power from Indians, it was not without some relation to contemporary thinking on the problem of adapting the practices of 'western' representation to 'non-western' societies. In his *Considerations on Representative Government*, for example, published in 1861, John Stuart Mill drew attention to the problem that was beginning to engage the attention of those of Britain's colonial adminstrators who were faced with demands for greater self-government. In his recommendations Mill called upon 'English politicians' to undertake 'a much more profound study of Indian experience and of the conditions of Indian government' before embarking upon the creation of 'representative institutions formed in imitation of [England's] own'.[16] Though Mill was unwilling to prescribe a system of representation best suited for India he was clearly persuaded that it was India's indigenous political traditions and not the political 'conceptions' supplied by 'English or European practice' that would prove to be the most durable foundations for good government.[17]

The second consideration that tended to impinge frequently upon the issue of Indian representation in the 1860s and 1870s was the inherent heterogeneity of Indian society. Officials and observers of India alike argued that European institutions presumed a degree of homogeneity that was notably absent in Indian society.[18] Others were persuaded that India's social and religious diversity radically pre-empted the emergence of a class that might properly be described as 'representative', that is, one which could reasonably command the support of a cross-section of society. In his speech to the Commons on the subject of Indian Councils reform, Sir Charles Wood explained why he thought the extension of 'western' representative institutions would be an impractical measure in India. An Indian electorate, he maintained, was bound to be so deeply divided as to preclude the emergence of a recognisable political consensus. The constitution of a 'western-style' representative body, he insisted, was 'impossible' where 'you cannot possibly assemble at any

[15] Moore, *Liberalism and Indian Politics*, pp. 9–10.
[16] John Stuart Mill, *Considerations on Representative Government* (Chicago, Henry Regnery, 1962, reprint of original edition of 1861), p. 365.
[17] *Ibid.*
[18] C.H. Philips, 'James Mill, Mountstuart Elphinstone and the History of India', in C.H. Philips (ed.), *Historians of India, Pakistan and Ceylon* (London, Oxford University Press, 1961), pp. 217–29.

one place ... persons who shall be the real representatives of the Native population of that empire'.[19]

Wood's categorical dismissal of India's capacity for consensus was to prove to be of immense political value to officials who sought later to question Congress's claim to speak on behalf of India including, by implication, rural India. While it is admittedly the case that the stress upon India's urban-rural divide as a part of official discourse on representation assumed much greater importance following the creation of Congress in 1885, its implications appear already to have become evident in the 1860s. 'The natives who are resident in the town' declared Wood 'no more represent the resident native population than a highly educated native of London, at the present, represents a highland chieftain or a feudal baron of half a dozen centuries ago. To talk of native representation is therefore, to talk of that which is simply and utterly impossible.'[20]

However it is clear that this preoccupation with Indian diversity, and indeed its significance for the development of Western representative institutions, was not exceptional. *The Times* of London reflected some of the more established notions about Indian diversity and its bearing upon the development of 'western' representative institutions by concluding that the people of India had 'no conception of national independence', of fellow-feeling or patriotism;[21] while others like John Stuart Mill underlined the importance of a 'united public opinion' as a necessary condition for 'the working of representative government'.[22]

The third important issue that tended to dominate official policy on Indian representation in the 1860s was the quest for efficient government. Since the Mutiny the feeling had grown that the basis of good, that is to say efficient, government depended in part upon a degree of Indian participation. The real value of extending representation to Indians was seen to lie in its capacity to ensure a government that could effectively stem political discontent and prevent the recurrence of events such as those witnessed in 1857. Political representation meant establishing channels of communication between Britain and her Indian subjects to serve the ends of good government. This, rather than any ideal of self-

[19] Charles Wood's speech in the House of Commons, 6 June 1861, *Hansard's Parliamentary Debates* (Commons) (1861), volume 163, columns 640–1.
[20] *Ibid.*
[21] *The Times*, 23 November 1858, quoted in Mehrotra, *The Emergence of the Indian National Congress*, p. 107.
[22] Mill, *Considerations*, p. 307.

government for Indians, was what dominated official thinking on Indian representation in the 1860s.[23]

Paradoxically, however, it was precisely those who were concerned to make a case for Indian representation as a means of strengthening government who were called upon also to dispel fears that such representation might weaken the Raj. They took great care, therefore, to stress that Council reforms would not be undertaken as part of a more general programme for the development of Indian self-government. Indeed, those officials in favour of reform tended precisely to underline the advantages that such reforms would bring to a government more skilled in the means of assessing the mood of its subjects. 'The addition of the native element', wrote Sir Bartle Frere in an official Minute in the spring of 1860, 'has, I think, become necessary owing to our diminished opportunities of learning through indirect channels what the natives think of our measures, and how the native community will be affected by them'.[24]

The thrust of Frere's comments lay also at the heart of Sir Charles Wood's defence of Council reform in the Commons in July 1861. 'I believe', he declared, 'great advantages will result from admitting Native chiefs to co-operate with us for legislative purposes, but they will no longer feel as they have hitherto done, that they are excluded from the management of affairs in their country. Nothing, I am persuaded, will tend more to conciliate to our rule the minds of natives of high rank'.[25] Implicit in Wood's statement was the suggestion that the association of Indians aimed to do no more than to forestall a crisis of political confidence and, by doing so, serve the interests of officialdom rather than contribute to the political education of its subjects. Indeed, he went so far as to maintain that if there was a sound reason for the introduction of Indian Councillors it was to conciliate India's 'natural leaders' whose hostility had been shown to be dangerous and whose co-operation could surely be assumed to strengthen the arm of government.[26]

The question about the proper ends of Indian representation proved also to be a variant of an ongoing debate amongst British intellectuals at the time. John Stuart Mill's influential treatise on representative government as well as James Fitzjames Stephen's *Liberty, Equality and*

---

[23] H.L. Singh, *Problems and Policies of the British in India, 1885–1898* (Bombay, Asia Publishing House, 1963), pp. 77–8.

[24] Quoted in Cross, *The Development of Self-Government in India*, p. 42.

[25] Charles Wood's speech in the House of Commons, 6 June 1861, *Hansard's Parliamentary Debates* (Commons) (1861), volume 163, column 643.

[26] Moore, *Sir Charles Wood's Indian Policy*, p. 62.

Fraternity,[27] had formed important elements of the contemporary discourse on representation. Among their many concerns was one singled out by Mill as the question of 'how the local business can be best done; and how its transaction can be made most instrumental to the nourishment of public spirit and the development of intelligence'.[28] Its relevance to Indian representation was to become much more noticeable in the late 1870s particularly in some municipalities like Calcutta where, as Furedy has demonstrated, a 'conservative civilians' model' with its stress on administrative efficiency confronted a counter-model espoused by Bengali nationalists who approached the Calcutta Corporation as something of 'a nursery of political education'.[29]

Indeed, it would be no exaggeration to maintain that Indians in the 1860s and 1870s tended to regard official proposals for the extension of representation to Indians as unduly cautious, if not conservative. The influence, above all, of Western education had rendered a predominantly Hindu intelligentsia eager to demonstrate their skills at managing modern European political institutions.[30] Their mood was aptly conveyed by Dr. Bahu Daji, a leading member of the influential Poona Sarvajanik Sabha, 'If we are today anxious for participation in the rights you Englishmen claim by virtue of your birth, it is you Englishmen who have taught us to aspire after them'.[31]

Many Indians came also to believe that the spread of Western education had contributed substantially to a degree of solidarity among the Indian middle classes which entitled them to European political institutions organised along European lines. A typical, if somewhat overblown, expression of the feeling that then prevailed among English-educated Indians was captured by a section of the burgeoning English language press, the *Hindoo Patriot*. 'English education has opened a new tie of fellowship between the different races of India... They now all breathe the same life and regeneration and share in one common feeling for the good of their common country'.[32] Educated Indians had no

---

[27] J.F. Stephen, *Liberty, Equality and Fraternity* (London, Smith, Elder and Company, 1873). See also his 'Foundations of Government in India', *Nineteenth Century*, 39 (1883), pp. 451–568. Also relevant is H.S. Maine, *Popular Government* (London, John Murray, 1885).

[28] Mill, *Considerations*, p. 286.

[29] Christine Furedy, 'Contrasting Models in the Development of Municipal Administration in Calcutta' in D. Rosenthal (ed.), *The City in India Politics* (Haryana, Thomson Press, India, 1976), pp. 152–72.

[30] Ghose, *The Western Impact on Indian Politics*, pp. 1–37.

[31] *Bombay Times*, 13 October 1859, quoted in Mehrotra, *The Emergence of the Indian National Congress*, p. 138.

[32] *Ibid.*, p. 139. See also Seal, *The Emergence of Indian Nationalism*, pp. 194–244 and J.C. Masselos, *Towards Nationalism: Group Affiliations and the Politics of Public Associ-*

doubt as what the next step should be. It was left to Surendrenath Banerjea, one of Bengal's leading political luminaries, to voice the aspirations of his class; 'Educated India is beginning to feel that the time has come when some measure of self-government must be conceded to the people of this country. Canada governs itself. Australia governs itself and surely it is anomalous that the grandest dependency of England should continue to be governed upon wholly different principles'.[33]

It is worth bearing in mind, however, that while men like Banerjea were persuaded that English education had 'uplifted all who had come under its influence to a common platform of thoughts, feelings and aspirations',[34] they did not deny that divisions of class and the hold of ignorance continued to persist elsewhere in society. But, while neither could readily be ignored, they could be made to serve the interests of this 'new' group of Western-educated, young Indians. For implicit in their political stance was the assumption that they were best qualified to represent all Indians. Their predominantly middle-class professions encouraged the view that the old aristocracy, entrenched as they were in their social prejudices, spoke only for themselves, while the 'voicelessness' of the illiterate masses rendered them quite incapable of doing so. The middle classes, placed strategically between these social extremes, were deemed by them to be the best qualified to represent India as a whole.[35]

The Liberal model of representation, 1880–1885

The return of the Liberals under Gladstone in the Spring of 1880 introduced a wholly new element into colonial discourse on Indian representation. This tended, at least apparently, to have less to do with the question of how best to improve the administration of colonial rule in India than with how to educate Indians for self government. In addition, the concern with the 'extension of native privileges'[36] at the

ations in Nineteenth Century Western India (Bombay, Popular Prakashan, 1974), pp. 56–62.

[33] R.C. Palit (ed.), *Speeches of Babu Surendrenath Banerjea, 1876–1880*, I (Calcutta, S.K. Lahiri, 1880), p. 168.

[34] *Ibid.*, p. 55.

[35] Leonard Gordon, *Bengal: The Nationalist Movement, 1876–1940* (New York, Columbia University Press, 1974), p. 28.

[36] Gladstone's famous phrase that was to lend fire to the Viceroyalty of Lord Ripon. For a comprehensive assessment of the period see S. Gopal, *The Viceroyalty of Lord Ripon, 1880–1884* (London, Oxford University Press, 1953). See also Seal, *The Emergence of Indian Nationalism*, pp. 147–57.

local and provincial levels which became the avowed aim of the new Viceroy, Lord Ripon, if not of the official establishment as a whole, brought a much more sustained discussion about the merits of elective representation than had hitherto been the case. It is clear however that even ardent Victorian Liberals were unwilling to alter what they deemed to be the essentially communitarian basis of Indian society by extending a system of territorial constituencies predicated upon notions of individual representation that were becoming increasingly familiar in Britain. In this, they shared many of their predecessors' assumptions about the nature of Indian society and their reservations about the extension of European institutions to Indians.

A new Liberal administration in India brought a fresh emphasis upon representative institutions as agents of popular education. Fired in part by a growing preoccupation in his native England with what political liberals termed 'public education', Ripon set about the task of injecting 'fresh life into the somewhat torpid system which at present exists'.[37] Although the Viceroy had initially set his sights upon the reform of the Provincial and Imperial Legislative Councils it is clear that few of his official colleagues were prepared to endorse his plans for greater Indian representation at these levels.[38] This, however, was not enough to discourage Ripon in his pursuit of political institutions that could obtain the political enlightenment of Britain's Indian subjects, albeit more modestly than he had originally hoped. Fortunately for him, the Viceroy was not altogether without support. Liberal-minded officials like Evelyn Baring, Courtney Ilbert and Charles Aitchison stood loyally by him while others drawn from among sections of non-official opinion appeared to be even more enthusiastic. Among these was Allen Octavian Hume, a close friend and confidante, who came later to enjoy prominence as a founder member of the Indian National Congress. Hume shared many of the Viceroy's ideas concerning the educational value of representative institutions and did much to enhance the credibility of Ripon's programme for municipal reform among Western-educated Indians.[39] Others, like R.D. Osborn the liberal editor of the *Indian Observer* and later of the *Statesman*, also campaigned publicly for the creation of 'independent municipal institutions' that

[37] Note by Ripon, 27 April 1882, *Ripon Papers*, MSS. 43576, quoted in Seal, *The Emergence of Indian Nationalism*, p. 155.

[38] *Ibid.*, pp. 152–3.

[39] Mehrotra, *The Emergence of the Indian National Congress*, pp. 308–17. See also Briton Martin, *New India: British Official Policy and the Emergence of the Indian National Congress* (Berkeley, University of California Press, 1969), p. 73.

would engender 'a common life and common interests' to make possible, eventually, the realisation of national self-government.[40]

The call for Indian reform, initiated by the new liberal spirit of the 1880s, provoked the resentment of local governments dominated by the civilian bureaucracy and did little to temper the anxieties of conservative public opinion. Although the fundamental issue at hand was clearly related to the wisdom of devolving power to Indians, the debate tended, not surprisingly, to be cast in terms that had become familiar to the discourse on representation in Britain, namely, the merits of good, that is to say, efficient, government against self-government. The reaction to Ripon's initial enquiries on the state of local government in the provinces and later to his famous Resolution on Local Self-Government, which sought to restructure municipal and local rural boards by incorporating a majority of elected non-official members, shows just how far the language of this discourse had permeated official and non-official opinion in India.[41]

In his reply to the Viceroy on the working of the Calcutta Corporation the Lieutenant-Governor of Bengal, Sir Rivers Thompson, underlined the danger of allowing 'ambitious young men whose chief aim is to . . . . acquire notoriety as speakers' to undermine the pursuit of 'real business'.[42] Even more unequivocal in his dislike of Ripon's scheme for political education through political control was Sir Alexander Mackenzie, who succeeded Thompson as Lieutenant Governor from 1895 to 1899. In a speech to the Bengal Legislative Council in April 1882 he dismissed the notion that 'India was all the same as Middlesex' and regretted that talk 'about local self-government and representation and the like' had compounded the difficulties of administering an Oriental city like Calcutta.[43] Elsewhere in Bombay the Governor, Sir James Fergusson, was unreservedly opposed to Ripon's proposals on much the same grounds. He castigated the Viceroy's scheme as an ill-advised measure that struck at the heart of efficient government in the name of obscure principles of Indian self-government.[44]

[40] *Statesman and Friend of India*, 13 August 1879, quoted in Mehrotra, *The Emergence of the Indian National Congress*, p. 301. See also R.D. Osborn, 'Representative Government for India', *Contemporary Review*, 42 (1982), pp. 931–53.
[41] For reactions to Ripon's initiatives in 1881 and 1882 see Seal, *The Emergence of Indian Nationalism*, pp. 154–8.
[42] *Government of Bengal to Government of India, July 12, 1881, Judicial and Public Proceedings*, quoted in Furedy, 'Contrasting Models in Municipal Development', p. 166.
[43] *Ibid.*, pp. 165–6.
[44] Seal, *The Emergence of Indian Nationalism*, p. 159.

The press and public opinion in India and Britain were equally sceptical about the merits of Ripon's grand design for Indian self-government. Many doubted whether his plans might not actually detract from the more urgent task of getting on with the business of governing India. This expression of views ranged from those known widely for the mistrust of liberal reform like James Fitzjames Stephen, who cast doubt upon the capacity of 'native committees' to discharge efficiently the burden of administrative functions,[45] to those like A.P. Sinnet, the sceptical editor of the *Pioneer* and a friend of Hume's, who wondered at the wisdom of transferring what were essentially the responsibilities of government to 'amateur committees'.[46]

Here it is worth bearing in mind that while there was certainly a division of opinion between the proponents of self-government on the one hand, and those of good government on the other, the issues were not always as clear cut or as simple for all. John Stuart Mill had been one of the first to appreciate some of the difficulties inherent in resolving the question of the proper ends of representative institutions. For while he recognised the value of representative institutions as 'talking bodies' necessary to the process of political education, he was equally persuaded that the task of administration was 'a skilled business' that could not be left to popular assemblies.[47] Some of these ambiguities about the purpose and the scope of representative institutions in India were to be embodied in the thinking of men like Sir George Campbell, Lieutenant-Governor of Bengal from 1871 to 1874, and Sir Richard Temple, his immediate successor. Both reflected the paternalist approach to Indian representation that was common to the majority of colonial officials in the mid-nineteenth century, and both remained deeply sceptical about its capacity to secure efficient administration. Yet both came also to believe that such an administration could best be obtained by winning the co-operation of Western-educated Indians and that such co-operation could justifiably be pursued not only in the interests of better government but also in the interests of the moral and political development of 'the educated middle class'.[48] For these men, Furedy

---

[45] James Fitzjames Stephen, 'Foundations of Government in India', p. 560.
[46] A.P. Sinnet, 'Anglo-Indian Complications and their Cause', *Fortnightly Review*, 40 (1883), pp. 408–9.
[47] Mill, *Considerations*, pp. 98–101.
[48] Sir Richard Temple, *Men and Events of My Time in India*, London, 1882, p. 501, quoted in Furedy, 'Contrasting Models of Municipal Administration', p. 158. Campbell believed that Britain ought to develop in educated Indians 'a capacity for self-government' that could, one day, lead to 'a Bengalee House of Commons'. C.E. Buckland, *Bengal under the Lieutenant Governors*, I, Calcutta, 1901, p. 552, quoted in *ibid.*, p. 157.

observes, there appeared not to be a fundamental or 'irreconcilable conflict between the principles of efficiency and political education in local government. Any temporary inefficiency... would ultimately be offset by the greater efficiency and smoother working which would be possible in popularly accepted administrative bodies'.[49]

What ultimately persuaded officials like Campbell and Temple to pursue that which many others had deemed detrimental to the cause of good government, was their confidence in the growing numbers of Western-educated Indians. In this they were not alone. The Viceroy and his Finance member, Evelyn Baring, were among the few highly placed officials who believed that Western education had wrought profound changes in Indian society which made possible the extension of some European political practices such as elections.[50] There was, of course, a more pragmatic component to these new attitudes to the question of Indian representation. As Ripon bluntly put it, there was 'an intelligent class of public spirited men, whom it is not only bad policy, but sheer waste of power, to fail to utilize.'[51] An extension of the elective principle would not only offer a measure of real power that could satisfy the ambitions of this class, but, and this was crucial, make 'the educated natives the friends, instead of the enemies of our rule'.[52]

Whilst there was clearly some appreciation of the need to institution-alise elections on a more routine basis than that which had existed in some municipalities since the late 1860s,[53] opposition to it was far too well entrenched to ensure its immediate success. In September 1881, Ripon enquired from local governments what items of administration could be transferred to local bodies 'comprising non-officials and, wherever possible, elected members'.[54] Implicit in his initiative was the belief that the time had come to associate Indians with government in a representative, rather than in a purely advisory capacity. Elected Indians would manage their own affairs independently, that is to say, with some claim to act on behalf of some more or less popularly-constituted electorate rather than in the interests of, or in subservience to, the *Burra Sāhib*.[55]

---

[49] *Ibid.*, p. 158.
[50] Seal, *The Emergence of Indian Nationalism*, p. 151.
[51] Resolution of the Government of India, 18 May 1882, *Parliamentary Papers* (1883), vol. L1, p. 30.
[52] Ripon to W.E. Forster, 19 May 1883, *Ripon Papers*, quoted in *ibid.*, p. 149.
[53] Hugh Tinker, *The Foundations of Local Government in India, Pakistan and Burma* (London, Pall Mall Press, 1968), pp. 34–42.
[54] Resolution of Government of India (Finance Department) 30 September 1881, number 3353, *Gazette of India*, 1 October 1881, pp. 449–50.
[55] Seal, *The Emergence of Indian Nationalism*, p. 154.

The reaction to Ripon's inquiries, and later to his Resolution on Local Self-Government issued in May 1882, confirmed the overwhelming official consensus against any proposal to extend elective government to Indians.[56] Two sets of arguments were used. First, those which held that Indians were, as a whole, temperamentally disinclined to take to elective representation.[57] This was a view most commonly expressed by local governments who claimed to have a more intimate knowledge of Indian political practice. Second, and this was more characteristic of the response from London, those that asserted that elections would introduce fundamental changes in the structure of government which could eventually undermine the basis of British authority in India.[58]

In their replies to the Viceroy, the governments of Bengal and Madras stressed that elections had tended to generate little popular enthusiasm.[59] Both governments suggested that the principal deterrent lay in the deeply hierarchical nature of Indian society where the better class of men were unwilling to subject themselves to the votes of those they considered their social inferiors. In Bengal it was reported that elections were preferred only by politically ambitious *arrivistes* and were actively shunned by Calcutta's more eminent notables.[60] In Madras differences in social class were seen to be the single most important reason for the existence of only four elected municipalities out of nine.[61] In Bombay considerations of caste tended to assume overriding importance in official explanations of the general apathy towards elective representation. Here, none but a handful of restless Brahmins were seen to be interested in elections while the vast majority were believed to prefer firm official control on the assumption that it matched the more

---

[56] For Ripon's views on local self-government see Resolution of the Government of India, 18 May 1882, *Extension of Local Self-Government in India. Parliamentary Papers* (1883), LI, pp. 25–32. For reactions to his Resolution see Correspondence between the Secretary of State for India in Council, the Government of India and the Various Local Governments on the Proposed Measures for the Extension of Local Governments in India, *ibid.*, 93-I and 93-II.

[57] Gopal, *The Viceroyalty of Lord Ripon*, p. 87.

[58] A typical expression from London was that of Lord Lytton, the conservative Viceroy who had been Ripon's predecessor. He accused Ripon of 'gradually transferring power in India from European to native hands'. See his speech in the House of Lords, 9 April 1883, *Hansard's Parliamentary Debates* (Lords) (1883), volume 277, column 1737.

[59] For a detailed treatment of their reactions see Gopal, *The Viceroyalty of Lord Ripon*, chapters 2 and 3.

[60] Letter from the Government of Bengal, 12 July 1881, *Extension of Local Self-Government in India Parliamentary Paper* (1883), LI, pp. 148–9.

[61] Letter from the Government of Madras, 3 August 1881, *ibid.*, p. 145.

authoritarian forms of government with which they were familiar.[62] What is significant about these observations is that while it was certain that self-government had nowhere been 'fairly tried', traditional perceptions about the 'unfitness' of Indian society for the institutions and practices of modern European democracies remained more firmly in place than ever.[63]

Ripon's proposals for electoral reform were subject also to intense criticism in Britain. Some members of the India Council believed that the Viceroy was becoming 'more radical everyday' and that his doctrinaire approach to Indian representation was both naive and deleterious to British rule in India.[64] In June 1882 Lord Hartington, the Secretary of State for India, advised Ripon that he might wish to temper the more radical recommendations of his scheme for Indian self-government in the interests of obtaining the support of the India Office and the India Council. Hartington intimated that it was particularly the fear of official power being steadily eroded that kept his colleagues from readily endorsing the thrust of the Viceroy's proposed measures.[65] Hartington's successor, Lord Kimberley, was rather less given to subtlety. When Ripon published his Resolution on Local Self-Government and pushed through its modest application in the Local Self-Government Bill of the Central Provinces in 1883, Kimberley bluntly told him that he should restore the precedence of official power. This, he asserted, was what Indians wanted and accepted as legitimate for, as he put it, elections were still foreign to India.[66]

The notion that representation in India could be more readily adapted through a mode of political consultation, rather than a measure of political control, also formed the thrust of other arguments against the devolution of power to Indians. Sir Alfred Lyall, the Lieutenant Governor of the North-Western Provinces who had confessed to having deliberately stalled the pace of Ripon's reforms,[67] believed that 'the best foundations of liberal institutions' in India lay in the association of 'leading natives' in the process of government, rather than

[62] Resolution of the Government of Bombay, number 3583, 19 September 1882, *ibid.*, pp. 39–57, and Seal, *The Emergence of Indian Nationalism*, p. 159.
[63] Note by A. Mackenzie, Home Secretary, 29 November 1881, *Ripon Papers*, quoted in Seal, *The Emergence of Indian Nationalism*, p. 155.
[64] Ripon to W.E. Forster, 26 May 1881, *Ripon Papers*, quoted in Mehrotra, *The Emergence of the Indian National Congress*, p. 303.
[65] Hartington to Ripon, 23 June 1882, *Ripon Papers*, cited in Seal, *The Emergence of Indian Nationalism*, p. 157.
[66] Kimberley to Ripon, 15 June 1883, *Ripon Papers*, cited in *ibid.*, pp. 157–8.
[67] *Ibid.*, p. 150.
[68] Quoted in E.C.T. Chew, 'Sir Alfred Comyn Lyall: A study of the Anglo-Indian Official Mind', unpublished Ph.D. thesis, University of Cambridge (1969), p. 202.

in the election of a small class of professional politicians.[68] Lyall's preference for a system that would endorse the co-optation of Indian notables without actually recognising their right to represent Indians or to act creatively on their behalf, had become a familiar theme in the 1860s. It was to continue to exercise a noticeable hold upon the formulation of official policy until the turn of the century.

So too did the notion of the communitarian basis of Indian society which was later to assume overwhelming importance in the debate on Muslim communal representation. The relevance of India's communal make-up had of course already been implicitly recognised by early British administrators who had pointed to it as a serious constraint in the way of implementing Western representative institutions. Victorian Liberals too were conscious of its bearing upon the question of Indian representation insofar as it sought to emulate the model of modern European democracies. Curiously enough, therefore, despite their penchant for political innovation, Liberals in India were reluctant to advocate measures that might, in their view, have disturbed the fundamental organisation of the society over which they ruled.

Ripon, for example, who was clearly persuaded of the merits of introducing elections, had no hesitation in recommending that such elections should be 'by caste or occupation' as these 'would be more consonant with the feelings of the people'.[69] Not surprisingly, the Viceroy had nothing to say about dismantling the fairly well established practice of communal and caste representation that had been in existence in some municipalities since the 1870s. In Sind, for example, elected representatives on city boards were chosen by special caste *panchāyats*, while in the Central Provinces, representation on rural boards was organised along lines of occupational 'interests'.[70] In the Punjab, increasing political hostility between Hindus and Muslims had led to the reconstitution of several municipalities along communal lines and in some instances had forced the introduction of separate electorates, as in Amritsar in 1895.[71] But while Liberal advocates of electoral reform in India tended, apparently, to accept the forms of communal and corporate representation at the local level it was not until the twentieth century that the political implications of relying upon caste and creed as the bases of representation were most fully realised.

Nor was there much in the response of Indians to suggest a reappraisal of the question. Indeed, Indians, and particularly Western-

---

[69] Quoted in L. Wolf, *Life of the First Marquis of Ripon* II (London, John Murray, 1921), p. 98.
[70] Tinker, *The Foundations of Local Government*, p. 49.
[71] *Ibid.*, p. 50.

educated Indians, were too deeply absorbed in the larger question of Indian self-government. The 1870s and 1880s had witnessed growing numbers of Indians travelling abroad, especially to Britain where many had been impressed by the intellectual and political changes stimulated by European liberalism and nationalism. Few were able to resist the appeal of ideas then being propagated by Britain's more radical crusaders who were engaged in the task of electoral reform, and who stressed the role of representative institutions as agents of political education.[72] The creation of Indian political associations in England, as well as the election of men like Dadabhai Naoroji to Parliament, did much to contribute to the growing enthusiasm among educated Indians for the practices familiar to Western democracies.[73]

When Ripon announced, therefore, his intention to pursue the cause of Indian self-government, his move was hailed widely as laying the 'foundation of the great future of Representative Government'.[74] Few Indians doubted that his proposals would promote political self-awareness and many believed that they would also prepare Indians for 'an independent political existence'.[75] And although not all Indians, most notably the Muslims, were inclined to endorse the new 'liberal' spirit, many Western-educated Indians were clearly prepared to press for an extension of Ripon's reforms to higher levels of government. Indeed, the actual implementation of the reforms caused some dismay among Indians. They pointed to the proportion of elected members in local governments and claimed, with some justification, that this was less than Ripon had envisaged.[76] It was clear that increasing numbers of Western-educated Indians were no longer prepared to forego elections on the basis that they were 'unfit' for the political practices enjoyed by Britain and some of her overseas dominions.[77] The theme of Indian

[72] S. Chakravarty, 'The Evolution of Representative Government in India, 1884–1909, with special reference to Central and Provincial Legislative Councils', unpublished Ph.D. thesis, University of London (1954), pp. 484–6.

[73] Mehrotra, *The Emergence of the Indian National Congress*, pp. 221–9.

[74] G. Subramania Aiyar, quoted in Mehrotra, *ibid.*, p. 307.

[75] *The Mahratta*, May 28, 1882, *ibid.*

[76] *Proceedings of the First Indian National Congress held in Bombay on the 28th, 29th and 30th December 1885* (Bombay, Indian National Congress, 1886), p. 23.

[77] Speaking to the Mysore Representative Assembly, of which he was the founder, Dewan Rangu Charlu declared 'If the spread of any degree of education among the great mass of people were to be insisted upon as a *sine qua non* [for representative institutions] we may have to wait for ever; meanwhile every year under an autocratic system of government we will find the people less fit for representative institutions'. Quoted in S.K. Ghosh, 'The Influence of Western, particularly English, Political Ideas on Indian Political Thought, with special reference to the Political Ideas of the Indian National Congress, 1885–1919', unpublished Ph.D. thesis, University of London (1949), pp. 38–9.

unity which had begun to surface in the 1860s now became more persistent as educated Indians pointed to the homogeneity of a class that had been exposed to Western education and used English as a medium of communication. The early sessions of the newly-founded Indian National Congress in 1885 emphasised the capacity of India's educated middle classes to manage elected institutions modelled along 'western' lines.[78] Curiously enough, some early Congressmen even pointed to India's indigenous institutions as evidence of their society's familiarity with the forms of democratic practice. They referred, for example, to studies by Chisholm Anstey and Bartle Frere, both of whom had attempted to demonstrate that the system of *panchāyatī rāj*, or local councils, equipped Indians for a measure of self-government that could not readily be envisaged for Britain's other less 'advanced' colonies.[79]

The reaction of educated Indians to 'class' or 'interest' representation was somewhat more complex. For while growing numbers of urban-based, educated Indians pressed for Western representative institutions, few were prepared to accept a more broad-based, or popular, franchise. Indeed, some even advocated elections through specially constituted electorates consisting of municipalities, district boards, and chambers of commerce to counter the effects of popular representation.[80] It is important to underline however that this preference for the representation of 'interests' did not always signify representation on the basis of caste, class or creed. Indeed, territorial constituencies, with their potential for cutting across rigid barriers of caste and creed, were sometimes positively endorsed. 'The value and serviceableness of a municipal representative', argued S.S. Bengali, a member of the Bombay Legislative Council in 1878, 'lies in his residence ... I do not see why individuals should be compelled to vote for their caste men alone when they find it more to their advantage to elect the most competent representative on the spot'.[81] These views were to become even more common in subsequent decades when many, though by no means all, Western-educated Indians reacted sharply to the introduction of separate electorates under the reforms of 1909.

[78] S.K. Ghose, *The Western Impact on Indian Politics, 1885–1919* (Bombay, Allied Publishers, 1967), pp. 1–15.
[79] *Ibid.*, p. 10.
[80] Daniel Argov, *Moderates and Extremists in the Indian Nationalist Movement, 1883–1920* (Bombay, Asia Publishing House, 1967), p. 34.
[81] Quoted in S.S. Majumdar, *History of Indian Social and Political Ideas: From Ram Mohun to Dayananda* (Calcutta, Bookland Private, 1967), pp. 211–12.

'Interest' representation: ideology and social engineering

The last two decades of the nineteenth century witnessed a more
conscious attempt by officials to structure a system of political
representation better suited to India's complex social structure. Her
heterogeneity and lack of social differentiation had led many to
conclude that political institutions which had flourished in more
compact societies like Britain were unlikely to succeed.[82] Notwithstanding these reservations, however, few officials could afford to ignore the
growing pressures to extend the practices of 'western' representation to
Indians. Many sought, therefore, to design a system that would bestow a
measure of political responsibility to Indians, as well as conform
somewhat to the essential make-up of the society for which it was
intended. This society, as officials saw it in the late 1880s and 1890s, was a
conglomeration of disparate and mutually antagonistic social groups.
Indeed, the emphasis upon the representation of groups rather than of
individuals was shaped decisively by contemporary perceptions of
Indian society some of which were embodied in historical studies by
those who subsequently came to influence the evolution of Indian
representation.

In an influential series of lectures entitled *The Rise and Expansion of
British Dominion in India*, Sir Alfred Lyall described contemporary
India as a 'mere loose conglomeration of tribes, races and castes' which
resembled early feudal Europe.[83] He argued however, that while Europe
had witnessed the growth of occupational groups which had enabled
individuals to assume indentities distinct from those imposed by creed
or race, Indians continued to define themselves pre-eminently in terms
of their religious and caste affiliations.[84]

The idea of India as an undeveloped, undifferentiated and, by
implication, 'barbarous' society influenced contemporary British political thinkers, whether jurists, historians and ethnologists. All drew
attention to India's diversity and its state of historical and social under-
development. James Mill saw India as lacking in civilisation, while Sir
Henry Maine characterised her as 'primitive'. William Hunter's ethnological research led him to conclude that the evolution of a homogen-

---

[82] The introduction of Western representative institutions in India, declared *The Times* in
1885, was precluded by 'the conflict of races, the diversity of creeds, [and] the isolating
effect of caste, all separating influences and disintegrating forces'. *The Times*,
17 August 1885.
[83] Alfred Lyall, *The Rise and Expansion of British Dominion in India* (London, John
Murray, 1924), p. 321.
[84] *Ibid.*

ous society in India had been constrained by the unwillingness of conquering Aryan races to cohabit with indigenous groups.[85]

These reflections on Indian society tended to permeate official thinking, particularly in its assessment of India's fitness for institutions that were seen to be part of more 'advanced' civilisations. India's 'backwardness' raised questions not only about the merits of applying to a predominantly rural society the political practices of an industrial society like Britain, but also about the wisdom of accepting as 'representative' the claims of a small class of chiefly urban-based Indians whose access to Western education had estranged them from the majority of their countrymen. Sir Henry Maine, for example, warned his official colleagues of the danger of regarding the 'educated classes' in India as in any way representative of the 'barbaric majority which filled the vast interior'.[86] While the thrust of Maine's observations could scarcely be faulted, it is important not to lose sight of their political utility. For as long as officials could point to the sociological discontinuity between India's increasingly articulate, if minute, middle classes and its seemingly inert rural masses the pressure for representative institutions could effectively be restrained.

This primarily sociological image of India had other implications as well. Of these, not the least important was the assumption that Indian 'political society' was essentially an extension of its 'civil society'. Indeed, it was this assumption that accounted, in part, for the official preoccupation with the representation of groups of caste, creed and class. Because the primary categories in use were almost always sociological, officials were led increasingly to rely upon a notion of representation that stressed social correspondence, rather than any aspect pertaining to political activity as such. Being representative, then, was pre-eminently a question of *being typical* of the represented, rather than of *acting politically* for or on their behalf. Political groups and associations like Congress, which in the late 1880s and 1890s tended to be dominated by Indians who were not, for the most part, socially representative of those for whom they claimed to speak, namely the vast Indian masses, could therefore readily be dismissed as 'unrepresentative'. For what officials sought, and believed possible, was not so much the representation of an evolving political consensus of individuals, but

---

[85] T.G.P. Spear, 'British Historical Writing in the Era of the Nationalist Movement', in C.H. Philips (ed.), *Historians of India, Pakistan and Ceylon* (London, George Allen and Unwin, 1961), pp. 404–15.

[86] Sir Henry Maine, *The Effects of Observation of India on Modern European Thought* (London, John Murray, 1875), p. 220.

the representation of an established order of distinct, and sometimes warring social groups; not the representation of individuals voluntarily organised as groups, but the groups – 'Kayasths', 'Muslims', 'landlords', 'peasants' – to which individuals belonged.[87] The representation of 'Indians', with which political associations like Congress were preoccupied, therefore, found little or no recognition except as one more social category alongside the many others which clamoured for official recognition.

This was to become even more manifest as part of official policy under Lord Dufferin, who succeeded Ripon as Viceroy in the summer of 1885. Although Dufferin, like Ripon, was keen on political reform, he was no less conscious of the need for a system that would reflect the inherent complexities of Indian society – 'circumstances' which, he asserted, 'we found and did not create'.[88] Dufferin declared that his government, in its approach to the problem of Indian representation, would proceed on the assumption that there were 'other communities and interests' besides those professed by 'nimble witted students from Bengal'.[89] Indeed, it seemed hardly necessary to caution Dufferin, as the Secretary of State, Lord Cross, was later to do, against the danger of accepting the 'interests of the noisy Bengalee Baboo' as in any way synonymous with those of the rest of India, and particularly of its great Muhammadan community.[90]

The quest for a system of representation that would balance the 'interests' of the *Baboo* class with those of the non-*Baboo* classes was one of the principal considerations that faced the Committee, appointed by Dufferin in September 1888, to evaluate the problem of Indian representation.[91] The predominant assumption upon which the Committee undertook to formulate its recommendations was that the 'interests' of the 'hereditary nobility' and 'the superior and influential landed classes' should receive as much recognition as those of the 'trading, professional and agricultural classes'. It also recommended that religious groups, like the Muslims and the Parsis, should receive representation in proportion

---

[87] Lucy Carroll, 'Colonial Perceptions of Indian Society and the Emergence of Caste (s) Associations', *Journal of Asian Studies*, 37, 2 (1978), pp. 233–49.
[88] Dufferin to G. Allen, 1 January 1887, *Dufferin Papers*, 51, quoted in Seal, *The Emergence of Indian Nationalism*, p. 189.
[89] Dufferin to Kimberley, 21 March 1886, *Dufferin Papers*, MSS. Eur. F. 130/5.
[90] Cross to Dufferin, 14 April 1887, *Dufferin Papers*, 20, quoted in Seal, *The Emergence of Indian Nationalism*, p. 189.
[91] See the Report on the Subject of Provincial Councils by Chesney, Aitchison and Westland, 1888 and Summary of Conclusions, Enclosures numbers 1 and 2. Dufferin to Cross, 20 October 1888, *Dufferin Papers*, MSS. Eur. F. 130/11 b.

to their population in order to ensure that their interests were not overlooked. The Committee was clearly not concerned to devise a system that could generate the means of obtaining a 'national' consensus. Rather, it saw its task to lie in the creation of a political framework that would reflect as accurately as possible the range and the diversity of 'interests' in society. What made such 'interest' represent-ation significant in the context of the India of the late 1880s, was that these 'interests' were seen to flow not from the voluntary coalitions of individuals, but from broad objective social groupings that were deemed to be 'fixed' and intrinsic parts of Indian society. Indeed, the thrust of the Committee's report demonstrates that individuals were rarely, if ever, held to profess interests: they were presumed merely to 'belong to' or 'partake of' 'interests'.

The official consensus in favour of the representation of 'types and classes', rather than 'areas and numbers', was formally endorsed in 1892 under a new scheme of reforms which sought to increase the numbers of elected Indians to the provincial Councils.[92] The purpose of these reforms however, was definitely not seen to be the creation of 'national' representative institutions such as existed in Britain. These, Lord Curzon declared, were impossible in a society that was divided into 'irreconcilable camp' where 'differences of caste, of religion of custom ... hold ... men fast bound during their life-time'.[93] Rather, the pattern of Indian representation envisaged by the new reforms was designed precisely to establish those very ingredients which had been implicit in official discourse since the 1860s.

There was firstly the belief that the practice of elections was an essentially Western phenomenon 'alien to the Indian mind';[94] it was deemed not to be, nor ever to have been, 'an Eastern idea', nor to conform to 'Eastern traditions' or 'Eastern minds'.[95] In his defence of the Bill on Indian Councils reform in the House of Lords, the new Viceroy, Lord Lansdowne, explained that his government's reluctance to extend elections more widely stemmed from its impression that 'in many parts of India any system of election is entirely foreign to the

---

[92] Lord Lansdowne's Speech in *Proceedings of the Legislative Council of the Governor General of India, XXXII (1893)* (Calcutta, 1893), pp. 105–11, quoted in Cecil Cross. *The Development of Self Government in India, 1858–1914* (Chicago University Press, 1922), p. 161.

[93] Curzon's speech in the House of Lord's, 28 March 1892, *Hansard's Parliamentary Debates* (Lords) (1892), volume 3 (new series), columns 66–7.

[94] Lord Cross's speech in the House of Lords, 6 March 1890, *ibid.* (1890), volume 342, column 85.

[95] Lord Salisbury's speech in the House of Lord's, 6 March 1890, *ibid.*, column 98.

feelings and habits of the people'.[96] Others, like Lord Curzon, relied upon their understanding of Indian normative standards to categorically reject elections as a workable basis for greater Indian representation. Popular representation, he argued, may well have been important for England but it was unlikely to present itself as such to those who, in his estimation, 'have no instinctive sense of what political equality is'.[97]

There was secondly the notion that constituencies defined along territorial lines were unlikely to result in the representation of the 'real' interests in society. In the 1870s, Sir Bartle Frere had drawn attention to the value of 'natural' constituencies like village *panchāyats* (or rural councils). These, he maintained, were a more suitable means of obtaining Indian representation than the territorial constituency which tended to impose forms of solidarity that were foreign to Indians.[98] Later, Dufferin was to reject the idea of elections through territorial constituencies by calling for representation organised along 'ethnical' lines or, failing that, representation through 'responsible bodies'.[99] These, the Viceroy believed, would ultimately help secure the representation of 'bonafide interests'.[100] His Committee appointed in 1888 went some way towards incorporating these preferences by recommending that the election of Indians to the Provincial and Supreme Councils be obtained primarily through existing bodies 'prescribed and ... determined by Law' such as municipal boards and corporations.[101]

Doubts about the merits of the territorial constituency as a mechanism for obtaining Indian representation extended also to officials at the India Office in London. In January 1889, the Secretary of State, Lord Cross, wrote to Lansdowne expressing reservations about elections in any form. Cross confessed that his difficulties stemmed in part from the problem of devising a suitable constituency to obtain Indian representation. He implied that territorial constituencies were unlikely to succeed where division and inequality were so deeply entrenched. 'The ryot', he wrote, 'cannot be represented. The other classes are against the ryot,

---

[96] Lansdowne's speech, *Proceedings of the Legislative Council of the Governor General of India, XXXII* (Calcutta, 1893), pp. 106–7, quoted in Cross, *The Development of Self-Government in India*, p. 160.

[97] See his speech in the House of Lords, 28 March 1892, *Hansard's Parliamentary Debates* (Lords) (1892), volume 3 (new series), column 66.

[98] Bartle Frere, *The Means of Ascertaining Public Opinion in India* (London, John Murray, 1871), p. 16.

[99] Cited in Chakravarty, 'The Evolution of Representative Government in India', pp. 56–7.

[100] Dufferin to Cross, 20 March 1887, *Dufferin Papers*, MSS. Eur. F. 130/8 a.

[101] Report on the Subject of Provincial Councils by Chesney, Aitchison and Westland, 1888, and Summary of Conclusions, Enclosures numbers 1 and 2. Dufferin to Cross, 20 October 1888. *Ibid.*, 130/11 b.

whose sole protector is the British government. Nor would the Mohammedan for a moment consent to be outvoted by the Hindu'.[102] The scepticism of officials like Cross on the question of territorial constituencies was later to be embodied in the Bill on Indian Councils reform which restricted the number of Council seats allocated according to geographical areas. In his assessment of the Bill, Lord Lansdowne explained that the decision against extending territorial constituencies more widely owed much to the difficulties of distributing seats 'according to strict numerical proportions'. He implied that in a society like India, the representation of 'real' interests was unlikely to be obtained by applying the kind of criteria that were more common to elections organised on the basis of territorial constituencies.[103]

The debate about the nature of the constituency suggests that official discourse on Indian representation continued to be dominated by a sociological perspective. It is clear that when officials referred to the constituency, what they had in mind was one or other of the many social groups, or 'interests' with which they had come to be familiar and which they had done so much to define. Indeed, what the 'colonial' model aspired to was precisely the equation of constituency with social group or 'interest'. For the vision which inspired such a model was a notion of representation as a descriptive activity, a matter of accurate resemblance between representative and represented with the purpose not so much of engaging in creative political activity as of providing government with the means of ensuring its own stability. However the absence of any conceptual distinction between a political constituency on the one hand and an administratively defined social category like the 'peasantry' or 'Muslim' on the other, also served specific political ends. For as long as the constituency of organisations like Congress, which clamoured for 'western' representation, could be shown to be restricted to the 'minute'[104] educated middle classes, their political claims were likely to appear highly tenuous.

It is interesting that while their political concerns were quite distinct from one another and were dictated by wholly different ends, officials tended, perhaps unwittingly, to espouse a notion of representation that would have been familiar to English Utilitarians engaged in the task of parliamentary reform in the nineteenth century. They too were anxious

---

[102] Cross to Lansdowne, 18 January 1889, *Lansdowne Papers*, MSS. Eur. D. 558/2.
[103] Lord Lansdowne's speech, *Proceedings of the Legislative Council of the Governor General of India* XXXII (Calcutta, 1893), pp. 105-11.
[104] Curzon's speech in the House of Lords, 28 March 1892, *Hansard's Parliamentary Debates* (Lords) (1892), volume 3 (new series), column 68.

to check what they believed amounted to the over-representation of particular classes on the grounds that they constituted only a small proportion of society. They too were concerned to secure a 'representative' assembly that could accurately reflect the society of which it was a part.[105] But there were inherent contradictions in applying this notion of representation to the case of colonial India. In their stance against the claims of Western-educated Indians, officials had maintained that being Indian could not, in itself, establish representative status as the very notion of 'Indian' was subject to question in so diverse a society. What was essential was to demonstrate a given connection between representative and represented that rested upon a set of shared social, cultural, religious or racial affinities. Yet it was manifestly the case that officials like Cross, who believed that they best represented the interests of India, could fulfil none of the criteria they so rigidly demanded of Indian representatives.[106] On what grounds then did they hope to speak on behalf of those 'vast interests which we have undertaken to represent'?[107] On the grounds, quite simply of 'good' government, that is to say, a government that rested in the hands of men 'far more advanced than those among whom it exists'.[108] The alternative, namely self-government, they believed, with its concomitant stress upon majority-rule, would, in a society like India, inevitably imply peasant-rule and a government of ignorance and superstition'.[109]

Indeed, the theme of 'good' government was far from exhausted. Lord Dufferin had emphasised early in his Viceroyalty that the reformed Councils he envisaged were neither harbingers of self-government in disguise, nor the instruments of constitutional revolution. They were merely props, sounding boards of Indian opinion, that would act to ensure a more efficient administration.[110] In October 1888, Dufferin's Committee underlined the function of the Councils as handmaidens of

[105] A.H. Birch, *Representative and Responsible Government: An Essay on the British Constitution* (London, George Allen and Unwin, 1964), pp. 45–7.

[106] In February 1887, Cross wrote to the Viceroy warning him that 'the masses of the people do not want to be ruled by Baboos, and it is our duty, as well as our interest, and still more the interest of our people, that there is to be English rule...'. Cross to Dufferin, 25 February 1887, *Dufferin Papers*, 20, quoted in Seal, *The Emergence of Indian Nationalism*, p. 186.

[107] Lord Salisbury's speech in the House of Lords, 6 March 1890, *Hansard's Parliamentary Debates* (Lords) (1890), volume 342, columns 85–6.

[108] A.O. Hume and Auckland Colvin, *Audi Alteram Partem* (Simla, 1888), pp. 22–3.

[109] *Ibid.*, p. 25.

[110] Dufferin's Minute on Reform Proposals, November 1888, *Public Letters from India, 1888*, volume 9, pp. 1190–3. See also J.L. Hill, 'Congress and Representative Institutions in the United Provinces, 1886–1901', unpublished Ph.D. thesis, Duke University (1966), p. 341.

administration by recommending that their powers be no more than advisory, though possibly somewhat larger in scope than those provided under Wood's Indian Councils Act of 1861. Although members of the Committee recognised the Council's right of interpellation in matters pertaining to local administration, they stressed that only such questions would be raised as to enable the government to assess public opinion more effectively.[111]

Later, Dufferin was to justify the primarily consultative powers of the Councils by pointing out that they were never intended, in any way, to be representative. Nor, he maintained, was there any question of Indian Councillors acting as mandate-bearers of the community or as agents charged with the task of making government more responsible. Indeed, he concluded, under the circumstances it would be wholly impracticable to extend to the educated classes, 'this infinitesimal and only partially qualified fraction of the people of India anything beyond consultative, critical and suggestive powers'.[112] Nor did he believe, was it quite appropriate. For, as he was subsequently to confess to Cross, 'you cannot apply constitutional principles to a conquered country'.[113] Dufferin's conception of the role of representative institutions in India merely echoed the prevailing official view which tended to regard them as no more than links between rulers and subjects, devoid of any creative potential or capacity to forge a political consensus. They were not 'debating societies' but instruments to gauge public reaction to public policy. They were above all, as Lord Northbrook observed drily, merely 'practical bodies' for 'practical business'.[114]

[111] Report on the Subject of Provincial Councils by Chesney, Aitchison and Westland, 1888, and Summary of Conclusions, Enclosures numbers 1 and 2. Dufferin to Cross, 20 October 1888, *Dufferin Papers*, MSS. Eur. F. 130/11 b.
[112] See Dufferin's Minute on Reform proposals, November 1888, *Public Letters from India*, 1888, volume 9, pp. 1195–6.
[113] Dufferin to Cross, 20 October 1888, *Dufferin Papers*, MSS. Eur. F. 130/11.
[114] Lord Northbrook's speech to the House of Lords, 6 March 1890, *Hansard's Parliamentary Debates* (Lords) (1890), volume 342, column 162.

3

Mughals and Muslims:
Muslim attitudes to representation:
1860–1900

The response of Indian Muslims to the introduction of Western representation constituted one of the most significant features of Indian political life in the last half of the nineteenth century. Like other, politically aspiring Indian groups, privileged Muslim gentlemen, concentrated mainly in the urban centres of the North-Western Provinces, Bengal and Bombay, surmised in the government's programme for council reform rich possibilities for an assured place in the colonial establishment. However, it is for their resistance to the modes of what they termed 'western' representation that Indian Muslims at the turn of the century are chiefly remembered. Their opposition to such representation was guided by a set of considerations which led them to an understanding of the nature and purpose of representation that was to have a significant impact on the subsequent history of the sub-continent.

These considerations stemmed from four quite distinct, if not always easily distinguishable, sources. There were those that were shaped by the specific interests which these Muslims deemed politically advantageous to themselves and their followers. There were others that owed more to the ideology of British power in India and to the notions of representation such ideology helped sustain. Yet others derived from a cultural tradition that had been closely associated with Muslim dominance in India. Finally there were considerations that were moulded by the political assumptions of a faith whose influence among Muslims, whether as a set of religious doctrines or as a more diffuse cultural ethic, was widely acknowledged.

The sociological premises with which colonial officials approached the question of representation in India were keenly adopted by many Indian Muslims. Like their colonial masters, well-placed Muslims in Calcutta and Bombay, Bihar and the North-West Provinces, prefaced their political observations with ritual reflections on Indian social heterogeneity. Categories of race and religion were indiscriminately superimposed on complex social and political phenomena, while group conflict was accepted as the dominant mode of interaction in Indian society. At the same time, a contradictory image of India as one vast

76

peasantry whose salvation lay in good, namely British government rather than in Indian self-government, was enthusiastically marshalled to sustain a profound scepticism of the claims of a fledgling nationalist movement.

However, if Indian Muslims did appear to take easily to official modes of describing and explaining Indian society and politics, what precisely were their motives in doing so? Furthermore were there perhaps, apart from calculated motives, real constraints which left them with few options in the realm of political action and belief?

There is now a fairly widely held and quite convincing view that Indian Muslims, particularly after the Mutiny of 1857, were concerned primarily to restore their political credibility as loyal allies of the colonial government.[1] Their perception of Indian society and their public stance on the merits or otherwise of 'western' representation, it is argued, derived principally from their understanding of how British officials expected loyal subjects to think and behave. In short, it is claimed that Muslim attitudes to society and representation flowed from a calculated position which was designed to ensure a place in the existing political hierarchy engendered by colonial rule.[2]

There is indeed very little, apparently, that could displace the power of this argument. The politics of Sayyid Ahmad Khān and his immediate followers, who were to dominate Muslim political thinking into the first decades of the twentieth century, appear to point decisively to a penchant for political expediency. Their programme of political action, embodied in the anti-Congress campaign, as well as their pronouncements on the dangers of Indian political representation, appear to have been dictated by their anticipation of political rewards rather than by any inner conviction about the merits of their case. Their stance on issues like pan-Islamism in the 1870s, for example, seem to have been prompted more by a wish to be consistent with official policy in India than by a concern to promote an institution that Muslims had traditionally cherished.[3]

---

[1] David Lelyveld, *Aligarh's First Generation: Muslim Solidarity in British India* (Princeton University Press, 1978), pp. 302–20; Margaret Case, 'The Aligarh Era: Muslim Politics in North India, 1860–1910', unpublished Ph.D. dissertation, University of Chicago, 1970; Ram Gopal, *Indian Muslims: A Political History (1858–1947)* (Lahore, Book Traders, 1976), pp. 44–52; A. Hamid, *Muslim Separatism in India* (Lahore, Oxford University Press, 1965), pp. 2–20; S.R. Mehrotra, *The Emergence of the Indian National Congress* (New York, Barnes and Noble, 1971), pp. 212–21.

[2] Anil Seal, *The Emergence of Indian Nationalism* (Cambridge University Press, 1971), pp. 298–340. See also his 'Imperialism and Nationalism in India', *Modern Asian Studies*, 15, 3 (1981), pp. 415–54.

[3] In his assessment of Sayyid Ahmad's position on the *khilāfat* issue in the 1870s, Aziz

Notwithstanding this quite ostensible pursuit of political advantages for themselves and their community, however, it is clear that these Indian Muslims were also subject to constraints within which many were bound to conduct their politics. Of these the influence of the language of colonial discourse cannot be easily dismissed. Indian Muslims, like many other groups in colonial India, found themselves constantly engaged in adapting and adjusting to this language. They acted on the assumption that it was the only language the colonial government understood and were prepared to accept. The idiom of race and religion, of conflict and dissension defined the parameters within which Indian Muslims manoeuvred in order to sustain their claims to representation.[4]

Attention has already been drawn to the tendency among British officials to emphasise corporate representation as a particularly appropriate political device for Indian society as they saw it. Partly because of the tenacious influence upon officials of the ideology of British Whiggery, and partly because it provided the rationale with which to cut at Congress's political claims, corporate representation quickly assumed the status of a dominant political norm among the official classes. It constituted both the yardstick and the principal criterion by which officials chose either to deny or legitimise indigenous claims to representation. Insofar, therefore, as the demand for Muslim communal representation can be seen to have been 'encouraged' by official prodding, it owed much to the pre-existing ideological discourse with which officials interpreted Indian society and sought to devise its institutions.[5]

However aside from these constraints which Muslims shared to a greater or lesser degree with other groups bound by the order of official expectations, there were yet others that were unquestionably peculiar to them. These essentially evaluative considerations were the expressions

---

Ahmad wryly observes 'Sayyid Ahmad Khān had been pro-Turkish as long as this was British policy ... But the change in Britain's foreign policy and the growing anti-Turkish trend in the measures taken by Rosebury and Salisbury were soon reflected in his writings. He had witnessed the tragedy of anti-British insurgence in 1857, and his lifelong mission had been to salvage the wreck of his community on the raft of loyalism. He could not cut loose from this sheet anchor'. Aziz Ahmad, *Islamic Modernism in India and Pakistan* (London, Oxford University Press, 1967), p.125.

[4] For a sense of the ingredients of colonial discourse and its influence upon the emerging pattern of politics in British India see Bernard S. Cohn, 'The Census, Social Structure and Objectification in South Asia', paper read at the Second European Conference on Modern South Asia, Elsinore, Denmark, June 1970 and Lucy Carroll, 'Colonial Perceptions of Indian Society and the Emergence of Caste(s) Associations', *Journal of Asian Studies*, 37, 2 (1978), pp. 233–49.

[5] A point developed at some length in Peter Hardy, *The Muslims of British India* (Cambridge University Press, 1972).

of two separate, yet inseparable, identities. There were those that Indian Muslims espoused as part of a ruling class culture of which they had at one time constituted the apex; and others which represented for them the recognisable elements of a Muslim political ethic. The former owed more to the influence of what might be termed 'Mongol-Mughal' ideas which had formed a characteristic element in Indo-Muslim political thinking since at least the mid-sixteenth century. The latter were more obviously 'Islamically-derived', in that they reflected the dominant assumptions familiar to Muslim political discourse since the consolidation of Islam as a world religion.

The adherence to a set of cultural norms that had become common to an Irano-Semitic tradition had a considerable impact upon the conduct of Indo-Muslim politics. These norms, which had crystallized in the sixteenth and seventeenth centuries at the height of Muslim dominance in India, were widely espoused by the ruling Muslim gentry.[6] The edifice of this 'Mongol-Mughal' tradition, which came later to form the heart of *sharīf* culture, was grounded primarily in the premise that an essential part of being a Muslim consisted of belonging to, and identifying with, the ruling power. Closely related to this, and flowing from it, was the notion that Muslims (or at least those who counted politically) formed part of a superior race whose noble foreign origins entitled them to a degree of deference beyond that commonly accorded to indigenous Indian groups.[7]

For those Indian Muslims who believed in the validity of these claims, the organisation and ends of 'western' liberal representation proved to be fundamentally inadmissible. The slogan of 'one-man, one-vote' that had become increasingly characteristic of its philosophy in Britain, if not as yet in colonial India, suggested to Indian Muslims the preoccupation with an altogether different set of commitments.

It implied, in the first instance, the rejection of any *a priori* claims to power, but it also signified the denial of all social and political distinctions based on class and race as legitimate grounds for claims to representation. Above all, for those Indian Muslims whose foreign ancestry had been the hallmark of their distinction, 'western' representation signalled the decline of their community to the status of 'just one more Indic caste'.[8]

The reaction of Indian Muslims to the prospect of Western

---

[6] Some of the cultural values that shaped the outlook and the political pre-occupations of the ruling classes of this 'Timuri Empire' are discussed in Marshall Hodgson, *The Venture of Islam: Conscience and History in a World Civilization* III (University of Chicago Press, 1974), pp. 60–86.

[7] Lelyveld. *Aligarh's First Generation*, pp. 20–34.

[8] Hodgson, *The Venture of Islam*, III, p. 148.

representation in the decades following the 1860s suggest that many found it difficult to accept such representation as legitimate. It is also clear that their inability to respond positively stemmed from the very different assumptions they made as Muslims about the basis of politics and its relation to men's religious beliefs. Many were profoundly disturbed by the steady emergence of political norms which ostensibly questioned the most cherished values of their faith. They viewed with alarm the possible introduction of territorial constituencies that threatened to undermine the primacy of the communal group as the only authentic basis of representation. For those whose faith had led them to presuppose that men's political loyalties were an extension of their religious commitments, Indian Muslims reacted sharply to the suggestion that non-Muslims might conceivably and legitimately represent them.

It could of course be argued, as indeed it has been, that Muslims engaged in the issue of political representation manipulated religious ideology to serve political ends.[9] These ends concerned privileges which Muslims as a dominant ruling minority had once enjoyed and were unwilling to relinquish. This claim is at the most only half true. For it ignores the very real pre-occupation of a deeply self-conscious group of men for whom the practice and profession of their faith was at least as important as the temporal destiny of their community (though many would admittedly have denied that the two were separable).[10]

Muslim attitudes to representation before 1880

The decades between the end of the Mutiny of 1857 and the return to power in Britain of a Liberal government in 1880, were a period of intense and often painful introspection for many Indian Muslims. There were those who ceaselessly questioned the causes of their community's decline both politically and culturally; and others who wondered how best to adjust their community to the new British presence on the subcontinent. Though each sought solutions in different means – the former by purifying the faith of the believer,[11] the latter by regenerating his social

---

[9] Paul Brass, *Language, Religion and Politics in North India* (London, Cambridge University Press, 1974). See also his 'Elite groups, symbol manipulation and ethnic identity among Muslims in South Asia', in David Taylor and Malcolm Yapp (eds.), *Political Identity in South Asia* (London, School of Oriental and African Studies, 1979), pp. 35–77.

[10] A position forcefully defended in Francis Robinson, 'Islam and Muslim Separatism' in Taylor and Yapp (eds.), *Political Identity*, pp. 78–112.

[11] Barbara D. Metcalf, *Islamic Revival in British India: Deoband, 1860–1900* (Princeton University Press, 1982).

and political life[12] – both contributed substantially to the consolidation of an Indian Muslim identity.[13]

Their very different preoccupations however dictated their attitudes towards political issues, including those which concerned the representation of Indian Muslims in the corridors of official power. For Muslims engaged in the task of religious reform there was little interest, at least for the time being, in the organisation of the state and its politics.[14] Theirs was a life devoted to the cultivation of the moral qualities of the individual believer in the hope that therein lay the way to communal advancement.

For another, and relatively much smaller group of Western-educated and primarily urban Muslims engaged in government service, the professions and land-holding, political issues were of the utmost importance. For many of them, Muslim political participation provided the only really effective means to reaffirm the vitality of their community and its pre-eminence in the colonial hierarchy of power.[15]

Despite these seeming differences however, it would not perhaps be correct to suggest that the concerns of these groups of Muslims were mutually exclusive. Barbara Metcalf has shown how Muslim religious movements like Deoband, through their teaching, provided the class of urban Muslim *ashrāf*, with the means of confronting the existing political situation.[16] This, she argues, they accomplished by endorsing the legitimacy of accepting government jobs and by sharing 'the

---

[12] David Lelyveld, *Aligarh's First Generation*.

[13] Comparing the orientations of the reformist *'ulamā'* with those of students from Aligarh, Metcalf concludes 'The *'ulama* held more clearly to the ideal of Islamic norms in all aspects of life, and accepted the limitations imposed on them more guardedly and more unwillingly than did people at Aligarh. They tended, in these early decades, to avoid political issues, whereas the Aligarh people sought out a place for themselves in the councils of the rulers. But both groups,... moved towards an acceptance of "Indian Muslim" as their fundamental social identity'. Metcalf, *Islamic Revival*, p. 335.

[14] *Ibid.*, p. 11.

[15] In a passionate letter to his friend and colleague, Sayyid Husain Bilgrāmī, Sayyid Ahmad stressed that although he regretted the passing of Muslim dominance in India, he was unwilling merely to wallow in its past glories. Nor was he persuaded that 'religious works' alone were enough to raise Muslims from the 'torpor' into which they had fallen. For him only a programme of 'communal reform' which could equip Muslims, both socially and intellectually, to face the consequences of British rule would enable them to regain something of their former status. Sayyid Ahmed Khān to Imdadul Mulk Sayyid Husain Bilgrāmī, 5 September 1895, in Shaikh Muhammad Ismā'īl Pānīpatī (ed.), *Maktūbāt-i-Sir Sayyid*, I (Lahore, Majlis-i-tarraqī-e Adab, 1976), pp. 290–1.

[16] Metcalf, *Islamic Revival*, pp. 252–3.

increasing concern that more of these jobs should be in Muslim hands'.[17]

Nor was politics altogether unfamiliar to the rather more peripatetic though less urbane world of the rural-based religious preacher, otherwise known as the *mullah*. In his study of the relationship between the process of 'Islamisation' and the origins of communalism in Bengal at the end of the nineteenth century, Rafiuddin Ahmed has shown how itinerant *mullahs* espoused and propagated political interests otherwise associated with a sophisticated Bengali urban elite.[18]

A reverse portrait appears in David Lelyveld's seminal work on Aligarh's 'first generation'. This reveals the way in which a group of Muslims led by Sayyid Ahmad Khān, succeeded in pursuing a programme of religious and educational reform along with a strategy of communal political survival.[19]

There are other examples which suggest that the traditional religious elite were not altogether unfamiliar with the concerns of their more worldly counterparts, and Western-educated Muslims not wholly dismissive of the perspectives of their faith. The members of the Muslim religious seminary, Nadvāt-ul-'ulamā' founded in Lucknow in the 1890s for instance,[20] shared with Western-educated Indian Muslims the view that what was needed was a much closer involvement with the ruling power.[21] Like their more urbane co-religionists they came to espouse a notion of political representation which regarded it as synonymous with official recognition. Like them, they also aspired to be 'spokesmen for Muslims to the government' and clearly realised that good relations with government was a necessary part of the claim to leadership and representation.[22]

However, if saintly pursuits were open to the expediency of politics, politics itself was sometimes hallowed by the incursion of a certain piety.

---

[17] *Ibid.*, p. 253.
[18] Rafiuddin Ahmed, *The Bengal Muslims, 1871–1906: A Quest for Identity* (Delhi, Oxford University Press, 1981).
[19] Lelyveld, *Aligarh's First Generation*. See also Metcalf, *Islamic Revival*, pp. 317–35.
[20] There is some controversy surrounding the precise date of its foundation. Aziz Ahmad, S.M. Ikram and David Lelyveld have set its date at 1894, see Aziz Ahmad, *op. cit.* p. 109; S.M. Ikram, *Modern Muslim India and the Birth of Pakistan* (Lahore, Shaikh Muhammad Ashraf, 1970), p. 125, and Lelyveld, *op. cit.*, p. 244. Others, like Francis Robinson, appear to concur by concluding that the first Congress of the Nadva 'met two years after the 1892 Councils Act'. See Francis Robinson, *Separatism Among Indian Muslims: The Politics of the United Provinces Muslims, 1860–1923* (Cambridge University Press, 1974), p. 275. Yet others, like Barbara Metcalf, believe that the seminary was created in 1891. Metcalf, *Islamic Revival*, p. 335.
[21] Metcalf, *Islamic Revival*, pp. 335–47.
[22] *Ibid.*, p. 336. See also Aziz Ahmad, *Islamic Modernism*, pp. 109–12.

Though few Muslim political leaders at the end of the nineteenth century were men of formal religious training, the traditions and the practices of their faith were by no means marginal to the conduct of their politics. Many applied, some more consciously than others, traditional Muslim criteria of good government to their understanding of modern representation. Political associations like the Anjuman-i-Islāmi invoked the notion of *shūrā*, or consultation, to stress their commitment to the principle of just and open government.[23] Others, like Sayyid Amīr 'Alī, developed the concept of *ijmā'* to sustain their claims for constitutional checks on executive authority.[24]

The 'politics' of Muslim representation

To begin to understand how Indian Muslims apprehended the question of representation in the decades immediately following the Mutiny of 1857, one must first draw attention to their intense concern with the political survival of their community. For many Muslims these years were fraught with the demanding task of restoring their tarnished image as loyal and committed subjects of the Raj. None were so keenly aware of this at the time as those Muslims drawn variously from the service and landed classes of the North-Western Provinces and Bengal.[25] They saw themselves as part of an embattled minority whose role in the uprising of 1857 had been vastly exaggerated. Many believed that a gross misunderstanding between themselves and their British masters had led their political opportunities to be dramatically and wrongfully arrested. A number were persuaded that under the circumstances, the restoration of their political influence depended upon and could be secured only by pursuing a policy of active loyalty to British rule in India.

It is not surprising therefore that Muslim attitudes to the question of representation in the last quarter of the nineteenth century should have been shaped principally, though by no means exclusively, by their quest for self-preservation. Concerned as they were with the political fortunes of their class and the lure of government patronage, urban and Western-educated Muslims came increasingly to espouse a view of representation that had little or nothing to do with popular support or political

---

[23] Founded in May 1855 by a group of lawyers and government employees, the Anjuman was designed partly to counter the effects of Christian missionary activity, but partly also to secure a voice for Muslim gentlemen in the corridors of official power. S.R. Mehrotra, *The Emergence of the Indian National Congress*, pp. 212–16.

[24] Aziz Ahmad, *Islamic Modernism*, p. 96.

[25] Robinson, *Separatism*, pp. 10–83, and Rafiuddin Ahmed, *The Bengal Muslims*, pp. 1–27.

mandates. Many were aware that the 1860s and 1870s were still characterised by profound official hostility to claims for popular representation. To them this suggested the development of an effective loyalist credo which would incorporate official attitudes as an essential part of their stance on representation.

Thus it was that political considerations and the pursuit of political favours led many Muslims to assume that representation depended upon, and was primarily a measure of political loyalty to the Raj. Individuals and associations were seen to be representative to the extent that they obtained official recognition. They accepted as axiomatic the notion that the purpose of representation was to legitimise official policy by engaging in orchestrated deliberations rather than to initiate that policy by responding to popular consensus.

One of the first, and perhaps most influential Muslims, to have embodied these assumptions in any coherent form was Sayyid Ahmad Khān. Born into a family with a long tradition of service to the East India Company he was able, perhaps more easily than others, to cultivate and extend his friendship with Europeans.[26] His own professional career with the Company, which began in 1837, allowed him to develop a degree of appreciation for the merits of British rule.[27] This was later to help crystallise a sustained policy of loyalty with which Sayyid Ahmad would always be identified.

However, as the historian Aziz Ahmad has emphasised, the object of Sayyid Ahmad's loyalism tended to vary considerably over the years.[28] Between 1859 to 1870 it was not, as in later years, concerned either with keeping pan-Islamism at bay or undermining the claims of the Indian National Congress. The purpose of Sayyid Ahmad's loyalism at this time, he maintains, was essentially 'to wean his own community "from its policy of opposition" to one of acquiescence and participation, and to wean the British Government "from its policy of suppression to one of paternalism"'.[29]

This was to become eminently clear in Sayyid Ahmad's *Essay on the Causes of the Indian Revolt* first published in 1858. In it he drew attention to the need for 'intermediaries' between the government and the people and argued that it was the absence of communication that had contributed decisively to the revolt of 1857. In what was, for its time, a

---

[26] Altāf Husain Hālī, *Hayāt-i-Jāwed* (Lahore, Ishrat Publishing House, 1965), pp. 39–55. See also Case, 'The Aligarh Era', p. 15.

[27] See for example his enthusiastic response to the royal Proclamation of 1858 in Hālī, *Hayāt-i-Jāwed*, pp. 102–5.

[28] Aziz Ahmad, *Islamic Modernism*, pp. 33–4.

[29] *Ibid.*, p. 33.

powerful moral indictment of British colonial rule in India, Sayyid Ahmad appealed for an end to the commercial exploitation of his people. He called instead for the inclusion of Indians in an advisory capacity to government and proposed the creation of consultative councils. These, he presumed, would consist of worthy Indians, who would provide officials with information concerning 'Indian habits and customs'.[30]

In order to assuage official fears Sayyid Ahmad underlined the essentially conservative purpose of Indian participation as he saw it. He emphasised its strictly advisory dimension and stressed its usefulness in the promotion of a common interest shared by government officials and men of his class – namely maintaining British rule in India. Though he chose not to spell it out, it was clear that Sayyid Ahmad expected officials to understand that by representation he meant neither the claim to a popular mandate, nor the institutions of self-government. On the contrary, what he did hope to convey was a notion of representation as the co-optation of Indian notables who would act as sounding-boards in the service of government.[31]

Sayyid Ahmad's views on representation were exemplified and enlarged upon by the two most important Muslim associations of the period, the Mahomedan Literary Society and the National Mahommedan Association. Founded in 1863 and 1878 respectively, both were Bengal-based organisations led by men whose social backgrounds and political persuasions encouraged them to adopt a stance of unswerving loyalty to British rule. Both were distinguished by their being 'controlled by men having close links with the government and holding high government appointments.'[32] Both were enabled thereby to acquire not only a degree of insight into the workings of the official mind, but also to grasp the rules of government patronage.

From the outset, the Mahomedan Literary Society relied entirely upon its close links with officialdom to gain political credibility. The political influence of the Society and indeed its standing with British officials, owed much to the endeavours of its founder, Nawāb 'Abdu'l Latīf, a prominent figure belonging to the older Calcutta elite who had served the government with 'distinction'.[33] As an active member of the officially endorsed Calcutta-based Anjuman-i-Islāmi in the 1850s. Latīf

[30] Sayyid Ahmad Khān, *Asbāb-i-Baghawāt-i-Hind* (Lahore, Munshi Fazluddin, n.d.), chiefly pp. 11–15, 27–30, 31–42.
[31] See G.F.I. Graham, *The Life and Work of Syed Ahmad Khān, K.C.S.I.* (London, Hodder and Stoughton, 1909), pp. 26–36.
[32] Rafiuddin Ahmed, *The Bengal Muslims*, p. 116.
[33] *Ibid.*, p. 36.

was no stranger to the art of cultivating official support and obtaining government recognition.[34] The Anjuman, which had publicly declared its loyalty in 1857, had been rewarded at the time by being called upon to advise government officials on ways of appeasing Muslim opinion.[35]

The Literary Society continued, in more ways than one, to function like the Anjuman. Composed almost entirely of members of the Calcutta establishment, including government employees, pleaders and a solid *corpus* of resident nobility, it neither possessed nor sought a mass following.[36] What it did aspire to however, was the protection of the privileged status of its members by affirming their loyalty to British rule and securing, in turn, government patronage and recognition. This objective was not, in itself, beyond the reach of the Literary Society. For although it was not ostensibly a political association, the inclusion of large numbers of Muslims drawn from the wealthiest and most influential families in Bengal actually served to transform a *conversazione* club into a powerful pressure group for a select elite.

At the same time, the Society also helped reinforce some dominant assumptions concerning the meaning of representation common amongst Muslim *ashrāf*. Nawāb 'Abdu'l Latīf sought to establish his representative credentials on the realistic assumption that these depended ultimately on official recognition. Convinced that such recognition was almost always a reward for a show of political loyalty, Latīf laboured tirelessly to persuade some eminent members of the *'ulamā'* in Bengal like Maulvī Karāmat 'Alī to issue *fatāwā* in support of British rule.[37] His efforts did not go unnoticed. By the 1870s, officials were in the habit of regularly consulting the society on matters affecting Muslims in areas of social and educational policy. By the time he came to write his autobiography, Latīf felt confident enough to proclaim himself the first 'true' representative of Indian Muslims in the last thirty-two years.[38]

Latīf's Society was not of course the only Muslim organisation that vied for government recognition or helped sustain similar notions of

---

[34] Mehrotra, *The Emergence of the Indian National Congress*, p. 217.
[35] *Ibid.*, pp. 215–16.
[36] A somewhat blunt assessment of the Society was offered by the *Urdu Guide* which declared that 'its sham literary meetings and showy ostentatious Town Hall conversaziones... [were] not exactly the means to work out a revolution in the stagnant Mahomedan mind, or to exercise much perceptible influence on a society the most conceited and exclusive in the world'. Quoted in *ibid.*, p. 217. See also Rafiuddin Ahmed, *The Bengal Muslims*, p. 163.
[37] Mehrotra, *The Emergence of the Indian National Congress*, p. 217; Rafiuddin Ahmed, *The Bengal Muslims*, pp. 51–2 and Seal, *The Emergence of Indian Nationalism*, p. 310.
[38] Nawab Abdool Luteef Khan, *A Short Account of my Public Life* (Calcutta, 1885) quoted in Rafiuddin Ahmed, *The Bengal Muslims*, p. 28.

representation. Sayyid Amīr 'Alī's Central National Mahommedan Association made identical claims on behalf of a younger generation of Western-educated Muslims. The Association started out originally as a breakaway faction of the Literary Society which had opposed its leadership's decision in 1876 to adopt a categorically loyalist stance on the issue of the caliphal claims of the Sultan of Turkey.[39] In reality, however, the rebel faction expressed the predictable tensions between an older generation of Bengali *ashrāf* Muslims drawn from the landed and service classes who were more conversant with Arabic, Persian and Urdu than English, and a younger, professionally-oriented and Western-educated elite, many of whose prominent members came from Bihar.[40]

The fact that the former were predominantly Sunnī and the latter Shī'a may well have aggravated their differences, though they clearly did not do so along expected lines. Many of 'Abdu'l Latīf's Sunnī colleagues were evidently prepared to compromise their sympathies for a universal Muslim Caliphate to sustain their loyalist politics; while Amīr 'Alī, himself a Shī'a, led Muslim intellectuals in India to work out a philosophical justification for the Caliphate as the only effective political solution for *dār al-Islām*.[41]

Notwithstanding these differences in their social origins and intellectual outlook, the Mahomedan Literary Society and the National Mahommedan Association nevertheless shared common principles.[42] Both were committed to British rule in India although some have suggested that the Mahommedan Association was characterised by a markedly 'conscientious' loyalism which rendered its political attitudes somewhat more discriminating than those of the Literary Society.[43] Its statement of objectives, for example, underlined its intentions 'to represent ... from a loyal but independent standpoint, the legitimate wants and requirements of the Musalman Community'.[44] This however was clearly not enough to set the two fundamentally apart. At least one subsequent assessment regarded them not so much as 'opposite camps

[39] Mehrotra, *The Emergence of the Indian National Congress*, p. 218.
[40] Leonard Gordon, *Bengal: The Nationalist Movement, 1876–1940* (New York, Columbia University Press, 1974), pp. 65–6.
[41] Aziz Ahmad, *Studies in Islamic Culture in the Indian Environment* (Oxford, Clarendon Press, 1964), p. 63, and Aziz Ahmad, *Islamic Modernism*, p. 140.
[42] Rafiuddin Ahmed, *The Bengal Muslims*, p. 164.
[43] Gordon, *Bengal*, p. 66.
[44] *Rules and Objects of the Central National Mahommedan Association and its Branch Associations with the Quinquennial and Annual Reports and Lists of Members (1885)*, pp. 2–3.

with antagonistic political ideals but... rival institutions of the same school of political persuasion'.[45]

It would certainly be fair to say that as far as their assumptions about representation were concerned, there was little that distinguished them. Like the Literary Society, the Mahommedan Association's narrow social base encouraged it to regard representation as the exclusive claim of the well-born and the outcome of official recognition rather than of ostensible popular support. Although much has been made of the Association's contribution to the growth of Muslim political conscious-ness in the late nineteenth century, its activities did not, in fact, differ much from those of a typical organisation of select notables. It prepared memorials and engaged in petitioning the government for measures that would help protect the interests of educated Muslims. Above all, it sought contacts with government officials to advise them, and whenever possible, to do so as the representatives of Indian Muslims as a whole.

Like their erstwhile colleagues in the Literary Society then, members of the Mahommedan Association were scarcely inclined to equate representation with any form of popular mandate. Amīr 'Alī condem-ned the still fledgling demands for Indian self-government and denoun-ced the 'obsession with democracy'.[46] For him, as for members of his class, the instinct of self-preservation demanded a cautious approach to political reform. Like Sayyid Ahmad Khān, with whom he was otherwise sometimes politically at odds, Amīr 'Alī shared the premise that the object of Indian Muslim participation was to strengthen and preserve British supremacy in India. Both were persuaded that the effective representation of their interests and those of their followers could only be accomplished by acting as adjuncts of the colonial administration rather than as spokesmen of Muslim popular opinion.

These views of representation were not, however, peculiar to privileged Muslim gentlemen. Hindu contemporaries of Amīr 'Alī and Sayyid Ahmad characteristically denied notions of popular represent-ation on the grounds that the illiterate Indian masses were unable to speak for themselves. Surendrenath Banerjea, leader of the predomi-nantly Hindu, Indian Association, contended that representation should be confined to the Indian 'middle classes';[47] while Romesh Chunder Dutt, later to become famous as Congress's chief ideologue,

---

[45] *The Musalman*, 14 October 1906, quoted in Rafiuddin Ahmed, *The Bengal Muslims.*, p. 164.

[46] Ameer Ali, 'Memoirs' in K.K. Aziz (ed.), *Ameer Ali: His Life and Work, part 2*, (Lahore, Publishers United, 1968), p. 566.

[47] Gordon, *Bengal*, p. 28.

felt that *zamīndārs*, native princes and spokesmen, of 'native associations' were India's natural leaders.[48] Both were part of a generation, Hindu and Muslim, which believed 'that men of position should rightfully dominate Indian politics and serve to communicate Indian opinion to officials in India and Britain'.[49]

However, even if Muslims like Amīr 'Alī and Hindu Kayasths like Romesh Dutt did indeed share the same ideas about who should participate in the process of governing their country, their political visions were altogether quite distinct. It is more than apparent, as Leonard Gordon has so convincingly shown, that Amīr 'Alī, despite his modernist pretensions, was deeply ambiguous about the merits of political reform.[50] He shared with many Muslims of his class a profound fear that extended political representation for Indians would spell anarchy and disorder. For them, the demand for Muslim participation and representation did not, and could not, signify a step towards some future golden age of Indian self-government. On the contrary, it seemed to be the only remaining means to recapture what little they could of the time when Muslims still decisively influenced the political destiny of India, although few could have had any illusions about the vastly reduced scope of their influence.

On the other hand, it is clear that for early Indian nationalists, like Banerjea and Dutt, the demand for greater Indian representation was part of an overall commitment to Indian self-government. The dominant political vision of these men was of an India where Western representative government and national freedom would usher in an unquestionably advanced stage in her people's history. For men like Romesh Dutt, whatever their reservations about a too-hasty extension of popular representation, there seemed to be few doubts about the desirability of Indians eventually aspiring to the political institutions of modern Western civilisation.

Official concepts of representation

It would be fallacious to suggest that it was the pursuit of political favours and fears concerning their own future as a dominant minority alone that led privileged Muslims in Bengal, the North-Western Provinces and Bihar to fashion so restricted a view of representation. Many were also responding to, and reflecting, a profound awareness of

[48] *Ibid.*, p. 57.
[49] *Ibid.*
[50] *Ibid.*, pp. 72–4.

the constraints generated by the existing colonial framework.[51] These bore testimony to the emergence of an essentially partial view of representation that was increasingly encouraged by colonial officials in their approach to Indian representation.

It was a view which emphasised representation as a medium of description rather than as a substantive activity. Its purpose was defined primarily as one of yielding information about the community as a whole, or parts of it, rather than one of engaging in political action on behalf of the whole or its parts. It was a notion which assumed, to quote Hannah Pitkin, that 'the representative does not act for others; he "stands for" them by virtue of a correspondence or connection between them, a resemblance or reflection'.[52] The fundamental principle of such representation is to 'secure a representative assembly reflecting... the various divisions in the electorate'.[53]

Nevertheless, it would not be correct to maintain that this pre-occupation with representation as a descriptive rather than a substantive activity led officials in the 1860s and 1870s to conceive of Indian representation merely in symbolic terms. Nor would it be true to say that the mere inclusion of selected Indians, drawn from a variety of social backgrounds, in the processes of official deliberations was seen by officials to be sufficient to demonstrate the fact of Indian representation. On the contrary, as we have seen, British officials were deeply concerned, particularly after 1857, that Indian representation should and ought to presuppose a degree of activity, but they were equally concerned that such activity should not entail claims to act for or on behalf of others, nor, for that matter, claims to be accountable to others. In short, some of the commonest assumptions pertaining to theories of modern represent-ation were to form no part of Indian representation as fashioned by colonial officials.

What then was the 'activity' that officials expected 'representative' Indians to engage in and how did Indian Muslims interpret official

[51] A bald statement of these constraints is provided by Seal. He writes '... the government of India held sway over all India ... These administrative lines formed a grid which at first rested loosely upon the base. Later it was pressed down more firmly by the heavier intervention of the Raj in local matters and the growth of representative institutions. Indians needed to treat with the Raj, and increasingly they came to do so by exploiting its structure and the forms in which its commands were cast'. Anil Seal, 'Imperialism and Nationalism', p. 326.

[52] Hanna F. Pitkin, *The Concept of Representation* (Berkeley, University of California Press, 1972), p. 61.

[53] *Ibid.* A view derived in part from John Stuart Mill who defined a representative body as 'an arena' in which each opinion in the nation 'can produce itself in the full light'. John Stuart Mill, *Considerations on Representative Government* (Chicago, Henry Regnery, 1962), p. 111.

preferences? Perhaps no better, and no more significant expression is to be found than in Sayyid Ahmad's blueprint for Indian representation. This provides as keen a sense of the limits imposed by official preferences as it did of how best to manoeuvre within those limits. It is notable for example that when Sayyid Ahmad appealed for 'intermediaries' between officials and the people he stressed their role principally as sources of information, rather than as makers of political consensus.[54] The 'activity' of representation was seen primarily as the means of conveying to officials the views of the dominant section of Indian society, so that government could more easily be rendered effective. At the heart of Sayyid Ahmad's understanding of representation lay the unquestioned premise, relentlessly fostered by colonial officials, that representation was one thing, and governing quite another.[55]

The implications were significant. It denied that Indian representation could presume either initiative or creative political action; it denied that it could generate political consensus or the formulation of policy. These, as officials had emphasised and many Indians obliged to accept, were the preserve of the governors of India – men who were beyond the mêlée of representation with its noisy deliberations and clamour for participation.

It is of course true that the social backgrounds and political culture of those Muslims who were engaged in issues of political representation in the 1860s and 1870s, were hardly such as to incline them to a broader or more liberal understanding of representation. Few, for example, would have accepted the notion of political responsiveness as essential to the activity of representation. Fewer still might have conceded that their claims to representation needed to be founded on, or authorised by, some general popular consent or mandate. Nevertheless, and notwithstanding the general truth of these observations, it is also clear that the institutional and ideological framework of colonial rule provided few incentives to Muslims or other Indians to assume otherwise. It is questionable, for example, whether a man as conscious of his community's aspirations to power as Sayyid Ahmad would have

---

[54] He wrote '... participation by the people is a *sine qua non* of the goodness and soundness, and indeed the stability, of a government. It is from the voice of the people only that the rulers can learn whether their projects are good or bad before the evils inherent in them reach a stage where it becomes impossible to remedy them'. Sayyid Ahmad Khan, *The Causes of the Indian Revolt*, translated by Auckland Colvin and G.F.I. Graham (Benaras, Medical Hall Press, 1873), p. 51.

[55] A view also propounded by John Mill and some advocates of proportional representation who 'tend to distinguish between representation, on the one hand, and activity – government, law-making, decision-making – on the other'. Pitkin, *The Concept of Representation*, p. 64.

confined his understanding of representation to as modest an activity as 'communication' had he not also realised that it was the only acceptable form of 'representation' that officials were willing to countenance at the time.

Indeed, it was precisely their unwillingness to consider representation as a substantive form of political activity that led many officials to rely upon an alternative view of representation as a mode of resemblance.[56] What tended to be stressed was a notion of representation that was concerned more with the attributes of the representative than with his activity as such. Muslims like Nawāb 'Abdu'l Latīf and Sayyid Amīr 'Alī reflected the pervasive influence of this officially preferred view of representation. Both, through their respective associations, sought to represent Indian Muslims not so much on the grounds that they actually acted for them, but that they *stood* for them, or at least those of them that counted.[57] What in effect they claimed was that each was more representative because each was a more typical example of the constituency at large, namely, Indian Muslims.

From the official point of view such a view of representation made sense only because officials themselves were inclined to see the sole purpose of political representation to lie in the supply of information about the people. The usefulness of such information lay precisely in being able to establish an accurate correspondence between the representative and his particular constituency.[58] For men like 'Abdu'l

---

[56] For a thoughtful exposition of the differences that characterise these two approaches to representation see *ibid.*, pp. 60–91, 207–40. For some other discussions of the inherent tensions between 'representing' and 'acting' as these are developed in the existing theoretical literature see Charles A. Beard and J.D. Lewis, 'Representative Government in Evolution', *American Political Science Review*, 26, 2 (1932), pp. 223–40; Harold Stoke, 'The Paradox of Representative Government' in John M. Mathews (ed.), *Essays in Honor of W.W. Willoughby* (Baltimore, John Hopkins Press, 1937), pp. 77–99; Alfred de Grazia, 'Representation: Theory', in *International Encyclopaedia of the Social Sciences*, 8 (London, Macmillan, 1968), pp. 461–5; and A.H. Birch, *Representation: Key Concepts in Political Science* (London, Pall Mall, 1971).

[57] Latīf's Literary Society took pride in having secured the support of prominent Muslims from all parts of India and in 1867 boasted of some 500 members. Mehrotra, *The Emergence of the Indian National Congress*, p. 217. The Central National Mahommedan Association, on the other hand, made much of having obtained, within five years, the support of 'all the men of "light and leading"'... among the Mussulmans of this country'. *Rules and Objects of the Central National Mahommedan Association*, p. 3.

[58] It suggested that 'the representative legislature is a sufficiently accurate copy, a perfect replica ... [of] the whole people, ... Here the purpose is action by the representative, but that activity is not itself representation. Representation is, rather, a matter of accurate resemblance or correspondence, and a precondition for justifying governmental action'. Pitkin, *The Concept of Representation*, p. 82.

Latīf and Amīr 'Alī, it did not really matter that neither was a typical specimen of Indian Muslims as a whole. Both were shrewd enough to realise that the true test of representation at least in the 1870s had less to do with acting as political data-banks or claiming to be communal prototypes than with the grace of official recognition.

The influence of Mughal political culture

Political constraints resulting from the fact of colonial domination were not, however, the only considerations which defined the meaning and scope of representation for Indian Muslims. Many of them were no less subject to the influence of political norms that once characterised a peculiarly Mughal tradition of government to which they had previously been accustomed.

It has been suggested that Sayyid Ahmad's plea for a system of government that recognised the importance of socially established individuals as interpreters between ruler and ruled was grounded in his familiarity with 'the patterns of life of the Mughal empire'.[59] These led him to believe that rulers ought actively to seek the co-operation of eminent lay Muslims in the administration of the state.

Other, more recent interpretations appear to concur with this view. David Lelyveld has argued that the basic thrust of Sayyid Ahmad's political thinking was derived from 'a theory of universal empire that had its origins in the Mughal concept of society'.[60] Similarly, Barbara Metcalf has seen Sayyid Ahmad's stress upon representation as consultation between ruler and society's notables to be the very embodiment of a quintessentially Mughal view of good government.[61]

There can be little doubt that Sayyid Ahmad was a man deeply immersed in the essentials of Mughal culture. He had himself been born into a noble family which had served loyally under the Mughals.[62] Later, he chose to extend his knowledge of Mughal traditions by pursuing

[59] Sheila McDonough, *The Authority of the Past: A Study of Three Muslim Modernists* (Chambersburg, Pennsylvania, American Academy of Religion, 1970), p. 12. S.M. Ikram observes that Sayyid Ahmad's treatise on the *Causes of the Indian Revolt* is 'noteworthy as embodying the political wisdom of a well-informed Muslim who was unacquainted with the (sic) modern political thought but who was a true heir to the traditions of Mughal statesmanship'. S.M. Ikram, *Modern Muslim India*, p. 23. See also the discussion of Sir Sayyid's theory of participatory rule in Hafeez Malik, *Sir Sayyid Ahmad Khan and Muslim Modernization in India and Pakistan* (New York, Columbia University Press, 1980), pp. 103–2.
[60] Lelyveld, *Aligarh's First Generation*, p. 344.
[61] Metcalf, *Islamic Revival*, p. 319.
[62] Lelyveld, *Aligarh's First Generation*, pp. 72–6. See also Malik, *Sir Sayyid Ahmad Khan*, pp. 59–66.

scholarly works in Mughal history and architecture.[63] Studies of Sayyid Ahmad suggest that even his avowed admiration for things British did not diminish his intense and lasting pride in his Mongol-Mughal heritage.[64] It was a heritage that had imparted to him not only the norms of *sharīf* culture ranging from social manners to styles of dress; from architecture to athletic skills, but also the rules governing political authority and power.[65]

These presupposed that the basis of strong and secure government rested upon the ruler's ability to establish 'ritual ties of loyalty... with strategically significant lineage groups'.[66] It was a model which assumed that rigid vertical alliances, based principally on family and kin relations, could alone ensure absolute loyalty to the emperor and the political stability of his realm. It generated a profound appreciation of the importance of wealth and social status as the principal determinants of one's relation to ruling power. It led to the consolidation of a ruling class comprising of *zamīndārs*, officials and nobility who served to justify Mughal rule and provide links between the imperial government and society at large.[67]

Sayyid Ahmad was of course acutely aware, as indeed were many of his contemporaries, that the days of Mughal supremacy were gone forever. Nevertheless, the basis of political legitimacy remained for him much the same as in the days of the Mughal emperors. As Lelyveld has suggested, it is likely that at the political level Sayyid Ahmad regarded the new situation as no more than a mere change of hands: 'the sultanate now belonged to Queen Victoria'.[68] The criteria that had once defined good government under the Mughals continued to be just as relevant.

To understand this feature in Sayyid Ahmad's thinking is to appreciate why even one so committed to British rule as he should have seen fit to confront the authorities in 1858 with so apparently forthright an appeal for more open government. By doing so Sayyid Ahmad was not heralding some new 'democratic' spirit but issuing a call to return to legitimate rule as he saw it. This involved restoring to men of influence their erstwhile role as intermediaries whose privileged access to ruling

---

[63] Malik, *Sir Sayyid Ahmad Khan*, pp. 72–6.
[64] This is the assessment of a recent biographer: 'Despite their residence in India for nearly 200 years, Sir Sayyid's family retained a consciousness of their foreign origin. This extraterritorial consciousness basically determined Sir Sayyid's ancestors' and other upper-class Muslim's *weltanschauung* in the Indian environment'. *Ibid.*, p. 60.
[65] Lelyveld, *Aligarh's First Generation*, pp. 20–68.
[66] *Ibid.*, p. 23.
[67] *Ibid.*, pp. 24–5.
[68] *Ibid.*, p. 344.

power would help convey popular reaction as well as the 'true' intent of official policy. Government would be rendered more responsive as well as more stable precisely because of its legitimation by members of the ruling classes.

Men like Nawāb 'Abdu'l Latīf and Sayyid Amīr 'Alī whose links to Mughal culture were perhaps more tenuous than those of Sayyid Ahmad, were also influenced by the political norms governing that tradition. Both espoused the ethos of the Mughal *ashrāf* even when, as in the case of Nawāb 'Abdu'l Latīf, they did not actually belong to that category.[69] Both 'regarded themselves as custodians of Mughal culture and guarded it as their most precious possession'.[70] Both were fundamentally persuaded of the notion that wealth and social status qualified them to be 'natural leaders'.

Leonard Gordon has compared Amīr 'Alī's political attitudes to those of 'Mughal officials sent to Bengal, an outsider at the top with no roots in the soil'.[71] There is little to suggest that Amīr 'Alī himself cared at all to identify with Bengal; indeed like many a Mughal nobleman his greatest pride lay in his foreign origins, whether these pertained to his Persian ancestry or Arab Sayyid heritage.[72] Nor did he ever pretend that his claims to representation were founded on a genuine association with his Bengali domicile or with the Bengali people.

On the contrary Amīr 'Alī saw himself as the representative of a cosmopolitan ruling class such as had flourished under the Mughals. Its members acted not so much as agents of some territorial constituency – indeed this was actively discouraged by Mughal rulers apprehensive of alternative foci of loyalty – but as links between rulers and subjects. Like Sayyid Ahmad, Amīr 'Alī often harked back to the glories of the Mughal past.[73] For Amīr 'Alī, as for Sayyid Ahmad, Western education

---

[69] Rafiuddin Ahmed, *The Bengal Muslims*, p. 14.

[70] *Ibid.*

[71] Gordon, *Bengal*, p. 61. This was not however unusual among the mobile ruling classes of the Mughal empire. Lelyveld notes 'Until Mughal authority began to weaken in the eighteenth century, every effort was made to shift members of the ruling class from place to place every few years to prevent them from building up a territorial base'. Lelyveld, *Aligarh's First Generation*, p. 25.

[72] Ameer Ali, 'Some Racial Characteristics of Northern India and Bengal' in K.K. Aziz (ed.), *Ameer Ali*, part 2, p. 279. See also Amīr 'Alī's comments on the situation of Muslims from other parts of India living in Bengal in 'A Cry from the Indian Mahomedans' in *ibid.*, pp. 49–50.

[73] No better summary of his views can be gained than from his classic statement: 'It can hardly be disputed that the real history of India commences with the history of the Mussalmans'. Ameer Ali, 'The Mohammedans of India and their Place in the Empire' in *ibid.*, part 2, p. 376. See also *ibid.*, part 2, p. 243 ff., 335, 383, 468, and his 'Islamic Culture under the Moguls' in *ibid.*, part 2, pp. 457–508.

as such could do little to displace the essential validity of a political
culture they cherished so deeply and of which they were so ostensibly
proud. This is not to say that both were not acutely conscious of the
emergence of competing criteria of political participation and governmental legitimacy, but these in themselves could do little to erode their
fundamental appreciation of the norms of their Mughal heritage.

The force of Muslim political tradition

It is unlikely however that these ideas of representation and legitimate
rule were inspired by Mughal values alone. Sayyid Ahmad, Amīr 'Alī
and 'Abdu'l Latīf were also Muslims for whom the profession and
practice of their faith was quite obviously vital.[74] For them the
exposition of their religious tradition, as they understood it, formed an
integral part of their intellectual lives. An assessment of their political
attitudes must depend therefore, to some degree, upon their relation to
conventional Muslim discourse on representation and the political
responsibility of rulers.

This is not to say that Indian Muslims like Sayyid Ahmad and Amīr
'Alī who were deeply engaged in the problem of political representation,
were prompted at all times by a consciously religious purpose. Nor
indeed that they sought, in their approach to this problem, to be wholly
consistent with classical Islamic political prescriptions. At the same
time, however, both men can certainly be seen as part of a tradition of
political realism that was indigenous to Muslim discourse. It was a

---

[74] This is borne out as much by modern as by contemporary assessments. Sayyid
Ahmad's approach to social and educational reforms, for example, has been seen to be
closely tied to his broader religious concerns. 'In consequence of the introduction of
modern knowledge into Muslim India', writes Baljon, 'he was charged with the task of
procuring also a new interpretation of Islam, through the support of which the
Muslim youth could remain faithful to their religious convictions.' J.M.S. Baljon, *The
Reforms and Religious Ideas of Sir Sayyid Ahmad Khan* (Leiden, E.J. Brill, 1949), p. 89.
See also Altāf Husain Hālī, *Hayāt-i-Jāwed*; Lelyveld, Aligarh's First Generation,
pp. 111–13; Metcalf, *Islamic Revival*, p. 322. On Amīr 'Alī, in comparison with
another Hindu contemporary, Leonard Gordon observes, 'Religion which was of
scant importance to Romesh Dutt, was vital to Ali. Religion and Muslim law were tied
to the fate of Ali's community, which was, he felt, in danger of disintegration . . . Ali,
the marginal man from the minority sect of the minority religion, was often fearful of
the continuity of his community.' Gordon, *Bengal*, p. 73. A contemporary assessment
of 'Abdu'l Latīf is provided by Wilfred Scawen Blunt, traveller, politician and poet,
who visited India in 1878 and 1883–4. For him Latīf was a Muslim committed to
reform along religious lines. Latīf's knowledge of religious languages like Arabic and
Persian rendered him, in the eyes of Blunt, one of those rare men of faith who would
soon belong to 'the past'. Wilfred Scawen Blunt, *India Under Ripon: A Private Diary*
(London, T. Fisher Unwin, 1909), pp. 98–9.

tradition which, while being firmly grounded in the religious and ethical teachings of Islam on the subject of good government did not, in the interests of effective rule, seek always to conform to the precise provisions of its constitutional law, the *Sharī'a*.[75]

Its earliest manifestations can be traced to the brand of utilitarian morality espoused by the twelfth-century Iraqi jurist, Ibn-al Tiqtaqā.[76] His treatise, *al-Fakhrī*, sought to combine a concern for the ethical and religious duties of the ruler with a particular interest in the principles of stable rule. These he saw as being primarily derived from the ruler's ability and willingness to consult with those whose influence could be relied upon to control the lower orders. Wealth and social status constituted, in his mind, the principal determinants of influence, and Ibn-al Tiqtaqā was persuaded that a careful handling of the classes that enjoyed these assets was essential to the ruler's stay in power.[77]

Ibn-al Tiqtaqā's counsels were clearly more relevant to a society of political subjects than to a community of faithful Muslims. They were designed to reflect a state where well placed, lay Muslims would occupy pivotal positions of influence to sustain a benevolent despotism. In India, the essence of this tradition appeared in the form of doctrines embodied in the set of political manuals for rulers, otherwise known as the 'Mirrors of Princes'. It is of course the case that these doctrines predated the rise of Islam, having originally been conceived for the Sassanian rulers of Persia. Nevertheless they were extensively adapted to rationalise Muslim absolutist rule in India without entirely disregarding the demands of just government and the limits of political powers.[78]

It was common, for example, among medieval Muslim historians and men of letters under the sultans of Delhi in the thirteenth century, to glorify the institution of monarchical rule. At the same time however, many also referred frequently to the importance of *shūrā* or consultation as an essential part of the Muslim polity enjoined by the *Sharī'a*.[79] This has led to the contention that despite their preference for monarchy, medieval Muslim scholars were rarely ever inclined to dismiss or 'underrate the value of the democratic institution of *shūrā*'.[80]

---

[75] E.I.J. Rosenthal, *Political Thought in Medieval Islam* (Cambridge University Press, 1958), p. 113.
[76] *Ibid.*, pp. 62–7.
[77] *Ibid.*, p. 66.
[78] Sayyid Athar Abbas Rizvi, *A History of Sufism in India: From Sixteenth Century to Modern Century*, II (Delhi, Munshiram Manoharlal, 1983), pp. 348–89.
[79] Khaliq Ahmad Nizami, *Some Aspects of Religion and Politics in India During the Thirteenth Century* (Bombay, Asia Publishing House, 1961), p. 111.
[80] *Ibid.*

To some extent the same was also true, though with some important caveats, of the political perspectives common to Sayyid Ahmad, Amīr 'Alī and Nawāb 'Abdu'l Latīf. For although they and indeed many of their followers were admittedly prepared to remain loyal to British rule in India, few were willing to exonerate it altogether from the standards of moral conduct which they, as Muslims, had come to expect of their rulers.

This, for example, is eminently clear from the tone of Sayyid Ahmad's essay on the causes of the Indian Mutiny. In it, he invoked notions of political justice and responsibility that would not traditionally have been uncommon among Muslims concerned with the excesses of political power. And though Sayyid Ahmad did not, like some of his medieval forebears, appeal to the institution of *shūrā* as the basis of good government in British India, he did point to mutual consultation between rulers and subjects as the single most important foundation of legitimate rule. It is of course wholly plausible that Sayyid Ahmad's understanding of representation as consultation between rulers and notables and his belief that this is what made for good government, owed much to his participation in Mughal political culture. At the same time it would be highly unlikely, given what we know of Sayyid Ahmad's profound religious commitments, if his political judgements were not also shaped by a tradition that he knew to be both relevant and authoritative. It is significant, for example, that in his assessment of the Indian Mutiny, Sayyid Ahmad singled out the absence of social intercourse between rulers and subjects which, he believed, had been an integral feature of Muslim political practice. 'There was', he wrote, 'no real communication between the governors and the governed, no living together or near one another, as has always been the custom of the Mohammedans in countries which they subjected to their rule.'[81]

To say that Sayyid Ahmad was moved by the political values of his faith is not however to ignore the specific meaning that he sometimes imparted to these values, nor to deny their differences with those common to a more classical understanding of Muslim religious tradition. This was perhaps particularly true of his views concerning political representation and consultation. It has, for example, traditionally been assumed by Muslim political theorists that the practice of consultation entailed regular discussions between the ruler and members of the body of *'ulamā'*. They believed that the purpose of

---

[81] Quoted in Graham, *The Life and Work*, p. 33.

consultation was primarily to ensure that the ruler acted in accordance with *Sharī'a* and argued that the *'ulamā'*, as custodians of that Law, should therefore occupy pre-eminent positions as his advisors.[82]

It is clear that in making his own recommendations for closer consultations between British officials and their more eminent Indian subjects, Sayyid Ahmad did not envisage a similar role for the *'ulamā'*. His religious perspectives which tended, in the words of Hodgson, to stress the 'practical reasonableness of Islam'[83] rendered him deeply sceptical of the ability of the *'ulamā'* to accommodate or interpret the feelings of a community desirous of change.[84] Moreover, as one scholar has observed, his own understanding of Indo-Muslim, particularly Mughal, history led Sayyid Ahmad also to assume that 'the *'ulemā'* would not exercise political control'.[85] It is not surprising, therefore, that Sayyid Ahmad's plea for greater representation should have been founded on the premise of mutual consultations between British officials and their lay subjects among Indian Muslims.

Admittedly Sayyid Ahmad's views reflected the steady erosion of the political influence of the *'ulamā'* much in evidence since the decline of a universal Caliphate in the eleventh century. The emergence of independent Muslim *amīrates* founded in part, though by no means exclusively, on the *Sharī'a*, had led to a much less intense preoccupation with the moral purposes of the State than with the mechanisms of effective power. This in turn had generated a tradition of political realism which sought good government without expecting it necessarily to conform to the letter of the *Sharī'a*.[86] It presupposed a degree of political

---

[82] This is not to say that there were no tensions within the body of Indo-Muslim *'ulamā'* concerning their right to be consulted. Rizvi notes that Indo-Muslim political tradition continued, at least into the reign of Aurangzeb, to be characterised on the one hand by the call for active involvement by the *'ulamā'* to enable the ruler to implement the Sharī'a, and on the other, by Sufi *pīrs* 'pursuing a traditional policy of political aloofness' but who 'continued to support the Emperor and the Muslim community'. Rizvi, *A History of Sufism*, p. 370.

[83] Hodgson, *The Venture of Islam*, III, p. 335.

[84] Commenting on the *'ulamā'*'s claim that there was no further scope for *ijtihād* or individual judgement as a basis for social change or innovation, Sayyid Ahmad wrote 'By this erroneous belief we do harm the Islamic religion and society seriously. We should be aware of the fact that times change and that again and again we are confronted with new questions and new needs... In other words: to-day also we want mujtahidin'. Quoted in J.M.S. Baljon, *The Reforms and Religious Ideas of Sir Sayyid Ahmad Khān* (Leiden, E.J. Brill, 1949), pp. 66–7.

[85] McDonough, *The Authority of the Past*, p. 12.

[86] The emergence of this tradition and its evolution in the early and mid-twentieth century is examined in Peter Hardy, *Partners in Freedom and True Muslims. The Political Thought of Some Muslim Scholars in British India, 1912–1947* (Lund, Scandinavian Institute of Asian Studies, 1971).

responsibility or accountability on the part of rulers such as was embodied in the traditional notion of *shūrā*, without assuming that rulers were accountable pre-eminently to the community's religious authorities. It was part of an emerging tradition within contemporary Muslim discourse that was later to go by the name 'modernist'.[87]

Sayyid Ahmad's views on representation, to the extent that they were expressive of certain emerging political norms within Muslim discourse, must be seen as a contribution to that tradition. So too were those of Sayyid Amīr 'Alī. Deeply influenced by the brand of modernism advocated by Maulvī Karāmat 'Alī Jawnpūrī which flourished in Calcutta in the 1860s and 1870s, he devoted much of his intellectual life to the re-evaluation of Muslim social and political thought in the light of nineteenth-century liberal values. Like Sayyid Ahmed, he also sought a society where authority would lie primarily in the hands of lay Muslims. Like him, he envisaged a political arrangement where rulers would consult with members of a Muslim lay elite as the representatives of a potentially modern and progressive community.

Amīr 'Alī's approach to the question of political representation cannot be fully grasped without appreciating his vision of a modern Muslim state. This is not to say that he actually believed British officials could be led to conform to this vision, nor indeed that they could be persuaded of its merits. But it does provide some insight into the way in which he, as a Muslim, sought to arrive at an understanding of representation that would be in keeping with the spirit of his faith as he hoped to preserve it. For Amīr 'Alī as for Sayyid Ahmad, the notion of representation was grounded primarily in the idea of mutual consultation between rulers and their subjects.[88] It implied a degree of political responsibility on the part of the ruler which he deemed essential to the constitution of a just and modern Muslim society. For him this idea of representation was perhaps most fully contained in the traditional Muslim institution of *ijmā'*.

He envisaged its modern adaptation to lie in its capacity to act as a constitutional check on executive authority. Like Sayyid Ahmad he rejected the idea of *ijmā'* as the prerogative of the *'ulamā'*. Indeed for him, *ijmā'* signified no less than the right of a Muslim lay elite to constitute the

---

[87] For a comprehensive discussion in the Indo-Muslim context, see Aziz Ahmad, *Islamic Modernism*. See also Fazlur Rahman, *Islam* (Chicago University Press, 1979), pp. 212–34.
[88] Syed Ameer Ali, *The Spirit of Islam: A History of the Evolution and Ideals of Islam* (London, Christophers, 1922, reprinted 1961), pp. 278–9.

communal consensus.[89] It was precisely such an elite that would, through periodic consultations with the ruler, ensure that government was answerable to the community as a whole. But its authority to do so, he believed, stemmed not from any popular mandate as such. Rather it grew from its pre-eminence in society which endowed it with a degree of moral integrity and a capacity for learning and intellectual training. This was what, in his view, *ijmā'* was designed to embody, and a modern system of representation ought to aspire to.

It would be naive to suppose that Amīr 'Alī or, for that matter, Sayyid Ahmad, whatever the intensity of their religious commitments, believed that Muslim notions of *ijmā'* and *shūrā* could be invoked to render British rule more accountable to Indians. At the same time however, it is clear that their *expectations* of good government and their understanding of representation owed much to their familiarity with, and acceptance of, some traditional norms of Muslim political behaviour. Given also what we know of their ceaseless efforts to readapt the political principles of their faith to modern conditions, it would not be unreasonable to assume that both sought sincerely to extend these principles to the realm of actual political conduct.

Nor was this uncommon among other Muslims who, while not being members of the established religious elite, that is to say, the *'ulamā'*, were deeply concerned about the transformation of their community's religious and political values. One such group, consisting mostly of lawyers and government employees, was the Anjuman-i-Islāmi founded in 1855. The Anjuman defined its task as one which was essentially 'in keeping with the precepts of our religion'. It projected itself as a body concerned with the modern expression of eternally valid principles enjoined by the Qur'ān and practised by the Prophet, Muham mad. Of these, 'the habit of holding consultations together' was held to constitute the principal impetus of the association. For members of the Anjuman it signified the most desirable model for the evolving relationship between officials and 'the great and learned of our [Muslim] community'.[90]

This then was the repertory of assumptions with which many Indian Muslims approached the issue of political representation in the 1880s. It was to help generate one of the most sustained critiques of Western liberal-democratic institutions in colonial India.

---

[89] *Ibid.*, p. 251.
[90] Mehrotra, *The Emergence of the Indian National Congress*, p. 212.

Muslim attitudes to representation, 1880–1900

The declared intention of the newly elected Liberal Party to institute some form of political representation for Indians along Western lines generated widespread concern among significant sections of Indian Muslims. Many perceived the proposed reforms to be deeply antithetical to their customary understanding of politics in India and to the political values of their faith.

Lord Ripon's decision to extend the basis of Indian representation by introducing elections to local councils led Indian Muslims to seriously reassess the implications of 'western' representation for Muslim political conduct and doctrine. The enactment of Ripon's Local Self-Government Bill for the Central Provinces in 1883, stimulated intense debate as well as opposition to it among certain groups of Indian Muslims. Of these, clearly the most articulate were those associated closely with Sayyid Ahmad Khān. Others tended to revolve around Sayyid Amīr ʿAlī whose National Mahommedan Association had already conveyed its dissatisfaction with forms of political selection based on competitive examinations and elections for Indians.[91]

There were essentially three sets of arguments which Indian Muslims used to counter the merits of 'western' representation. Firstly, they claimed that such representation naively assumed that common political interests could emerge in a society whose hallmarks were its intense religious and racial differences. Secondly, they maintained that the notion of individual representation, central to 'western' political systems, was founded on the inadequate premise that society consisted of isolated persons rather than of members of well-defined social and religious groups. Finally, they contended that 'western' representation failed to acknowledge that men's claims to political power were determined not only by their numerical strength, but by their moral attributes and social worth.

The denominational foundations of society

One of the most powerful arguments used by Indian Muslims opposed to 'western' representation was the claim that it ignored the political significance of racial and religious tensions in society. It was argued that the notion of common political interests implied by 'western' elective representation would be radically undermined by the prevalence of fundamental and irrevocable social and religious divisions.

[91] See its Memorial presented to the Viceroy Lord Ripon in 1882 in K.K. Aziz (ed.), *Ameer Ali*, part 2, pp. 23–40.

It is of course true that the Indian Muslim case against Western representative institutions drew heavily upon existing Indian reality as this was elaborated by British officials in public statements and policy. Sayyid Ahmad, for example, rested his critique of Ripon's Local Self-Government Bill of 1883 on much the same grounds as had become familiar to parts of the official establishment opposed to 'western representation for Indians.[92] He argued that the system of 'western' elective representation, such as was incorporated in the Bill, was unsuitable to a heterogeneous society like India which was characterised by 'the dominancy of race over race, of religion over religion'.[93]

It is also worth noting that Sayyid Ahmad frequently acknowledged his debt to eminent British contemporaries and political observers who had raised doubts about applying the practices of Western democracy to socially and religiously divided societies. He referred publicly to the arguments of J.S. Mill and James Fitzjames Stephen, both of whom had written extensively on the importance of a homogeneous society as an essential condition for Western representative institutions.[94]

Like Sayyid Ahmad, Amīr 'Alī shared the view that elective representation was fundamentally unsuitable to India. In a series of letters to the Viceroy's private secretary, H.W. Primrose, in March and April 1884, he drew attention to the existing constraints in Indian society and religious divisions in India, or, for that matter, diminish their Amīr 'Alī shared Sayyid Ahmad's conviction that Western education and improved communications had done little to erode the intensity of social and religious divisions in India, or, for that matter, diminish their political salience. Although he did acknowledge the unifying effects of

---

[92] See his speech on the Central Province Local Self-Government Bill, 12 January 1883, in Shan Mohammad (ed.), *Writings and Speeches of Sir Syed Ahmad Khan* (Bombay, Nachiketa Publications, 1972), pp. 156–7.

[93] *Ibid.*, p. 156.

[94] In an article published in the *Aligarh Institute Gazette* in the autumn of 1893, Sir Sayyid confessed 'Long before the Indian National Congress was even thought of I had pondered over the question of representative government for India, and had arrived at the conclusion, after careful study of the late Mr. John Stuart Mill's views vindicating representative government... that as the first essential... it is indispensable that there should be a tangible homogeneity among the voters'. *Aligarh Institute Gazette*, 3 October 1893. By this time Sayyid Ahmad was also familiar with James Fitzjames Stephen's 'Foundations of Government of India', *Nineteenth Century*, October 1893, pp. 541–68, in which Stephen had categorically rejected the wisdom of instituting representative government in so diverse a society as India. See Sayyid Ahmad to Stephen, 17 February 1888, cited in Lelyveld, *Aligarh's First Generation*, p. 310.

[95] Amir Ali to H.W. Primrose (private secretary to the Viceroy), 10 March, 12 March, 12 April 1884, Ripon Papers, B.P. 7/6, numbers 104a, 107a, 158a, cited in Mehrotra, *The Emergence of the India National Congress*, p. 219.

the cosmopolitan policies pursued by some Mughal emperors like Akbar, he remained deeply sceptical of their success in bridging the religious gap between India's various communities.[96]

It would not be correct to suggest however that these were mere reflections of official bias, or simply routine observations on Indian social reality. Much of it also concealed the real political fears of a minority who had sensed that political competition such as was embodied in the principle of election, was certain to affect their political future. Many believed that elections were likely to benefit those who, like the Hindus of the coastal presidency towns of Calcutta, Bombay and Madras, had had the privilege of Western education and become familiar with the art of modern political organisation. They were persuaded, rightly or wrongly, that Indian Muslims as a whole had fallen behind in these areas and were likely, as a consequence, to be denied any effective representation whatever under the new rules.[97]

One expression of these fears was contained in an article written by Sayyid Husain Bilgrāmī in 1888. Bilgrāmī, who was among the small group of Western-educated Muslims associated with Sayyid Ahmad in the 1860s and who was later to become one of Aligarh's 'elders',[98] shared many of his colleague's apprehensions about Britain's liberal experiment in India. He argued that 'western' representation was not only unsuitable because it ignored the hostility between India's 'races, castes and classes': it was also deeply unjust because it failed to acknowledge the unequal 'intellectual and moral development' of India's diverse communities.[99]

Other Muslims, like those belonging to the Mahomedan Literary Society chose also to express their apprehensions publicly. In a memorial submitted to the government in 1890, they 'pray[ed]' for the withdrawal of political practices such as elections. They contended that such practices could only lead to injustice where different levels of education and social mobility were dominant features.[100]

The emphasis upon Indian social, and particularly religious, hetero-geneity as insurmountable obstacles to Western representative institutions, was also reflected in wider Muslim circles. The Siddon's Union

---

[96] See his 'Some Racial Characteristics of Northern India and Bengal' in K.K. Aziz (ed.), *Ameer Ali*, part 2, pp. 265–86.

[97] Francis Robinson, *Separatism*, pp. 46–66.

[98] Lelyveld, *Aligarh's First Generation*, pp. 93, 337.

[99] *Aligarh Institute Gazette*, 6 October 1888.

[100] S. Chakravarty, 'The Evolution of Representative Government in India, 1884–1909', unpublished Ph.D. thesis, University of London, 1954, pp. 141–2.

Club, which formed part of the Mohammedan Anglo-Oriental College founded by Sayyid Ahmad in 1875 at Aligarh, also debated the issue of representative institutions for India. In September 1887, the Club resolved that religious divisions in India posed a formidable, if not insuperable obstacle, to the evolution of 'western' representation on the subcontinent.[101] In January 1888, the general consensus of Union members held that 'the complicated nature of the ethnological and religious differences' of India would substantially undermine any notion of common representative institutions.[102]

Not all Indian Muslims however were opposed to what they termed 'western' or liberal political institutions; nor were they were all agreed on the fundamental and irrevocable nature of religious divisions and their decisive impact upon politics. The participation of a small but influential group of Muslims led by the eminent Bombay lawyer, Badruddin Tyabjī, in the Indian National Congress's campaign for representative government suggested an alternative perspective. Although they also believed that religious differences were an important consideration in the organisation of Indian political life, they did not accept their causal influence to be such as always to inhibit the development of common representative institutions. Nor did they believe religious differences to be significant enough to determine all other forms of social and political cleavages. Indian Muslims as Muslims, argued Tyabjī, admittedly had their 'own peculiar social, moral and educational and even political difficulties to surmount'.[103] Nevertheless, he insisted, there were 'some general questions affecting the whole of India from which Muslims could not be excluded'.[104]

The position of Tyabjī and his group of 'nationalist' Muslims was however deeply problematic. The close collaboration between colonial officials and influential Muslims, like Sayyid Ahmad and Amīr 'Alī, had helped to sustain a view of Indian society and of the nature of political representation which made alternative claims appear to be devoid of credibility.[105] Ideologically, the 'nationalist' Muslim case seemed even

[101] *Aligarh Institute Gazette*, 3 September 1887.
[102] *Ibid.*, 24 January 1888. See also Lelyveld, *Aligarh's First Generation*, p. 225.
[103] Tyabjī's presidential address to the third annual session of the Indian National Congress, December 1887, quoted in Anil Seal, *The Emergence of Indian Nationalism* (Cambridge University Press, 1971), p. 332.
[104] *Ibid.*, pp. 332–3.
[105] Tyabjī and his men were dismissed by Muhammad Shafi, who was later to emerge as a leading figure in Muslim League politics in the Punjab, as unrepresentative and 'self-selected'. Muhammad Shafi to the editor, *Pioneer*, 13 July 1888, quoted in *ibid.*, p. 335.

more difficult to support when seen against the background of traditional Mughal and Muslim assumptions.

'The basic principle of Mughal political structure', Lelyveld has observed, 'was that society consisted of a great multiplicity of conflicting segments that could only be brought into harmony by virtue of their subordination to the apex of the system, namely the ruling dynasty'.[106] Although these 'segments' were not conceived of as 'simple, separate units' being often bound as they were by ties of ancestry and kinship, the Muslim *birādarī*, or exogamous patrilineage, was inclined to be much less fragmented than its Hindu counterpart.[107] Whether this was, as Lelyveld has suggested, because 'it had less power to proliferate' or because as a Muslim *birādarī* it tended, naturally, towards a degree of internal solidarity and exclusivism, it contributed substantially to the notion of *qaum*, a people of common descent, which was later to form the basis of the Muslim separatist position on representation. It presumed that Indian Muslims were an ethnic community whose identities and interests were determined at birth and who were, as a consequence, unlikely to be open to the politics of persuasion espoused by Congress and favoured by its group of 'nationalist' Muslims.[108]

However, there was also much in the 'nationalist' position that went against the grain of Muslim thinking. By refusing to accept the centrality of religious heterogeneity in society and politics, 'nationalist' Muslims removed themselves even farther from those of their fellow Muslims who, like some members of the *'ulamā'*, chose to co-operate with Congress, but who stressed the distinction of a Muslim ethos. The Deoband *'ulamā'* are notable examples of those whose co-operation with Congress in the 1880s did not dissuade them from issuing *fatāwā* to discourage Muslims from social and business contacts with Hindus.[109]

In contrast to 'nationalist' Muslims, men like Sayyid Ahmad and Amīr 'Alī appeared more obviously in keeping with Muslim preconceptions. For them, social and religious heterogeneity was not a phenomenon that could be wished away by the mere injection of man-made

---

[106] Lelyveld, *Aligarh's First Generation*, p. 21.
[107] *Ibid.*, p. 22.
[108] I owe a recognition of these considerations almost entirely to Lelyveld. *Ibid.*, pp. 22, 311–12.
[109] Metcalf writes '[Maulana] Rashid Ahmad [Gangohi of Deoband], particularly from the 1880s, issued *fatawa* that discouraged social and business intercourse with Hindus, forbad attendance at Arya Samaj lectures (unless one were skilled in debate), and deemed illegitimate the appearance of being Hindu, whether in dress, hair style, or the use of brass instead of copper vessels'. Metcalf, *Islamic Revival*, p. 153.

institutions and laws. As Muslims, and as men whose faith was deeply authentic, they had come to regard such heterogeneity as a necessary part of human society so long as that society itself was not united on Muslim principles. It formed an essential part of the assumption that Islam and its adherents were an exclusive category whose preservation along these lines remained a desirable norm until the incorporation of non-Muslims was finally achieved.

What they, as Muslims, expected of political institutions was the means to pursue the specific, exclusivist impulses of their faith. What appeared to them insidious was not only that 'western' representation presumed political homogeneity to exist in the face of religious differences, but that it sought to persuade men that homogeneity on other than Muslim principles was both workable and worthwhile.

The communitarian basis of politics

One compelling objection raised by Muslims opposed to 'western' representation was that such representation assumed that the fundamental units of society were individuals rather than discrete communities based on race, religion and language. Many deplored the features of a system which expected individuals to act politically as isolated units with little or no relation to their creed or caste. They emphasised the powerful influence of religious loyalties upon individual political behaviour, not withstanding the effects of Western education, and asserted that individuals would continue, more often than not, to regard themselves and others in relation to such 'primary' affiliations.[110]

At the heart of the Muslim argument against 'western' representation lay the assumption that far from being autonomous of men's religious values, the sphere of politics constituted the most important forum for their expression. Political action was an extension of men's religious obligations and the religious community was often the bearer of men's worldly interests. Men acted as members of their religious community and, in a political contest based on numbers, it was inevitable that the largest religious community would also form a permanent political majority. Numerically superior religious groups, it was argued, would proceed to consolidate their own interests and legitimise their political domination over smaller communities.

These issues were to appear repeatedly in Indian Muslim political

---

[110] See Sayyid Ahmad Khan, 'What will be the feelings of Indian Muhammedans after they have obtained Higher Education in English?', in *Aligarh Institute Gazette*, 6 February 1897.

discourse in the last quarter of the century. In his biography of Sayyid Ahmad Khān, the poet Altāf Husain Hālī suggested that Sayyid Ahmad was persuaded that Ripon's proposals grossly overlooked the decisive contribution of religion to the conduct of men's lives.[111] That men's religious beliefs constituted a central imperative in their lives was perhaps not altogether unusual in a man whose devotion to his faith was described as 'terrifying'.[112] Although his interpretation of its principles may not always have met with universal approval from other Muslims, few doubted the depth of his commitment.[113]

Sayyid Ahmad's conviction in the power of religion to shape men's minds and actions was evidenced in numerous public declarations. He warned the Viceroy's Imperial Legislative Council in January 1883 that religious influences continued to affect 'matters connected with the administration and welfare of the country at large'.[114] Under these circumstances, he argued, 'the system of election pure and simple cannot be safely adopted'.[115] Later in 1887, at a meeting in Lucknow he was to be more specific. Proceeding on the premise that men's political interests were always dictated by their religious persuasions, he concluded that Muslim electors would vote for Muslim candidates while Hindu electors for Hindu members. Their discrepancy in numbers would ensure that 'Hindu members will have four times as many [votes] because their population is four times as numerous'.[116]

These assumptions concerning the religious impulses underlying political behaviour found wider currency in the contemporary Muslim press. In January 1887, the *Mahomedan Observer* offered this view on the merits of elective representation to its readers:

To ask for representative institutions without sufficient guarantees for the representation of the minority means the swamping of the minority by the majority ... there is more hope of a fair equilibrium being maintained from the political wisdom of a neutral Government than from the generous instincts of a majority looking primarily, but *naturally*, to the interests of its own bulk.[117] [my emphasis]

In March 1888, the *Central Indian News* summarised the outcome of Western representative institutions as one which 'would be overwhelm-

---

[111] Hālī, *Hayāt-i-Jāwed*, p. 253.
[112] *Ibid.*
[113] Robinson, 'Islam and Muslim Separatism', p. 92.
[114] Shan Mohammad (ed.), *Writings and Speeches*, p. 157.
[115] *Ibid.*
[116] *Ibid.*, p. 210.
[117] *Mahomedan Observer*, 1 January 1887, quoted in Seal, *The Emergence of Indian Nationalism*, p. 315.

ingly in favour of the Hindus'.[118] In September 1893, Nawāb Muhammad Ismā'īl Khān, later to become a prominent member of the League, in an article prepared for the *Aligarh Institute Gazette* sought to cast doubts upon the application of the terms 'majority' and 'minority' in the Indian context. He argued that the understanding of these terms in Western liberal-democratic theory and practice was irrelevant to a society 'inhibited by two totally distinct races, unequal in number'.[119] In September 1896, the Nawāb once again denounced attempts to organise Indian politics along the lines of Western political configurations, and rejected the assumption that individuals could vote on the basis of other than religious considerations. 'In a country where the Hindus and Muslims are in a ratio of five to one, the Muslims must go to the wall, if any elective or representative system of government came to be established. This is not an imaginary bug-bear presented to scare the Muslims away from the Congress camp, but a stubborn fact...'.[120]

The assumption that groups, not individuals, determined the course of politics and that these groups were sufficiently well-defined to withstand the vagaries of shifting political coalitions presumed by Western representation, was a view that was undeniably nurtured by colonial perceptions and their influence on policy. There was, as we have seen, an implicit understanding at the official level that membership of a religious community was the fundamental organising principle in Indian society. Its political implications were perhaps nowhere as readily evident as in the area of political representation. Anil Seal has shown how the prevailing political content in the 1880s and 1890s encouraged forms of corporate and communal organisation. Officials, anxious to identify areas of group support 'carved [India's] people's into large administrative blocks... for the ambitious politicians the entrance fee was to assert or pretend affinities with those who had been bundled into the same category'.[121] The political bargain at hand has been described by Paul Brass: 'the British would recognise the existence of a Muslim community in India, with Muslim aristocrats and government servants as its spokesman... In return the Muslim landlords and government servants were expected not only to avoid opposing government but to provide positive support for it.'[122]

---

[118] Quoted in *Aligarh Institute Gazette*, 20 March 1888.
[119] Muhammad Ismail Khan, 'Causes of the Riots Between Hindus and Mohammedans', *Ibid.*, 2 September 1896.
[120] *Ibid.*, 12 September 1896.
[121] Seal, 'Imperialism and Nationalism', p. 338.
[122] Paul Brass, 'Elite Groups', p. 57.

To Sayyid Ahmad and Amīr 'Alī, who had already invested much in establishing their credentials as the 'natural' spokesmen of Indian Muslims, the benefits of 'playing politics couched in [the Raj's] own formulae' could scarcely have gone unnoticed.[123] Their emphasis upon the communal group which they knew to be favoured by official policy, contributed substantially to their political stance against Congress and 'nationalist' Muslims allied with it. As long as the communal group could be held up as the decisive factor in politics, Congress's claim that individuals could come together regardless of their religious affiliations was susceptible to the charge of self-deception.

This was certainly the thrust of the attacks levied against Congress and its Muslim supporters, like Tyabjī, by Sayyid Ahmad and his supporters. They dismissed as 'madness' Congress's contention that all Indians, as individuals, had certain common interests which bound them and made possible the institutions and practices of 'western' representation.[124] The reality of Indian politics, they asserted, was to be found not in the large-minded impulses of individuals, but in 'the ethnological and religious differences that divided the people resulting in dis-union and dissimilitude of interests.'[125] It was, they argued, impossible to conceive of individual representation such as was being proposed by Congress under conditions where Hindus and Muslims were likely to behave as spokesmen of their religious groups.[126]

The claim that individuals pursued their interests primarily as members of religious groups was necessarily founded on the assumption that there was a clearly defined 'Muslim' interest. This was believed to be both coherent and homogeneous, as well as profoundly resilient to the modifying effects of cross-cutting economic interests or shared cultural attributes. These perceptions had been particularly hardened in the last decades of the nineteenth century. It was a period characterised by intense competition for education and employment between Hindus and Muslims and the emergence of bitter communal animosity resulting

---

[123] Seal, 'Imperialism and Nationalism', p. 341.
[124] Sayyid Ahmad's letter to editors of 'all leading newspapers' in Shan Mohammad (ed.), *Writings and Speeches*, p. 220.
[125] Report on Siddon's Debating Club in *Aligarh Institute Gazette*, 24 January 1888.
[126] See article by 'an anonymous Muslim' entitled 'Is a National Congress in India possible and what benefits would it confer upon the country?' in *Aligarh Institute Gazette*, 20 March 1888; Salar Jung's letter to Sayyid Ahmad in *ibid.*, 16 October 1888, and Nawab Muhammad Ismail Khan's letter to *The Times* (London), 20 September 1893. In addition, see also the views of Theodore Beck, principal of Aligarh College who campaigned vigorously against representative institutions for India, in Theodore Beck, *Essays on Indian Topics* (Allahabad, Pioneer Press, 1888), pp. 39–87, 93–127.

from the Hindi–Urdu controversy.[127] Both had contributed substantially to the view that Muslims and Hindus represented mutually exclusive interests at every level in society, politics and culture. The process was not unlike that described by Paul Brass as 'nationality formation'. In the case of Indian Muslims, it involved bringing other symbols, like Urdu, 'into congruence with the leading symbol', in this case Muslim religious identity, 'either by choice or out of conflict with competing or antagonistic groups'.[128]

Its consequences for the introduction of elective representation in India were significant. In 1882, Amīr 'Alī's National Mahommedan Association drew the Viceroy's attention to a distinct 'Muslim' interest and in 1884 called for its representation as such under a system of separate electorates.[129] In May 1883, Muhammad Yūsuf 'Alī, a Muslim member of the Bengal Legislative Council, called for separate Muslim representation. He argued that the institution of territorial constituencies implied by the system of 'western' representation would enable Hindus to dominate the outcome of electoral results. More importantly, such constituencies would contribute to the anomalous condition where Hindus could claim to act as the legitimate representatives of Muslims. This, he asserted, would radically undermine the 'Muslim interest'. He suggested the creation of separate communal electorates to enable Indian Muslims to select members of their own community as their representatives. This alone, he concluded, would ensure both the unity of Indian Muslims as well as the protection of their interests.[130]

In December 1896 Sayyid Ahmad, with the help of Theodore Beck, then principal of the Mohammedan Anglo-Oriental College at Aligarh and a staunch supporter of Sayyid Ahmad's campaign against Western elective representation, drew up a memorial calling on the government to introduce separate Muslim electorates.[131] In a subsequent letter to the English-language daily, the *Pioneer*, Sayyid Ahmad defended separate electorates as the only means to ensure that Muslims were really represented by Muslim councillors who would be elected by exclusively Muslim constituencies. The system of 'western' representation, he alleged, was inherently unacceptable because it endorsed

---

[127] On the Urdu–Hindi controversy see Robinson, *Separatism*, pp. 69–76, and Brass, *Language, Religion and Politics*, pp. 127–38.

[128] Brass, *Language, Religion and Politics*, p. 410.

[129] Amir Ali to H.W. Primose. 10, 12 March, 12 April 1884, Ripon Papers, B.P. 7/6, numbers 104a, 107a, 158a, cited in Mehrotra, *The Emergence of the Indian National Congress*, p. 219.

[130] B.B. Majumdar, *History of Indian Social Ideas: From Ram Mohun to Dayananda* (Calcutta, Bookland Private, 1967), pp. 242–3.

[131] See the petition of the Indian Defence Association in the *Pioneer*, 22 December 1896.

predominantly Hindu territorial constituencies which could, in the absence of a Hindu candidate, elect Muslim councillors who would be obliged to act primarily for the promotion of Hindu interests.[132]

The case against Western representation made out by these proponents of separate Muslim electorates stemmed from two vital concerns that had always been central to traditional Muslim political thinking. The first pertained directly to the common Muslim assumption that the communal group was the basic unit of society and its solidarity the individual's primary concern. The principle of individual representation embodied in the institution of territorial constituencies implicitly challenged this view. It stressed the multiplicity of individual interests and regarded solidarity when it existed, as an expression of common political interests rather than as the extension of combined religious fervour.

The second derived more obviously from the traditional Muslim premise that religious loyalty constituted the only authentic basis of political loyalty. Indeed, this may be seen to form much of the theory pertaining to the institution of the Caliphate. Here, representation was nothing if not primarily a pledge: the Caliph, as the representative of his people, was endowed with a trust whose real test lay in his capacity to demonstrate his loyalty and devotion to the community of faithful.[133] That non-Muslims could undertake this commitment or legitimately aspire to represent Muslims would have been inconceivable. It is reasonable to assume that for many Indian Muslims, the principle of elections embodied in Western representation could not in itself therefore, provide a sufficient basis for legitimate representation if it resulted in non-Muslims acting in the name of Muslim constituents.

However this understanding of representation as a trust also revealed other more complex considerations. It suggested a radically different approach to the activity of representing than that which was seen to be common to 'western' representation. Indian Muslims did not deny that the system of representation which the British hoped to institute in India aspired, at least in part, to ensure that representatives would act in the interest of the represented or, in other words, to obtain what Pitkin has termed 'substantive representation'.[134] What many questioned was the assumption that there was *an* interest to be represented. They argued

---

[132] Cited in M.S. Jain, *The Aligarh Movement: Its Origin and Development, 1858–1906* (Agra, Sri Ram Mehra, 1965), pp. 128–9.

[133] T.W. Arnold, *The Caliphate* (London, Routledge and Kegan Paul, 1965, reissued), pp. 70–7. 'Some Considerations on the Sunnī Theory of the Caliphate', *Archives d'histoire droit Oriental*, 3, 1948, pp. 401–10.

[134] Pitkin, *The Concept of Representation*, p. 213.

that the substantive representation presumed by Western systems was meaningless where men disagreed so profoundly in their values and commitments. Institutions like separate communal electorates, they contended, were necessary precisely so that some groups such as Muslims could elect those with whom they shared specific value-commitments, namely other Muslims.

But was this merely an echo of the notion of descriptive representation that had for so long been encouraged by official policy? Was it simply the political reflex of a group of privileged Muslims who had grown accustomed to, and indeed had benefited from, the restricted colonial definition of representation as a mode of resemblance rather than a creative political activity? Did it imply that these Muslims rejected altogether any notion of representation as a substantive activity because it was likely to threaten their claims to be the spokesmen for Indian Muslims?

It is, as we have suggested earlier, highly plausible that Indian Muslims, like other Indians, were influenced by the assumptions of colonial policy which tended to stress affinity as a basis for political representation. It is also true that many saw in the notion of representation as resemblance a convenient means by which they, as Muslims, could sustain their claims to speak authentically for Indian Muslims at a time when political competition and open elections threatened to displace this privilege. At the same time however, it is clear that there was also some concern about a kind of substantive representation which it was believed was in danger of being undermined by the norms of Western representation.

It was an understanding of substantive representation that was intimately related to a peculiarly Muslim conception of politics and political life. It assumed fundamental cleavages in society which resulted in profound differences in value-commitments. These, in turn, were seen to be inseparable from political issues and were held not to be open or accessible to rational debate. The meaning of substantive representation in this kind of society, as Pitkin has suggested, is likely to involve 'an increasing desire ... for representativeness in its legislators, a desire to pick them from a particular group as the only safe guarantee of action in the interest of that group'.[135]

At one level it could be argued that this interpretation of substantive representation is potentially explosive, as well as unacceptable to the theory of Western liberal representation. It would introduce into the legislature the antagonisms that pervaded society and make

[135] *Ibid.*, pp. 213–14.

impossible the evolution of common political institutions or a common political society. This indeed was what the opponents of separate communal electorates were to argue in later years. For many Muslims, however, unaccustomed to the idea of a common society other than one founded on Muslim principle, the issue of separate electorates was less problematic.

The 'weighted' significance of social groups

A common objection levied by the well-born followers of Sayyid Ahmad and Amīr 'Alī against 'western' representation was that it tended to overlook the traditional pre-eminence of groups like the Indian Muslims. It was claimed that the application of strictly numerical criteria in determining claims to representation and power was grossly unfair to Muslims whose historical importance in India's political life had been considerable. They demanded a degree of preferential treatment from the government that would not only counter some of the disadvantages that Muslims were likely to suffer as a result of 'western' representation, but also symbolise a gesture of recognition for their special status in Indian society.[136]

The significance of these claims lies in the powerful justification they were later to provide for the demand for Muslim 'weightage': a measure designed to endorse Muslim representation in excess of the actual numerical proportion of Muslims in British India. At the outset these claims appeared to be little more than expressions of political vanity and crude social snobbery. At the same time, however, they also suggested a more profound set of concerns. The first reflected the fears of a minority whose claims to political recognition were steadily being questioned by new ideas of how power and prestige were to be distributed in society; the second pointed to a fundamental unwillingness to compromise on the premise that Indian Muslims, as Muslims, were endowed with an unqualified right to power. As Lelyveld has observed, whether it was as a *qaum*, that is, a subculture with peculiar moral attributes which made them a ruling people, or as an *umma*, namely the community of believers who had accepted in full God's final revelation, the idea of being Muslim was deemed to entail 'a special relationship to the political order'.[137]

---

[136] In its memorial presented to the Viceroy, Lord Ripon in 1882, the National Mahommedan Association demanded preferential treatment for Indian Muslims on the grounds that they were a backward, but nevertheless politically important, community. K.K. Aziz (ed.), *Ameer Ali*, part 2, pp. 23–40.

[137] Lelyveld, *Aligarh's First Generation*, p. 345.

Their Mughal heritage which had taught them the importance of ancestry as a determinant of power, led many Muslims opposed to Western representation to demand that social position be considered as a factor in the selection of India's future representatives. Speaking to an audience of like minded Muslims in Lucknow in December 1887, Sayyid Ahmad demanded, 'Would our aristocracy like that men of low caste or insignificant origin, though he be a BA or MA, and have the requisite ability, should be in a position among them and have power in making laws that affect their lives and property? Never.'[38] His own response was predictable enough. 'Men of good family would never like to trust their lives and property to people of low rank with whose humble origins they are well-acquainted'.[139]

Rather more fetching expressions of these sentiments were heard later in the autumn of 1888. Nawāb Imād-ad-daulāh, secretary to the Nizām of Hyderabad, feared that 'western' representation would result in the election 'of B.A.'s and M.A.'s from ordinary families ... hardly the sort of men [one] would care to hob-nob with'.[140] Political ability, in the minds of these Muslims, was no substitute for the 'high devoir' of Empire.[141] Musalmans, argued one, were entitled to power for no other reason than that for centuries they have been rulers, 'the principles of a monarchy have become their second nature'.[142]

One important consideration which was seen to justify this claim to power, was the belief that Muslims were descended from the ruling races. This, as Lelyveld has so effectively demonstrated, was what underlay Muslim anxieties in the face of the political competition implied by Western representation. Muslims from the *sharīf*, or well-born classes, amongst whom were many opponents of Western representation, found it difficult to countenance the prospect of 'the withdrawal of deference'.[143] The idea that those who spent much time tracing their ancestry to foreign Turkish and Arab aristocracies should

---

[138] Shan Mohammad (ed.), *Writings and Speeches*, p. 204.
[139] *Ibid.*, p. 208.
[140] See his letter to the editor of the *Aligarh Institute Gazette*, 11 September 1888.
[141] *Ibid.*
[142] *Ibid.*, 10 August 1894. These views appear not to have been exceptional. Fateh Nawaz Jung, a leading Muslim notable in the state of Hyderabad, explained his community's resistance to the idea of representative institutions in terms of its 'strong predilection for that form of rule which is known as despotism'. *Ibid.*, 24 April 1888. In May, an editorial in the *Aligarh Institute Gazette* doubted whether elections could be made part of Muslim political practice. It observed ' ... we have yet to learn that the Empire of Islam was governed by a parliament, the members of which were chosen by election'. *Ibid.*, 26 May 1888.
[143] Lelyveld, *Aligarh's First Generation*, p. 309.

have to subordinate themselves to inferior breeds of men appeared to them to be fundamentally unacceptable.[144]

In a letter to his friend and biographer, Altāf Husain Hālī, Sayyid Ahmad explained some of his own difficulties with Ripon's proposals to extend elective representation to India. He wrote, 'I am a Muslim, an inhabitant of India and descended from the Arabs... The Arab people neither seek, nor do they desire that instead of ruling themselves, someone else should rule them'.[145] These sober tones of regret were soon to give way to a much more aggressive defence of a political order which endorsed the differences between ruling races and subject people, and which acknowledged that power was the natural dispensation of the former. 'Our nation' declared Sayyid Ahmad in 1887, 'is of the blood of those who made not only Arabia, but Asia and Europe to tremble. It is our nation which conquered with its sword the whole of India'.[146]

Similar sentiments, differently expressed, prevailed also in contemporary works by Amīr 'Alī, written largely for the consumption of official decision makers. Their tone is characteristic of 'a nation... with great traditions but without a career'.[147] Much is made of Muslims as 'the paramount race in India' and considerable space devoted to the descent of Indian Muslims from the Turkish or Afghan aristocracy, and in some rare instances 'from the higher Hindoo castes, like the Rajpoots'.[148] Everywhere, there was, as Leonard Gordon observes, a marked 'identification with the just and the powerful'.[149] All around there was a profound sense that Muslims as members of a ruling race, deserved more than the vagaries of 'western' representation could assure them.

It is of course important to bear in mind, as Lelyveld reminds us, that both Sayyid Ahmad and for that matter Amīr 'Alī probably realised that not all Indian Muslims were descended from the ruling races. However, by stressing the element of kinship, they were able to provide a basis of solidarity that was later to prove crucial in the face of non-Muslim competition.[150]

It is also true that this Muslim self-image was in large part fostered and reinforced by prevailing official views. Theodore Beck's impressions of Indian Muslims and his apprehensions concerning their reaction to

---

[144] *Ibid.*
[145] Hālī, *Hayāt-i-Jāwed*, p. 562.
[146] Shan Mohammad (ed.), *Writings and Speeches*, p. 213.
[147] K.K. Aziz (ed.), *Ameer Ali*, part 2, p. 71.
[148] *Ibid.*, part 2, p. 49.
[149] Gordon, *Bengal*, p. 70.
[150] Lelyveld, *Aligarh's First Generation*, p. 311.

official policy was by no means untypical of the opinion of the British colonial establishment in India. He warned in 1886 that

It must be remembered... that Mahomedans ruled this part of India for five centuries, and are not prepared to accept a position of political insignificance... If the Government shut to them the door by which they may hope to gain legitimate influence, it will give a dangerous impetus to those with whom the idea of the *jehad* is not yet dead...[151]

Nor was the response from Indian-Muslims at all reassuring. Sayyid Ahmad's picturesque threat of a Muslim backlash was particularly compelling: 'Pathans, Syeds, Hashimi and Koreishi whose blood smells of Abraham, will apppear in glittering uniforms... But we must wait for that time'.[152]

But were social and racial ancestry the only factors that persuaded these Indian-Muslims that they were entitled by right to partake of power? Were there perhaps other considerations which inspired a belief in the innate superiority of Muslims over non-Muslims? Is there some evidence that their difficulties in accepting the terms of eventual majority rule stemmed in part from the conviction that as a divinely constituted community, their destiny lay in their role as the superior arbiters of power?

To seek answers to these questions one must go beyond the immediate milieu of public politics to the realm of contemporary Muslim literary and religious discourse. One must appreciate the political impact and the significance of major Muslim literary achievements such as Hālī's epic poem, *Musaddas Madd-o-Jazr-i-Islām* which appeared in 1879.[153] Written originally at the instigation of Sayyid Ahmad, it is a profound lament on the fate of a decaying Muslim ruling class. At heart, however, it remains a powerful attempt to show how the political dominance of Islam was intrinsic to the logic of civilization. It asserts that Islam represented a superior culture imparted by Muhammad to the Arabs. It suggests that an important element of this Islamic heritage was political power which had been deeply compromised by a decadent and inactive Muslim elite in India.[154] The

---

[151] Beck's evidence before the Public Services Commission (North Western Provinces and Oudh), quoted in Seal, *The Emergence of Indian Nationalism*, p. 323.

[152] Sayyid Ahmad's speech in Lucknow in 1887 in Shan Mohammad (ed.), *Writings and Speeches*, p. 215.

[153] On Hālī and the 'historical poem' see Aziz Ahmad, *Islamic Modernism*, pp. 97–100. See also S.M. Ikram, *Modern Muslim India*, pp. 59–71.

[154] The following extract expresses the mood of the *Musaddas*:

Let someone go and see the ruins of Cordova,
The arches and the doors of its magnificent mosques,

sentiments that moved Hālī to compose his poem lay somewhere in the world-view he acknowledged to be part of his personal and intellectual quest. He wrote in the 1870s, 'I was given wholly to religious fanaticism ... I considered the Muslims the very cream of creation.'[155]

This belief in the superiority of Islam was axiomatic not only amongst traditional minded Muslims like Maulānā Altāf Husain Hālī but even amongst Muslim modernists like Amīr 'Alī, familiar with and sometimes sympathetic to the rationale of Christian doctrine. The cultivation of a sense of Muslim moral superiority also formed part of the teachings of those Muslims whose activities were confined principally to religious and educational ventures. Barbara Metcalf has shown how the *'ulamā'* associated with the theological seminary at Deoband encouraged such superiority, particularly in relation to the politically dominant British, on the grounds that it stemmed from divine sanction. Although the *'ulamā'* were not directly involved in questions of Muslim represent-ation, it is reasonable to assume that they shared with other Muslims the view that the superior moral attributes of their community equipped it specially for power.

> The mighty palaces of the Arab chiefs,
> And their decayed pomp and grandeur.
> The glory of their race shines from beneath the debris,
> Just as pure gold glitters in a heap of ashes.
> ...
> [Now] They possess neither wealth, nor prestige, neither learning, nor art,
> Faith alone remains – and that too is like a tree without leaves or flowers.

Quoted in *ibid.*, pp. 62, 63.

[155] Quoted in M. Sadiq, *A History of Urdu Literature* (Delhi, Oxford University Press, 1984), p. 346.

4

The quest for community
Muslims and the demand for separate
electorates, 1900–1909

The decisive moves by government and Congress towards electoral representation in the late nineteenth century contributed substantially to Muslim unease. Already, the effects of the existing system of limited elections had led some Muslims to engage in a more sustained campaign against Western representation. By the spring of 1890, Sayyid Ahmad Khān had obtained 40,000 signatures on a petition appealing to the House of Commons to restrain any further extension of the elective principle in India. It emphasised the dangers inherent in elections and stressed the importance of retaining the system of nomination as the only means of guaranteeing the interests of groups unable or unwilling to participate in the new system.[1] Yet, scarcely a decade was to elapse before the submission of an apparently quite distinct set of proposals which called for elected Muslim representatives accountable to exclusively Muslim electorates. In December 1896 the Indian Defence Association, founded by Sayyid Ahmad Khān as an alternative to the Indian National Congress, called for the existing system of nomination to be replaced by the institution of separate Muslim electorates.[2]

What lay behind this unexpected change of heart? The most obvious explanation lies in the direction of official policy which, since the late 1880s, had begun to show signs of a much greater concern for the forms, if not the substance, of popular representation in India. This was to become much more marked following the return to power of a Liberal government in early 1906. Muslims, particularly those who were closely associated with the politics of Sayyid Ahmad Khān, realised that the time had come for them to accommodate some at least of the practices of

---

[1] See Rafiq Zakaria, *Rise of Muslims in Indian Politics: An Analysis of Developments from 1885–1906* (Bombay, Somaiya Publications, 1970), p. 131 and Appendix C for a full text of the petition.

[2] *Ibid.*, pp. 140–2; M.S. Jain, *The Aligarh Movement: Its Origin and Development, 1858–1906* (Agra, Sri Ram Mehra, 1965), pp. 128–9 and Shan Mohammad (ed.), *The Aligarh Movement: Basic Documents, 1864–1898*, III (Meerut, Meenakshi Prakashan, 1978), pp. 1063–8, for a full text of the petition.

Western popular representation. At the same time many were also reassured by the government's intention to continue to pursue its policy of 'interest' representation which allowed minority groups like the Muslims a degree of participation they might otherwise not have enjoyed. These considerations were to become all the more pertinent following the partition of Bengal in 1905 when Muslims chose, on the whole, to refrain from joining movements of public protest. Anxious about the consequences of liberal reform, Muslims now collaborated with officials to restore a system of representation that would function as a means of patronage whereby officials would dispense political recognition in return for political support.

There were other factors too which had little or nothing to do with official policy as such, which encouraged Muslims opposed to Western representation to revise their traditional attitudes. Not the least important was the dismal level of Muslim representation in local and provincial councils. Here the system of nomination upon which Muslims like Sayyid Ahmad Khān had tended to rely as a means of securing the interests of their class, failed to contain the emergence of predominantly Hindu majorities. Many came to believe that separate Muslim electorates with their stress upon the exclusive right of Muslims to elect Muslim representatives, offered the best chance of counteracting the effects of popular elective representation. Others were persuaded that elections could be made more acceptable to Muslims if they were predicated upon some notion of equality between Hindus and Muslims, regardless of their actual numerical strength. The growing sentiment in favour of a political party committed to the representation of Muslim 'interests' which began to gather momentum at this time, also helped to instil a feeling of confidence among Muslims. Those who had tended in the past to believe that Congress gave Hindus an unfair advantage in the art of political organisation and electioneering now felt able to participate, however, reluctantly, in the institutions of Western representation.

However despite these changes, provoked in part by the evolution of government policy and partly by developments within groups of Indian Muslims, there remained nevertheless a profound scepticism in relation to the assumptions that were deemed to underlie Western representation. Such scepticism issued as much from the anxieties of a political minority faced with the admittedly distant prospect of majority rule as from an understanding that Muslims in India (as elsewhere) formed a distinct religio-political community; that they were innately superior to non-Muslims and that they were endowed with special claims to political power and representation. Its hold on Muslim thinking was reflected in the Simla Memorial of October 1906, which remains not only the most systematic defence of separate Muslim electorates but also a telling indictment of 'western' representation. Above all, it shaped the preoccupations of men like Amīr 'Alī, and later Muhammad Iqbāl, for whom Muslim communal representation in the form of separate electorates was as much a pragmatic as it was an imperative measure to secure the integrity of their religious community, its place in the life of the individual and the nature of its exclusive pursuits.

The Colonial context

The direction of Liberal initiatives

The return to power of the Liberal Party in the early part of 1906 had a dramatic effect upon Muslim attitudes to political representation in India. The Party's enthusiasm for 'a good start in the way of reform in the popular direction',[3] gave rise to new fears that Muslim interests might be overlooked in the process of future Councils reforms. Many believed that there were good reasons to be concerned. The Act of 1892 had persuaded them that Britain intended to concede, at least in part, some of the measures then being proposed by Congress on Indian representation. There was particular anxiety about the implementation of the Act especially as it concerned the selection of members to provincial Councils. For although the Act did not formally sanction elections, the practice of accepting the recommendations of Congress, which tended to dominate the specially constituted electorates, did little to assuage Muslim fears.[4]

Muslim apprehensions were scarcely mitigated by the statement of policy contained in the Secretary of State Lord Morley's budget speech of July 1906 in which he stressed the importance of expanding 'the representative element' within Indian legislative councils.[5] Muslims, particularly those who had been closely associated with Sayyid Ahmad Khān, like Mohsin-ul-Mulk, lost no time in expressing their reservations.[6] At the heart of their objections lay established arguments about the diversity of Indian society and its constraints upon the development of 'western' representative institutions. In a wry comment designed to

---

[3] Morley to Minto, 15 June 1906, *John Morley Papers*, MSS. EUR. D. 573, volume I.
[4] Reginald Coupland, *India: A Restatement* (Oxford University Press, 1945), p. 101.
[5] John Morley's budget speech, 20 July 1906, in *Hansards Parliamentary Debates* (Lords), (1906), volume 161, columns 587–8.
[6] Mohsin-ul-Mulk to W.A. Archbold, 4 August 1906 (enclosure), *Morley Papers*, MSS. EUR. D. 573, volume 3.

expose the doctrinaire approach which characterised members of the Liberal establishment, including Morley, Mohsin-ul-Mulk described the new government as a body of 'philosophers' in need of practical statesmen. The pursuit of principles, he feared, could blind them to 'the real conditions of India', which in turn would lead to policies that were seriously misguided.[7]

Muslim unease was also intensified by the Liberal Party's public sympathy for Congress's campaign for the extension of popular representation in India. In the summer of 1905, Congress had sent its president, Gopal Krishna Gokhale, to publicise its case for the reform of Indian Councils beyond the terms stipulated in the Act of 1892. Gokhale argued that Congress's demands were essentially consistent with the stated objectives of British rule in India, namely to prepare Indians for self-government. He maintained that although Congress did not demand an immediate transition of power to Indians, it did call for unequivocal efforts in that direction.[8] In his presidential address to Congress later that year, Gokhale declared that the only real and permanent remedy for Indian discontent lay in the institution of self-government based on a system of popular elections.[9]

Gokhale's views elicited a warm response in England. Lord Morley, who spent long hours in discussion with Gokhale, emerged broadly persuaded of the reasonableness of Gokhale's claims.[10] Elsewhere, prominent members of the Liberal Party, notably Henry Fawcett, Allen Hume, Henry Cotton and William Wedderburn, also lent their enthusiastic support for changes in the substance of Indian representation,

[7] Mohsin-ul-Mulk to W.A. Archbold, 18 August 1906 (enclosure), *Minto Papers Correspondence*, volume 2, quoted in M.N. Das, *India Under Minto and Morley* (London, George Allen and Unwin, 1964), p. 196. His views were not exceptional. Sayyid Husain Bilgrāmī, a friend and colleague of Sayyid Ahmad Khān and one of the authors of the Simla Memorial, wrote, 'I see that Mr. Morley is going ahead in the most reckless manner. Ministers who know nothing of the condition of life in India and yet wish to carry out their theories at any hazard can only bring about the ruin of the country ... I am afraid that Mr. Morley knows more about Voltaire and 18th century literature than the condition of contemporary India'. Sayyid Husain Bilgrāmī to C.S. Bayley, 24 July 1906, enclosed with Bayley to Dunlop Smith, 25 July 1906, *Minto Papers Correspondence*, 1906, volume 2, quoted in *ibid.*, p. 18.

[8] Gokhale's speech to the National Liberal Club, 15 November 1905, issued as 'The Awakening of India', published by the Political Committee of the National Liberal Club, London, 1905, *India Office Library Tracts*, Pol. 993, pp. 3–5.

[9] Gokhale's presidential address to the annual session of Indian National Congress, in D.G. Karve and D.V. Ambedkar (eds.), *Speeches and Writings of Gopal Krishna Gokhale*, II (London, Asia Publishing House, 1966), pp. 187–209.

[10] Morley's budget speech, 20 July 1906, *Hansard's Parliamentary Debates* (Lords), 1906, volume 161, columns 587–8.

particularly at the higher levels.[11] Muslims now felt that whatever assurances to the contrary they might have received in the past, the present government was unlikely to check the pace of liberal reform in India.[12] Some were led to take prompt action. The more influential among them like the Āgā Khān, who was known to command the ear of government, were despatched to London to lobby Whitehall and the India Office against the introduction of popular elective representation.[13]

However, the public image conveyed by the Liberals as a party of reform gradually led growing numbers of Muslims to conclude that if they were to survive the prevailing political climate, they needed somehow to accommodate the practice, if not the theory, of Western representation. The demand for separate Muslim electorates which was formally mooted in the Simla Memorial of 1906 constituted in essence a step in this direction. It purported to conform to the model of Western liberal representation but decisively rejected the assumptions upon which such representation was founded. It accepted the principle of popular representation but denied that it involved the representation of individual interests; it endorsed elections but only on condition that electorates were organised on religious lines. Finally, while it recognised numerical considerations as important to the distribution of power, it held that they were essentially secondary to questions of social status and moral virtue.

Officials and communal representation

Among the factors that shaped official thinking on Indian represent-ation, few were as decisive as the question of the representation of 'interests'. This entailed the representation of groups and classes rather than of individuals, and implied that 'interests' were the attributes of broad social categories rather than the outcome of shifting political alignments.

[11] S.R. Wasti, *Lord Minto and the Indian Nationalist Movement* (Oxford, Clarendon Press, 1964), p. 19.
[12] In April 1905, Mohsin-ul-Mulk is said to have enquired of Harcourt Butler, then secretary to the government of the United Provinces, how he could keep 'our boys from agitation' if they 'see a man like Gokhale treated as an equal by the Viceroy'. Harcourt Butler to H.E. Richards, 28 April 1905, *Harcourt Butler Papers*, MSS. EUR. F.116, volume 18.
[13] The Āgā Khān, *The Memoirs of Aga Khan: World Enough and Time* (London, Cassell, 1954), p. 91. In correspondence with Morley about his contacts with the Āgā Khān, Minto noted approvingly 'The Aga Khan agrees...that India is quite unfit for popular representation in our sense of the word'. Minto to Morley, 4 October 1906, *John Morley Papers*, volume 9.

Some scholars have attempted to explain this preoccupation with 'interest' representation as part of a general endeavour whereby officials sought to comprehend a society that appeared to them both immensely complex and fundamentally alien.[14] They point to the propensity of British officials to classify and categorise Indian society in order to make it more accessible. These social constructs, which often bore little relation to the 'structural reality' of the society officials were attempting to grasp, they argue, had enormous practical consequences for Indian representation.[15] It encouraged 'the emergence of a ... consciousness to fit that official communal view ...' so that 'those seeking patronage or protesting proscription had to speak in the name of a bureaucratically recognized category'.[16]

There were few signs that the Liberal government was any less subject to the perceptions that had shaped the policy of their predecessors, or indeed that they or their colleagues in India intended at all to question them. In a despatch to the Government of India, Lord Morley urged officials to recognise the importance of obtaining the 'true representation, within the narrow limits thus imposed, of the vast diversity of classes, races and interests in the Indian Empire'.[17] The Government of India, in its turn, reaffirmed its commitment to 'the broad principle that Indian society lives, thinks and acts according to castes, races and religions'.[18] In April 1907, the Viceroy's Council unanimously proposed a system of corporate and communal representation which asserted that 'the national division of Indian society is not territorial, but sectional'.[19]

The emphasis upon the representation of 'interests' may not in itself have proved to be so significant had it not also tended, implicitly, to

[14] Bernard S. Cohn, 'Notes on the History of the Study of Indian Society and Culture' in M. Singer and B. Cohn (eds.), *Structure and Change in Indian Society* (Chicago, Aldine Press, 1968), pp. 3–28; 'The Census, Social Structure and Objectification in South Asia', Second European Conference on Modern South Asia, Elsinore, Denmark, June 1970; Peter Hardy, *The Muslims of British India* (Cambridge University Press, 1972), pp. 116–25; Francis Robinson, *Separatism Among Indian Muslims: The Politics of the United Provinces Muslims* (Cambridge University Press, 1974), pp. 99–100; David Washbrook, 'The Development of Caste Organisation in South India, 1880–1925' in C.J. Baker and D. Washbrook (eds.), *South India: Political Institutions and Political Change* (Delhi, Macmillan, 1975), pp. 150–203; and Lucy Carroll, 'Colonial Perceptions of Indian Society and the Emergence of Caste(s) Associations', *Journal of Asian Studies*, 37, 2 (1978), pp. 233–49.

[15] Bernard S. Cohn, 'Anthropological Notes on Disputes and Law in India', *American Anthropologist*, 67, part 2 (1965), p. 114.

[16] Carroll, 'Colonial Perceptions', p. 249.

[17] Paragraph 22 of the Secretary of State's secret despatch no. 71 of 17 May 1907, *John Morley Papers*, MSS. EUR. d. 573, volume 32.

[18] See note by W. Lee Warner, 18 April 1907, *ibid.*, volume 32. See also the Government of India's Despatch of 21 March 1907, especially paragraphs 52–8, *ibid.*

[19] Note by W. Lee Warner, 18 April 1907, *ibid.*

underrate the value of a political majority. By assuming that groups like the Muslims, Western-educated Indians, traders and landlords rather than individuals were the constituent units in society, it opened the way for claims to the kind of equality commonly reserved for individuals in the theory, if not the practice, of Western democratic representation. Parity, not political majorities came steadily to dominate the debate on Indian representation.[20]

Its implications were not lost upon Indian Muslims. Throughout the last decades of the nineteenth century those who had opposed the application of majority rule in India had argued that they and their community could not accept a political system which required them to be subject to those over whom they had once ruled. By the early part of this century, many realised that their claims might substantially be augmented if they could obtain official recognition for Muslims as a distinct social category – a separate 'interest'. Many are likely to have believed that by doing so, their actual numerical size could become far less decisive in estimating the extent of their community's representation and its participation in power. The tone was set by Nawāb Salīmullāh, East Bengal's wealthiest landed magnate and a convener of the first session of the Muslim League in Dacca in December 1906. He told his fellow Muslims, 'We are today prepared to enter on a political career as a community, which the spirit of the times compels us to do'.[21]

It would be tempting to suggest that Muslim representative politics in the twentieth century was simply a product of administrative definitions of Indian society. Indeed this is a view that has been espoused by distinguished scholars who have sought to explain the emergence of Muslim separatism in colonial India. Peter Hardy, for example, has argued that political mobilisation around a cultural category namely, Muslim communalism, was more a response to official constructs of a Muslim 'community' than it was a reflection of the actual organisation of Indian Muslim society which was highly diverse.[22] Others like Francis Robinson have also drawn attention to the importance of official perceptions as one of the many important sources of Muslim separatism. He believes they encouraged a view of India as a vast

[20] The spirit that pervaded the making of the new reforms of 1909 was summed up by Sir Alfred Lyall. He wrote, 'I do not believe that any system of electing members to the councils by majorities can profitably produce fair representation of the Indian people whose whole society is founded upon division of religion and race'. Lyall to Morley, 15 February 1909, *John Morley Papers*, volume 49.

[21] Cited in Abdul Hamid, *Muslim Separatism in India: A Brief Survey, 1858–1947* (Lahore, Oxford University Press, 1965), p. 78.

[22] Hardy, *The Muslims*, pp. 116–18.

organisation of communal groups characterised along lines of religion, language, race and caste. Officials, he argues, handed out patronage and accorded representation to Muslims as Muslims and, in doing so, consolidated a sense of Muslim communal identity.[23]

Although these explanations are valid to a point, they are inclined to suggest too decisive an influence exercised by the permutations of colonial policy. By concentrating too closely upon the consequences of official policy, they fail to account adequately for the normative constraints which often directed Muslim political action.[24] The idea that Muslim separatism was inspired primarily by administrative measures is apt to draw attention away from the very real value that Muslims themselves attach to the organisation of their politics on grounds of religion and community. Indeed, as we shall see, the issue of separate Muslim electorates did in fact embody for large numbers of Muslims, a quest for political identity as the extension of their religious solidarity, whether real or imagined.

The partition of Bengal and Muslim representation

The partition of Bengal and the emergence of political radicalism among groups of Hindu politicians and intellectuals acted as major catalysts in the transformàtion of Muslim attitudes to Western representation. It was a time when anxious British officials let it be known that support for the Raj could confer considerable political benefits and when influential Muslims, like the Āgā Khān and Nawāb Mohsin-ul-Mulk, concluded that political loyalism could finally obtain the concessions on represent- ation that had eluded them and their followers.

The partition of Bengal which precipitated a political crisis was justified by officials as a necessary 'administrative measure' designed to facilitate the task of governing a large province.[25] Many Hindus however, saw it as a political move which sought to weaken their political

---

[23] Robinson, *Separatism*, pp. 98–105, 345–54. For further developments of this argument, especially in relation to studies by Paul Brass see Francis Robinson, 'Nation Formation: The Brass Thesis and Muslim Separatism', *Journal of Common- wealth and Comparative Politics*, 15, 3 (1977), pp. 215–30 and his, 'Islam and Muslim Separatism' in David Taylor and Malcolm Yapp (eds.), *Political Identity in South Asia* (London, School of Oriental and African Studies, 1979), pp. 78–112.

[24] A question recognised at some length in Robinson, 'Islam and Muslim Separatism'.

[25] There is no dearth of literature on the partition of Bengal. One of the most comprehensive accounts of the subject, albeit from a Muslim point of view, is Z.H. Zaidi, 'The Partition of Bengal and its Annulment, 1902–1911', unpublished Ph.D. thesis, University of London, 1964. See also his 'The Political Motive in the Partition of Bengal', *Journal of the Pakistan Historical Society*, volume 12 (1964), pp. 113–48.

influence by forcibly dividing them.[26] More importantly, they were persuaded, not without reason, that the creation of a Muslim majority province of Eastern Bengal and Assam was a concession to Indian Muslims with the intention of consolidating their role as a political counter-weight to Congress.[27]

The idea that government and Muslims began, at this time, to discover interests in common has some foundation.[28] Much of it is based on the active disassociation of Bengali Muslims from the widespread protest movements against partition. But the reasons for Muslim aloofness were more complex than proponents of an Anglo-Muslim rapprochement have been prepared to acknowledge. It is worth noting, for example, that in Bengal the movement tended to assume, if unwittingly, a distinctly Hindu flavour which led to the steady alienation of large numbers of Muslims. The invocation of traditional Hindu cultural and historical symbols, accompanied by the suggestion that these had forcibly been eroded as a result of centuries of Muslim rule, also served to distance the majority of Indian Muslims.[29]

The spread of Hindu revivalism was not, admittedly, the only reason for Muslim indifference. Muslims, especially those opposed to Congress, were also persuaded that there were concrete political benefits to be enjoyed by their aloofness. They believed that the creation of a separate province where Muslims would constitute a majority was likely to ensure them a major share in its administration. Prominent political associations like the National Mahommedan Association and the Mahomedan Literary Society urged Muslims in various parts of Bengal 'to exert your greatest influence to prevent all ignorant members of the

---

[26] R.C. Majumdar, *History of the Freedom Movement in India*, II (Calcutta, Firma Mukhopadhyay, 1963), pp. 12–28.

[27] Ram Gopal, *How India Struggled for Freedom* (Bombay, The Book Centre, 1967), pp. 139–48.

[28] The idea of an Anglo-Muslim rapprochement is developed in M.N. Das, *India Under Morley and Minto: Politics behind Revolution, Repression and Reform* (London, George Allen and Unwin, 1964); Ram Gopal, *Indian Muslims: A Political History, 1858–1947* (Lahore, Book Traders, 1976) and S. Gopal, *British Policy in India, 1858–1905* (Cambridge University Press, 1965).

[29] See Mustafa Nurul Islam, 'Bengal Muslim Public Opinion as Reflected in the Vernacular Press Between 1901 and 1930', unpublished Ph.D. thesis, University of London, 1971, pp. 171–2; J.R. McLane, 'The 1905 Partition and the New Communalism', in Alexander Lipski (ed.), *Bengal, East and West* (East Lansing, Michigan, Asian Studies Centre, 1969), pp. 39–77 and Sufia Ahmed, 'Some Aspects of the History of the Muslim Community of Bengal, 1884–1911', unpublished Ph.D. thesis, University of London, 1960, pp. 273–4.

Mohammedan community of your district from directly or indirectly opposing the policy [of partition]'.[30]

Whatever the reasons for Muslim apathy, however, officials themselves were more concerned to discover what, if anything, it signified about Muslim loyalty.[31] In the context of growing political unrest, the advantages of retaining such loyalty could not be underestimated. Muslim political support was cultivated and much was done to redress 'Muslim under representation' in the services. Yet, as some officials realised, there were inherent dangers in pursuing too zealous a programme of Muslim welfare. In December 1906, the Viceroy, Lord Minto, confessed that he was concerned not to be seen to give 'any appearance of playing off Muhammedans against Hindus'[32] or, indeed, of endorsing the overtly pro-Muslim policies of Sir Bampflyde Fuller, the Lieutenant Governor of Eastern Bengal.

However the dilemmas were inescapable. The dismissal of Fuller on grounds of blatant Muslim partiality provoked widespread resentment among Bengali Muslims who regarded it as giving in to Hindu pressure to have Fuller removed from his post. Many threatened civil disobedience and the government's political credibility was in question among its staunchest allies. There was talk of 'agitation' among Muslims and the withdrawal of Muslim loyalty.[33] The message was clear: fundamental political concessions or the risk of Muslims going 'their own way'.[34]

• Its impact upon British officials was immediate and profound. The Āgā Khān recalled that by the summer of 1906 his colleagues in India had assured him that 'at last the Government were (sic) beginning to realise that there was something called a Muslim problem in India'.[35] Evidence suggests that his assessment came close to the truth. Officials were persuaded that it would be nothing short of a 'calamity' if Indian Muslims were alienated and 'driven into the arms of Congress'.[36] Many appreciated the need to steer Muslims towards a 'natural and legitimate

30 *The Muslim Chronicle* (Calcutta), 11 November 1905, quoted in Zakaria, *Rise of Muslims in Indian Politics*, p. 101.
31 Lancelot Hare to Minto, 27 April 1907, *Minto Correspondence*, volume 1, cited in M.N. Das, *India Under Morley and Minto*, p. 179.
32 Minto to Morley, 19 December 1906, *John Morley Papers*, volume 4.
33 Mohsin-ul-Mulk to W.A. Archbold, 18 August 1906, enclosed in Archbold to Dunlop Smith, 22 August 1906, *Minto Papers* (4E383), cited in Robinson, *Separatism*, p. 143.
34 Mohsin-ul-Mulk to Archbold, 4 August 1906, enclosed in Minto to Morley, 8 August 1906, *Morley Papers*, volume 9.
35 The Aga Khan, *Memoirs*, p. 91.
36 Denzil Ibbetson to Dunlop Smith, 10 August 1906, *Minto Papers Correspondence*, volume 2, cited in Das, *India Under Morley and Minto*, p. 169.

direction' grounded in closer co-operation between officials and 'the old fashioned and conservative element' who could restrain the 'young and advanced school' of Muslims.[37]

Curiously, and perhaps significantly, there also prevailed a feeling among officials that a Muslim uprising might prove rather more difficult to control than one led by non-Muslims. Sir Lancelot Hare, who replaced Fuller as Lieutenant Governor of Bengal, drew attention to the potentially greater threat posed by Muslims who tended to organise their movements around religious values. Political mobilisation dependent upon the skills of 'Moulavies' ready to exploit religious symbols, he believed, could be more ominous than any modern, predominantly Hindu organisation consisting of a few 'agitators'.[38] Not even the fierce anti-partition riots led by Hindu extremists, it seemed, could displace the power that the spectre of a Muslim uprising exercised upon the official mind.[39] This alone might have encouraged Muslims into believing that the consequences of elective representation were unlikely to affect the special attention they commanded among members of the colonial establishment.

The transformation of Muslim attitudes to elective representation

The dismal level of Muslim representation in local and provincial Councils at the turn of the century, and the emergence of groups of Muslims who felt less bound by the loyalist politics of Sayyid Ahmad Khān, prompted a fresh interest in the means of participating more effectively in the institutions of liberal reform without necessarily accepting their premises. Muslims agreed therefore to accept elections, but denied their formal purpose, namely to establish legitimate political majorities, by insisting upon statutory parity between Hindus and Muslims; and while they recognised the numerical criteria which underlay elections, they sought also to assert their historical and political importance as a basis for their claim to additional representation.

Muslim representation in local and provincial councils

The cautious acceptance by Indian Muslims of political institutions they had earlier opposed stemmed, curiously enough, from their adverse

---

[37] Lieutenant Governor of Punjab to Minto, 23 March 1907, *Minto Papers Correspondence*, Volume 1, cited in *ibid.*, p. 156.
[38] Lancelot Hare to Dunlop Smith, 1 September 1906 (enclosure), Minto to Morley, 10 September 1906, *Morley Papers*, volume 9, cited in Robinson, *Separatism*, p. 166.
[39] Minto to Morley, 29 August 1906, *Morley Papers*, volume 4.

electoral fortunes at the turn of the century. Elections to the municipalities in the 1880s had returned few Muslim candidates and official nominations had not succeeded in offsetting their dwindling numbers. Moreover, recommendations by specially designated constituencies under the provisions of the Councils Act of 1892 had tended in the Punjab, for example, to favour the appointment of Muslims loyal to Congress which already wielded considerable influence in the area.[40]

The results obtained in the municipal and provincial elections held between 1880 and 1906 in the three provinces of the Punjab, the United Provinces and Bengal – areas where Muslims were either in a majority or in positions of influence – bear some evidence of these trends. In the Punjab, for example, of a total of ninety-six reported elections held between 1883 and 1884 in the central and eastern towns, Muslims won a majority on only twelve committees, whereas Hindus controlled seventy-two.[41] The discrepancy between the representation of the two communities was considered so great that local officials systematically resorted to nomination in order to achieve a more equal balance.[42] Muslims in these areas also relied frequently upon government gerrymandering to obtain some advantages in precincts that would otherwise have tended to return Hindu majorities.[43] In some areas like Delhi and Amritsar, Muslims found themselves at a disadvantage owing to economic pressure from Hindu money-lenders who frequently obliged indebted Muslim clients to vote for Hindu candidates.[44]

In the United Provinces, particularly in the western regions and the Doab, Muslim representation on municipal boards between 1884/5 and 1907/8 declined, though less noticeably, from 34.1% to 30.1%.[45] In the same period, Muslim representation in the municipalities over the whole province also declined marginally from 32.7% to 31.1%. As in the Punjab, Muslims tended to rely heavily upon official nominations to restore the balance although, in some instances, as in the western town of Pilibhit, even this was not enough.[46]

[40] Gerald Barrier, 'The Punjab Government and Communal Politics, 1870–1908', *Journal of Asian Studies*, 27, 3 (1968), p. 536.
[41] *Ibid.*
[42] *Ibid.*, p. 537.
[43] This occurred, for example, in Delhi, where Muslims were able to obtain an advantage in almost half the precincts as a result of government gerrymandered wards. *Ibid.*
[44] *Ibid.*
[45] Francis Robinson, 'Municipal Government and Muslim Separatism in the United Provinces, 1883–1916' in John Gallagher *et al.* (eds.), *Locality, Province and Nation: Essays on Indian Politics, 1870–1947* (Cambridge University Press, 1973), p. 92.
[46] *Ibid.*, pp. 91, 94. One of the factors that went against the representation of larger numbers of Muslims was their failure to meet the stringent economic qualifications for

Even at the level of provincial councils, Muslim representation fared poorly. Between 1895 and 1906, the total percentage of Muslim representatives in the Bengal Legislative Council declined drastically from 50% to less than 13%.[47] Of a total of nineteen non-official members in 1895, Muslim membership stood at three, while that of the Hindus at six. In 1901, of a total of twenty non-official members, Muslims numbered two while Hindus claimed eight. In 1906, Muslim membership stood at one and that of Hindus at eight out of a total body of nineteen non-official members.[48]

In the Governor-General's Legislative Council these trends showed little sign of improvement. Muslim representation among non-official members fell in 1895 from two against six Hindus out of a total of eleven, to nil against five Hindus out of a total of nine in 1901. As late as 1904, Muslim representation failed to revive substantially: out of a total of eleven non-official members, six were Hindus and only two Muslim.[49]

The decline in Muslim representation at the turn of the century may have proved to be less consequential had it not also been characterised by the steady political exclusion of those Muslims critical of liberal reform who had been close to Sayyid Ahmad Khān. It is noteworthy, for example, that until 1909, only two Muslims who could readily be identified as political colleagues of Sayyid Ahmad Khān were nominated to provincial Councils. Two others who were nominated to the provincial Councils at the same time, although not members of Congress, were politically obscure.[50]

Alternative Muslim schemes for representation

The limitations of the existing system prompted some Muslims to Consider means of obtaining Muslim representation without having to accept Western elective representation, or the rules of 'political arithmetic'. A step in this direction was taken by the Indian Defence Association in the winter of 1896. In a memorial to the government, it outlined what it claimed to be the position of Indian Muslims on the question of elective representation.[51]

franchise. See also J.L. Hill, 'Congress and Representative Institutions in the United Provinces, 1886–1901', unpublished Ph.D. dissertation, Duke University, 1966, p. 129.
[47] Zakaria, *Rise of Muslims in Indian Politics*, p. 139.
[48] *Ibid.*
[49] *Ibid.*, p. 138.
[50] *Ibid.*, pp. 139–40, 145.
[51] A full of the Memorial was published in the *Pioneer* (Allahabad), 22 December

Its authors underlined their community's opposi⁺ion, in principle, to elective representation, but conceded that it would be 'useless and foolish' to continue to press for its withdrawa.. What was important, they stressed, was to secure for Indian Muslims 'a reasonable and just representation'. This postulated 'one cardinal fact, that the Muhammedans are for political purposes a community with separate traditions, interests, political convictions and religion'. This demanded the abolition of existing electorates dominated by Hindus, and the creation in their place, of separate Muslim electorates which would enable Muslims to elect their 'true' representatives instead of mere agents of a Hindu majority.

Superficially considered, the memorial bears the hallmarks of a democratic manifesto. It aimed after all at a more complete, indeed substantive, relationship between the representative and the represented by attempting to ensure that Muslim candidates did indeed represent Muslim electors. At the same time, by insisting that such electorates be designated mutually exclusive from non-Muslim electorates, it tended inevitably to deny the premise of an 'emancipated electorate'.[52] The thrust of the memorial however suggests one important trend, namely the growing impatience of a section of Indian Muslims with official nomination, even if such impatience was constrained somewhat by the unwillingness to espouse too 'liberal' and 'western' an understanding of political representation.[53] Some sought to resolve these tensions by advocating elections on the basis of statutory parity between Hindus and Muslims. In January 1897, Hājī Muhammad Ismāʿīl Khān, a prominent Muslim publicist and close political colleague of Sayyid Ahmad Khān, urged Congress to consider a proposal on Indian representation which would ensure that 'in the Councils of the government and Municipal and Local Boards the Hindus and Musalmans may have an equal number of elected members'.[54] Congress dismissed Ismāʿīl Khān's plea on the grounds that it stemmed partly from the erroneous assumption that Hindus wished to dominate Indian Muslims and partly from an

---

1896 and is reproduced in Jain, *The Aligarh Movement*, III, pp. 128–9. See also Zakaria, *Rise of Muslims in Indian Politics*, pp. 140–1.

[52] That is to say, one 'among which a free party system will operate towards an aggregation of interests. The representation of permanently defined sectional interests is the very antithesis of this system...' Dietmar Rothermund, 'Emancipation or Re-Integration: The Politics of Gopal Krishna Gokhale and Herbert Hope Risley' in D.A. Low (ed.), *Soundings in Modern South Asian History* (London, Weidenfeld and Nicolson, 1968), p. 152.

[53] Mohsin-ul-Mulk to W.A. Archbold, 4 August 1906 (enclosure), Minto to Morley, 8 August 1906, *John Morley Papers*, Volume 9.

[54] Quoted in Zakaria, *Rise of Muslims in Indian Politics*, pp. 85–6.

exaggerated sense of Muslim self-importance.[55] Whatever the merits of Congress's assessments (and these were not altogether misplaced) it remains the case that it was proposals like those of Ismāʿīl Khān's that were to become the germ of later Muslim claims to parity of representation.

Moves towards a Muslim political organisation

By the end of the nineteenth century, growing numbers of Muslims had come to believe that their claim to representation as a separate community would be vastly enhanced, if not amplified, by a body working primarily for the promotion of Muslim political interests. Many were persuaded that the representation of Muslims as a community demanded an organisation that would speak for all Indian Muslims – a privilege which they believed had wrongfully been appropriated by Congress. What was intended was not only to question Congress's credentials as a nationalist movement but, more importantly perhaps, to undermine the credibility of Muslims who chose to conduct their politics on other than avowedly communal lines by seeking election on a Congress ticket.

The necessity of a Muslim political organisation had not always been obvious. Indeed many Indian Muslims in the 1870s and 1880s, with the exception of those who were members of Congress, had tended on the whole to refrain from political activity on the understanding that it was inclined to incur official disapproval. Here, Sayyid Ahmad Khān's influence was decisive. This is not to say that his preferences dominated the approach of all groups of Indian Muslims even when they happened, in fact, to share many of his own perspectives on the delicate relationship between the Raj and its Muslim subjects. Among those who expressed their disagreement with Sayyid Ahmad on the issue of a Muslim political organisation, only Sayyid Amīr ʿAlī commanded enough influence to found a political association with substantial support from Muslim notables in parts of Bengal and Bihar.

It was not until well after the creation of the Indian National Congress in 1885 that the need for a Muslim political organisation assumed greater urgency,[56] but the support it received from members of

[55] *Ibid.*, pp. 86–8.
[56] The government's Nagri resolution of April 1900 which allowed the use of the Devanagri script in conjunction with Persian, until then the language of official business between Britain and her Indian subjects, also acted as a major catalyst. Muslim political organisation and the need for a Muslim political association acquired a new intensity from then on. Robinson, *Separatism*, pp. 135–40.

the Aligarh establishment like Nawāb Mohsin-ul-Mulk, and later from others, like the Āgā Khān, was crucial in lending it momentum. Although both had previously expressed serious reservations about the merits of such an organisation, they came increasingly to share the view that it remained an indispensable condition of Muslim 'communal' representation.[57]

There were other developments as well which encouraged organised Muslim politics. Among these was the emergence of a number of 'young Muslim gentlemen' led by ex-Aligarh graduates like Maulānās Muhammad ʿAlī and Zafar ʿAlī Khān who pressed for a more independent stance vis-à-vis the government.[58] The Urdu–Hindi controversy which raged between 1900 and 1901 had a profound effect upon the outlook of these men. Many became deeply sceptical of the government's good faith and of its willingness to respond to Indian Muslims without the pressure of organised political action,[59] but, above all, they were aware that an authoritative Muslim organisation remained the only credible means to question Congress's claim to represent Indian Muslims.

The mood of this younger generation of Muslims was reflected in ever wider circles. Between 1901 and 1903 a series of attempts were made to establish a Muslim political party. One of the key figures behind these moves was Nawāb Viqār-ul-Mulk, whose appreciation of Sayyid Ahmad's loyalist stance was tempered by a degree of sympathy for those like Muhammad ʿAlī who stood for a more critical Muslim posture in relation to government.[60] Viqār-ul-Mulk's campaign for a Muslim political organisation was supported by others like Muhammad Shafīʿ, the prominent Punjabi barrister who was later to become instrumental in establishing the League's provincial branch in the Punjab.[61] Elsewhere, as in Bengal, Sayyid Amīr ʿAlī opted to cast his own political creation into oblivion in favour of a 'recognised organisation' that would express 'the sentiments and opinions of the Mohammedans as a body'.[62]

---

[57] *Ibid.*, pp. 147–8. Shan Mohammad, *Successors of Sir Syed Ahmad Khan: Their Role in the Growth of Muslim Political Consciousness in India* (Delhi, Idarah-i-Adabiyat-i-Delhi, 1981), pp. 26–7, 43, 80.

[58] Robinson, *Separatism*, pp. 138–40.

[59] On the origins of this controversy, *ibid.*, pp. 69–76.

[60] *Ibid.*, pp. 139–40. Viqār-ul-Mulk inaugurated the first of a series of branches of the Muhammadan Political Association at a meeting in Lucknow in October 1901. One of its stated objectives was 'to oppose the main demand of the Congress regarding representative government'. Zakaria, *Rise of Muslims in India*, p. 99. See also Shan Mohammad, *Successors of Sir Syed Ahmad*, p. 45.

[61] *Ibid.*

[62] Ameer Ali, 'India and the new Parliament' in K.K. Aziz (ed.), *Ameer Ali: His Life and Work*, part 2 (Lahore, Publishers United, 1968), p. 208.

It was during a session of the Muslim Educational Conference, originally founded by Sayyid Ahmad in 1886 as a medium to disseminate the views of the class of Muslim *ashrāf* opposed to Congress, that the All Indian Muslim League was formally established.[63] In December 1906, the Conference resolved to create a body that would henceforth constitute the sole authoritative representative of Muslim interests in India.[64] By doing so, many sought to restrict, once and for all, Congress's role as spokesman for Hindu, or at least non-Muslim, interests and thereby, implicitly, to reaffirm the essence of Sayyid Ahmad's own political credo.[65]

The Simla Memorial – an analysis

The question of whether or not the exclusively Muslim deputation that met the Viceroy, Lord Minto in Simla in October 1906, was a 'command performance'[66] engineered by British officials to encourage Muslim political aspirations as a counterweight to Congress;[67] or merely an idea that emerged independently among Muslims dissatisfied with the government's scheme for political reform,[68] has long been the subject of much controversy.

While the importance of these issues is not to be denied, attention here will focus primarily on an understanding of the Simla Memorial as expressive of the values that governed the Indo-Muslim notion of representation. Its purpose is to suggest that although Muslim attitudes to Western representation were clearly subject to considerable reassessment, Muslim discourse on representation was still shaped, if not constrained, by a set of normative considerations that was a part of

---

[63] Robinson, *Separatism*, pp. 125–6.

[64] The political rivalries that lay behind an organisation that was ostensibly designed to represent an Indian Muslim 'consensus' are examined in *ibid.*, pp. 147–9.

[65] In his address to the Muslim Educational Conference in December 1906, Nawāb Salīmullah, one of its principal conveners, declared that the creation of an exclusively Muslim party owed much to the existence of separate Muslim interests which had not, in the past, been adequately or justly represented. *Englishman Weekly Summary*, 3 January 1907, cited in Rahman, *From Consultation to Confrontation*, p. 37.

[66] A phrase first used with reference to the Simla Deputation by Maulānā Muhammad 'Alī in his presidential address to the Coconada session of the Indian National Congress in December 1923, *Congress Presidential Addresses* (Madras, Natesan, n.d.), volume 2, p. 620.

[67] M.N. Das, *India Under Morley and Minto*; Asoka Mehta and Anand Patwardhan, *The Communal Triangle in India* (Allahbad, Kitabistan, 1942); Lal Bahadur, *The Muslim League: Its History, Activities and Achievements* (Agra Book Store, 1954).

[68] Hafeez Malik, *Moslem Nationalism in India and Pakistan* (Washington, Public Affairs Press, 1963); Matiur Rahman, *From Consultation to Confrontation*; S.R. Wasti, *Lord Minto and the Indian Nationalist Movement*.

Muslim political thinking in India as elsewhere. Three features in particular stand out as reflections of these concerns. First, the Memorial's emphasis on communal representation which reaffirmed the primacy commonly accorded by Muslims to their communal group as the centre of political activity. Second, the demand for separate Muslim electorates which pointed to a vision of society as consisting of two exclusive political groupings – Muslims and non-Muslims. Finally, the Memorial's rejection of the 'law of numbers' which drew attention to the value that Muslims attach to moral righteousness, backed by Divine sanction, as the basis for political authority.

At the heart of the Simla Memorial lay the demand for the constitutional recognition of the communal group as the principal unit of representation.[69] It took as its starting point a critique of personal enfranchisement which, its authors maintained, reflected a grave limitation of 'institutions of the European type'.[70] Its application, they argued, would be 'entirely opposed to the genius and traditions of Eastern Nations' where the diversity of race and religion had always played an important role in the conduct of human politics.[71] Individuals in these societies, they claimed, acted as members of distinct communal groups and not as the autonomous units upon which much of 'western' representation was predicated. To demonstrate the force of their contention, the memorialists pointed to the effects of the existing system of personal enfranchisement which, they asserted, had encouraged Hindu voters to return Hindu candidates or such others as were likely to further Hindu interests.[72]

Like many of their predecessors in the late nineteenth century, these Muslims denied that individuals could be free agents in politics. Like them, they assumed that individuals were primarily members of religious groups and conducted themselves as such. This, and the allegiance individuals owed to their community, they argued, was what enabled groups with the largest number of members to succeed in

---

[69] A full text of the Address of the Simla Deputation is enclosed in Minto to Morley, 4 October 1906, *John Morley Papers*, volume 9. For an account of the political differences among those responsible for its formulation see Rahman, *From Consultation to Confrontation*, pp. 20–3.

[70] Address of the Simla Deputation, enclosed in Minto to Morley, 4 October 1906, *Morley Papers*, volume 9, paragraph 8.

[71] *Ibid.*

[72] It declared 'It is most unlikely that the name of any Mohammedan candidate will ever be submitted for the approval of the Government by the electoral bodies as now constituted unless he is prepared to forego the right of private judgement and undertake to vote with the majority in all matters of importance'. *Ibid.*

obtaining the greatest representation.[73] Equitable representation demanded, therefore, the enfranchisement of communal groups *as groups* regardless of considerations relating to size and number.

The memorialists' assertion that individuals in politics were prompted primarily by religious motives characteristic of their group as a whole, tended also to shape their conception of the role of the political representative. In theory, if not in practice, Western liberal representation has usually presumed that the representative acts in defence of individual, as against class or communal, interests.[74] In theory also, political representatives are deemed to be responsible to a variety of individual and group interests organised within territorially demarcated constituencies.[75] The Simla Memorial, however, categorically rejected these principles of 'western' representation. It maintained that a Muslim elected from communally mixed constituencies would be unrepresentative of his community and, at best, only 'a mere mandatory of the Hindu majority'.[76] Elected status could not, in itself, guarantee the 'substantive representation' of Muslims.[77] 'Really representative men' would emerge when Muslims themselves, organised as a separate electorate, were empowered to elect Muslim representatives.[78]

The memorialists' observations on the nature of representation point to a set of noticeably distinct assumptions from those which have commonly been associated with the practice of political representation in liberal-democratic societies. They supposed, firstly, that political representation was pre-eminently a descriptive activity, it existed when and so long as the representative could be held to be typical of his constituency. It implied that shared features signified shared values. It held that when a representative 'stood for' his constituency, he also 'acted for' it.[79] Secondly, they assumed that authentic political responsibility was a function of communal, that is to say, religious,

---

[73] 'Nor can we in fairness', they conceded, 'find fault with the desire of our Hindu fellow-subjects to take full advantage of their strength and vote only for the members of their community'. *Ibid.*

[74] Hanna Fenichel Pitkin, *The Concept of Representation* (Berkeley, University of California Press, 1972), pp. 190–208.

[75] A.H. Birch, *Representative and Responsible Government: An Essay on the British Constitution* (London, George Allen and Unwin, 1964), pp. 45–84.

[76] Address of the Simla Deputation, enclosed in Minto to Morley, 4 October 1906, *John Morley Papers*, volume 9.

[77] On the issue of 'substantive' representation see Pitkin, *The Concept of Representation*, pp. 209–40.

[78] Address of the Simla Deputation, enclosed in Minto to Morley, 4 October 1906, *John Morley Papers*, volume 9, paragraphs 8, 10, 11 and 12.

[79] On the notion of descriptive representation as 'standing for' see Pitkin, *The Concept of Representation*, pp. 60–91.

loyalty. The proper focus of a representative's concerns was deemed to be his communal group, and a system which postulated its separation from the political constituency was held to be profoundly unacceptable. It is of course true, as a number of assessments have made eminently clear, that the demand for separate Muslim electorates, and presumably its rationale, were shaped by sound political considerations. The members of the Simla Deputation were after all well-placed, politically conservative Muslims, many of whom subscribed to Sayyid Ahmad's view of Western representation as damaging to the political aspirations of the class of ashrāf Muslims to which they belonged.[80] At a time when hitherto accepted criteria of political influence and power were being increasingly questioned, it made sound political sense for these Muslims to opt for a system which, by focussing attention on their 'Muslim-ness', promised to guarantee them a measure of authority among their traditional followers.

No doubt colonial policy too had contributed much to the evolution of the demand for separate Muslim electorates. Colonial officials had readily resorted to a view of representation as a descriptive activity in order to draw attention away from representation as a substantive, creative activity. As such, communal representation could be seen to embody what was essentially a colonial understanding of representation as a measure of accurate correspondence between a representative and his constituency. Officials did not, of course, always define represent- ation along communal or religious lines – the category of landlords being a case in point – but they did constitute vital considerations which tended, more often than not, to override the economic and political interests common to a variety of different groups. This became especially marked after the creation of the Indian National Congress which sought, for the first time, to seriously question the official view of Indian representation.

An awareness of these issues must not however cloud the significance of other more intangible, but nevertheless real, concerns which underlay the demand for separate Muslim electorates. The question is not whether the Simla Deputation and its Memorial were consciously inspired by specifically religious concerns, but whether or not they expressed a view of the conduct and the ends of political action that can reasonably be construed as common to Muslim tradition. That this tradition formed an essential, and indeed authoritative, basis of the lives

---

[80] On the composition of the Simla Deputation and the background of those who were signatories of the Memorial see Rahman, From Consultation to Confrontation, pp. 8–9. See also Wasti, Lord Minto and the Indian Nationalist Movement, p. 70.

of these Muslims would appear not to be in doubt. Francis Robinson has drawn attention to the degree to which Sayyid Ahmad Khān and many of his associates were in fact 'men of deep faith'.[81] Some, like the poet Altāf Husain Hālī and the theologian Shiblī No'mānī, whose political influence upon later generations of Muslims cannot be underestimated, were dedicated to reviving pride in the grandeur and superiority of Islam.[82] Others, like the Nawābs Mohsin-ul-Mulk and Viqār-ul-Mulk were men known not only for their intellectual interest in issues of religious reform, but also for their intense piety and devotion to their faith.[83] Yet others, like Sayyid Husain Bilgrāmī, a close friend of Sayyid Ahmad, who is sometimes credited with the authorship of the Simla Memorial, although seemingly worldly were nevertheless deeply preoccupied with the traditions of the faith and its relation to a modern Muslim community.[84]

Given what we know of these men, it would be surprising if they did not sometimes draw upon a tradition they so highly valued and of which they were a part. It would be unusual indeed if, as Muslims, they did not regard the communal group as the proper object of a Muslim representative's concerns. It would be curious if they did not, as Muslims, take as axiomatic the notion that in order for there to be Muslim representation, representatives must *ex hypothesi* be Muslims.[85]

However, these were not the only issues that concerned the Muslim Deputation. Central to their Memorial was the contention that numerical criteria were wholly inadequate as the bases for representation and power. Numerical strength alone could provide no real measure of a group's political importance which, it was argued, depen-

[81] Robinson, 'Islam and Muslim Separatism', p. 92.
[82] Aziz Ahmad, *Islamic Modernism in India and Pakistan, 1857–1964* (London, Oxford University Press, 1967), pp. 77–86, 97–102.
[83] S.M. Ikram, *Modern Muslim India and the Birth of Pakistan* (Lahore, Shaikh Muhammad Ashraf, 1970), pp. 74–5; Shan Mohammad, *Successors of Sir Syed Ahmad Khan*, p. 91.
[84] Speaking at Aligarh College in February 1900, he declared '... we Mahomedans have received a nobler and more sacred inheritance than our secular literature and learning, namely our God and our Religion, and were our children to forget these in the turmoil of worldly pursuits however desirable, they shall surely perish...'. Nawāb Imād-ul-Mulk Bahādur, Syed Hossain Bilgrāmī *Speeches, Addresses and Poems* (Hyderabad, Government Central Press, 1925), p. 86.
[85] Hardy interprets this insistence upon a Muslim ruler, or representative, as the final means of containing 'teleological dualism', that is to say, the complete disassociation of the life of the Muslim community from the ends embodied in the Sharī'a. Peter Hardy, *Partners in Freedom and True Muslims. The Political Thought of Some Muslims Scholars in British India, 1912–1947* (Lund, Scandinavian Institute of Asian Studies, 1971), p. 19.

ded ultimately upon its historical role in society ι nd politics. What the memorialists clearly wished to stress was that any system of representation which failed to accommoda.c Muslim claims to power owing to the paucity of their numbers was fundamentally inadmissible. It was also, under the circumstances, profoundly unjust for it relied upon evidence that was highly contentious. They pointed to the existence of erroneous calculations which represented Indian Muslims as a fifth instead of a fourth of the total population, and maintained that these figures stemmed from the unjustified inclusion of parts of the population of Burma and of 'uncivilised portions... [including] Animists and other minor religions'.[86]

However it was clearly with the admission of subjective or 'nonnumerical' criteria as legitimate grounds for representation that the memorialists were more directly concerned. For them 'western' representation as it then existed in India, albeit in limited form, would continue to be problematic so long as it did not recognise the 'political importance' of Muslims in India. They proposed therefore that Muslims be granted representation not only in proportion to their actual numerical strength, but also in recognition of 'the prestige and the influence'[87] they exercised 'a little more than a hundred years ago'.[88] To them, as they presumed to many of their fellow Muslims in India, it was inconceivable that the bearers of an hitherto dominant tradition should be subject to those over whom they had once held sway.

As an expression of the sentiments of well-born Muslims, many of whom saw themselves as the repositories of Mughal *sharīf* culture, these views were far from surprising. The bulk of those who made up the Simla Deputation were, after all, products of a background steeped in Mughal values. Like Sayyid Ahmad Khān, they shared a keen appreciation of the worth of social status, high birth and wealth as essential qualities for the exercise of political influence and power.[89]

However there were other standards too which shaped and directed the Deputation's thinking. These had less to do with Mughal norms than

[86] Address of the Simla Deputation, enclosed in Minto to Morley, 4 October 1906, *John Morley Papers*, volume 9, paragraph, 5.

[87] *Ibid.*, paragraph 9.

[88] *Ibid.*, paragraph 5.

[89] This culture was certainly believed by some, like Sayyid Husain Bilgrāmī, to be 'intimately connected' with Muslim 'well-doing (sic) in the world'. 'We Mahommedans', he observed with some pride, 'have received from our ancestors the acknowledged gift of good manners. We have in our life time set an example to the world in this respect,... of dignified deportment and courtly manner – accomplishments that add to the worth and respect in which their possessors are held'. Address presented at Aligarh, 18 February 1900 in Bilgrami, *Speeches, Addresses and Poems*, pp. 87–8.

with the characteristic assumptions of Muslim political tradition. At heart lay the belief that Muslims were endowed with superior moral attributes which derived from their unquestioned obedience to God's Law and which qualified them especially for power. This is not to say that the memorialists consciously professed these claims: it is to suggest that their position on what was later to be referred to as Muslim 'weightage' exemplified a peculiarly Muslim conception of the basis of political power in society. It might also be argued, by the same token, that the memorialists' reservations on the 'law of numbers' as the determining factor in representative politics owed something at least to the notion common to Muslims which presumes that power ought to be the consequence of righteousness rather than of mere numerical clout. Traditional Muslim discourse in India as elsewhere has tended to be deeply sceptical of the merits of rule by majority on the grounds that it ignored the far more legitimate claims of moral force. The memorialists may not explicitly have drawn on Muslim values; but it is hard not to conclude that theirs was an appeal for the restoration of a moral force in politics which, as Muslims, they tended naturally to equate with members of their own community.

Separate electorates: the ideology of Muslim representation

The period between 1906 and 1909 witnessed a growing momentum among Indian Muslims in favour of separate Muslim electorates.[90] Although the public campaign, conducted mainly by the Muslim League, was given mainly to defending the political merits of the case, the demand for separate electorates reflected important intellectual concerns which had dominated Indo-Muslim thinking since the turn of the century. There were of course large numbers of Muslims, both 'traditional', like Maulānā Abū'l Kalām Āzād, and 'modern', like the eminent 'nationalist' Muslim and member of Congress, Dr. Sayyid Mahmūd, who chose not to support separate Muslim electorates. Their position however said more about their distinct vision of how modern Muslims met the challenge of Western civilisation and foreign rule than it did about their commitment to the values they shared with those of their fellow Muslims who opted for alternative political solutions. Like them, they partook as Muslims, of a common understanding of the purpose of human action and the limits within which that action assumed significance.

---

[90] For a comprehensive survey of these developments see Wasti, *Lord Minto and the Indian Nationalist Movement*, especially Chapters 2 and 5.

For Maulānās Muhammad 'Alī and Muhammad Iqbāl, both staunch advocates of separate Muslim electorates, these limits were unquestionably those imposed by a man's religious creed. In December 1908, Muhammad 'Alī told an assembly of the Muslim League that the demand for communal representation stemmed from the conviction that men's political orientations were directed and inspired by their religious faith.[91] That such inspiration could enrich the quality of men's political lives was also the dominant theme of much of the speculative and political writing of Amīr 'Alī and Muhammad Iqbāl. For the former, deeply concerned with the moral and political decline of his community, communal representation was essential to guarantee 'the value of communal life and activity'.[92] For the latter, it expressed Muslim 'communal consciousness' without which the 'civic significance' of the Muslim polity could not be fully realised.[93]

Iqbāl's emphasis upon the centrality of community was of course more complex than of Amīr 'Alī. He was after all deeply persuaded, in a way that Amīr 'Alī appears not to have been, that the essence of his faith lay in the growth of individuality.[94] At the same time, he was also certain that this growth could only occur within the community 'which is the source of my life and behaviour ... a living operative factor, in my present consciousness'.[95] Not surprisingly for one whose vision was essentially poetic, Iqbāl's conception of the relationship between the individual and his community is most fully elaborated in his contemplative poem *Rumūz-i-Bekhudī* (The Mysteries of Selflessness).[96] In it he expounds upon his notion of *millat* or community which postulates a homogeneity based on the ethics of a common faith while constituting also the centre of human activity and thinking. Although Iqbāl is loath to equate communal aspirations with the individual Muslim's desires, and goes so far as to recognise a degree of tension between the two, it is clear that he conceived of the ultimate 'good' in collective, not individual terms.[97]

[91] Muhammad 'Alī's address to the All India Muslim League, 31 December 1908, in S.S. Pirzada (ed.), *Foundation of Pakistan*, I (Karachi, National Publishing House, n.d.), p. 70.

[92] See his speech at Aligarh, 1908, in Aziz (ed.), *Ameer Ali*, part 2, p. 309.

[93] Muhammad Iqbāl's address to the All India Muslim League on 29 December 1930, in Pirzada (ed.), *Foundations of Pakistan*, II (Karachi, National Publishing House, 1970), p. 157.

[94] Anne-Marie Schimmel, *Gabriel's Wings* (Leiden, E.J. Brill, 1963).

[95] Muhammad Iqbāl's address to the All India Muslim League, 29 December 1930 in Pirzada (ed.), *Foundations of Pakistan* II, p. 158.

[96] Muhammad Iqbal, *Rumuz-i-Bekhudi The Mysteries of Selflessness*, translated by R.A. Nicolson (London, J. Murray, 1953).

[97] He believed that it was only within the community that the human self could attain the

The nature of the relationship between men's faith and the conduct of their politics which provided these Muslims with the conviction that communal representation was both worthwhile and necessary, was accepted as axiomatic even by those who refrained from its active espousal. For Maulānā Āzād, who stood out amongst a small group of eminent Muslims allied with Congress's nationalist politics, the question of the separation of religion from politics was more complex. Although Āzād recognised the power of religion in the conduct of men's lives[98] and endeavoured to lend it substance in the years which witnessed the rise of the *khilāfat* movement in India, he sought also, particularly in his later years, to impart to his religious faith a more universalistic dimension.[99] It is significant however that despite his efforts to conceive of a framework that would endorse the political co-operation of Muslims with non-Muslims, he remained committed to the consolidation of a separate, distinctly Islamic order in India. Although the objective of this autonomous order, or *imārat* was ostensibly to strengthen allegiance to a universal Muslim Caliphate, the assumptions upon which it was founded differed little from those which impelled the politics of separate Muslim electorates.[100]

However the views of Āzād and his colleagues in the Jamʿīyyat al-ʿUlamāʾ-i-Hind who also stood for a distinct Muslim order in India were by no means exceptional, nor can they be dismissed as merely the preserve of traditional-minded Muslims. Other, more worldly Muslims, like Mian Fazl-i-Husain, leader of the powerful Unionist Party in the Punjab in the 1920s and 1930s and Dr. Sayyid Mahmūd, an active member of Congress and a contemporary of Jawaharlal Nehru, also deferred to the authority of the religious tradition within which they were raised. Fazl-i-Husain's politics like Iqbāl's poetry, did not lend itself easily to a communal interpretation. His Unionist Party, although predominantly Muslim, was founded on avowedly non-communal principles. Yet, his defence of separate Muslim electorates is interesting precisely because it was couched in terms unusual for a man whose

perfection that was prophethood. Aziz Ahmad, *Islamic Modernism in India and Pakistan*, p. 152.

98 In his journal *Al-Hilāl* he wrote, in 1912, 'We have learnt all our politics from religion ... We believe that every idea which is derived from any source other than the Qurʾān is patent heresy, and this applies to politics also'. Quoted in Ali Ashraf, 'Khilafat Movement: A Factor in Muslim Separatism' in Mushirul Hasan (ed.), *Communal and Pan-Islamic Trends in Colonial India* (Delhi, Manohar, 1981), p. 72.

99 Aziz Ahmad, *Islamic Modernism in India and Pakistan*, pp. 175–85.

100 Maulānā ʿAbduʾl Halīm Siddīquī (Nazim, Jamʿīyyat al-ʿUlamāʾ-i-Hindi); *Jamʿīyyat al-ʿUlamāʾ-i-Hind ki chand ahm khidmāt-i-millī kā muhkhtsar tazkirā* (Delhi, Jamʿīyyat al-ʿUlamāʾ-i-Hind, 194–); Hardy, *Partners in Freedom*, pp. 32–6.

political impulses seemed otherwise to be ecumenical in style.[101] In March 1923, while initiating a Bill to extend separate Muslim electorates to local and municipal councils in the Punjab, Fazl-i-Husain acknowledged that 'religion is an important part of the individuality of the person and it is impossible to entirely ignore it'.[102] While few would deny that Fazl-i-Husain's politics were grounded in pragmatic rather than religious considerations, it is worth bearing in mind his commitment to the aims of influential bodies like the Lahore-based Anjuman-i-Himàyàt i-Islām which shaped some of the more persistent concerns of his political career. Of these, one of the most significant was his critical involvement in the foundation and promotion of the Islamia College in Lahore which served as a model for the extension of communal representation in institutions of higher education, and as a bastion of resistance against Congress's scheme for a unified system of 'national' education in the 1920s.[103]

Sayyid Mahmūd's devotion to his faith was, unlike Fazl-i-Husain's, less the result of any public endeavour than of his own upbringing. Born into a family of devout Muslims who were followers of the well-known leader of the *jihād* movements of the early nineteenth century in India, Sayyid Ahmad of Rae Bareilli, he showed a lifelong adherence to Islam.[104] Although Sayyid Mahmūd opposed separate electorates for Muslims and is said even to have been drawn to Jawaharlal Nehru's brand of secularism he confessed that his politics owed most to his concern for a strong 'Muslim bloc' in Congress.[105]

This notion of a 'Muslim bloc' whose ends were deemed to be inherently different from those of non-Muslims, was also crucial to Muslims who stood for separate Muslim electorates. For many, it signified the most accurate description of society as they were accustomed to regard it, that is, as a religious federation whose separate units shared a common space without a sense of a common purpose. In February 1907, Maulānā Muhammad 'Alī suggested that the demand

---

[101] Ayesha Jalal and Anil Seal, 'Alternative to Partition: Muslim Politics Between the Wars', *Modern Asian Studies*, 15, 3 (1981), pp. 425–6.
[102] Quoted in Azim Husain, *Fazl-i-Husain; a Political Biography* (Bombay, Longmans, Green, 1946), p. 185. See also Mushirul Hasan, 'Communalism in the provinces: A Case Study of Bengal and the Punjab, 1922–1926', in Mushirul Hasan (ed.), *Communal and Pan-Islamic Trends*, pp. 270–3.
[103] Ikram, *Modern Muslim India*, p. 214.
[104] V.N. Datta and B.E. Cleghorn (eds.), *A Nationalist Muslim and Indian Politics: Being the Selected Correspondence of the late Syed Mahmud* (Delhi, Macmillan, 1974), p. xii.
[105] *Ibid.*, p. xv. His lasting commitment to such a 'bloc' was expressed in his support of, and active participation in, the Muslim Majlis-e-Mashawarat in the 1960s. See Brass, *Language, Religion and Politics*, pp. 247–50.

for Muslim communal representation actually embodied an attempt 'unconsciously [to work] on the lines of a federation of religions'.[106] Nor was this an unusual sentiment. For, as he was later to confess to Gokhale, as a Muslim, 'denominationalism has no terrors for me'.[107] On the contrary, it reflected not only a realistic understanding of the lines of cleavage in India as denominational rather than territorial, but a recognition of 'the logical and correct division of the world . . . according to religion and religious communities'.[108]

For Iqbāl, communal representation was both desirable, because it protected 'the Islamic principle of solidarity', as well as necessary because 'the units of Indian society are not territorial' but religious. 'The principle of European democracy', he maintained, 'cannot be applied to India without recognizing the fact of communal groups. The Muslim demand for the creation of a Muslim India within India is, therefore, perfectly justified'.[109] There were other Muslims who shared this vision of societal organisation. The Āgā Khān, leader of India's large Shī'a Ismā'īlī community and an active proponent of separate Muslim electorates, also defended communal representation on the grounds that men's differences were not so much political as religious.[110] In December 1925, Sir 'Abdu'r Rahīm, one of Bengal's prominent Muslim politicians, explained what he thought to be the basis of Muslim communal representation. 'In our country', he told the annual session of the Muslim League, 'the majority and minority are sharply determined . . . by their respective religion, . . . in short by communalism and not at all by any political principles. . .'[111]

The purpose of drawing attention to these observations is not so much to demonstrate how often or indeed how consciously proponents of separate Muslim electorates expressed themselves in an explicitly religious idiom. It is rather to raise questions about the relation of

---

[106] See his lecture at Allahbad, 24 February 1907 in Mushirul Hasan (ed.), *Mohamed Ali in India Politics: Select Writings*, I (New Delhi, Alantic Publishers, 1982), p. 7.

[107] Muhammad 'Alī to G.K. Gokhale, 8 February 1908, *ibid.*, p. 25.

[108] Mohammad Sarwar (ed.), *Mazāmīn-i-Mohamed Ali*, I, p. 185, quoted in Ali Ashraf, 'Khilāfat Movement: A Factor in Muslim Separatism' in Hasan (ed.), *Communal and Pan-Islamic Trends*, p. 75. See also Muhammad 'Alī's proposals for a 'federation of faiths' where the religious prescriptions of each group would provide the bases of parallel systems of law. Muhammad Ali, *My Life: A Fragment*, edited by Afzal Iqbal (Lahore Shaikh Muhammad Ashraf, 1966), pp. 33–6.

[109] Muhammad Iqbal's presidential address to the All India Muslim League, 29 December 1930, in Pirzada (ed.), *Foundations of Pakistan*, II, pp. 158–9.

[110] Aga Khan, *India in Transition: A Study in Political Evolution* (London, Philip Lee Warner, 1918), p. 57.

[111] Sir Abdur Rahim's presidential address to the All India Muslim League, 30 December 1925, in Pirzada (ed.), *Foundations of Pakistan*, II, p. 55.

separate Muslim electorates to a tradition that has consistently denied the notion of a common political society or the desirability of a common law, other than one that is founded on Muslim principles. This is not to say that this tradition was not, like all traditions, subject to the political constraints of its time or that it did not witness, like others, both change and diversity among its followers. But whatever the real political interests that separate Muslim electorates were designed to protect (and there were many) and however varied the response of different Muslims to the issue, they did little to displace the authority of this tradition among its followers or the resilience of its assumptions in the conduct of their politics.

Although the demand for separate Muslim electorates was, in the first instance, concerned to defend a particular view of the organisation of society, it was also a statement about the nature of political consensus. The Simla Memorial was predicated on the premise that Indian Muslims were a community whose representation as such demanded that it elect its own, Muslim, representatives. It called for an end to Muslim 'mandatories' accountable to predominantly non-Muslim constituencies and emphasised the urgency of obtaining 'really representative' Muslims accountable to exclusively Muslim electorates.

In March 1908, the Muslim League formalised the gist of these demands by calling for measures which would enable 'Mohammedan voters to elect their own representatives' to legislative Councils and local boards.[112] Later that year, it asserted that mixed, non-denominational electorates precluded 'the successful election of the real representatives of the minorities' and resulted instead in 'the return of such members . . . as are only mandatories of the majority'.[113] At the heart of the League's claims lay the assumption that the political responsibility of the Muslim representative was an extension of his communal or religious obligation. The absence of a conceptual distinction between the two owed much to an understanding of political consensus as an agent of conformity designed to ensure the unity of Muslims. Historically, Muslims have sought to establish such consensus or *ijmāʿ* by pointing to a recognisable degree of unanimity among the body of religious scholars, the *ʿulamāʾ*. But this implied the acceptance of the *ʿulamāʾ* as the sole interpreters of a Muslim consensus – a condition that Muslim modernists in India, and elsewhere, in the late nineteenth century were no longer prepared to endorse. For them, the power to formulate consensus rested primarily with the community as a spiritual whole, although some Muslims like

---

[112] *Ibid.*, I, p. 32.
[113] *Ibid.*, p. 59.

Sayyid Ahmad Khān and Sayyid Amīr 'Alī were inclined to regard it as the prerogative of lay Muslims. But whatever the range of permutations concerning the issue of who ultimately was qualified to represent the Muslim consensus, few appeared to question its purpose as an instrument of social and political cohesion whose sources lay in the 'charismatic' quality of the Muslim community.

This notion of consensus was not, of course, acceptable to all Indian Muslims. Dr Sayyid Mahmūd expressed the opinion held by the body of 'nationalist' Muslims as far as prevailing ideas of consensus and communal representation were concerned. In February 1909, he wrote defiantly to Maulānā Muhammad 'Alī, 'We can elect as our representative even a Hindu if he is fit for our purpose'.[114] Whilst it is certainly useful to bear in mind the diversity that characterised Indo-Muslim thinking on separate electorates, it would be foolish to dismiss as self-deception the concern of Muslims who aspired to a form of representation which they believed to be consistent with the traditions of their faith. Men like Hakīm Ajmal Khān, who were known widely both for their piety and their 'modernism',[115] expressed serious reservations about an electoral system that presumed 'joint representatives' for 'all classes and creeds'. For them denominationally mixed electorates cut at the very heart of a substantive Muslim consensus by questioning a Muslim's obligation to speak 'solely' for his community.[116]

The idea that Muslim representation ought to reflect a substantive Muslim consensus was a persistent strain in the public campaign for separate Muslim electorates both in India as well as in Britain. The campaign owed much to the endeavours of Sayyid 'Alī Imām, the eminent Bihari barrister who acted as the League's chief negotiator with the Government of India between 1909 and 1910, and Sayyid Amīr 'Alī who headed the League's London branch until 1913.[117] Both men did

---

114 Syed Mahmud to Mohamed Ali, 26 February 1909, in Datta and Cleghorn (eds.), *A Nationalist Muslim*, p. 5.
115 Barbara Metcalf, 'Nationalist Muslims in British India: The Case of Hakim Ajmal Khan', *Modern Asian Studies*, 19, 1 (1985), pp. 1–28. See also M. Mujeeb, *The Indian Muslims* (London, George Allen and Unwin, 1967), pp. 533–6.
116 See his reception speech to the All India Muslim League session, 29 January 1910, in Pirzada (ed.), *Foundations of Pakistan*, I, p. 91.
117 This is not to say that others did not also engage in similar endeavours, albeit at a more modest level. One example was that of Muhammad 'Azīz Mirza, who, as a Secretary of the League in 1910, embarked upon the task of expounding the purpose of Muslim representation and the nature of a Muslim consensus by issuing a pamphlet cast in the form of a dialogue between a *maulānā* and a Muslim rustic. In it the *maulānā* defines Muslim representation as essentially a defence brief in a court of law, and asserts that even if the communal 'plaintiff' in question comprised *muqallid* and *ghair muqallid*, Shī'a and Sunni, it was nevertheless a *Muslim* community, bound by its belief in one

much to promote the view that Muslim representation depended fundamentally upon the community's exclusive right to elect Muslim candidates.[118] When Lord Morley suggested that his government might, in the interests of promoting a more cohesive political society in India, introduce a joint electoral college with a proviso for the statutory reservation of seats for Muslims, Muslims in India reacted sharply. The core of their objections was summed up by Sayyid 'Alī Imām. Morley's proposals, he maintained, were unacceptable because they assumed, as Muslims did not, that Muslim representatives could be truly representative without also being exclusively accountable to a Muslim electorate.[119]

Later in January 1909 Sayyid Amīr 'Alī, who led a Muslim League Deputation to the India Office in London, elaborated upon these objections. The Deputation's address, which was very likely to have been drafted by Amīr 'Alī, stressed that the 'nominees of another body, not altogether in agreement with Mohammedan opinions, cannot really or effectively represent Mohammedan wishes and feelings'....[120] At the same time, in a much publicised interview in *The Times*, Sayyid Husain Bilgrāmī, now something of an elder statesman among Muslims in India and a member of the Secretary of State's Council, asserted that Muslims elected from joint electorates were certain to represent the interests of a predominantly non-Muslim electorate instead of those in whose name they were ostensibly designated to act.[121]

It could be argued that the demand for separate Muslim electorates was, in essence, a radical plea for a form of substantive representation and as such consistent with the desired end, if not the final outcome, of political representation in Western representative democracies. Whilst it is likely that many Indian Muslims conceived of separate electorates in precisely these terms, it is questionable whether they did so on the basis of a conception of politics that would have been familiar to such democracies. For what rendered it distinct was its reference to the prevailing colonial discourse on representation and the normative considerations of a wider Muslim tradition. Colonial definitions of political representation which restricted its meaning to descriptive

God and the finality of his Prophet. Muhammad. 'Azīz Mirza, *Muslim Pālītiks* (Lucknow, All India Muslim League, 1910), p. 4.

[118] Wasti, *Lord Minto and the Indian Nationalist Movement*, pp. 166–90 and Rahman, *From Consultation to Confrontation*, pp. 116–55.
[119] See his speech while moving the third resolution of the All India Muslim League, 31 December 1908, in Pirzada (ed.), *Foundations of Pakistan*, I, p. 62.
[120] See the address of the Deputation of the London League to the Secretary of State, 27 January 1909, in Aziz (ed.), *Ameer Ali*, part 2, p. 318.
[121] *The Times*, 4 January 1909.

rather than creative forms of political activity, established the parameters within which the demand for separate Muslim electorates developed and took place. One of those who acknowledged these constraints was Sayyid Amīr 'Alī. In an essay on the direction of constitutional reform in India, published in 1910, he concluded that the demand for separate Muslim electorates was, among other things, the outcome of specific circumstances where legislation and government were unlikely 'to be delegated to any kind of representative assembly' for some time.[122]

However the imperatives of colonial domination were not the only considerations that prompted Muslims to insist upon separate electorates. No less important was a genuine concern with the unity of Muslims not only as a political objective in the context of colonial India, but as the very condition of 'Muslimness', that is to say, of a consciousness of one God, one Law and one Community. While it would scarcely be credible to maintain that the proponents of separate Muslim electorates were oblivious to the fragmentation of their community or indeed, that they always acted in a manner that was designed to counteract such fragmentation (Sayyid 'Alī Imām's political somersaults in 1909 being just one example),[123] the ideal of a community bound in substantive consensus seems never to have lost its powerful appeal. Muslim opposition to the Indian Councils Bill in April and May 1909 which failed to guarantee separate electorates for all Muslim candidates, brought together Muslims who otherwise shared little in common: 'western-educated and orthodox, Shia and Sunni, landlord, professional man, shopkeeper and priest all joined their voices to the protest'.[124] Although some did so from motives that had little or nothing to do with the promotion of Muslim consciousness, many are likely to have been moved by this consciousness and the urgency of obtaining it by political means.

However, this sense of Muslim consciousness was more complex than it appeared. For it reflected not only a sense of being Muslim, but also of being part of a superior culture whose definition had once been the preserve of a predominantly Muslim ruling class. Its significance for Muslim representation was recognised by officials at the very highest levels. The Viceroy, Lord Minto, had no hesitation in reassuring members of the Simla Deputation that 'your position should be

---

[122] Ameer Ali, 'The Constitutional Experiment in India', in Aziz (ed.), *Ameer Ali*, part 2, p. 339.
[123] Rahman, *From Consultation to Confrontation*, pp. 136–50.
[124] Robinson, *Separatism*, pp. 158–9.

estimated not only on your numercial strength but in respect of your political importance and the service it has rendered to the Empire'.[125] Although neither Minto nor his distinguished company cared to define the term 'political importance', it was to provide the single most compelling rationale for the representation of Muslims in excess of their actual proportion in the population.

Despite its obscurity, therefore, it is essential to obtain some coherent sense of what the notion signified to those who chose to uphold it. It is clear, for example, that for some Muslims the phrase 'political and historical importance' implied the participation of their community in a larger pan-Islamic world stretching from south-east Asia to the Middle East.[126] Others used it to emphasise their community's contribution to the 'social economy' of colonial India.[127] But above all, it seems, many relied upon the term to draw attention to the position that their community, or, more properly, sections of it had once occupied as the dominant power in the subcontinent. For them, it was this that entitled members of their community to a measure of substantial representation or 'weightage' in excess of their actual numerical strength.[128]

Political events at the turn of the century were undeniably crucial to the development of the demand for 'weightage'. The partition of Bengal in 1905 and the widespread political unrest it generated, persuaded officials of the need to obtain and cultivate whatever indigenous political support there was to be had. Many were tempted by the possibility of groups of influential Muslims who would be prepared to stand by the government in return for some concessions on the question of Muslim representation. Some believed, rightly or wrongly, largely as a consequence of the Mutiny, that Muslims were likely to react violently if some at least of their traditional privileges were not restored to them.[129]

Muslims working for separate electorates did not fail to seize upon these misgivings. Much was made, not all of it in innocence, of the military potential of Muslims in the subcontinent not only historically as rulers, but as subjects, in the service of the Raj. In an address in December 1908, that was clearly intended for official consumption,

[125] Minto's reply to the Simla Deputation enclosed in Minto to Morley, 4 October 1906, *John Morley Papers*, volume 9.

[126] See Sayyid 'Alī Imam's comments while moving the third resolution of the All India Muslim League, 31 December 1908, in Pirzada (ed.), *Foundations of Pakistan*, I, p. 61.

[127] See address of the Deputation of the London League to the Secretary of State, 27 January 1909, in Aziz (ed.), *Ameer Ali*, part 2, p. 319.

[128] See address of the Simla Deputation, paragraph 5, enclosed in Minto to Morley, 4 October 1906, *John Morley Papers*, volume 9.

[129] Some of these considerations are examined in Robinson, *Separatism*, pp. 163–9.

Sayyid 'Alī Imām underlined the government's good fortune in being able to rely upon Indian Muslims for 'the defence of the Empire', and to count upon them for their stability and political loyalty. Muslims, he hinted darkly, did not however expect the value of their loyalty to be taken lightly.[130] Others, like Amīr 'Alī, warned against the dangers of disregarding 'an asset' as crucial as 'Mohammedan loyalty'.[131] Mian Muhammad Shaf'ī, the blunt Punjabi spokesman for the League, also stressed that the time had come for the government to show its appreciation of the 'unswerving devotion' of Muslims 'to the Raj'.[132]

The full implications of just what Muslims intended to convey about their 'importance' was to become even more manifest when, in the Spring of 1909, the government announced that it intended to obtain additional Muslim representation from mixed rather than separate electorates. This met with a storm of protest from Muslims, many of whom clearly felt moved to adopt the language befitting of warrior-rulers. Rājā Naushād 'Alī Khān, secretary of the United Provinces' League, warned of a violent Muslim backlash such 'as to make one's hair stand on end'.[133] In a somewhat subtler vein, the Muslim League endorsed a resolution which called upon the government to grant additional Muslim representation on the basis of separate electorates or risk provoking 'a dynamic force'.[134] Sayyid 'Alī Imām, one of the movers of the resolution, 'trembled to pronounce the effects of any departure by the government of pledges towards the Muslims';[135] while Muhammad Shaf'ī warned the government that 'a breach of faith in an oriental country was a most dangerous thing'.[136]

By the summer of 1909, it was clear that the threat of Muslim unrest in India was beginning to have its effects upon government policy. The Indian Councils Bill of 1909 had provided Muslims with four out of twenty-seven elected seats on the Viceroy's Imperial Council.[137] These separately elected Muslim seats constituted a total of 14.8% as against 23% which represented the proportion of Muslims in

---

[130] Sayyid 'Alī Imam's speech at the All India Muslim League session, 31 December 1908, in Pirzada (ed.), *Foundations of Pakistan*, I, p. 61.
[131] See his letter to *The Times*, 14 January 1909.
[132] See Muhammad Shaf'ī's correspondence with Dunlop Smith in January, April and June, 1909, *Minto Papers Correspondence*, India 1909, volume 1, cited in Das, *India Under Morley and Minto*, pp. 234–7, 242.
[133] Quoted in Rahman, *From Consultation to Confrontation*, p. 127.
[134] The phrase used by Sayyid 'Alī Imām at an 'extraordinary' session of the Muslim League on 23 May 1909, quoted in *ibid.*, p. 136.
[135] *Ibid.*
[136] *Ibid.*
[137] Wasti, *Lord Minto and the Indian Nationalist Movement*, pp. 191–220.

the population of British India. By retaining the system of joint electorates for the election of Muslim candidates, however, the government hoped to obtain a total Muslim representation that would exceed the actual percentage of Muslims in the population.[138] But the extent of Muslim dissatisfaction and its ominous overtones persuaded officials both in Calcutta and in London that they would have to reconsider their proposals for Muslim representation. In London, the Āgā Khān and Amīr 'Alī battled relentlessly to convince the Secretary of State to re-open the question of Muslim representation. By October 1909 Morley had succumbed and, much against the Viceroy's own wishes, agreed, in the interests of justice and expediency, that Muslim representation on the Viceroy's Council should be raised to eight – a total of 29.6%.[139] In elections held under the terms of the new Act in January 1910, Muslims obtained a total of eleven candidates (separately and jointly elected) which brought the total Muslim representation on the Council to approximately 40.7% – well in excess of the actual proportion of Muslims in the population.[140]

The configurations of politics and the prospects of Council reform cannot however, in themselves, provide enough insight into other, more subtle considerations that contributed to the claim for 'weightage'. In September 1908, a deputation of the Deccan Provincial League explained to the governor of Bombay that it did not envisage the extension of 'weightage' to other communities as none were comparable to Muslims.[141] In October 1908, the Muslim daily, *Khabardār*, disseminated these views to a wider audience. It suggested that 'weightage' be restricted to Indian Muslims on the grounds that other minorities were unlikely to be endowed with the special attributes of Muslims.[142] The claim lay also at the heart of the Muslim League memorial submitted to the Secretary of State in London in January 1909. 'The position of the Muslim community', it asserted, 'has no analogy to that of the minor communities of India'. Muslim claims to representation and 'weightage' needed to be placed 'on a totally different footing' and 'be considered on a totally different basis'.[143]

What is most striking in these attitudes is the assumption that Muslims were a superior community imbued with special moral

---

[138] Rahman, *From Consultation to Confrontation*, p. 150.
[139] *Ibid.*, pp. 143–51.
[140] Minto to Morley, 6 January 1910, *John Morley Papers*, volume 23.
[141] Cited in Rahman, *From Consultation to Confrontation*, p. 88.
[142] *Ibid.*, p. 88, footnote 14.
[143] See the address of the London League presented to the Secretary of State, 27 January 1909, in Aziz (ed.), *Ameer Ali*, part 2, p. 319.

attributes. This belief owed much, at least among Muslims in the early twentieth century, to their espousal of the *sharīf* culture that had grown around the Mughal courts, and with which many of them were familiar. As participants of a culture that was predominantly, although by no means exclusively, associated with a Muslim ruling class in India, they took for granted their access to political power and influence.[144] Through this culture which assumed a distinctly cosmopolitan flavour particularly under the Mughal emperor, Akbar, social class came gradually to compete with explicitly religious criteria as a necessary condition for the dispensation of power. It implied the acceptance of non-Muslims, drawn from among society's well-born classes, who were willing to partake of and contribute to the development of this culture as members of the ruling elite.

These perspectives, in all their complexity, were to find their way into the question of 'weightage'. In December 1908 Sayyid 'Alī Imām, whose distinguished ancestry went back to the Mughal emperor, Aurang-zēb,[145] recommended the exclusion of 'the uncivilised portions of the country classified as Hindu' so as to obtain a form of representation that would be more acceptable to Muslims.[146] In January 1910, while re-assessing the implications of the Councils Act, Amīr 'Alī told members of the Muslim League in London that the 'juggling' with census figures had effectively deprived Indian Muslims of a share in political power that was commensurate with their 'historical and political importance'.[147] Such 'juggling' he contended, stemmed from the unjustified inclusion of India's lowly classes, namely the Chandals, Chamars and Musahirs, as parts of an already sizeable Hindu electorate.[148] Although both 'Alī Imām and Amīr 'Alī were admittedly most concerned with the effects of revised census figures upon the extent of Muslim represen-tation, they were manifestly disturbed by the degeneration of politics as the property of the ignoble. As those whose political preferences were directed by the norms of a cosmopolitan Mughal culture, they were inclined to believe that the business of government was the preserve of

---

[144] Underlining the significance of Muslim rule in India, Amīr 'Alī concluded 'It is idle to say that Mohammedans in India possess no historical importance . . . I may say again, without presumption, it is idle to say that they are of no political importance'. See his address to the London Muslim League in *ibid.*, p. 334.

[145] Robinson, *Separatism*, Appendix IV, p. 431.

[146] Sayyid 'Alī Imām's presidential address to the All India Muslim League, 30 December 1908, in Pirzada (ed.), *Foundations of Pakistan*, I, p. 48.

[147] See Amīr 'Alī's address to the London League on 23 January 1910, in Aziz (ed.), *Ameer Ali*, part 2, p. 336.

[148] See his letter to *The Times*, 14 January 1909, in *ibid.* p. 313. See also the address of the London League to the Secretary of State, 27 January 1909, *ibid.*, pp. 316–17.

'the best minds' in society, both Hindu and Muslim, and that such excellence was the consequence of high birth.[149]

However, social class and culture were only one aspect of the superiority with which these Muslims believed their community to be imbued. More central perhaps to their self-image was what Marshall Hodgson has described as 'the sense of the high ultimate destiny of Islam'.[150] Men like Sayyid Amīr 'Alī, Viqār-ul-Mulk, Muhammad Iqbāl, Maulānā Muhammad 'Alī, to name only a few, who were actively and passionately committed to the representation of Indian Muslims as a community, were also those who were deeply persuaded of the distinction and pre-eminence of their faith and of those who subscribed to it. The intellectual endeavours for which Amīr 'Alī and Muhammad Iqbāl are best known, the spirit of which they sought to express in the course of their political activity, are underpinned by a belief in the supremacy of Islam and the excellence of its prophet, Muhammad.[151]

Even those like Muhammad 'Alī for whom the consciousness of Islam is said by some to have been less pronounced (at least until his internment in 1915), seem rarely to have questioned their community's divinely endorsed claim to worldly power.[152] For although Muhammad 'Alī was inclined to the view that political power was not essential to sustain the spiritual resources of his faith, he was deeply reluctant to minimise its importance in the temporal life of his community.[153] To discern values derived from Muslim religious tradition in the formulation of political demands is not to engage in *ex post facto* analysis. At least one contemporary assessment of 'weightage' regarded it as 'tantamount to saying that it should be declared that Islam has something in it which is not to be found in other religions – a something which entitles the followers of Muhammad to special consideration'.[154]

---

[149] See the Memorial presented by the Deputation of the London League to the Secretary of State on 27 January, 1909, reproduced in 'Memoirs', *ibid.*, part 2, p. 603.

[150] Marshall Hodgson, *The Venture of Islam: Conscience and History in a World Civilization*, III (Chicago University Press, 1974), p. 351.

[151] Syed Ameer Ali, *The Spirit of Islam: A History of the Evolution and Ideals of Islam* (London, Christopher's, 1961) and Muhammad Iqbāl, *The Reconstruction of Religious Thought in Islam* (London, Oxford University Press, 1934).

[152] Mushirul Hasan, *Mohamed Ali: Ideology and Politics* (Delhi, Manohar, 1981), pp. 36–7, 41–3.

[153] *Ibid.*, p. 42.

[154] *Advocate* (Lucknow), 18 February 1909, *Selections from the Native Newspaper Reports, NWP & United Provinces.*

The official view of separate Muslim electorates

The acceptance of separate Muslim electorates by the colonial government remains one of the most controversial aspects of modern Indian historiography. There are, broadly speaking, two lines of argument. The first sees it as a classic expression of the policy of 'divide and rule';[155] others, in opposition, have treated it as the consequence of the social fragmentation of India and of the animosity between Hindus and Muslims.[156]

Neither explanation is entirely satisfactory.[157] While the former is inclined to over-emphasise the decisive role of official policy in shaping political events in colonial India, the latter rests on the dubious hypothesis that Muslim separatism was an inevitable consequence of existing social and religious divisions. A more fruitful approach to the question lies, we believe, in establishing the complex interaction between official perceptions of representation and its purpose in colonial India, and the 'model' of Muslim political action.

The central question confronting British officials at the turn of the century was whether, and to what extent, Western representation could be applied to a society like India. Many believed that the persistence of caste, race and religion as organising categories effectively precluded the extension of Western representative institutions. Others sought to deal with the problem by adapting a form of representation that would endorse the representation of 'interests' which was deemed to be more suited to Indians and India.

Among those preoccupied with the relationship between political representation and the 'natural' social order in India, was Herbert Hope Risley, Home Secretary to the Government of India from 1907 to 1909. Risley, whose role in shaping the reforms of 1909 is known to have been crucial, was a man deeply cognisant of the 'traditional patterns of social and political life' in India.[158] He was persuaded that these patterns

---

[155] Das, *India Under Morley and Minto*; Mehta and Patwardhan, *The Communal Triangle*; S. Gopal, *British Policy in India*.

[156] Hafeez Malik, *Moslem Nationalism in India and Pakistan*; Sayeed, *Pakistan: The Formative Phase*. There were also good reasons related to the internal politics of the Liberal Party in Britain which accounted for the acceptance of separate Muslim electorates by the colonial government. See Robinson, *Separatism*, pp. 169–70.

[157] For some studies less marked by the partisan nature of contemporary Indo-Pakistani historiography see Stanley Wolpert, *Morley and India, 1906–1910* (Berkeley, Los Angeles, University of California Press, 1967), and Stephen Koss, *John Morley at the India Office, 1905–1910* (New Haven, Yale University Press, 1969).

[158] Dietmar Rothermund, 'Emancipation or Re-Integration: The Politics of Gopal Krishna Gokhale and Herbert Hope Risley' in Low (ed.), *Soundings in Modern South Asian History*, p. 135.

demanded the 'representation of communities and interests' and suggested that such representation, far from being divisive as nationalists maintained, would ensure 'a sense of order and proportion in Indian society'.[159] He believed that the true end of representation, namely integration, could be obtained not by the creation of new and unstable constituencies dominated by Western-educated Indians, but by the consolidation of those existing social groups which had contributed, historically, to India's 'traditional' balance.[160]

This idea of a 'balanced' society as the end of political representation shared some of the features of eighteenth-century Whig theory. Order in society was presumed to be the outcome of a delicate equilibrium between the landed 'estates', the ecclesiastical hierarchy and the commercial classes.[161] These, and not individuals, were seen to be the constituent units of society: it was their 'interest' rather than the rational pursuits of individuals that were deemed to contribute to the common 'good'. Like his Whig forebears, and steeped in the ideas of the German historical school, Risley was inclined to believe that social peace would ensue only when India's 'traditional' classes were recognised as the real bases of social and political organisation and as the proper sources of legitimate political activity.[162]

Whilst these considerations were obviously important to some officials, many others believed that Muslim communal representation was a necessary, if regrettable, response to the inherent constraints of traditional Indian society as they understood it. Like John Stuart Mill, they assumed that India was a society still unfit for representative government;[163] like Charles Dilke, they were inclined to believe that India had yet to pass 'through the present transition stage from a country of many peoples to a country of only one'.[164] Even if some, like Lord Morley, were quite prepared to accept the principle of popular

---

[159] Ibid., p. 139.
[160] Ibid., pp. 143, 137.
[161] R.J. Moore, Liberalism and Indian Politics, 1872–1922 (London, Edward Arnold, 1966), pp. 42–62. See also his 'The Twilight of the Whigs and the Reform of the Indian Councils, 1886–1892', Historical Journal, 10, 4 (1967), pp. 400–14.
[162] Rothermund, 'Emancipation or Re-Integration' in Low (ed.), Soundings in Modern South Asian History, pp. 135–7.
[163] Of societies like India Mill wrote 'But there are others which have not attained that state [fitted for representative government], and which, if held at all, must be governed by the dominant country, or by persons delegated for that purpose by it. This mode of government is as legitimate as any other, if it is the one which in the existing state of civilization of the subject people, most facilitates their transition to a higher state of improvement'. J.S. Mill, Considerations on Representative Government (Chicago, Henry Regnery, 1962), p. 346.
[164] Sir Charles Dilke, Greater Britain, II (London, Macmillan, 1868), pp. 257–8.

reform along lines familiar to Britain, they too were led to conclude that ultimately 'the forms of government are much less important than the forces behind them'.[165]

Morley's close friend and confidante, Alfred Lyall, upon whom he relied for advice while dealing with an intransigent London League in February 1909, also shared these perceptions. Unlike Morley, however, Lyall appeared not to be beset with the intellectual dilemma that confronted Liberals on the question of popular representation for India. He wrote, 'I do not believe any system of electing members to the Councils by majorities can profitably produce a fair representation of the Indian people, whose whole society is founded upon divisions of religion and race...'[166] Others like Lord Asquith, the Liberal minister closer in heart to Morley, observed that even if separate Muslim registers did appear 'objectionable' from the advanced vantage point of Britain, they remained the only practical solution for a society still characterised by traditional social affiliations.[167]

There were other considerations as well. Separate Muslim electorates appeared to fit neatly into the mould of descriptive representation which had for so long led officials and Indians to assume that 'real' representation was a matter of accurate correspondence. The notion that separate electorates embodied a form of 'true' representation in the Indian context was a theme taken up by influential sections of the media as well as established commentators on Indian affairs in Britain, who tended usually to be retired civil servants. A *Times* editorial warned in January 1908 that Morley's scheme for a joint electoral college would result in 'illusory representation'. It went on to observe, 'the type of Muslim who secures Hindu support secures it by virtue of his utility to Hindu rather than Muslim interests; yet this is the type most likely to be elected under the provisions of the scheme'.[168] Others, like Sir Valentine Chirol and A.E. Duchesne, concluded that without separate electorates, Muslim representation would be reduced to a mockery characterised by 'puppet' Muslim representatives.[169]

---

[165] John Morley, 'Democracy and Reaction', *The Nineteenth Century and After*, 62 (1905), p. 538.
[166] Lyall to Morley, 15 February 1909, *John Morley Papers*, 49, quoted in Robinson, *Separatism*, p. 170, footnote 5.
[167] See Asquith's speech in the House of Commons, 1 April 1909, *Hansard's Parliamentary Debates* (Commons) (1909), volume 3, column, 533.
[168] *The Times*, 29 December 1908.
[169] See A.E. Duchesne, 'The Indian Mohammedans and the Reforms', *Empire Review*, 17, 100 (1909), pp. 254–63 and Sir Valentine Chirol, *Indian Unrest* (London, Macmillan, 1910), p. 128.

Whilst some officials saw communal representation as a measure designed to preserve the 'traditional' stability of Indian society, and others as essential to guarantee substantive Muslim representation, it is important not to lose sight of the explicitly political considerations that dictated official policy. The search for political allies during the widespread unrest which followed the partition of Bengal prompted growing numbers of officials to consider more seriously Muslim demands for concessions on representation. Some believed that Indian Muslims constituted 'a strong conservative element' whose enlistment 'as allies and auxiliaries on the side of the British government' should be obtained at whatever cost.[170] Others felt that separate electorates were definitely a lesser evil when compared to the prospects of a 'Mussalman Jehad'.[171]

The preoccupation with separate Muslim electorates tended to overwhelm all other issues relating to Muslim representation. This was certainly the case as concerned the question of 'weightage'. In a preliminary statement to the House of Commons in December 1908 T.R. Buchanan, the Under Secretary of State for India, scarcely touched upon the potential problems posed by 'weightage' for Muslims as a basis for the proposed reforms in Indian representation.[172] Few appeared to query the justice of a claim to representation grounded in patently subjective considerations.[173] Even those like Morley who believed that numerical strength alone should determine representation, were led to concede that 'modifying influences' would be necessary to estimate the degree of Muslim representation.[174]

This apparent lack of any real concern for the wider implications of 'weightage' for Muslims is less surprising if one considers that the notion of special claims to representation was by no means unfamiliar to colonial discourse. The participation of the 'natural leaders' of Indian society in a process of mutual consultation between rulers and subjects had become a common theme in the debate on Indian representation, particularly after the Mutiny. Although the representation of India's 'natural leaders' was never formalised as 'weightage' was later to be,

[170] Lyall to Morley, 4 February 1909, *John Morley Papers*, 49, quoted in Robinson, *Separatism*, p. 170.
[171] Gilbert Martin, *Servant of India* (London, Longman, 1966), p. 56.
[172] See Buchanan's speech in the House of Commons, 17 December 1908, *Hansard's Parliamentary Debates* (Commons) (1908), volume 198, column 2158.
[173] A notable exception was A.J. Balfour. See his speech in the House of Commons, 26 April 1909, *ibid.* (1909), volume 4, columns 53–5.
[174] See Morley's reply to the Deputation from the London League in *The Times*, 28 January 1909.

nor held to apply exclusively to Muslims, it presumed, as did 'weightage', that social class was a legitimate basis for political power and representation in India. Here it is perhaps worth noting that those Muslims upon whom officials had customarily relied as interpreters of society and politics, were for the most part men of influence and wealth; Sayyid Amīr 'Alī, the Āgā Khān and the Raja of Mahmūdabād to name only a few. They tended also to be those whom officials associated, naturally, with the former ruling classes and with the image of Muslim dominance in India. Although aristocrats were by no means the preserve of Indian Muslims, officials appear to have been influenced by prevailing historiography which tended to regard the differences between Hindus and Muslims as much in religious as in social terms. 'What was assumed all along ... was that with the advent of the Arabs and the Turks into India, a valid distinction could be made between rulers and ruled on cultural and social grounds'.[175]

It is likely that if British officials did not fundamentally question the legitimacy of Muslim 'weightage' it was because they regarded Muslims as the 'gentlemen' of the East, entitled to special consideration. In this sense, 'weightage' was the manifestation of a shared affinity between India's past rulers and its present masters. It embodied, in the words of Lord Ampthill, a common desire to protect Indian Muslims from the 'humiliation' of having 'to seek favours from a peasantry or proletariat in the hope of being invited by the Government to take part in their deliberations'.[176]

[175] J.S. Grewal, *Muslim Rule in India: The Assessments of British Historians* (Calcutta, Oxford University Press, 1970), p. 168. See also Kenneth Ballhatchet, *Race, Class and Sex under the Raj: Imperial Attitudes and Policies and their Critics, 1793 1905* (London, Weidenfeld and Nicolson, 1980).

[176] See Lord Ampthill's speech in the House of Lords, 23 February 1909, *Hansards Parliamentary Debates* (Lords) (1909), volume 3, columns 159–60.

5

Representation and consensus
the Muslim League,
1909–1939

One important consequence of the League's involvement in the movement for separate Muslim electorates was its claim to be the authoritative spokesman for Muslim India. Much of the authenticity of this claim stemmed from the government's recognition of a party whose political impulses and understanding of representation were congruent with colonial policy and official notions of representation. Yet, developments within the League after 1911, and its steady political decline among Muslims in the Punjab and Bengal, seriously eroded its claim to speak on behalf of Muslim India. However, its resilience during these years can largely be explained by the hold of a 'modernist' tradition among Muslims in India, which tended to interpret the idea of *ijmā'* as the prerogative of a lay community and as a form of consensus that was distinct from one founded on explicitly democratic criteria.

The League's representative standing in the early years owed much to its commitment to British rule in India.[1] This was particularly significant at a time when anti-British feeling in Congress was running high on the question of the partition of Bengal. The predominance within the League of Aligarh Muslims, who were closely associated with Sayyid Ahmad's loyalist politics, also encouraged colonial officials to regard it with particular sympathy.[2] Their perception of the League as the model of unqualified political support for a British presence in India was critical to the influence it exercised in official circles in later years. This is all the more noteworthy as the party itself underwent important

---

[1] At its first session in December 1906, the League resolved 'to promote among the Mussalmans of India, feelings of loyalty to the British Government, and to remove any misconception that may arise as to the intention of Government with regard to any of its measures', *Home (Public) Proceedings*, February 1907, volume 7587, quoted in Matiur Rahman, *From Consultation to Confrontation: A Study of the Muslim League in British Indian Politics, 1906–1912* (London, Luzac, 1970), p. 38.

[2] Many were also 'men of property and influence'. See Francis Robinson, *Separatism Among Indian Muslims: The Politics of the United Provinces' Muslims, 1860–1923* (Cambridge University Press, 1974), p. 148, footnote 4. For their hold over the party in its early years see Rahman, *From Consultation to Confrontation*, pp. 52–60.

changes in the 1920s and 1930s which rendered it, or at least important sections of it, neither manifestly loyal to government nor ostensibly representative of Indian Muslims.[3]

However, if the League's representative credentials after the First World War were questionable, its standing as the pre-eminent Muslim organisation in India, at least until 1916, seemed not to be at issue. The conclusion of the Lucknow Pact with Congress in 1916 was an important measure of the League's political standing. For it not only obliged Congress to accept separate Muslim electorates, which it had always roundly condemned as detrimental to the evolution of a common political society, but it also established the League as the authoritative representative of Muslim interests.[4] More importantly, it implicitly restricted Congress' role to one of spokesman for a predominantly Hindu, or non-Muslim, constituency. This was to contribute substantially to the League's contention that Congress was essentially a Hindu, that is to say a non-Muslim, party, fundamentally unqualified to represent Muslim interests.

The League's bid to pose as the exclusive representative of Muslim interests in India in 1916 was vastly enhanced by the absence of rival Muslim groups, with the exception, that is, of the handful of 'nationalist' Muslims allied with Congress, who challenged its authority. The introduction of political reforms in 1919 which brought power to the provinces, led however to the emergence of competing Muslim parties with substantial bases of support in Muslim majority provinces like Punjab and Bengal. As a party whose support was drawn chiefly from Muslims in the United Provinces, Bombay and Bihar, the League could do little to check its own political demise in the 1920s.

There were other developments too which had a direct bearing upon the League's claim to represent Indian Muslims. The post-War period witnessed the rise to prominence of Mahatma Gandhi and a new style of politics which went by the name of 'non-cooperation'. At the same time, the humiliation of Turkey by the Allied Powers and Muslim concern about the fate of the Ottoman Caliph, led growing numbers of Muslims to become disillusioned with the government's policies. The League's traditional loyalism and its brand of 'drawing-room' politics became less

---

[3] For the emergence of a 'young party' more critical of government and its impact upon the League see Robinson, *Separatism*, pp. 236–344. For an account of the tenuous representative standing of the League in the 1930s see Ayesha Jalal, *The Sole Spokesman: Jinnah, The Muslim League and the Demand for Pakistan* (Cambridge University Press, 1985), pp. 7–50.

[4] Hugh Owen, 'Negotiating the Lucknow Pact', *Journal of Asian Studies*, 31, 3 (1972), pp. 561–87.

relevant and were no longer credible. Many turned to the political activism of a younger generation of Western-educated Muslims and were increasingly drawn to those, like the *'ulamā'*, who promised a more effective defence of the faith and of its institutions.[5]

If it is the case that the political standing of the League in the 1920s and early 1930s could not sustain its representative claims, how then did it come to exercise such a decisive influence upon the subsequent course of Muslim politics in the 1940s? Few would deny that the abolition of the Caliphate in 1924, or the prospects of change at the centre, were crucial to the resuscitation of the League; but explanations of its resilience must also be sought in the concerns of a religious and political tradition which were congruent with prevailing official definitions of representation. In the period leading up to the War, the League's representative claims hinged almost exclusively upon a notion of descriptive representation fostered and developed by official thinking on Indian representation. What was emphasised was the League as a Muslim organisation whose 'Muslimness' was deemed by officials to be a sufficient criterion for representation. This is not to say that explicitly political considerations, namely the League's loyalist credo, were not important to obtain for it the recognition that it aspired to. Nor is it to deny that many of its own members did not also believe that 'real' Muslim representation was conditional upon there being Muslim representatives, or an avowedly Muslim organisation. Whilst both these factors were clearly indispensable to sustain the political claims of the League, it is in their relation to a highly developed colonial 'ideology of representation' that a more complete picture of the League as a 'representative' organisation is to be found.

In the 1920s and early 1930s, other kinds of concerns came also to have a significant bearing upon the League's right to speak on behalf of Indian Muslims. There were two issues in particular that tended to dominate Muslim discourse on representation in this period. Both had been central to Indo-Muslim political thinking on *ijmā'*, or consensus, and both were to account decisively for the League's claim to represent Indian Muslims. The first concerned the right of the *'ulamā'* to constitute *ijmā'* and to represent a modern Muslim community. The question assumed particular relevance during the *khilāfat* movement of the early 1920s. The Indo-Muslim modernist tradition within which the League was firmly established had sought, since the late nineteenth century, to redefine the classical understanding of *ijmā'* by denying that it could be

---

[5] Gail Minault, *The Khilafat Movement: Religious Symbolism and Political Mobilization in India* (New York, Columbia University Press, 1982), pp. 45–67.

the exclusive preserve of the *'ulamā'*. Indeed, some Muslims like Sayyid Ahmad Khān and Amīr 'Alī had gone so far as assert that *ijmā'* was the prerogative of the lay community. The hold of this tradition with its emphasis upon the right of lay Muslims to constitute *ijmā'* and to express the consensus of the community was far from eroded in the 1920s. Although large numbers of lay Muslims, most notably the Western-educated, did indeed turn to the *'ulamā'* as political allies and, sometimes, religious guides,[6] many were clearly unwilling to accept a restoration of their traditional role as spokesmen for the community. It was by drawing upon this modernist interpretation of *ijmā'* that the League was able, as an almost exclusively lay party, to re-establish its claim to represent Indian Muslims.

However there was another, more complex dimension to the modernist understanding of *ijmā'*. This concerned a profound unwillingness to equate a Muslim consensus with a democratic majority. The significance of this question, and its bearing upon the representative standing of the League, emerged sharply following the provincial elections of 1937 when the electoral losses of the League in the Punjab and Bengal, appeared decisively to undermine its political credibility. Yet, what is particularly noteworthy about this period is precisely the affirmation of the League as a 'representative' organisation. It suggests a renewed concern to uphold a specifically Muslim conception of consensus whose ultimate sanction, as opposed to a democratic consensus, was seen to lie beyond the force of numbers. This was not, however, some commonplace theory of minority rule, although it is clear that the League itself spoke only for a minority of Indian Muslims at the time. Rather, it reflected some of the ambivalence which had already characterised Indo-Muslim modernist thinking in relation to the norms of Western popular democracy. For while Muslims like Muhammad Iqbāl were loathe to restrict the right to constitute *ijmā'* to a minority, namely the *'ulamā'*, they were deeply sceptical about the merits of reducing the idea of a Muslim consensus to the rules of 'arithmetical democracy'. Furthermore, whilst men like Jinnah clearly recognised the League's failure to meet the democratic criteria which alone could substantiate its claim to speak on behalf of Indian Muslims, they too were persuaded that such criteria could not, in the final analysis,

---

[6] The most notable example being the relationship between the 'Alī brothers, Shaukat and Muhammad, and Maulānā 'Abdu'l Bārī of Firingī Mahal. Mushirul Hasan, *Mohamed Ali: Ideology and Politics* (Delhi, Manohar, 1981), p. 66 and Robinson, *Separatism*, p. 212. See also Afzal Iqbal, *The Life and Times of Mohamed Ali* (Lahore, Institute of Islamic Culture, 1974), pp. 336–41, for an account of their subsequent estrangement over the issue of 'Ibn Saūd and his Wahhābī policies in the Hejaz.

constitute the basis of an authentic Muslim consensus. For what mattered, ultimately, was not the sum of votes cast, but the espousal of that which was deemed to be Islamically 'just'.

The League's claim to representation, 1909–1918

The creation of the Muslim League in December 1906 was undertaken on the premise that it constituted the authoritative voice of Muslim India.[7] Its founder members, many of whom had participated in the Simla Deputation which Lord Minto had described as a 'representative gathering',[8] lent it a degree of pre-eminence that few Muslim organisations had commanded. The inclusion of Muslims like the Āgā Khān [9] and the Rājā of Mahmūdabād whose influence and wealth prompted officials to treat them as 'natural leaders' of Indian society, also added something to the weight of its claims. It was the Āgā Khān, for example, who persuaded the Governor of the United Provinces, J.P. Hewett, in 1909 to accept the League as the sole authority on all matters concerning Indian Muslims.[10] The government's trust in a party whose leadership tended, on the whole, to be instinctively loyal was also reflected in the Viceroy's judgement of the League as 'a very representative Muhammedan body'.[11]

Whilst it may be true that the League's status in official circles was enhanced by the participation of trusted friends of the government like the Āgā Khān, its credibility on the question of Muslim representation owed much more to its espousal of an understanding of Indian society that was familiar and acceptable to contemporary official discourse. The League's emphasis upon its role as a Muslim organisation, designed to represent Muslim interests, endorsed the social and political diversity which lay at the heart of official thinking on Indian representation.[12] It

---

[7] Rahman, *From Consultation to Confrontation*, pp. 36–7.
[8] See Minto's reply to the Simla Deputation, enclosed in Minto to Morley, 4 October 1906, *John Morley Papers*, MSS. EUR D. 573, volume 9.
[9] The Āgā Khān's enthusiasm for the League, as the expression of Muslim political organisation, was, however, distinctly lukewarm. His financial support for the party was limited and he did not attend any of its sessions until 1910. Robinson, *Separatism*, p. 150.
[10] Hewett to Minto, 3 February 1910, *Minto Papers Correspondence, India, 1910*, volume 1, cited in Rahman, *From Consultation to Confrontation*, p. 180.
[11] Minto to Hewett, 15 February 1910, *Minto Papers Correspondence, India, 1910*, cited in *ibid.*, p. 181.
[12] See Nawāb Salīmullah's speech on the first resolution passed by the All India Muslim League on 30 December 1906, in S.S. Pirzada (ed.), *Foundations of Pakistan: Documents of the All India Muslim League*, I (Karachi, National Publishing House, n.d.), pp. 6–9.

assumed that representation was pre-eminently a function of correspondence and that it existed when and if such correspondence could be established between the representative and those he claimed to represent. It implied a notion of representation which stressed its descriptive quality and undervalued its significance as a substantive activity involving creative political action. When applied to a highly fragmented society like India, it tended to hinder the development of political consensus by encouraging different groups to believe that their interests could best be secured by representatives drawn exclusively from amongst themselves. Thus, even as the League's founder members paid lip service to the value of inter-communal co-operation, they were concerned foremost with ensuring that Muslim representatives acted in keeping with the notion of a 'community' endowed with its own 'religious, social and ethical ideals'.[13]

Official notions of representation did not, however, merely provide a rationale for the representation of sectional interests. Far more significant was the degree to which they contributed to the confusion of crucial conceptual definitions which enabled avowedly communal organisations like the League to claim that being representative of Indian Muslims was synonymous with actually representing Indian Muslims. The early sessions of the League point overwhelmingly to the impression that the majority of its members assumed that the League's unquestionable credentials as a Muslim party amounted to its designation as a party which represented Muslims.[14]

However, there were clearly other reasons apart from those which stemmed from the prevailing 'ideology of representation' which prompted officials to accept the League as a representative Muslim organisation. Here the significance of the League's political heritage as a party nurtured within the tradition of loyalist politics associated with Sayyid Ahmad Khān cannot be lightly dismissed.[15] For it was by no

---

[13] The Āgā Khān's presidential address to the All India Muslim League, 29 January 1910, *ibid.*, p. 101.

[14] At its first session, in December 1906, Nawāb Salīmullah drew attention to 'this meeting composed of Mussalmans from all parts of India' dedicated to 'protect and advance the political rights and interests of the Mussalmans of India'. *Home (Public) Proceedings*, February 1907, volume 7587, quoted in Rahman, *From Consultation to Confrontation*, p. 38. See also the presidential address of Sir Adamjee to the All India Muslim League, 29 December 1907, in Pirzada (ed.), *Foundations of Pakistan*, I, pp. 17–20 and Sayyid 'Alī Imām's presidential address to the All India Muslim League, 30 December 1908, *ibid.*, pp. 49–50.

[15] This was not, of course, obvious at the start when initiatives taken by the Bengali Muslim establishment, led by Nawāb Salīmullah, to found a Muslim political organisation, threatened to upstage the conservative Aligarh leadership, dominated

means the case that Muslims associated with the League were the only ones concerned to protect the interests of their fellow-Muslims. Others, like the small group 'nationalist' Muslims led by Badruddin Tyabjī from Bombay, were also committed to the representation of Muslim interests, although they believed that this could best be obtained by working within Congress.[16] Yet others, with potential claims to the leadership of Indian Muslims, were groups of influential *'ulamā'* associated with the seminaries at Deoband and the Nadvāt-ul-'ulamā' in Lucknow, although they tended to believe that the survival of Indian Muslims depended less upon political, than upon religious, reform.[17] While there might be a temptation to exaggerate the differences between these groups of Muslims,[18] there is no doubt that Sayyid Ahmad's commitment to Muslim modernisation in the service of government encouraged officials at the highest levels like the Viceroy, Lord Minto, to declare, 'We have much to gain politically by our goodwill to Mussalman enlightenment'.[19]

Official enthusiasm for the League as an authoritative Muslim organisation was, however, to diminish steadily by the second decade of this century. Political events at home and abroad were to decisively alter the political orientations of the League at its highest levels. Although the party's more established notables, like the Āgā Khān, the Nawāb of Dacca and Sayyid Amīr 'Alī, continued to gain privileged access to the corridors of official power in Calcutta and London, they were unable to stem the growing tension that now existed between the government and the League. Much of it reflected a wider Muslim dissatisfaction with government policy in India. In 1911, the government revoked the

by Nawābs Mohsin-ul-Mulk and Viqar-ul-Mulk. The means by which the men from Aligarh succeeded in fashioning an organisation 'in their own image', is discussed in Robinson, *Separatism*, pp. 147–50. As late as 1917, those who were to continue to dominate the League's politics were still deeply conscious of being 'the first born of Sir Sayyid and Aligarh'. Mohamed Ali to the Raja of Mahmudabad, 16 April 1917, quoted in Minault, *The Khilafat Movement*, pp. 53–4.

[16] Tyabjī clearly believed that for Muslims in India, 'the proper course is to join the Congress and take part in its deliberations from our peculiar stand-point'. Tyabji to Amir Ali, 3 December 1887, quoted in Anil Seal, *The Emergence of Indian Nationalism* (Cambridge University Press, 1971), p. 332.

[17] Barbara Metcalf, *Islamic Revival in British India: Deoband, 1860–1900* (Princeton University Press, 1982). On the Nadvāt-ul-'Ulamā', *ibid.*, pp. 335–47.

[18] Minault, who has drawn attention to this, writes, 'The contrast between the traditional and the Westernizing cultural movements, however, should not be overstressed. More significant are the parallels in their development which show the interconnection between early cultural and educational movements and later political associations'. Minault, *The Khilafat Movement*, p. 12.

[19] Minto to Morley, 29 July 1908, *Morley Papers*, 16, quoted in Robinson, *Separatism*, p. 167.

partition of Bengal causing intense resentment among Bengali Muslims who had benefited hugely from the creation of a separate province.[20] In 1912, it provoked the anger of Western-educated Muslims in the United Provinces by refusing to accept a Muslim University at Aligarh without effective government control.[21] In the summer of 1913, the government's handling of the issue surrounding the demolition of a mosque in the northern town of Kanpur led to serious disturbances among the Muslim population, some of which resulted in the loss of Muslim lives.[22]

Things were no better on the international front. Britain's involvement in the Balkan Wars generated widespread concern among Indian Muslims who were unhappy about the treatment of Turkish troops. Many were disturbed by Britain's declaration of war in 1914 against the Turkish Sultan whom they regarded as the Caliph of Islam. Finally, Britain's support for the Arab revolt of 1916 and her failure to guarantee the sanctity of Muslim holy places in the Arab Peninsula, convinced large numbers of Indian Muslims that the true intent of Britain's Turkish campaign was far from honourable.[23]

The cumulative effect of these events upon the Muslim League was dramatic. It called into question, more urgently than ever before, the wisdom of pursuing a policy of sustained loyalty to Britain and her Indian Government. A younger generation of Muslims in the League emerged to denounce the moderation of their political elders. Many rejected the value that had once been attached to government patronage as a means of securing the interests of their community, and called for self-government for India. Indeed, what is significant about developments at this time is that it was sections of the League, rather than Congress, that seized the initiative in the movement towards self-government.[24] In provincial branches across India the trend was

---

[20] Mushirual Hasan, *Nationalism and Communal Politics in India, 1916–1928* (Delhi, Manohar, 1979), p. 52.

[21] Gail Minault and David Lelyveld, 'The Campaign for a Muslim University, 1898–1920', *Modern Asian Studies*, 8, 2 (1974), pp. 145–88.

[22] Robinson, *Separatism*, pp. 212–15 and Minault, *The Khilafat Movement*, pp. 46–8.

[23] Robinson, *Separatism*, p. 204; Minault, *The Khilafat Movement*, p. 52.

[24] By March 1913, well before the consolidation of Congress's 'Home Rule Movement', the League had already gone as far as to call for 'the attainment under the aegis of the British Crown of a system of self-government suitable to India'. Reginald Coupland, *The Indian Problem*, part I (New York, Oxford University Press, 1944), pp. 46–7. Sayeed reminds us however that the League's vision of self-government continued to distinguish between 'the kind of unadulterated representative government that the Congress was agitating for, and the sort of representative government modified by reservations and separate electorates that the Muslim League believed in'. Khalid bin Sayeed, *Pakistan: The Formative Phase* (London, Oxford University Press, 1968), p. 37.

unmistakable. In Bengal, H.S. Suhrawardy and Fazlul Haq called upon Muslims to adopt an independent stance against government;[25] in the United Provinces, a radical faction led by Maulānā Muhammad 'Alī and Zafar 'Alī Khān argued against the League's loyalist credo and pressed for a rapprochement with Congress;[26] while in the Punjab, the League's 'old guard' were on the defensive against newly politicised young Muslims like Mian Fazl-i-Husain who favoured co-operation with Congress.[27]

International events affecting Muslims abroad also engendered profound changes in the complexion of the League. Of these, the most significant was the alliance between Western-educated Muslims and the '*ulamā*'. The involvement of the '*ulamā*' in relief work to aid Turkish soldiers wounded in the War, and their participation in a newspaper industry given over to promote the cause of Turkey brought a large number amongst them to the forefront of public life. This in turn led to their association with other Muslims like Maulānā Muhammad Alī and Dr. M.A. Ansārī, who shared with them a commitment to the fate of Turkey and the Caliphate, but who sought also to mobilise Muslim public opinion of India in the cause of Indian self-government.[28]

The reorientations of the League between 1911 and 1914 took their toll upon its traditional standing in official circles as a 'representative' organisation. The resignation of Muslim League loyalists, like the Āgā Khān[29] and Sayyid Amīr 'Alī, prompted officials to question the credentials of the new leadership.[30]

There were other factors too which led officials to question the wisdom of continuing to regard the League as a representative body. Many who were likely to have been reassured by the distinctly 'lay' preoccupations of the League were clearly disturbed by the growing co-operation between leading sections of the party and the '*ulamā*'. The '*ulamā*''s traditional hostility to British rule was well known[31], and some

---

[25] Hasan, *Nationalism and Communal Politics*, pp. 53–4, 82.
[26] *Ibid.*, pp. 83–4.
[27] *Ibid.*, pp. 79–81.
[28] Robinson, *Separatism*, pp. 261–2, 279–88, and Minault, *The Khilafat Movement*, pp. 65–110.
[29] Āgā Khān to Wazir Hasan, 3 November 1913, cited in Minault, *The Khilafat Movement*, pp. 49–50.
[30] Amir Ali to Wazir Hasan, 22 October 1913, *ibid.*, p. 49. Not surprisingly, officials soon began to question the credentials of the new leadership which was variously described as 'a gang' of 'no importance'. Hasan, *Nationalism and Communal Politics*, p. 78.
[31] Shiblī No'mānī's series of articles entitled 'Musalmānon kī pālītical karwat' written at around this time shows that this hostility was still firmly in place. Shiblī No'mānī, 'Musalmānon kī pālītical karwat', in *Maqalāt-i-Shiblī*, volume 8, Sayyid Sulaimān

feared that such co-operation could further erode the loyalist impulses of the League.[32] To the extent that claims to representation in colonial India were founded, in part, upon official recognition, the League's credentials on the eve of the First World War looked distinctly tenuous.

However, colonial India was also in the throes of change, and although notions of representation were still determined largely by the parameters of colonial ideology and the dictates of political collaboration, these changes ensured that the League's claim to be the voice of Muslim India was not altogether jettisoned. The emergence of new kinds of political discourse among Indian parties which stressed the idea that Indian self-government depended upon Indians being able to speak for themselves provided the League with a fresh opportunity to reaffirm its representative standing. The conclusion of the Lucknow Pact between Congress and the League in December 1916 was a triumphant demonstration of the League's claims.[33] This is all the more remarkable in the light of its implicit challenge to Congress to speak on behalf of all Indians, including Muslims.

The efforts to forge unity between Congress and the League on the question of Indian self-government were not, however, without their inherent difficulties. The introduction of separate electorates and 'weightage' for Muslims in 1909 had generated widespread resentment in Congress;[34] and even those, like Gopal Krishna Gokhale, who had been sympathetic to Muslim demands were alienated by what they perceived to be Muslim greed for additional representation in excess of their numbers.[35] By 1915, however, the influence of moderate leaders in Congress like Tej Bahadur Sapru and Motilal Nehru, had persuaded growing numbers of their colleagues in the party of the expediency of adopting separate Muslim electorates in the interests of obtaining a

Nadwī (ed.) (Azamgarh, Ma'aref Press, 1938), pp. 148–81. Mushirul Hasan, 'Religion and Politics in India: The '*Ulama* and the Khilafat Movement' in Mushirul Hasan (ed.), *Communal and Pan-Islamic Trends in Colonial India* (Delhi, Manohar, 1981), pp. 1–26.

[32] By the middle of 1913, some officials were persuaded that the alliance of Western-educated young Muslims and the '*ulamā*' had forged 'a militant bond' that posed a new and unfamiliar threat to British authority in India. Meston to Hardinge, 25 March 1915, *Hardinge Papers*, 89, quoted in Hasan, *Nationalism and Communal Politics*, p. 147, n. 36.

[33] This is still important even if the Pact itself was, admittedly, an agreement not so much 'between representatives of the Congress and the Muslims of all India, or even the Muslims of the UP, but a deal between Congress and the UP "Young Party" leaders of the Muslim League'. Robinson, *Separatism*, p. 256.

[34] See *Report of the twenty-fifth session of the All India National Congress*, held at Lahore, 27–29 December 1909 (Lahore, Indian National Congress), 1910, p. 47.

[35] Bombay Presidency Association, Council Minutes, 1 July 1909, cited in Hugh Owen, 'Negotiating the Lucknow Pact', p. 563.

joint programme for constitutional change and self-government for India.

The conclusion of the Lucknow Pact endorsed the principle of separate Muslim electorates and postulated Dominion status for India. It recommended 'weightage' for Muslims in the Muslim minority provinces and demanded that India be granted a representative government elected on as broad a franchise as possible.[36] For those in the League, like Wazīr Hasan and Muhammad 'Alī Jinnah, who had pressed relentlessly for closer co-operation with Congress, the Pact signified a decisive step towards the definition of a common 'nationalist' programme for change.[37] However for them, as for some others, its greatest import lay in the formal recognition of the League as the authoritative spokesman for Indian Muslims or, as Jinnah put it, 'the chief representative of Muslim India'.[38] It was, first and foremost, an agreement between Congress and League as 'the two chief representative organisations of India', representing Hindu and Muslim opinion, respectively.[39] That this should be so, was crucial to the political identity of the League as a 'representative' organisation, that is to say, as a Muslim party that stood for Muslims. In December 1917, the Rājā of Mahmūdabād assured his party that those like him who had favoured an agreement with Congress had been heartened by the recognition of a distinct Muslim entity whose representation was deemed to be the exclusive responsibility of the Muslim League.[40] The mood of the League was, perhaps, most tellingly summed up in the observation, 'Far from the Congress having captured the League', the members of the Muslim League might as well claim that 'the League had captured the Congress'.[41]

Whilst these heady statements may have fended off immediate fears concerning the authoritative status of the League, the Pact provoked other kinds of misgivings, some of which were later to seriously threaten the party's standing among its Muslim followers in the Punjab and Bengal. There were essentially two kinds of Muslim opposition to the Pact. The first, and most obvious, concerned the extent of Muslim representation granted under the terms of the Pact. Critics in Bengal

[36] Sayeed, *Pakistan: The Formative Phase*, pp. 38–42.
[37] *Ibid.*, pp. 40–1.
[38] See his speech while moving resolution V of the All India Muslim League session on 1 January 1916, in Pirzada (ed.), *Foundations of Pakistan* I, p. 354.
[39] *Ibid.*
[40] See his address to the All India Muslim League on 30 December 1917, *ibid.*, p. 431.
[41] 'Abdu'l Latīf Khān's speech at the All India Muslim League session on 30 December 1917, *ibid.*, p. 416.

expressed bitter disappointment with the Pact's provisions to accord 'weightage' to Muslims in minority provinces at the expense of reducing the number of seats reserved for Muslims in the majority provinces, especially Bengal.[42] In the Punjab opposition to the Pact was no less fierce, although the cut in the extent of Muslim representation was less drastic than in Bengal. It is worth noting, however, that while the application of 'weightage' for Muslims in the Punjab was subject to the same restrictions as in Bengal, the Punjab actually gained by obtaining, for the first time, a recognition of separate Muslim electorates in the province.[43]

The second, and more significant kind of opposition, centred on the Pact's implications for the recognition of social status and gentility as bases of representation. Members of the 'old guard' who had been close to Sayyid Ahmad Khān, most notably Sayyid Husain Bilgrāmī, raised questions about the Pact's emphasis on self-government and expressed fears that it would lead to Indians being ruled by men 'of very low birth' like Mr. Jinnah.[44] In Bengal, established notables, like Sayyid Nawāb 'Alī Choudhry and Sir 'Abdu'r Rahīm, claimed that the Pact had unjustly deprived Muslims of the gains they had obtained under the reforms of 1909 and forced the League to seriously compromise the principle of 'weightage'. As men drawn from the class of Muslim *ashrāf*,[45] many of whom regarded their claims to leadership as self-evident, both were deeply disturbed by the Pact's apparently cavalier attitude to the 'political importance' of Muslims as a basis for their additional representation.[46] In the Punjab, well-heeled Muslims like Mian Muhammad Shafī, who was later to lead a rival faction of the League, also expressed concern at the absence of any clear understanding in the Pact about the 'political importance' of his community which entitled its members to 'weightage'.[47]

[42] Hasan, *Nationalism and Communal Politics*, pp. 91–4.
[43] Owen, 'Negotiating the Lucknow Pact', p. 581. See also Hasan, *Nationalism and Communal Politic.*, p. 94, n. 97.
[44] Sayyid Husain Bilgrami to James Meston, 14 November 1917, *Meston Papers* (4), quoted in *ibid.*, p. 90.
[45] Both had been members of the Simla Deputation in 1906; the one, Sayyid Nawāb 'Alī Choudhry, had become Bengal's premier notable after the death of Nawāb Salīmullah, while the other, was a scion of one of Bengal's leading families and an eminent lawyer in his own right. S.M. Ikram, *Modern Muslim India and the Birth of Pakistan* (Lahore, Shaikh Muhammad Ashraf, 1970), pp. 275, 283. See also Hasan, *Nationalism and Communal politics in India*, pp. 223–5.
[46] G. Allana, *Pakistan Movement – Historic Documents* (Lahore, Islamic Book Service, 1977), p. 40.
[47] Ikram, *Modern Muslim India*, p. 208 and Hasan, *Nationalism and Communal Politics*, p. 94.

172   *Community and consensus in Islam*

However it was not so much Muslim dissatisfaction with the Pact, but the consequences of constitutional reform initiated in 1917 that contributed, in the first instance, to the steady erosion of the League's political authority in the Punjab and Bengal. In August 1917, the Liberal Secretary of State, Lord Montagu, announced that his party intended to take 'substantial steps' towards 'a progressive realisation of self-government in India'.[48] For the men who now led the League and the Indian National Congress, Montagu's signal provided the first real opportunity to submit a joint programme for liberal reform based on the Lucknow Pact. Yet it was clear that the Pact's central demand for a self-governing Indian Dominion was too radical a measure yet for the British government to concede. The recommendations of the *Report on Indian Constitutional Reforms*, put out by the government in July 1918, fell far short of self-government. Educated Indians, both Hindus and Muslims, were outraged that Britain should still chose to formulate reforms on the assumption that Indians were not fit for responsible government.[49]

There were other issues too, of particular interest to Muslims, that caused anxiety. Of these, the most significant was the *Report*'s manifest reluctance to endorse the merits of communal representation and separate Muslim electorates.[50] Although the authors of the *Report* agreed to continue such representation as an expedient device to secure the interests of a minority, they stressed its adverse effects upon the evolution of a common citizenship.[51] The *Report's* position on a question of palpable importance to large numbers of Indian Muslims generated a degree of political unanimity among those otherwise divided over the Lucknow Pact. Leading figures in the League objected to the government's disregard of 'the peculiar position of the Musalmans of India' and regretted its cursory treatment of a matter that Muslims espoused with an 'intensity of conviction'.[52]

[48] *Report on Indian Constitutional Reforms, Parliamentary Paper*, Cmd. 9109 (London, 1918), paragraph 6. For events leading up to the August Declaration see S.R. Mehrotra, 'The Politics Behind the Montagu Declaration of 1917', in C.H. Philips (ed.), *Politics and Society in India* (London, Oxford University Press, 1963), pp. 89–92.
[49] Hasan, *Nationalism and Communal Politics*, p. 127.
[50] In its view, separate electorates had inhibited 'the give and take which is the essence of political life and discouraged one side to forbear, or . . . the other to exert itself'. *Report on Indian Constitutional Reforms, Parliamentary Paper*, Cmd. 9109, p. 187.
[51] The *Report* underlined the 'divided allegiance' to religious community and State fostered by separate electorates and concluded, 'The division of creeds and classes means the creation of political camps against each other, and teaches men to think as partisans and not as citizens; and it is difficult to see how the change from this system to national representation is ever to occur'. *Report of Indian Constitutional Reforms*, pp. 187, 188.
[52] See the resolution passed by the special session of the All India Muslim League on

However this show of unity was not enough to check the League's steady decline as a representative political organisation. For what was eventually to gnaw at its power to represent Muslims in the councils of the State was the introduction, under the Montagu–Chelmsford reforms, of 'dyarchy' which granted to the provinces the right to appoint political executives accountable to elected majorities. As a party that had become increasingly bereft of the support of Muslims from the majority provinces of Bengal and Punjab, the League found itself unable to compete for its share of 'transferred subjects' which were now the responsibility of provincial legislatures. Yet, even if its political resources were sharply depleted by the implementation of the reforms, the League's ideological reserves were still of some considerable import. It was these, as much as the political skills of those who were to lead the League in the next few decades, that were to contribute to its re-emergence as the authoritative voice of Muslim India.

The League's claim to representation, 1919–1927

The end of the War witnessed the political eclipse of the Muslim League and the emergence of new forces which seriously questioned its right to represent Indian Muslims. The League's narrow political base and its penchant for polite petitioning were a clear liability at a time when India was in the thrall of Mahatma Gandhi's non-cooperation movement. By 1919, growing numbers of Indians believed that their only recourse as subjects of the Raj lay in popular agitation and mass disobedience. The authorities' recent rebuff of Indian demands for political change; their treatment of Indians under the provisions of the Rowlatt Bill and the appalling tragedy at Jallianwala Bagh in Amritsar made Gandhi's appeal for non-cooperation all the more compelling.

The League was also politically undermined by developments within its own constituency. Muslims in India were becoming increasingly restive about the fate of the Turkish Sultan and his Muslim Caliphate. Britain's role in dismantling the Ottoman Empire at the Peace Conference in Versailles had stirred profound religious emotions and many had turned for guidance to the *'ulamā'* who had traditionally acted as custodians of the faith and its institutions. For the *'ulamā'*, the issue of

31 August 1918, in Pirzada (ed.), *Foundations of Pakistan*, I, p. 468 and the Rājā of Mahmūdabād's address at the same session, *ibid.*, p. 465. See also Hasan, *Nationalism and Communal Politics*, pp. 120–1 for reactions against the *Report* in the Muslim press.

the *khilāfat* provided an important opportunity to reaffirm their role as the authoritative representatives of a Muslim consensus.[53]

The impact of Gandhian politics and the emergence of rival Muslim political organisations dominated by the *'ulamā'* took their toll upon the political standing of the League. By 1919, its total membership stood at a mere 777, and four out of six Council meetings had to be adjourned for lack of a quorum.[54] It was clear that neither the League's customary political methods nor its loyalist credo, were likely to survive a climate which encouraged mass participation and which regarded the operative principle in politics to be confrontation not co-operation. Although some in the League sought actively to direct its politics in the course of non-cooperation,[55] the party was unable to match the attention that was commanded by alternative Muslim bodies like the newly-founded all-India Khilāfat Committee and the JamʿIyyat al-'Ulamā'-i-Hind.

The party was being rendered moribund in other ways as well. The enactment of the Montagu–Chelmsford reforms in 1919 placed a new emphasis on provincial politics which fitted uneasily with the League's all-India aspirations. The result was the consolidation of provincial-based Muslim parties, especially in Bengal and the Punjab, whose emphasis upon the local alignments of politics was often at cross-purposes with the interests of an all-India Muslim organisation like the League.[56] By the mid-1920s, shunted to a side by *khilāfatists* and over-ridden by provincial parties, the League was left with neither a political role nor a constituency to speak for.

Yet, if it is the case that the League was a party in decline in the 1920s, how then did it claim to represent Indian Muslims during these years? Few would deny the impact that Turkey's voluntary abolition of the *khilāfat* in 1924 had upon the good fortunes of the League in relation to rival Muslim organisations like the Khilāfat Committee;[57] nor would it be possible to disregard the importance of impending constitutional changes at the centre which contributed to the revival of all-India

---

[53] For 'Abdu'l Bārī of Firingī Mahal, for example, the problem of defending the *khilāfat* was essentially a matter of elaborating the *Sharī'a* for which task the *'ulamā'* would undertake to lead and guide the community. Cited in Minault, *The Khilafat Movement*, p. 79.

[54] Sayyid Zahur Ahmad, *Annual report of the All India Muslim League for the year 1919* (Lucknow, All India Muslim League, 1919), cited in *ibid.*, p. 72.

[55] See in particular the account of M.A. Ansārī's contributions to the 1918 session of the League in *ibid.*, pp. 60–2.

[56] The tensions between these diverse orientations is treated in full in Jalal, *The Sole Spokesman*.

[57] Minault, *The Khilafat Movement*, pp. 201–7.

politics and the resurrection of the League in the late 1920s.[58] However while these political developments were obviously crucial to the survival of the Muslim League, they are inclined to produce explanations which impart too decisive a role to events abroad and to the meanderings of official policy at home. At least as significant for the re-emergence of the League as a 'representative' organisation was the part played by a religious and political tradition whose roots lay deep in Indo-Muslim 'modernist' thinking. It was this tradition and the assumptions it fostered that enabled the League finally to withstand both the pressures of the *'ulamā'*s claims to represent a modern community, as well as the challenge of provincial Muslims' parties who sought to redefine a Muslim consensus in terms of exclusively democratic criteria.

The greater part of 1919 witnessed the mobilisation of Muslim public opinion in favour of the Turkish Caliphate and, by definition, against Britain's wartime record. Allied in this endeavour, though motivated sometimes by quite distinct purposes, were young Westernised Muslims, on the one hand, and members of the *'ulamā'* on the other. Both expressed the prevailing mood of political activism, although it was the *'ulamā'* who had the kinds of resources required to launch a mass movement.[59] Not surprisingly, the task of promoting Muslim political consciousness and representing Muslim public opinion, fell not to the League but to bodies like the All India Khilāfat Committee and the Jamʿīyyat al-ʿUlamāʾ-i-Hind which comprised, or were dominated by, the *'ulamā'*.[60] Their emergence was symptomatic of some of the limitations that had become characteristic of the political style of the League at the time, but their significance, for Muslim representation more generally, lay in their attempts to restore a classical understanding of the relationship between the Muslim lay community and its religious leaders, the *'ulamā'*.

While some scholars, like Minault, believe that organisations such as the Khilāfat Committee served to offset the League's tradition of political loyalism and its preference for constitutional methods,[61] it is clear that the Jamʿīyyat al-ʿUlamāʾ-i-Hind was concerned primarily to

---

[58] Jalal, *The Sole Spokesman*, pp. 10–15.

[59] Of these resources, Robinson writes, 'Islam was their stock in trade. All Muslims came within their ken, political or non-political, literate or illiterate, male or female. They could reach far beyond the English columns of the *Comrade* or the Urdu vituperation of the *Hamdard*. Other groups had not a tithe of their wide ranging influence ... The appeal of a group of ulama ... could transcend many of the divisions of Islamic society'. Robinson, *Separatism*, p. 272.

[60] For details of their organisation and composition see Minault, *The Khilafat Movement*, pp. 72–84.

[61] *Ibid.*, p. 73.

restore to the '*ulamā*' their traditional role as leaders of the community in all matters concerning its religious life. Since politics was seen also to constitute an extension of this life, the creation of a separate organisation that could exemplify the conduct of a right-minded community was deemed to be necessary.[62]

The manifest importance of the *khilāfat* and the influence of the '*ulamā*' upon political events in the early 1920s, were to have a significant bearing upon the League's representative standing during these years. It is now abundantly clear to historians of the period that the League was in no position to express the sentiments of the vast numbers of Indian Muslims who rallied around the *khilāfatists* in 1919 and 1920. It is ironic indeed that this most self-avowedly Muslim of bodies should have ceased to represent this most ostensibly Muslim of causes. Yet the reasons for its disengagement from the movement are more complex than have hitherto been acknowledged.

Two considerations need to be borne in mind when attempting to discern the grounds on which the League sought, in the face of these overwhelming political odds, to establish its claim to representation. Firstly, its espousal of a body of Indo-Muslim thinking which had tended to regard the *khilāfat* as an institution of symbolic, rather than political, value to Muslims. Secondly, its reliance on a prevailing 'modernist' discourse on *ijmā'* which rejected its classical interpretation as the prerogative of the '*ulamā*'. The one contributed to the assumption that so long as the League stood for the *khilāfat* as an issue of singular symbolic importance to Muslims, its claim to represent the dominant Muslim consensus could not substantially be eroded. The other shaped the view that the task of formulating the consensus of a modern Muslim community in the 1920s should ultimately be entrusted not to the class of '*ulamā*', but to an organisation of lay Muslims like the League.

The issue of the *khilāfat* had, for Indian Muslims, always been intimately bound by questions about their loyalty to British rule in India. One of the first to confront the problem in these terms was Sayyid

---

[62] *Ibid.*, p. 79. Many at this time are likely to have sympathised with the gist of Shiblī No'mānī's inaugural address to the Nadvāt-ul-'Ulamā' in 1894. He declared, 'In the days of Muslim rule the worldly as well as the religious affairs of the Muslims were in the hands of the '*ulamā*' . . . Now that things have changed, and worldly affairs have come under the authority of the [British] Government . . . it is generally felt that the link which they [the '*ulamā*'] retain with the community is merely religious . . . I believe this to be wrong the totally wrong'. Quoted in Ikram, *Modern Muslim India*, pp. 129–30. Not all '*ulamā*' were, however, prepared to share this view. In this they were motivated both by political differences as well as by personal rivalries. See Minault, *The Khilafat Movement*, p. 80, and Sayed Jamal-ud-din Ahmed, 'The Barelvis and the Khilafat Movement' in Hasan (ed.), *Communal and Pan-Islamic Trends*, pp. 344–57.

Ahmad Khān. In the 1880s and 1890s, when substantial numbers of Indian Muslims were beginning to regard with sympathy the claim of the Turkish Sultan to the Caliphate of Islam, Sayyid Ahmad chose to pronounce rather differently on the matter.[63] He maintained that Indian Muslims were obliged by law to be loyal not to some Muslim potentate, but to their British masters in India.[64] Ironically enough, the potential conflict between a Muslim's religious sentiments, on the one hand, and his political loyalties on the other, was dismissed by Sayyid Ahmad on grounds that would have been more familiar to Muslim orthodox thinking than to his own brand of 'naturalism'. He contended that as the true Caliphate had ceased to exist after the death of the fourth Caliph 'Alī in 661 A.D., Muslims were not religiously obliged to owe allegiance to subsequent caliphs. As far as Ottoman claims were concerned these, he suggested, were invalid because Turks did not, as a rule, descend from Muhammad's tribe of Quraysh who alone were entitled to constitute the Caliphate.[65]

Although some of Sayyid Ahmad's interpretations were by no means uncommon to traditional Sunnī Muslim discourse on the Caliphate,[66] neither he nor his biographers have cared to deny that his views were shaped by considerations of prudent political practice rather than by sound political theory.[67] His overriding preoccupation since the Mutiny had, after all, been to ensure that Muslims were never again made vulnerable to the charge of disloyalty – a charge he believed that had contributed decisively to their communal decline. Not surprisingly he was inclined to believe, therefore, that the espousal of the cause of *khilāfat* at a time when pan-Islamism was becoming synonymous with anti-imperialism could be nothing short of 'dangerous political adventurism'.[68]

If it is true, as some historians like Aziz Ahmad have maintained, that Sayyid Ahmad's pronouncements on the Caliphate went against the

---

[63] On a survey of pan-Islamic trends in this period see Ahmad, *Islamic Modernism in India and Pakistan*, pp. 123–31. See also I.H. Qureshi, *Ulema in Politics* (Karachi, Ma'aref, 1972), pp. 242–3, 253–6.

[64] Sayyid Ahmad Khān "Khilāfat aw/r Khalīfāh", Mazhabī wa Islāmīc Mazāmīn, (Lahore, Majlis-i-Tarqqī-i-Adab, 1962), pp. 164–8.

[65] *Ibid.*, p. 166. See also Aziz Ahmad, 'Sayyid Ahmed Khan, Jamal-ud-din Afghani and Muslim India', *Studia Islamica*, 13 (1960), pp. 55–78.

[66] E.I.J. Rosenthal, *Political Thought in Medieval Islam* (Cambridge University Press, 1958), pp. 21–51.

[67] See Sayyid Ahmad Khan, 'Khilāfat aur Khalīfāh' in Sayyid Ahmad Khan, *Akhri Mazāmīn* (Lahore, Majlis-i Tariqqī-i Adab, 1962), p. 161. Hafeez Malik, *Sir Sayyid Ahmad Khan and Muslim Modernization in India and Pakistan* (New York, Columbia University Press, 1980), pp. 237–8.

[68] Ahmad, *Islamic Modernism in India and Pakistan*, p. 33.

dominant Muslim *ijmā'* of his time,[69] then it was perhaps inevitable that his political successors in the Muslim League should have been keen to redress the balance. In June 1906, Sayyid Ahmad's friend and colleague, Nawāb Mohsin-ul-Mulk, reflected upon the state of the Caliphate and suggested that the present confusion between Sultan and Caliph was symptomatic of the degeneration of the institution. Nevertheless, he concluded, the sympathy that Muslims felt for one another through the medium of the Caliphate was genuine and this, more than political deference to the Turkish Sultan, was what accounted for their sentiments.[70] This recognition of Muslim religious sympathy as legitimate, although quite distinct from political loyalty, and of the Caliphate as a spiritual focus for Muslim unity, was to dominate thinking in the League into the next decade.[71]

Perhaps the most important theoretical contributions within the League to the question of the *khilāfat* in the twentieth-century came from the League's foremost ideologues, Sayyid Amīr 'Alī and Muhammad Iqbāl.[72] Their positions are significant, for they reflected something of the League's own stance on the *khilāfat* which combined a keen sense of the political constraints of colonial rule with a profound sentiment for one of the few surviving embodiments of Muslim civilisation. Neither Amīr 'Alī nor Iqbāl chose to be closely associated with the *khilāfat* movement as it evolved in the early 1920s. The loyalist instincts of the one, and the other's reluctance to endorse Gandhi's vision of Hindu–Muslim co-operation, contributed substantially to their aloofness from

---

[69] *Ibid.*, p. 126.

[70] He wrote, '... by denying Khilafat it does not follow that the Indian Musulmans have no love for the Sultan of Turkey ... sympathy for religion and for a community is quite distinct from political relations ... Loyalty towards our Government does not exclude the idea of sympathy with one's co-religionists. Those who think that the two are exclusive of each other, are ignorant both of their religious duties and of their political relations', Mohsin-ul-Mulk, 'Khilafa and Khilafat' *Aligarh Institute Gazette*, 20 June 1906, reprinted in Shan Mohammad, *Successors of Sir Syed Ahmad Khan: Their Role in the Growth of Muslim Political Consciousness in India* (Delhi, Idarah-i-Adabiyat-i-Delhi, 1981), Appendix IV, pp. 165–6.

[71] In 1911, Nawāb Viqār-ul-Mulk expressed the growing mood of Muslim discontent in India concerning Britain's relations with Turkey, and her disregard of the Caliphate, by stressing the need for Muslim solidarity and self-reliance to protect Muslim institutions. Cited in Lini May, *The Evolution of Indo-Muslim Thought after 1857* (Lahore, Shaikh Muhammad Ashraf, 1970), p. 184.

[72] For an account of their practical contributions to the pan-Islamic movement, see Minault, *The Khilafat Movement*, p. 49. On Amīr 'Alī's Red Crescent Mission of 1913, see also Ameer Ali, 'Memoirs' in Aziz (ed.), *Ameer Ali: His Life and Work*, part 2, pp. 627–45. For Iqbāl's participation in the Anjuman-i-Khuddam-i Kaaba, the organisation devoted to the protection of the Holy Places of Islam, see Mushirul Hasan, *Mohamed Ali: Ideology and Politics*, p. 45.

the movement.[73] Yet, it is clear that for both men the institution of the *khilāfat* was of the utmost symbolic importance.

Amīr 'Alī's view of the Caliphate was postulated on the distinction between its 'apostolical' and its 'pontifical' functions.[74] While he acknowledged that the 'apostolical' dimension was more authentic for Shī'as, who believed it to have been most fully contained in the Caliphate of 'Alī, its 'pontifical' role was not insignificant. Its importance, he claimed, rested pre-eminently upon its capacity to serve as a living reminder to Muslims of their collective history and civilisation.[75]

It is important to note, however, that while Amīr 'Alī's commitment to the Turkish Caliphate was not in doubt, he had always been careful to distinguish its spirit from the current of Muslim fervour that passed under the name of 'pan-Islamism'. As one whose impulses were deeply anchored in a tradition of political loyalism, he was unable to endorse a movement that was fuelled in part by anti-British feelings. On the eve of the Balkan wars, at a time when growing numbers of Indian Muslims found themselves responding to the ideal of Muslim unity, Amīr 'Alī chose to dismiss pan-Islamism as 'a figment of the brain'.[76] Like Mohsin-ul-Mulk before him, he sought to defuse its political content by drawing attention to its character as a spiritual fraternity which symbolised Muslim brotherhood, rather than as the proper focus of Muslim allegiance.

Amīr 'Alī's stress upon the religious, rather than the political significance of the *khilāfat*, was expressive of prevailing attitudes in the League. Its influence can be discerned in those, like Muhammad 'Alī, who were to abandon the League's loyalist politics in favour of a more determined stand against Britain's role in dissolving the Ottoman Empire. In November 1918, at the height of the *khilāfat* movement, Muhammad 'Alī asserted that 'Muslim interest in Turkey is essentially Islamic and not political'.[77] Like Amīr 'Alī, he denied that the issue of

---

[73] Here it is worth recalling that Amīr 'Alī was resident in England from 1911 to 1928, although this did not, apparently, keep him from taking a keen interest in the fate of the *khilāfat* or developments in India. See Aziz (ed.), *Ameer Ali: His Life and Work*, part 1, pp. 18–26.

[74] Ameer Ali, *The Spirit of Islam*, p. 37. See also his 'The Caliphate: A Historical and Juridicial Sketch', *Contemporary Review* (1915), pp. 681–94, and 'The Caliphate and the Islamic Renaissance', *Edinburgh Review* (1923), pp. 180–95, reprinted in Aziz (ed.), *Ameer Ali: His Life and Work*, part 2, pp. 387–403 and 424–40, respectively.

[75] Aziz (ed.), *Ameer Ali*, part 2, pp. 103–5, 293.

[76] *Proceedings of the Central Asia Society* (1912), cited in Dwight E. Lee, 'The Origins of Pan-Islamism', *The American Historical Review*, 67, 2 (1942), pp. 19–20.

[77] Mohamed Ali to B. Lindsay and Abdul Rauf, 27 November 1918, in Mushirul Hasan (ed.), *Mohamed Ali in India Politics: Select Writings*, volume 2 (Delhi, Atlantic Publishers, 1983), p. 122.

180   Community and consensus in Islam

the *khilāfat* was synonymous with pan-Islamism, and condemned pan-Islamism as 'absolute and utter infidelity.'[78] It is significant that although Muhammad 'Alī eventually subscribed to Maulānā Āzād's notion of the Caliphate as the political centre of the Muslim world, he remained unwilling to renounce its pre-eminently spiritual significance, or accept that its defence was in any way tantamount to a quest for Muslim political dominance.[79]

Muhammad 'Alī's understanding of the *khilāfat* suggests that his commitment to the movement may have had less to do with his rejection of prevailing interpretations of the *khilāfat* which stressed its spiritual significance, than with his differences concerning its implications for Muslim political practice. For while dominant thinking in the League was inclined to the view that the pre-eminently spiritual claims of the Caliphate obviated the need for explicitly political action, *khilāfatists* like Muhammad 'Alī were clearly persuaded that these claims depended in some measure upon restoring the Caliph's temporal power. In the increasingly repressive context of British India in the 1920s this demanded, in his view, a political statement, namely non-cooperation.[80]

Iqbāl's approach to the Caliphate was less concerned with the preservation of the institution, as such, than with its value and power to engender Muslim solidarity.[81] Unlike Amīr 'Alī and Muhammad 'Alī, Iqbāl was prepared to countenance the disappearance of an institution that the deemed, in some respects, to be antiquated and unsuited to the contemporary evolution of Muslim societies.[82] More importantly

[78] *Ibid.*, p. 124.
[79] 'It was not', he wrote, '... the fear of losing political dominance that troubled Muslims most. The spiritual force of Islam does not depend on political supremacy ... [but] the temporal power of Islam might be so weakened that it might become liable to suffer, without adequate power to prevent, the curtailment of its spiritual influence through the pressure of the temporal power of rival creeds'. Mohamed Ali to Lord Chelmsford, 24 April 1919, *ibid.*, p. 227. See also Hasan, *Mohamed Ali: Ideology and Politics*, pp. 41–2.
[80] For others, like Maulānā Āzād, the movement's chief theoretician, the re-possession of the Caliph's temporal power clearly extended, when necessary, to *jihād*, although such *jihād* was not interpreted exclusively as the use of violence. See Maulānā Abū'l Kalām Āzād, *Mas'ala-i-Khilāfat wa Jazīra-i-'Arab*, (Bombay, Central Khilāfat Committee), 1920. See also his speech on Islamic unity in Calcutta, 27 October 1914, in which he advocated the defence of the *khilāfat* by political means as the logical recourse of a community that was essentially a political entity. Maulānā Abū'l Kalām Āzād, *Khutbāt-i-Āzād*, Mālik Ram (ed.), (Delhi, Sahitya Academy, 1974), p. 29.
[81] It is unlikely however, whether Iqbāl would have so readily endorsed its abolition as some other Indo-Muslim modernists, like Khuda Bakhsh (1877–1931), for whom it signified the end of 'a fiction' which had acted as an 'embargo on liberalism'. Quoted in Hamilton Gibb, *Whither Islam?* (London, Victor Gollancz, 1932), p. 225.
[82] Muhammad Iqbal, *The Reconstruction of Religious Thought in Islam* (London, Oxford University Press, 1934), pp. 149–52.

perhaps, affected neither by Amīr 'Alī's loyalist preoccupations nor Muhammad Alī's political ambivalence, Iqbāl was persuaded that it was pan-Islamism, as a manifestation of Islamic brotherhood, and not the *khilāfat* as such, that was worth struggling for. His enthusiastic support for pan-Islamic endeavours, both organisational and intellectual, during the Balkan Wars, was a consequence of his lasting commitment to the idea of a worldwide Muslim fraternity. So intense was this commitment that it led him also to question, momentarily, the narrow Indo-Muslim orientations encouraged by the Aligarh tradition and propounded by the Muslim League.[83]

It is clear, however, that the development of the *khilāfat* movement as an extension of non-cooperation in the 1920s, led Iqbāl to reconsider his political stance. Unsure of the merits of Hindu–Muslim *entente*, he remained deeply sceptical of Gandhi's contribution to the promotion of Muslim interests in India and abroad.[84] But there were other more significant concerns that were fundamentally consistent with the 'modernist' preoccupations of Iqbāl, and with the intellectual heritage of the League more generally, that prompted his withdrawal from the *khilāfat* campaign. These reflected a profound unease in relation to a movement which threatened to restore to the *'ulamā'* their claim to be the pre-eminent representatives of a Muslim consensus. In April 1925, Iqbāl wrote to the historian, Akbar Shāh Khān Najībabādī:

The influence of the professional Maulvis had greatly decreased owing to Sir Syed Ahmed Khan's movement, but the Khilafat Committee, for the sake of political *fatwas*, has restored their influence amongst Indian Muslims. This was a very big mistake, [the effect of] which has, probably, not yet been realised by anyone.[85]

Iqbāl's understanding of the implications of the *khilafat* movement is crucial. It suggests that strictly political considerations, namely loyalty to British rule, cannot wholly explain why an important section of the League refused to endorse an ostensibly Muslim movement. Above all, it serves as a reminder of the pervasive influence of a tradition which had first flourished among Muslim 'modernists' in the late nineteenth century and which came later to be commonly associated with followers of the Muslim League. It was a tradition whose exponents, from Sayyid Ahmad to Chirāgh 'Alī, had tended to believe that the power to express *ijmā'* rested, or ought to have rested, primarily with lay Muslims.[86] In

---

[83] Ikram, *Modern Muslim India and the Birth of Pakistan*, p. 165.
[84] Anne-Marie Schimmel, *Gabriel's Wings* (Leidèn, E.J. Brill, 1963), p. 47.
[85] Quoted in Ikram, *Modern Muslim India and the Birth of Pakistan*, p. 175.
[86] See chapter 1.

the 1920s the intellectual hold of this tradition was still far from eroded. Amīr 'Alī's monumental *Spirit of Islam* published in 1922 was firmly grounded within this tradition, as was Iqbāl's *Reconstruction of Religious Thought in Islam*, which appeared in 1934. Both made significant contributions to the 'modernist' discourse on *ijmāʻ*, and it is reasonable to assume that the political reservations expressed by Amīr 'Alī and Iqbāl concerning the direction of the *khilāfat* movement stemmed in part from their doubts about the capacity of the *'ulamāʼ* to act as agents of modern Muslim public opinion.[87]

Nor did this 'modernist' interpretation of *ijmāʻ* fail to leave its mark upon those in the League known more for the adoption of its style of politics than for the direction of its contemplative philosophy. Muhammad 'Alī Jinnah is a case in point. In December 1920, he denounced the participation of the *'ulamāʼ* in politics as invidious and appealed for 'the intellectual and reasonable section' of Muslim opinion to regain the initiative.[88] While it is true that Jinnah's tirade was designed primarily to emphasise his distaste for mass politics, his rejection of the role of the *'ulamāʼ* as spokesmen for the community must be seen as expressive of a much wider tradition that was represented at the time by the Muslim League. It was precisely the weight of this tradition and its stress upon *ijmāʻ* as a lay prerogative that was to enable the League to assert that it, and not the *'ulamāʼ*, actually dominated the *khilāfat* movement, and most fully represented the Muslim consensus.

The influence of this tradition among Western-educated, young Muslims is also evident in the tensions which sometimes existed between them and the body of *'ulamāʼ* with whom they were allied in the cause of *khilāfat*. In 1921, the Jamʻīyyat al-'Ulamāʼ-i-Hind, under the influence of Maulānā Abū'l Kalām Āzād, mooted the idea of an *amīr-i-Hind*, or leader, drawn from among the *'ulamāʼ* who would be charged with the task of providing guidance to Muslims in matters relating to the *Sharīʻa*.[89] The purpose was to restore to the *'ulamāʼ* their role as the chief

---

[87] In the case of Iqbāl, it can certainly be said that he endorsed the fresh 'materialist orientation' that the Kemalist experiment in Turkey had brought to Islam which, in his view, 'has had too much of renunciation'. For him the contribution of Turkish 'secularism' lay not in its rejection of Islam, 'for no one can abandon Islam', but in its anti-mullah, anti-suficampaigns. See Muhammad Iqbal, *Islam and Ahmadism*, in Latif Ahmed Sherwani (ed. and compiler), *Speeches, Writings and Statements of Iqbal* (Lahore, Iqbal Academy, 1977), pp. 192–3.

[88] Jinnah's address to the Nagpur session of Congress in 1920, quoted in M.H. Saiyid, *Mohammad Ali Jinnah: A Political Study* (Lahore, Shaikh Muhammad Ashraf. 1962), p. 130.

[89] Maulānā 'Abdu'l Halīm Siddīquī (Nāzim, Jamʻīyyat al-'Ulamāʼ-i-Hind), *Jamʻīyyat al-'Ulamāʼ-i-Hind Kī chand ahm khidmāt-i-millī kā mukhtasar tazkirā* (Delhi,

custodians of the Law and as organisers of Muslim communal life. However, these proposals were fiercely resisted by Western-educated politicians, like the 'Alī brothers, who were unwilling to place lay Muslims under the control of the *'ulamā'*.[90]

By the mid-1920s, the growing importance of political issues surrounding Council entry and constitutional reform heightened the incipient differences between the two groups.[91] In September 1923, Maulānā 'Abdu'l Bārī wrote to Muhammad 'Alī claiming that 'western-educated sahibs, who have no respect for the guardians of Islam', were telling his men to return to their places in Qur'ānic schools and seminaries.[92] These differences between Muslim lay-men and *'ulamā'* suggest that although their alliance may have proved a workable basis for Muslim mass mobilisation during the *khilāfat* campaign, it could not conceal what Minault has termed 'their fundamentally different orientations to politics'.[93] There is no doubt that at the heart of this opposition lay their diverse interpretations of who was to constitute the *ijmā'* of Muslims in India.

The abolition of the Turkish Caliphate in March 1924 put an abrupt end to these controversies. Although the Khilāfat Committee continued to function intermittently during the 1920s, the energies of its members were increasingly channelled into other pursuits. Some like M.A. Ansārī, Hakīm Ajmal Khān and Dr. Sayyid Mahmūd went on to become active members of Congress. Others like the 'Alī brothers returned to the communal politics of the League. Yet others, like Maulānā Hasrat Mohānī and Saifuddin Kitchlew, devoted their energies to Muslim proselytisation through the *tablīgh and tanzīm* movements which crystallised in the late 1920s.[94] Among the *'ulamā'*, some like 'Abdu'l Bārī called for a withdrawal from politics, while others like

---

Jam'īyyat al-'Ulamā'-i-Hind, 1940), pp. 31–7 and P.C. Bamford, *Histories of the Non-Co-Operation and Khilafat Movement* (Delhi, Government of India, 1925), p. 168. See also Yohanan Friedmann, 'The Attitude of the *Jam'iyyat-Ulama-i-Hind* to the Indian National Movement and the Establishment of Pakistan', in Gabriel Baer (ed.), *The 'Ulama' in Modern History* (Jerusalem, Israeli Oriental Society, 1971), VII, pp. 157–83 and Peter Hardy, *Partners in Freedom and True Muslims: The Political Thought of Some Muslim Scholars in British India, 1912–1947* (Lund, Scandinavian Institute of Asian Studies, 1971).

[90] Minault, *The Khilafat Movement*, p. 154. Some among the *'ulamā'*, like Maulānā 'Abdu'l Bārī, who opposed the scheme appear to have done so more from their temperamental than from their doctrinal differences with Āzād. *Ibid.*

[91] Robinson, *Separatism*, pp. 335–7.

[92] Abdul Bari to Mohamed Ali, 7 September 1923, *Mohamed Ali Papers*, quoted in Hasan, *Nationalism and Communal Politics*, p. 196.

[93] Minault, *The Khilafat Movement*, p. 154.

[94] *Ibid.*, pp. 192–201.

Maulānā Abū'l Kalām Āzād opted to continue within the broad forum of Congress.

The League's claim to representation, 1927–1937

The disintegration of the *khilāfat* organisation in the mid-1920s led to a noticeable political vacuum at the level of all-India Muslim politics. Although the Muslim League was resuscitated somewhat in 1925, its total membership at the end of 1926 was scarcely impressive – a mere 1,184.[95] Indeed, its years of political inactivity since the end of the War had contributed to a distinct feeling in some quarters 'that to all practical intents and purposes it is dead'.[96] Nor had its part in provincial politics been such as to encourage a more optimistic forecast. In Bengal and Punjab, the party's image had been badly tarnished after its controversial endorsement of the Lucknow Pact and its provisions relating to 'weightage' in Muslim majority provinces. Finally, the introduction of 'dyarchy' which encouraged the development of provincial autonomy rendered the League's own preoccupations with power at the centre increasingly marginal.[97]

The provincial politics of Bengal and Punjab in the 1920s were characterised by the notable absence of the League at the centre of Muslim politics. Indeed, the hallmark of Bengali politics at the time lay in the competition among a variety of Muslim organisations, each of which claimed to be the most 'representative' spokesman for their community.[98] Who best established this claim depended on who succeeded, ultimately, in obtaining a measure of stable support in the midst of the province's highly volatile politics.[99] Stable support, however, demanded a willingness to co-operate with Bengal's sizeable Hindu population – a game at which the League, with its communal orientations, proved to be an abject failure. The revival of communal

---

[95] Choudhry Khaliquzzaman, *Pathway to Pakistan* (Lahore, Longmans, 1961), pp. 137–8.

[96] Sayyid Riza 'Alī's presidential address to the All India Muslim League, 30 December 1924, in Pirzada (ed.), *Foundations of Pakistan*, I, p. 16.

[97] David Page, *Prelude to Partition: The Indian Muslims and the Imperial System of Control, 1920–1932* (Delhi, Oxford University Press, 1982), pp. 36–72, and Jalal, *The Sole Spokesman*, pp. 82–125.

[98] Leonard Gordon, *Bengal: The Nationalist Movement, 1876–1940* (New York, Columbia University Press, 1974), p. 204.

[99] One eloquent testimony to the province's turbulent politics at this time was the creation of at least six different ministries between 1927 and 1936. Ayesha Jalal and Anil Seal, 'Alternative to Partition: Muslim Politics Between the Wars', *Modern Asian Studies*, 15, 3 (1981), p. 429.

politics in the province in 1926 did little to restore the credibility of the party. For such politics reflected not so much a concern with 'Muslim' issues as such, but a bitter struggle for power between advocates of Hindu–Muslim co-operation, who included younger Muslims, like Fazlul Haq and H.S. Suhrawardy, and established members of the Muslim 'old guard' led by Sir 'Abdu'r Rahīm, whose opposition to the Lucknow Pact was well known.[100]

In the Punjab as in Bengal, the intricacies of provincial political alignments, involving a three-cornered alliance between Muslims, Hindus and Sikhs, proved too much for the communal ethos of the League and its centrist concerns. Here the League was clearly no match for Fazl-i-Husain's National Unionist Party with its solid political base, drawn from all three communities and representing powerful rural interests.[101] Fazl-i-Husain's own objectives as leader of this coalition were both complex and varied.[102] While his policies were not ostensibly communal, he did little to check the growing imbalance in favour of Muslims in areas concerned with education and representation in municipal councils.[103] At the same time, while his immediate interests were clearly directed at the consolidation of Punjabi power under his leadership, he was not without some considerable ambition to win acceptance as the spokesman of Muslim interests at the level of all-India politics.[104] His reputation as a guardian of conservative interests, which had won his party the support of British officials, made him a likely successor to replace the League's loyalist 'old guard' whose influence had been sharply eroded by the *khilāfat* movement.

The re-emergence of competing claims for the representation of Indian Muslims at the all-India level was stimulated by the appointment of the 'all white' Simon Commission in November 1927, which was charged with the task of evolving a constitution to grant full Dominion status to India.[105] Two groups, representing rival factions of the

---

[100] Hasan, *Nationalism and Communal Politics*, p. 225.

[101] Page, *Prelude to Partition*, pp. 65–72; 143–4.

[102] His 'urban and rather humble origins and record of sympathy with Congress made him an unlikely person for this role ... Yet urban Muslim politicians ... had no political future in the Punjab after the reforms, except as spokesmen for the dominant agricultural interest'. Jalal and Seal, 'Alternative to Partition', pp. 425–6.

[103] Ikram, *Modern Muslim India and the Birth of Pakistan*, pp. 216–18 and Hasan, *Nationalism and Communal Politics*, pp. 228–30. On the Hindu backlash provoked by some of his policies, see *ibid.*, pp. 234–8.

[104] Jalal and Seal, 'Alternative to Partition', pp. 433–9.

[105] R.J. Moore, 'The Making of India's Paper Federation, 1927–1935', in C.H. Philips and M.D. Wainwright (eds.), *The Partition of India: Policies and Perspectives, 1935–1947* (London, George Allen and Unwin, 1970), pp. 54–76.

League, claimed to speak authoritatively for Muslims on the subject of India's future constitution. One, led by Jinnah and supported by Muslims drawn mostly from the minority provinces, stood for accommodation with Congress on the basis of an equal share of power for Hindus and Muslims in a strong centre. Another group, dominated by Muslims from the Punjab, most notably Mian Fazl-i-Husain and Mian Muhammad Shafī, was determined to press for a federal solution where provinces would be guaranteed a substantial degree of autonomy.[106] Their proposals were supported by Muslims from Bengal keen to establish their statutory majority in the province, as well as some others, like the Āgā Khān, who had become deeply suspicious of Jinnah's overtures to nationalists in Congress.[107]

The year 1928 witnessed the hardening of Muslim differences, with rival groups poised to contest one another's representative credentials ostensibly on the issue of whether or not to co-operate with a constitutional Commission that did not include any Indians among its members.[108] Although neither group possessed the means to establish its credentials, two important developments were to contribute decisively towards undermining, for a time, the credibility of the 'Jinnah group'.

The first was the resistance put up by Muslim politicians, in the Punjab and Bengal, to Jinnah's proposals for an Indian constitution based on a settlement with Congress at the all-India level.[109] They believed that these proposals were essentially tailored to suit the interests of Muslims from the minority provinces whose paucity in numbers kept them from endorsing constitutional schemes based on the consolidation of power in the provinces.[110] There were other objections too which deepened the provincialists' suspicions. For while Jinnah's scheme clearly endorsed statutory Muslim majorities in both Punjab and Bengal, it envisaged the abolition of separate Muslim electorates at all levels in exchange for substantial Muslim representation at the centre. This was deemed unacceptable by provincial politicians in

---

[106] Page, *Prelude to Partition*, pp. 144–62.
[107] *Ibid.*, pp. 245–7.
[108] See resolutions passed by the All India Muslim League (Jinnah Group), January 1928, in Pirzada (ed.), *Foundations of Pakistan*, I, p. 125, and Shafī's presidential address and resolution passed by the All Indian Muslim League, January 1928, *ibid.*, pp. 131, 134–5.
[109] Page, *Prelude to Partition*, pp. 187–92.
[110] The 'Punjab alternative' fashioned by Fazl-i-Husain was designed precisely to restore the claim of Muslims from the majority provinces who had little to gain from deals for a strong centre which involved an equal share of power for Congress and League. See Jalal and Seal, 'Alternative to Partition'.

Punjab and Bengal, many of whom regarded separate electorates as essential to protect their political majorities.[111]

The other development which cut at the representative standing of the 'Jinnah group' was the publication of the *Report of the All Parties Conference*, otherwise known as the 'Nehru Report' in August 1928.[112] In its recommendations, many of which embodied Congress's vision of a political arrangement for India, the *Report* called for an end to separate Muslim electorates and Muslim 'weightage'; its cruellest blow to Jinnah came, however, in the form of its proposals for Muslim representation at the centre. This, it suggested, should be a fourth instead of a third, thereby denying Muslims a share of power which Jinnah believed would ensure them a constituent status at the centre equal to Hindus.

The *Report* serves as an important indication of the League's overall decline as an organisation with an indisputable claim to represent Indian Muslims. Indeed, there was a sense that the League was 'totally discredited'.[113] In a context where the idea of representation had long been synonymous, above all, with recognition, Congress's attitude to the League became an important measure of its political standing and of the worth of its political claims. The implications were profound. Jinnah was forced to retreat into political isolation abroad and those, like Fazl-i-Husain, confident of their political following in the provinces stepped forward to assume the mantle of India's premier Muslim leader with an all-India organisation to boot. In December 1928, Fazl-i-Husain organised the All India Muslim Conference.[114] Its ostensible purpose was no less than to 'speak authoritatively on behalf of the Muslims of India';[115] its declared intention none other than to reaffirm the ingredients of Muslim communal politics: separate Muslim electorates, statutory Muslim majorities and 'weightage' for Muslim minorities.[116] However, even if the Conference's manifesto read remarkably like that of

---

[111] For some accounts of provincial Muslim reactions to Jinnah's proposals see Page, *Prelude to Partition*, pp. 144–5, 148–9.

[112] For details of the negotiations leading up to the *Report* see Uma Kaura, *Muslims and Indian Nationalism: The Emergence of the Demand for India's Partition, 1928–1940* (Delhi, South Asia Books, 1977), pp. 44–51. For Muslim reactions to the *Report* see Page, *Prelude to Partition*, pp. 174–91.

[113] A statement attributed to Motilal Nehru, *ibid.*, p. 51. Mahasabhites, like M.R. Jayakar and Lala Lajpat Rai who were active and influential in Congress at this time, advised Congress that Jinnah's faction had 'really no following'. *Ibid.*, p. 47.

[114] Page, *Prelude to Partition*, chapter 4. See also K.K. Aziz (ed.), *The All India Muslim Conference, 1928–1935: A Documentary Record* (Karachi, National Publishing House, 1972).

[115] Aziz (ed.), *The All India Muslim Conference*, p. 46.

[116] See the resolutions passed by the Conference on 31 December 1928, and 1 January 1929, in *ibid.*, pp. 53–6.

the League which it hoped to supersede, its immediate objectives were limited to the consolidation of provincial, mainly Punjabi Muslim, interests as the basis for a transition to responsible government at the centre.[117] This then was what Fazl-i-Husain expected his hand-picked Muslim delegation to achieve at the First Round Table Conference in London in November 1930. This too was what he hoped officials would accept as the 'representative' demands of the Muslims of India.[118]

There was little in 1930 that need have caused concern to Fazl-i-Husain on this account. Gandhi's non-cooperation movement had resurfaced after its disastrous turn at Chauri-Chaura in February 1922, and the government returned to its search for allies among its Muslim subjects. Officials, who had viewed with nervous apprehension the trend towards communal unity in the late 1920s, were reassured by the scale of Muslim dissatisfaction with the 'Nehru Report'. As in the past, they prepared to reward political support with recognition and represent-ation. The Muslims who 'really count', wrote Malcolm Hailey to Harry Haig, Secretary to the Government's Home Department, on the eve of the first Round Table Conference, were those who stayed away from Unity Conferences.[119]

Nor was the significance of this renewed emphasis on established notions of representation lost on those who sought official recognition. In the spring of 1930, Shafaʿāt Ahmad Khān, one of the United Provinces' most prominent Muslim politicians and a confidante of Fazl-i-Husain, impressed upon the Viceroy the value of his colleague's support in return for official recognition of their demands as representa-tive of Indian Muslims.[120] Others, like the Āgā Khān, were equally cognisant of the considerations that shaped official notions of represent-ation. In March 1932, he assured the newly appointed Secretary of State, Sir Samuel Hoare, that his group would be willing to secure 'the

---

[117] Jalal and Seal, 'Alternative to Pakistan', p. 433.

[118] In May 1930, Fazl-i-Husain wrote to Sir Malcolm Hailey, Governor of the United Provinces '. . . frankly I do not like the idea of Jinnah doing all the talking and of there being no one strong-minded enough to make a protest in case Jinnah starts upon expressing his views when those views are not acceptable to the Indian Muslims'. Fazl-i-Husain to Malcolm Hailey, 20 May 1930, *Hailey Collection*, quoted in Kaura, *Muslims and Indian Nationalism*, p. 60. On how Fazl-i-Husain's men worked hard to make Jinnah appear 'unrepresentative' see *ibid.*, pp. 59–62 and R.J. Moore, *The Crisis of Indian Unity, 1917–1940* (Oxford, Clarendon Press, 1974), p. 121.

[119] Malcolm Hailey to Harry Haig, 19 November 1932, *Hailey Collection*, quoted in Kaura, *Muslims and Indian Nationalism*, p. 91.

[120] He assured the Viceroy that 'Muslims' would not join the civil disobedience movement if the government was prepared, in its turn, to 'make a moral gesture' in favour of the demands of Fazl-i-Husain and his men. Shafaat Ahmad Khan to Captain Blunden, 12 May 1930, *Hailey Papers*, quoted in *ibid.*, p. 60.

permanence of ... the Imperial Crown throughout India' if its views at the Round Table Conference were endorsed as authoritative.[121]

However, questions of political support can only partly explain why the government opted to accept as 'representative' this, rather than any other, group of Muslims. Here it is important to bear in mind that a group dominated by eminent notables with vast economic and social resources at its disposal, such as was the Muslim delegation to the Round Table Conferences, most fully embodied the official conception of Muslims in India as a dispossessed ruling class ever prepared to restore, at whatever cost, something of their former status. In January 1931, the Viceroy, Lord Irwin, wrote to the Secretary of State, Wedgwood Benn, that the government's failure to concede the demands of the Muslim delegation could result in 'a situation of the utmost gravity'.[122] Benn's own feelings were likely to have been reinforced by the Āgā Khān's talk of a Muslim mass protest;[123] while Irwin's successor, Lord Willingdon, pressed Whitehall to give in to Fazl-i-Husain's men or risk 'a situation in this country which almost certainly will demand measures more drastic than we have yet taken.'[124] The Muslims, he emphasised, were 'a people emotional, suspicious, apprehensive of their future and apt to be hasty in opinion and violent in action'.[125]

The promise of political support, and atavistic fears of a Muslim uprising, ensured that Fazl-i-Husain's preferences dominated official thinking at the First and Second Round Table Conferences held in 1930 and 1931.[126] The 'representative' Muslim position was defined as one which postulated a weak federal centre for India and autonomous constituent units, within which Muslim majorities would be protected by statutory measures ranging from reserved seats to separate electorates. The Communal Award, granted by the government in the summer of 1932, incorporated the gist of this position. It guaranteed Muslims substantial representation in Muslim majority provinces and unequivo-

---

[121] Memorandum from Aga Khan to Samuel Hoare, 9 March 1932, *Private Office Records* L/PO/49.
[122] Telegram from Irwin to Wedgwood Benn, 15 January 1931, *Halifax Papers*, quoted in Kaura, *Muslims and Indian Nationalism*, p. 67.
[123] Wedgwood Benn to Irwin, 17 January 1931, *Halifax Collection* (6), quoted in Moore, *The Crisis of Indian Unity*, p. 163.
[124] Lord Willingdon to Samuel Hoare, 10 July 1932, *Templewood Papers*, quoted in Kaura, *Muslims and Indian Nationalism*, p. 85.
[125] *Ibid.*
[126] Fazl-i-Husain was in every sense the *éminence grise* of the Conference. His absence he owed to his appointment as the Muslim member of the Viceroy's Council. Moore, *The Crisis of Indian Unity*, p. 121.

190 Community and consensus in Islam

cally recommended complete self-government for the provinces.[127]

Fazl-i-Husain's spectacular gains might well have won him the acclamation of Muslim India, but already there were discontented rumblings which suggested that his political success had been won at the cost of setting aside the dominant assumptions that had shaped Indo-Muslim politics since the late nineteenth century. Of these, the idea of a Muslim 'community' predicated upon notions of Islamic solidarity was clearly central. While the exigencies of colonial politics had sometimes led Muslims to confront the difficulties of realising this most compelling vision, the power of its appeal was far from eroded. In December 1930, Iqbāl admonished Muslims against the 'narrow visioned sacrifice of Islamic solidarity in the interests of what may be called "Punjab Ruralism"'.[128] Iqbāl's censure was more than just a call to expose the pettiness of Punjabi provincialism against the grandeur of Islamic universalism. It was as much a statement about the proper limits of Muslim political conduct as understood and expounded by a high-minded scripturalist tradition in Islam.

For Iqbāl, Fazl-i-Hussain's brand of 'Ruralism' went against the very dynamic that had contributed to the strength of the Muslim community. It was this dynamic, which he referred to as the 'herd instinct', that had restrained individuals and groups in their pursuit of 'independent careers' devoid of communal purpose.[129] It was clear to Iqbāl that the orientations of Fazl-i-Husain's politics which had cut at all-India Muslim solidarity, were vastly more insidious than the 'sectional bickerings' common to his religion. For while these did not, in his view, question 'the sole principle of our structure as a people', and rarely ended in detachment 'from the general body of Islam', diversity in political action could be fatal to the life of the community. For it was a community whose political unity postulated God's own unity, and was its very *raison d'être*.[130]

Iqbāl's public reflections about the proper ends of Muslim political action were not exceptional. In January 1910, Sayyid Amīr 'Alī had drawn the attention of Indian Muslims to the dangers of political competition for the future of their community. The prospect of Council elections prompted him to remind his fellow-Muslims of the 'curse' of 'political individualism', or what classical jurists in another age might

[127] See *Communal Decision, Parliamentary Paper* (1932), Cmd. 4147.
[128] See Muhammad Iqbal's presidential address to the All India Muslim League, 29 December 1930, in Pirzada (ed.), *Foundations of Pakistan*, II, p. 166.
[129] *Ibid.*, p. 170.
[130] *Ibid.*, p. 159.

have dubbed the sin of *bidʿa*, or innovation.[131] For him, the solidarity of the Muslim community was bound by 'the dictates of religion' which condemned 'separate political platforms'.[132] Admittedly, both Amīr ʿAlī and Iqbāl were moved to a degree by political considerations; the former to establish the authority of the fledgling League over the claims of 'nationalist' Muslims allied with Congress, the latter to restore the influence of urban Punjabi Muslims for whom Fazl-i-Husain and his Unionist Party had had little time. At the same time, knowing what we do of these men in the context of their lives and the tradition they cherished, it would scarcely be appropriate to dismiss their concerns as either disingenuous or mere political froth.[133]

There is perhaps rather more to be said here for Iqbāl for whom the ideology of 'Ruralism' is likely to have represented a distinct move away from the tradition of scripturalist Islam fostered by the reform movements of the late nineteenth century, which both he and Amīr ʿAlī had done so much to promote. Its most characteristic feature was a universalism which sought to 'transcend the peripatetic religions of local pirs' who were, for the most part, rural-based. Their cultivation of a 'folk' Islam with its attendant evils of personal devotion to the *pīr*, symbolised precisely the cult of the individual which Muslims like Iqbāl and Amīr ʿAlī would have regarded as fundamentally opposed to Islam's emphasis on an impersonal Law.[134] While the agricultural bias of Fazl-i-Husain's Unionist Party may well have suited the conditions of Punjabi politics, they were unlikely to appeal to the proponents of a tradition whose denunciation of 'folk' Islam was shared by urban-based religious movements as varied and as different as Aligarh and Deoband.

However if Punjabi 'Ruralism' did not accurately represent the concerns of a dominant Indo-Muslim tradition, how then did the League confront the democratic verdict in 1937 which appeared decisively to endorse both 'Ruralism' and 'provincialism', not only in the Punjab, but in Muslim strongholds like Bengal, Sind and the North West Frontier Province?[135] How did the party hold resolutely to the

---

[131] See his address to the All India Muslim League, 29 January 1910, *ibid.*, I, p. 109.

[132] *Ibid.*, p. 113.

[133] Nor were the preoccupations with Muslim unity peculiar to men of ideas: both the Āga Khān and Shafaʿāt Ahmad Khān, intrepid politicians and allies of Fazl-i-Husain at the Round Table Conferences, appear also to have been disturbed by what they perceived to be Fazl-i-Husain's cynical disregard of Muslim solidarity in India. See Jalal and Seal, 'Alternative to Partition', pp. 445–9.

[134] Barbara Metcalf, 'Iqbal: Ideology in Search of an Audience', in C.M. Naim (ed.), *Iqbāl, Jinnah and Pakistan* (Delhi, Jinnah Publishing House, 1982), pp. 132–44.

[135] In the Punjab, the League won one out of eighty-four seats reserved for Muslims; in

view that it embodied the true expression of a Muslim *ijmā'* in India? How much did this conviction owe to prevailing assumptions about the nature of a 'Muslim consensus' as distinct from one founded on principles of 'arithmetical democracy'?

To pursue the inquiry along these lines is not to claim that the followers of the League were oblivious to the need to establish their claims on democratic grounds. Indeed it can be argued, if the League's annual session in October 1937 immediately after the elections is anything to go by, that it was painfully aware of the discrepancies between what it claimed to be and what in fact it was. This was eminently reflected in Jinnah's presidential address which remains not only an exercise in reviving the League's failing morale, but also a sober recognition of the party's dissociation from the current of Indo-Muslim consensus.[136] Nor was Jinnah alone in realising that without a popular organisation capable of securing a majority of popular votes, the League could make few claims to speak authoritatively on behalf of Indian Muslims. In May 1937, Iqbāl had written to Jinnah emphasising that the League's credibility as a medium of representative Muslim opinion in India would have to depend upon its transformation into a mass party concerned with popular issues like the eradication of poverty.[137]

Whilst these public and private reflections among Muslims in the League demonstrate a recognition of the need for a popularly based consensus as a measure of political representation, they are not without important caveats. To appreciate these, is to draw attention to the ambiguities that have characterised modern Muslim thinking on the nature of consensus and to suggest that the League reflected those ambiguities. Iqbāl's reservations about the merits of Western democracy, which he believed equated political consensus with the counting of heads, have already been discussed.[138] So too have those of Sayyid Amīr 'Alī, who was decidedly of the view that an authentic Muslim consensus depended not upon the force of numbers but upon a quest for God's law.[139] Even Muslims not known for their indebtedness to 'Islamic modes' of thinking, like Jinnah, drew upon and acknowledged

---

Sind, three out of thirty-three; in Bengal, thirty-nine out of 117; while in the North West Frontier, it won no seats at all. *Return Showing the Results of Elections in India (1937), Parliamentary Paper Cmnd.* 5589.

[136] See his address to the All India Muslim League, 15 October 1937, in Pirzada (ed.), *Foundations of Pakistan*, II, pp. 265–73.

[137] He wrote 'The question therefore is: how is it possible to solve the problem of Muslim poverty? And the whole future of the League depends on the League's activity to solve this question'. Iqbal to Jinnah, 28 May 1937, in S.S. Pirzada (ed.), *Quaid-e-Azam Jinnah's Correspondence* (Karachi, Guild Publishing House, 1966), p. 159.

[138] Chapter 1, pp. 34–5.

[139] *Ibid.*, p. 34.

the authority of such an understanding of consensus. The true expression of what Muslims really want, he declared in December 1938, was not always to be found in the sum of votes cast. 'The counting of heads', he confessed, 'may be a very good thing; but it is not the final arbiter of the destiny of nations'.[140] Later, in March 1939, he underlined his belief in a notion of consensus that was not, ultimately, open to common democratic criteria. 'You may think', he observed impatiently, 'that the counting of heads is the final judgement ... But let me tell you ... You will never be able to destroy the culture we have inherited, the Islamic culture'.[141]

What these observations suggest is that for Muslims, even as apparently diverse as Jinnah and Iqbāl, the final sanction of a Muslim consensus did not, and indeed could not, lie in mere numerical configurations. They point, some more explicitly than others, to the assumption that the real force of such a consensus rested in its conformity to that which was deemed to be divinely ordained. They imply that what was imperative was to aspire to the representation of what was held to be 'Islamic' (howsoever that was defined), rather than of what was constitutive of Muslim opinion at the time. In this they were consistent with the notion that the representation of a Muslim consensus was not, at heart, the representation of a self-governing aggregate but of a 'charismatic' community in the service of some higher end.

To attempt to grasp the League's understanding of its own representative status in these terms is not to mystify the politics in which it was palpably engaged. It is rather to suggest a deeply complex and subtle relationship between the dominant assumptions of a religious and political tradition and the activity of those who recognised its authority. It is to be able to comprehend, more fully, respected modern assessments of the League which attribute its success among Indian Muslims not in terms of how 'it stood at the time of elections' but in terms of 'the idea it represented'.[142]

---

[140] See his address to the All India Muslim League, 26 December 1938, in Pirzada (ed.), *Foundations of Pakistan*, II, p. 307.

[141] See his speech to the Legislative Assembly on 22 March 1939 in Jamil-ud-din Ahmad (ed.), *Speeches and Writings of Mr. Jinnah*, I, p. 84.

[142] Z.H. Zaidi, 'Aspects of the Development of Muslim League Policy, 1937–1947', in Philips and Wainwright (eds.), *The Partition of India*, p. 254.

6

Muslims and non-Muslims
the logic of parity,
1937–1947

The idea that Muslim representation should be liberated from the constraints of political arithmetic was to become an integral part of the League's constitutional discourse in the 1940s. Indeed, it lay at the very heart of its claim to parity of representation which led Jinnah, subsequently, to proclaim that Indian Muslims were a 'nation' entitled to equality of status and 'national self-determination'.[1]

There were of course good political reasons for the issue of Hindu–Muslim parity to surface more prominently in the late 1930s and 1940s than at any other time in the past. The results of the provincial elections of 1937 which returned Congress with decisive majorities in six out of eleven provinces in British India persuaded growing numbers of Indian Muslims that the pressures to devolve power to a Hindu majority at the centre could only intensify. Congress's demand for constitutional changes on the basis of majority rule led many to believe that Hindu–Muslim parity at the centre was the only means to ensure that Muslims had an effective voice at the all-India level. Many were drawn at this time to deal with the problem of their status as an Indian minority by attempting to redefine their community as a 'nation' entitled to equality of representation with a non-Muslim majority.[2] However, it was the outbreak of the War in September 1939, and Britain's readiness to accept the claims of those who promised to support her War effort, that helped finally to crystallise the demand for parity.

Although the right to parity as an extension of Muslim 'nationhood' was admittedly a response to the prospects of democratic self-government at

---

[1] According to one observer, the failure to obtain Western representative institutions commenced when the logic of democracy was met with the logic of nationalism. Reginald Coupland, *Indian Politics, 1936–1942, Report on the Constitutional Problem in India*, II (London, Oxford University Press, 1943), p. 243.

[2] 'If the Hindus believed in the rule of the majority, the Muslims denied that they were a minority ... To the Congress claim that India was a national state, the Muslims answered with a brand new idea of a separate Muslim nationalism'. K.K. Aziz, *The Making of Modern Pakistan: A Study in Nationalism* (London, Chatto and Windus, 1967), pp. 60, 61.

the centre, it is important not to lose sight of its historical antecedents in the development of Indo-Muslim politics. Its roots lay deep in the nebulous 'two-nation' theory, frequently attributed to Sayyid Ahmad Khān, and Iqbāl's rather more complex understanding of Muslim 'nationhood'. Although each tended to conceive of a distinct Indo-Muslim identity as flowing from quite different sources – the one from foreign ancestry, the other from God's final revelation to Man – both contributed to the idea of a separate Muslim 'nation' by emphasising that its bases lay beyond the immediate confines of India and the reach of a common 'Indian' nationalism. Whilst these cultural and religious definitions of a Muslim 'nation' were crucial to sustain the Muslim claim to parity, institutional measures too had contributed decisively to its evolution. The introduction of 'weightage' for Muslims under the reforms of 1909 was founded on the very assumption that their status as a minority was questionable. Although 'weightage' did not postulate, as parity was later to do, a Muslim 'nation', it did recognise a distinct community whose right to be represented was deemed not to be subject to strict numerical criteria.

The problems posed by the demand for Hindu–Muslim parity were not however confined only to questions about the proper nature, or the political status, of Muslims in India. What proved in the end to impinge directly upon the decision to partition India was whether or not parity could obtain the elements of a free electoral system. For parity, as understood and expounded by its proponents in the Muslim League, implied not only the right of Indian Muslims to equality of representation as a 'nation', but also the exclusive prerogative of a Muslim party to represent a Muslim electorate. Parity then was as much an assertion of the rights of Indian Muslims as it was a denial of the political freedom of non-Muslims to elect Muslim representatives of their choice. These complex, but nonetheless fundamental orientations, were to be expressed in the course of prolonged constitutional negotiations in the 1940s. The League's response to the government's 'August Offer'; its reactions to the Cripps blueprint for an Indian constitution; its conditions for an Interim Government during the War and its approach to the Cabinet Mission Plan, were all deeply suggestive of the real implications of parity as the basis of Indian representation.

Whilst the political imperatives underlying the demand for parity were unquestionably compelling, the issue is important for its significance to Muslims as a measure of 'just' representation, and its relation to their vision of societal organisation. At its most fundamental level, parity embodied the essential features of an alternative model of representation which Muslims have tended to regard as authoritative. It expressed profound reservations about the merits of the 'law of numbers' and of the capacity of a democratic consensus, in itself, to sustain a just 'constitution'. For such a 'constitution' entailed the recognition of a set of principles whose rational foundations were seen to be grounded not in some humanly devised system of democratic pluralism, but in the norms of a God-given law. It postulated a division between Muslims and non-Muslims and questioned the notion of a common political 'good'. It assumed that members of the 'charismatic' community were endowed with superior moral attributes which qualified them to an *a priori* claim to power and leadership. It held that 'justice' lay not in establishing the claims of men as members of a common society, but as those who participated in God's final compact for mankind. Parity then was not just an issue of immediate political urgency for Indian Muslim's in the 1940s, but a restatement of the most authentic values of their political tradition.

The transition to parity, 1937–1939

The aftermath of the elections of 1937 was marked by one of the most extraordinary contradictions in modern representative politics. For while the elections appeared decisively to have established that the League did not, in fact, represent Indian Muslims, the League for its part claimed that it was the only authoritative voice of Muslim India. This assertion in the face of adversity has been interpreted as a sign of Jinnah's unfailing capacity to make a virtue out of his party's every weakness.[3] This may well be true. But Jinnah's position also reflects his espousal of a complex set of assumptions about the nature of Muslim representation, its scope and its ultimate purpose.

In the Spring of 1936 Jinnah, who had been persuaded to return to India after a period of self-imposed isolation in England, threw himself into the task of revitalising a flagging League. Although the party had denounced the recently introduced Government of India Act of 1935 as 'wholly unacceptable'[4], it was obliged nevertheless to contest the elections under the new Act if only to establish its claim to be the premier Muslim party in British India. The task, however, was far from simple. The creation of a League Central Parliamentary Board to persuade Muslims in the provinces to return only such candidates as would be

---

[3] A point developed at some length in Ayesha Jalal, *The Sole Spokesman: Jinnah, the Muslim League and the Demand for Pakistan* (Cambridge University Press, 1985).
[4] Sharif-ud-din Pirzada (ed.), *Foundations of Pakistan, Documents of the All India Muslim League, 1906–1947*, II (Karachi, National Publishing House, 1970), p. 260.

prepared to run on purely communal tickets was fiercely resisted, especially in the Punjab and Bengal. Here, Fazl-i-Husain's Unionists and Fazlul Haq's Krishak-Praja Party, respectively, were determined to continue their tradition of inter-communal co-operation from which both had tended, on the whole, to benefit hugely. In the two other Muslim majority provinces of Sind and the North West Frontier, the League had little or no standing. In Sind, rampant factionalism among groups of Muslim notables rendered impossible any workable coalition, let alone one under the auspices of a political body as feeble as the League.[5] Indeed, it was the very absence of any real organisational power that accounted for the League's failure even to attempt to obtain a mandate from the Muslims of the North West Frontier Province. Here the Khudā'ī Khidmatgārs [Servants of God], led by Khān 'Abdu'l Ghaffār Khān had succeeded in mobilising a degree of popular support among the Pathans that the League's strife-torn tribal following was quite unable to match.[6]

The provincial elections demonstrated that the League's failure to come to terms with the realities of Muslim politics in the provinces, and its careless handling of organisational issues, had relegated it to the position of a second-class Muslim party. In the Punjab, only one out of eighty-four seats reserved for Muslims went to a League candidate. In Bengal, the League obtained a mere thirty-nine out of one hundred and seventeen seats; while in the North West Frontier and Sind, it claimed none.[7] Although the League did relatively well in the important constituencies of the United Provinces, winning twenty-seven of the sixty-four Muslim seats, its failure to arrive at an agreement for a coalition government with Congress only seemed to confirm its dismal prospects as a party forever excluded from office.[8] Its electoral rout was even worse compared to the impressive returns obtained by Congress. Of the 1,585 seats allocated to provincial assemblies, Congress won 716. Congress's actual standing was probably higher if one accounts for more than half the total number of seats reserved for or allocated to

---

[5] Jalal, *The Sole Spokesman*, p. 28.

[6] *Ibid.*

[7] See *Return Showing the Results of the Elections in India, 1937, Parliamentary Paper*, Cmd. 5589 (1937). For results in the Punjab see *ibid.*, pp. 277–85; in Bengal, *ibid.*, pp. 245–58; in the North-West Frontier Province, *ibid.*, pp. 311–13; in Sind, *ibid.*, pp. 318–21.

[8] For results in the United Provinces see *ibid.*, pp. 260–73. For some partisan perspectives on the United Provinces coalition controversy see Abul Kalam Azad, *India Wins Freedom* (Bombay, Orient Longmans, 1959), pp. 160–3 and Choudhry Khaliquzzaman, *Pathway to Pakistan* (Lahore, Longmans Green, 1961), pp. 152–63.

special electorates. Against this, the League won only 109 out of 482 seats reserved for Muslims and represented no more than 4.8 per cent of the total Muslim electorate.[9]

However the League's poor electoral standing in relation both to provincial Muslim parties and to Congress was offset by two vital considerations which drew something off the fire of their rival claims to representation. First, the scope of regionally based Muslim parties equipped them primarily to represent local interests which were of little or no relevance at the all-India level. In the event of British withdrawal, it was likely that many would have turned to the League to secure the representation of their Muslim constituents at the centre. Second, while it is true that Congress had obtained a resounding mandate from the non-Muslim electorate, its share of Muslim votes was decidedly disappointing. Of the fifty-eight Muslim candidates put up by Congress to contest separately elected Muslim seats, only twenty-six were successful.[10]

In its attempts to regain its political credibility as a representative party, the League sought to underline these limitations by drawing upon two powerful assumptions that had shaped Indo-Muslim political thinking since the turn of the century and that continued to dominate contemporary Muslim discourse. The first, which acted to check political competition from powerful Muslim groups in the provinces, was the idea of a Muslim political community, or 'nation', predicated upon the solidarity of those who adhered to God's final revelation to Man. The second, which tended more to cut at Congress's claim to carry a Muslim electorate, was the notion of Muslim representation as a 'trust' that could not, in the absence of a common 'good', be delegated to non-Muslims. To recognise the force of these ideas is not to suggest that they conveyed the same sense to all Muslims or indeed, that they were not put to quite diverse ends. For if the concept of 'nation' enabled some like Jinnah to see in it the only effective means to restore the League's political standing as a 'national' party at the all-India level equal in status to Congress, it allowed others like Iqbāl to restore what remained of the individual Muslim's relation to 'the community of believers'. At the same time, while some like Jinnah were aware that the League's Muslim credentials had proved to be of little use in winning the confidence of Indian Muslims, many Muslims were likely to have accepted the premise that a non-Muslim organisation like Congress could not obtain the authentic representation of a Muslim electorate.

[9] *Return Showing the Results of the Election in India, 1937*, Cmd. 5589.
[10] *Ibid.*

It was in the Muslim majority provinces of the Punjab and Bengal that the League's representative credentials were most severely tested. Fazl-i-Husain's death in the summer of 1936 had held out the promise of a possible settlement between the League and the Unionist Party, although one that was likely to be drawn up in line with Unionist preferences in mind, namely its exclusive control over Punjabi affairs.[11] However, it was not until after the elections that Fazl-i-Husain's successor, Sikander Hayāt Khān, agreed to draw up a pact which would bind Unionists to accept the League's *diktat* at the all-India level in return for its pledge to keep out of the Punjab.[12] While some have concluded that the Pact was essentially a victory for the Unionists[13], there is no denying that 'from a constitutional point of view [it created] a Muslim League Party out of nothing in the Punjab Assembly'.[14] In a context where constitutional recognition was seen to be an indispensable condition of representation, this was no mean achievement.

Things were not very different in Bengal. Here Fazlul Haq's Krishak Praja Party, 'non-communal in aim and objective' but 'dominantly Muslim in composition and leadership', was clearly the League's most formidable challenge;[15] but the Praja Party was deeply divided, and Congress's unwillingness to assume ministerial responsibility in a coalition government under the new Act led Haq to approach the League in the hope of securing his ministry.[16] Haq's offer to fuse his organisation with the League (rather than merely to coalesce with it), as well as the sheer urgency of obtaining a mandate from the Muslim majority provinces, proved irresistible to Jinnah.[17] The emergence of a 'Bengal Muslim League', albeit on the back of a Praja Party, ensured once again that the League could formally, if not actually, claim to represent a sizeable Muslim electorate.

The League's quest to establish its political standing in these years could prompt the historian to conclude that its survival owed everything

---

[11] Azim Husain, *Fazl-i-Husain: A Political Biography* (Bombay, Longmans Green, 1964), pp. 308–9; Sikander Hayat Khan to Fazl-i-Husain, 1 May 1936 in Waheed Ahmad (ed.), *Letter of Fazl-i-Husain* (Lahore, Research Society of Pakistan, 1976), p. 528. See also B.B. Misra, *The Indian Political Parties: An Historical Analysis of Political Behaviour up to 1947* (Delhi, Oxford University Press, 1976), p. 416.

[12] Stanley Wolpert, *Jinnah of Pakistan* (New York, Oxford University Press, 1984), pp. 151–2.

[13] Jalal, *The Sole Spokesman*, p. 39.

[14] Misra, *The Indian Political Parties*, p. 417.

[15] Humayun Kabir, *Muslim Politics, 1906–1942* (Calcutta, Firma Mukhopadhyay, 1944), p. 36.

[16] Leonard Gordon, *Bengal: The Nationalist Movement, 1876–1940* (New York, Columbia University Press, 1974), pp. 279–88.

[17] Jalal, *The Sole Spokesman*, p. 40.

to the good-will of Muslim bosses in the provinces and to the skills of men like Jinnah to make the right moves. It could lead to the conclusion that the demand for a separate Muslim homeland which the League was made to espouse, was no more than a bold attempt to play a dangerous hand of cards. However, this would be to suggest that the evolution of the League and the outcome of its politics progressed independently of the values that had influenced Muslim political action from the late nineteenth century. It would be to ignore the force of a persistent discourse on the political community as an extension of Muslim religious fellowship which explains not only what legitimised the League's politics, but what constrained it to accept a course that some have regarded as ostensibly against the 'interests' of the vast majority of Indian Muslims.

The basis of parity: the idea of a Muslim 'nation'

The growing preoccupation among groups of Indian Muslims in the 1930s with the notion of a 'Muslim India within India'[18] was far from new. In December 1921, as the euphoria of Hindu–Muslim co-operation waned steadily, the redoubtable Maulānā Hasrat Mohānī exhorted Muslims to act upon their power as a political majority in the north-west and east of India, and to demand their right to self-determination. This alone, Mohānī emphasised, would ensure that Muslims lived their lives as Muslims.[19] Although he is unlikely to have envisaged either partition or separate Muslim statehood, Mohānī's understanding of the practice of the true faith as dependent in some degree upon political control, was to lie at the heart of subsequent proposals for a separate homeland.

These focussed attention upon the right of Muslim majorities in the North, West, and East of India to govern autonomously and to constitute a 'nation' based upon the profession of a common faith. Such themes found their most coherent expression, in December 1930, when Iqbāl chose to use the occasion of the annual session of the League to expound upon the contemporary significance of Muslim solidarity in India. His vision of a 'consolidated North Western Muslim State'[20] stemmed in the first instance from a desire 'to obtain a territorial

---

[18] A phrase borrowed from Muhammad Iqbāl's famous presidential address to the All Indian Muslim League on 29 December 1930 in Pirzada (ed.), *Foundations of Pakistan*, II, p. 159.

[19] See Mohānī's presidential address to the All India Muslim League on 30 December 1921, in *ibid.*, I, pp. 556–63.

[20] See Iqbāl's presidential address to the All India Muslim League on 29 December 1930 in *ibid.*, II, p. 159. The thorny question of whether or not Iqbāl intended his proposed

solution to India's communal problem'.[21] At a more profound level
however, it expressed a concern for 'the life of Islam as a cultural
force'.[22] Whilst Iqbāl was willing to recognise that the survival of Islam
in India might ultimately have to depend upon its 'centralization in a
specified area',[23] he was not prepared to accept, in principle, a
nationalism predicated upon territorial boundaries. 'The construction
of a polity on national lines', he declared, 'if it means a displacement of
the Islamic principle of solidarity, is simply unthinkable to a Muslim'.[24]
To believe that the development of Muslim nationalism in Turkey could
reasonably be compared to European nationalism which assumed an
attachment to territory was, in his view, quite fallacious.[25] Muslims, he
contended, were a 'nation' not because they occupied a particular
territory but because they were bound by a common religious ideal.
What necessitated their 'national' development in India along territorial
lines was not so much the espousal of 'European political thinking'
(although Iqbāl could not altogether ignore its powerful appeal among a
younger generation of Muslims), but the fact that the ethical ideal of
Islam was incapable of fulfilment in India without its embodiment in a
polity.[26]

On the face of it Iqbāl's position appears to have been patently
inconsistent. For while he rejected European nationalism as inherently
incompatible with Islam's universalist impulse, he was apparently
prepared to set this aside in the interests of Muslims in India by
advocating a form of territorial nationalism. Yet, while there is no
denying the pragmatic component of his concern which led him to
favour a territorial base 'for the enforcement and development of the

Muslim State to be construed as an endorsement of the 'Pakistan Plan' was subject to
some debate amongst his contemporaries. Edward Thompson, the British journalist
for *The Observer* claimed that Iqbāl had privately expressed grave reservations about
the idea of 'Pakistan', but that as President of the League he had had no option but to
support it publicly. See Edward Thompson, *Enlist India for Freedom!* (London, Victor
Gollancz, 1940), p. 58. Others, like Āshiq Husain Batālvī, a close friend and confidante of Iqbāl's, hotly disputed Thompson's contention and maintained that it was
wholly lacking in substance. See Āshiq Husain Batālvī, *Iqbāl kē ākhrī dō sāl* (Lahore,
Iqbāl Academi, 1969, reprint), pp. 580–90.

[21] See Iqbal's presidential address in Pirzada (ed.), *Foundations of Pakistan,* II, p. 166.
[22] *Ibid.*, p. 159.
[23] *Ibid.*
[24] *Ibid.*, p. 157.
[25] Muhammad Iqbal, 'Islam and Ahmadism' in Latif Ahmed Sherwani (ed. and
compiler), *Speeches, Writings and Statements of Iqbal* (Lahore, Iqbal Academy, 1977),
p. 197. See also Anwar H. Syed, 'Allama Iqbal and the Quaid-i-Azam on Issues of
Nationhood and Nationalism' in A.H. Dani (ed.), *World Scholars on Quaid-i-Azam
Mohammad Ali Jinnah* (Islamabad, Quaid-i-Azam University, 1979), pp. 200–21.
[26] Pirzada (ed.), *Foundations of Pakistan,* II, p. 154.

Shariat of Islam' in India[27], it is important not to lose sight of the imperative determinants which shaped Iqbāl's position on Muslim nationalism. Here it is worth recalling his conviction that in order to obtain Islamic universalism as an 'effective ideal', it was necessary to commence with a society exclusive in organisation but cosmopolitan in purpose.[28] As early as 1921, Iqbāl had recognised that the endeavour to obtain Islamic universalism in 'actual life' might involve Muslim 'national organizations' as 'temporary phases in the unfoldment and upbringing of collective life'.[29] For what was eminently clear to him was that the ideal of Islamic universalism could not be obtained in political submission.[30] For Muslims in India to voluntarily accept a nationalism that postulated domination by non-Muslims would be to negate the very essence of their faith and its commitment to a universal society.[31]

It was precisely this profound appreciation of the political dimension of Islamic universalism that led Iqbāl to expound upon the philosophical unity of the *quam* (nation) and the *umma* (community) – a unity that lay at the heart of the claim to parity and Pakistan. Shortly before his death in March 1938, Iqbāl was engaged in a public debate with **Maulānā** Husain Ahmad Madanī, a Deobandi and a leading figure among the 'nationalist' *'ulamā'*.[32] It was a debate that commanded intense public attention among Indian Muslims and represented, for many, the most sustained discourse on the meaning of the political community as an extension of religious fellowship.[33]

---

[27] Muhammad Iqbal to M.A. Jinnah, 28 May 1937 in S.S. Pirzada (ed.), *Quaid-e-Azam Jinnah's Correspondence* (Karachi, Guild Publishing House, 1966), p. 159. In another letter to Jinnah, Iqbāl stressed the need for a 'federation of Muslim provinces' which could 'save Muslims from the domination of non-Muslims'. See Muhammad Iqbal to M.A. Jinnah, 21 June 1937, *ibid.*, p. 163.

[28] Muhammad Iqbal to R.A. Nicholson, 24 January 1921 in Bashir Ahmad Dar (ed. and compiler), *Letters of Iqbal* (Lahore, Iqbal Academy, 1978), p. 144.

[29] *Ibid.*, p. 145. For Iqbāl, Muslim nationalism was inherent in 'the conceptual structure' of Islam and in its relation to 'the process of time'. Muhammad Iqbal, 'Islam and Ahmadism' in Sherwani (ed. and compiler), *ibid.*, p. 198.

[30] *Ibid.*, p. 197.

[31] Saleem M.M. Qureshi, 'Iqbal and Jinnah: Personalities, Perceptions and Politics' in C.M. Naim (ed.), *Iqbal, Jinnah and Pakistan* (Delhi, Jinnah Publishing House, 1982), pp. 11–39 and Anwar Syed, 'Allama Iqbal', pp. 203–12.

[32] I.H. Qureshi, *Ulema in Politics: A Study Relating to the Political Activities of the Ulema in the South Asian Subcontinent from 1556 to 1947* (Karachi, Ma'aref, 1972), pp. 340–6 and Aziz Ahmad, *Islamic Modernism in India and Pakistan* (London, Oxford University Press, 1967), pp. 191–3. See also Parveen Feroze Hassan, *The Political Philosophy of Iqbal*, (Lahore, Publishers United, 1970), pp. 204–7.

[33] There had of course been other more obscure and less well thought out expositions, like those of Maulānā Muhammad 'Ibrāhīm whose pamphlet on the essentials of Muslim religious nationalism first appeared in 1911. In it, he sought to argue that the fundamental laws governing all societies were necessarily religious. This, he main-

The issue centred broadly on whether the Indian Muslims were a *qaum*, in the Qur'ānic sense, that is to say a part of a confederation of religious communities, or a *qaum* in the modern sense, that is to say a community defined by territory. Madanī, who opposed the movement for a separate Muslim state, held that to the extent that contemporary nations were formed and defined by reference to land, Muslims were not a nation. They were, he maintained, pre-eminently a religious fellowship, a *millat*, which could coexist with other religious communities as a *qaum* in the Qur'ānic sense.[34] Madanī's understanding of 'nation' and the nature of Muslim communal organisation is, at first glance, neither exceptional nor questionable. It recalled a fairly established tradition of *muttahida qaumīyyat*, or composite nationalism, that Maulānā Āzād had already done much to promote, and reaffirmed common definitions of both 'nation' and the nature of Muslim communal organisation.[35] At the same time, Madanī's views had profound implications for a solution to the Muslim problem in India. For it questioned the right of Indian Muslims to national self-determination and attempted to reconcile the pursuit of a common Indian nationalism with the conduct of Muslim religious fellowship.

Yet, while Madanī sought through definitions of 'nation' (*qaum*) and religious fellowship (*millat*) to legitimise Muslim support for Indian nationalism, he clearly overlooked the fundamental component that had tended to unify these concepts in classical Muslim thinking. That component was power, and it was left to Iqbāl to restate its contemporary relevance to the ends of Muslim collective endeavour and to show how it had sustained the modern Muslim's '*dīn-i-qā'yyim*': a faith coextensive with, not exclusive of, the nation 'in its true cultural or political sense'.[36] In his riposte to Madanī, Iqbāl denied that all nations

tained, was more true of Muslim societies where Islam acted as the sole uniting principle, or 'amr-i-jama'a. Neither territory nor lineage, he asserted, could ever be sufficient to define the basis of Muslim 'nationhood' for, he claimed, Muslims were as common to India as they were to Turkey and embraced Mughals no less keenly than Syeds. See Maulānā Muhammad Ibrahīm, *Qaum aur mazhab* (Amritsar, Munshi Abdul Rahman Shauq, 1911), pp. 5–12.

[34] Husain Ahmad Madanī, *Muttahida' Qaumīyyat aur Islām* (Delhi, n.d.), pp. 21–6.
[35] Aziz Ahmad, *Islamic Modernism in India and Pakistan, 1857–1964* (London, Oxford University Press, 1964), pp. 186–90. See also the diverse perspectives offered on Āzād and his theory of nationalism in Maulana Azad Memorial Committee (ed.), *Azad, Islam and Nationalism* (New Delhi, Kalamkar Prakashan, n.d.), especially the essays by Moin Shakir, 'Political Ideas of Maulana Azad', pp. 9–39 and Hafeez Malik, 'Abul Kalam Azad's Theory of Nationalism', pp. 56–65.
[36] Muhammad Iqbal, 'Statement on Islam and Nationalism in Reply to a Statement of Maulana Husain Ahmad [Madani]', originally published as 'Islām aur Qaumīyyat' in *Ehsan*, 9 March 1938 and reprinted in Sherwani (ed. and compiler), *Speeches, Writings and Statements*, p. 260.

were defined by land, although he did acknowledge that the development of European nationalism had contributed much to the hold of this idea. He contended that there were other 'principles of human association', such as Islam, which sought to organise men on a wholly different basis.[37] These principles, he believed, were radically incompatible with European nationalism which by its 'indifference to the social order' led inevitably to a secular atheism.[38] It was precisely this radical opposition, he argued, which made it imperative for Muslims in India to resist their inclusion in a common Indian *qaum* which sought to model itself on the lines of Western nationalism.[39]

Iqbāl was determined in his stance against Madanī to take on the whole terminological repertoire of composite nationalism. He began by denying that Muslims had ever partaken of a common contractual arrangement with non-Muslims, an arrangement which Āzād had taken to be the basis for composite nationalism in India, and pointed to the absence in the Qur'ān of any reference to Muslims as members of a *qaum*.[40] This, he maintained, was because the term *qaum* signified 'a mere group' which 'from the viewpoint of divine revelation and of a Prophet'... [was] 'not yet a guided one'.[41] Although Iqbāl did not quarrel with Madanī's description of Indian Muslims as a *millat*, he denied that it reflected the specificity of Muslims as a community. The term *millat*, he claimed, was commonly applied to *any* recognisably distinct group, as well as to the body of unbelievers.[42] What Iqbāl wished to stress was the special status accorded by the Qur'ān to the *umma* which, he asserted, was a term exclusively reserved for Muslims.[43] His purpose in doing so was to establish both the limits and the scope of the *umma*, neither of which he held to be consistent with the principles of composite Indian nationalism. For while Indian nationalism sought to encompass men within the confines of what were essentially arbitrary boundaries, the *umma* aspired to a much broader organisation of human society based on the division of Muslims and non-Muslims.[44]

---

[37] *Ibid.*, p. 253.
[38] *Ibid.*, pp. 254–6.
[39] *Ibid.*, p. 258.
[40] *Ibid.*
[41] *Ibid.*
[42] *Ibid.*, p. 259.
[43] *Ibid.*, p. 260.
[44] He wrote 'After getting the name of the *ummat-i-Muslimah* from the court of God was there any room left for merging part of the form of our society into some Arabian, Afghani, English, Egyptian or Indian nationality? There is only one *millat* confronting the Muslim community, that of the non-Muslims taken collectively'. *Ibid.*, p. 259.

Iqbāl's understanding of the *umma* invoked crucial elements of Muslim political tradition. It reaffirmed the vision of societal organisation along the lines of a division between Muslims and non-Muslims, and restored to the idea of the religious fellowship its dimension as a political order in the service of a higher end. Above all, as Hardy reminds us, it stressed the fundamental Islamic principle which holds that God's Law cannot be lived merely as a moral imperative.[45] Islam could not be reduced to the realm of private individual beliefs nor could the ends of the Muslim *millat* be obtained without a control of its own political destiny. While Iqbāl's exposition differed markedly from that of the nationalist *'ulamā'* like Āzād and Madanī, it is important to recognise precisely what these differences suggested about their hopes for the future of Muslims in India. For it would certainly be naive to pretend that the *'ulamā'*'s 'nationalist' vision had much in common with that of Congress. As commentators and partisans alike have stressed, the *'ulamā'* held tenaciously to the idea of a distinct Muslim component in independent India which would adhere not to a common law inspired by Congress's brand of secular humanism, but to rules grounded in the *Sharī'a*;[46] and while it is true that the 'nationalist' *'ulamā'* preached universalism, few were likely to have envisaged the inclusion of non-Muslims into the 'pious community'.[47]

Iqbāl's stress upon exclusivism as a necessary condition in the evolution towards Islamic universalism and his concern to restore the dynamic components of the *Sharī'a* found a more popular, if idiosyncratic, expression in the political endeavours of Indian Muslims like Chaudhri Rahmat 'Alī and 'Ināyetullāh Mashriqī. In the early 1930s, Rahmat 'Alī, who was still a student at Cambridge, used his Pakistan National Movement to propagate a Muslim 'land of the pure'. He dreamed of an independent Muslim federation whose borders would extend well beyond the Muslim majority areas of the north-west and east of India to encompass pockets of Muslim fiefdom scattered among a handful of princely states.[48] Like Iqbāl, Rahmat 'Alī believed that the

---

[45] Peter Hardy, *Partners in Freedom and True Muslims: The Political Thought of some Muslim Scholars in British India, 1912–1947* (Lund, Scandinavian Institute of Asian Studies, 1971), pp. 39–41.
[46] *Ibid*. See also Maulānā 'Abdu'l Halīm Siddīquī (Nāzim of the Jam'īyyat al-'Ulamā'-i-Hind), *Jam'īyyat al-'Ulamā'-i-Hind kī chand ahm khidmāt-i-millī kā mukhtasar tazkirā* (Delhi, Jam'īyyat al 'Ulamā'-i-Hind, 194-), cf. pp. 12, 13, 16–19, 20–4, 31–7.
[47] Lini May, *The Evolution of Indo-Muslim Thought after 1857* (Lahore, Shaikh Muhammad Ashraf, 1970), p. 194.
[48] Chaudhri Rahmat Ali, *The Millat and the Mission* (Cambridge, Pakasia Literature, 1942), pp. 1–18; see also his *Pakistan: the Fatherland of the Pak Nation* (Cambridge, Pakasia Literature, 1947).

ends of the Muslim *millat* depended in the first instance upon 'its integration with other Muslims' and upon the manifest control of its own political destiny.[49]

It is ironical that the man whose ideas are seen to be 'the practical expression of Iqbāl's dynamism'[50] should also have led one of the groups most opposed to the League's vision of a Muslim state which Iqbāl himself had done so much to promote. Yet it is the case that 'Ināyetullah Mashriqī's Khāksārs attempted, perhaps most fully, to embody the spirit of their faith as a code of action. Although they received little support from the Muslim religious establishment which was wary of the movement's radical overtones, their commitment to a range of charitable causes won them something of a popular following particularly among the urban poor.[51] Mashriqī saw the value of his religious faith to lie in its 'vitalism' and its capacity to generate a society with the means to establish its distinction from, and indeed its opposition to, non-Muslims. Like Iqbāl, he believed that the ultimate destiny of Islam as a universal principle could not be realised without the 'Islamic' dispensation of power.[52]

Between 1938 and 1939, these ideas concerning the scope and the proper ends of the Muslim community found their way into a plethora of constitutional schemes which were to lend credence, some more decidedly than others, to the League's claim to represent an Indian Muslim 'nation'.[53] Some, like the 1938 resolution of the Sind Provincial Branch which advocated self-determination for Hindu and Muslim 'nations', stemmed from within the League itself.[54] Others from individual dreams like those of a diffident 'Punjabi' who called upon the Muslim 'nation' in India to act as 'separationists-cum-federationists', and to demand 'absolute political power' in areas where they were a majority.[55] Yet others emanated from respected academic quarters in

---

[49] Chaudhri Rahmat Ali, *Pakistan*, p. 214. In his view, the most important task facing Muslims in India was 'the release of our nation from the bonds of minorityism'. *Ibid.*, p. 227.

[50] Anne-Marie Schimmel, *Islam in the Indian Subcontinent* (Leiden, E. J. Brill, 1980), p. 239.

[51] Qureshi, *Ulema in Politics*, pp. 324–7 and J.M.S. Baljon, 'A Modern Muslim Decalogue', *World of Islam*, n.s. 3 (1954), pp. 187–200.

[52] Schimmel, *Islam*, p. 240.

[53] For a comprehensive selection of these schemes see M. Gwyer and A. Appadorai (eds.), *Speeches and Documents on the Indian Constitution, 1921–1947*, II (London, Oxford University Press, 1957), pp. 443–73.

[54] Khalid bin Sayeed, *Pakistan: The Formative Phase, 1857–1948* (London, Oxford University Press, 1968), p. 107.

[55] See 'A Punjabi' (Nawab Sir Muhammad Shah Nawaz Khan of Mamdot), *A Confederacy of India* in Reginald Coupland, *The Indian Problem. Report on the*

Hyderabad and Aligarh. These ranged from proposal, for an Indian federation consisting of Hindu and Muslim 'cultural zones'[56] to models which envisaged the partition of the subcontinent into 'a Muslim India and Hindu India'.[57] Although differences of detail tended to separate these schemes from one another, particularly on the issue of whether or not a Muslim 'nation' was entitled to political self-determination and separate statehood, they shared a common repudiation of the ideology of Indian nationalism.[58]

By the spring of 1939, the League was ready to formalise its own position on the existence of a Muslim 'nation' with the inherent right to self-determination and parity of representation.[59] In March 1940, the party adopted what came later to be known as the 'Pakistan Resolution'.[60] Although its actual content was notoriously vague on the question of a constitutionally separate Muslim federation or federations, at least in the immediate future,[61] it clearly intended to redefine India's constitutional problem as 'international' not 'inter-communal' in character.[62] The Resolution has been seen as a spectacular demonstration of Jinnah's skills in harnessing the diverse interests of Indian Muslims with the intention of establishing the League's credentials as the authoritative spokesman of Muslims' interests.[63] Yet, it was more than just a spectacular *tour de force*. In the context of prevailing discussions about Muslim independence, it became a part of a more profound and persistent concern to restore to the religious community its significance as a political order where power, as an instrument of righteousness, would be a Muslim prerogative.

Constitutional Problem in India, II (London, Oxford University Press, 1944), pp. 203–4.

[56] Gwyer and Appadorai (eds.), *Speeches*, II, pp. 444–5.

[57] *Ibid.*, pp. 462–5.

[58] Jinnah rejected the 'cultural zones' proposal because he believed it did not explicitly endorse Muslim self-determination. M.A. Jinnah to S.A. Latif, 12 October 1940, in Nazir Yar Jung (ed.), *The Pakistan Issue: being the correspondence between S.A. Latif and M.A. Jinnah on the one hand, and between him and Maulana A.K. Azad, Dr. Rajendra Prasad and Pandit J. Nehru on the other and connected papers on the subject of Pakistan* (Lahore, Shaikh Muhammad Ashraf, 1943), p. 62.

[59] Sayeed, *The Formative Phase*, p. 108.

[60] See Resolution I passed by the All India Muslim League on 23 March 1940, in Pirzada (ed.), *Foundations of Pakistan*, II, pp. 340–1. See also Latif Ahmad Sherwani (ed.), *Pakistan Resolution to Pakistan, 1940–1947: A Selection of Documents presenting the case for Pakistan* (Karachi, National Publishing House, 1969).

[61] The resolution envisaged 'the assumption *finally*, by the respective regions, of all powers, such as defense, external affairs etc. etc. ...' (my italics). Pirzada (ed.), *Foundations of Pakistan*, II, p. 341.

[62] See Jinnah's presidential address to the All India Muslim League, 22 March 1940, in *ibid.*, p. 337.

[63] Jalal, *The Sole Spokesman*, pp. 54–60.

208 Community and consensus in Islam

The basis of parity: Muslims and non-Muslims

One of the most urgent tasks confronting Jinnah and his almost crippled organisation in the aftermath of the 1937 elections was to undermine, once and for all, Congress' claim to represent Indian Muslims. In December 1938, Jinnah declared, 'Congress is a Hindu body... The presence of the few Muslims... who are there with ulterior motives, does not, cannot, make it a national body'.[64] The refrain was a familiar one with a history stretching as far back as the days of Sayyid Ahmad Khān. However, the urgency of taking on Congress at a time when responsible government loomed as a distinct possibility was clearly of a different order. Congress had of course always claimed to be a national organisation whose gaze was set firmly on all-India heights. The elections had established that Congress could scale those heights and come well within reach of the top. The League, for its part, knew that this objective could be made hopelessly elusive if it could demonstrate that Congress as a predominantly non-Muslim organisation could not, by definition, hope to scale the summit on behalf of Muslims. Having failed to obtain a political mandate from the Muslim electorate and faced with the prospect of being overridden by Congress, the League now sought to revive an understanding of representation that was grounded, in part, in the assumptions of an Indo-Muslim religious tradition. What the League tried to establish was not whether Congress spoke for Indian Muslims, for that would surely have exposed the weakness of its own claims to do so, but whether non-Muslims could legitimately express a Muslim consensus.

The League's contention that Congress did not represent Indian Muslims was not therefore at issue, least of all it would seem for Congress. The election results were evidence enough that Congress did not, on the whole, command the confidence of the Muslim electorate, and the party's 'mass contact' campaign among Indian Muslims in the late 1930s clearly testified to its recognition of Muslim alienation.[65] Nor indeed, to be fair, did Congress maintain that it did or could represent the entire gamut of Indian political opinion. As Jawaharlal Nehru reminded Jinnah in the winter of 1939, Congress was a political organisation that 'does not represent everybody in India ... It does not represent those who disagree with it, whether they are Hindus or

---

[64] See Jinnah's presidential address to the All India Muslim League, 26 December 1938 in S.S. Pirzada (ed.), *Foundations of Pakistan*, II, p. 304.
[65] S.R. Mehrotra, 'The Congress and the Partition of India' in C.H. Philips and M.D. Wainwright (eds.), *The Partition of India: Policies and Perspectives* (London, George Allen and Unwin, 1970), p. 190.

Muslims. In the ultimate analysis it represents its members and sympathisers'.[66] However, whilst the League's 'descriptive' claim that Congress did not command Muslim support was probably consistent with Congress' self-image as a political organisation, its 'ideological' claim, that is to say that Congress *could not* as a non-Muslim organisation represent Muslims was less acceptable, for it hinged upon the premise that the representation of Indian Muslims was a Muslim prerogative.[67]

However, this is what the League sought to affirm. It did so by drawing upon two distinct sets of assumptions which sustained its claim to represent Indian Muslims more authentically than Congress. The first derived from a colonial ideology of representation which had shaped official policy and influenced the way in which many Indian Muslims conceived of representation. It tended to emphasise a view of representation as essentially a mode of resemblance rather than as a substantive political activity. Its political appeal lay in its capacity to resist claims by nationalists to represent an emerging Indian political consensus. In the nineteenth century, this understanding of representation proved to be a powerful weapon in the hands of those, like Sayyid Ahmad Khān, who sought to question the validity of Congress' claims to represent a national consensus. The thrust of his position had lain precisely in the contention that Congress could not represent Indian Muslims because it was not representative, that is to say typical, of Indian Muslims. This constituted also the essence of the League's claim against Congress in the late 1930s. Like Sayyid Ahmad Khān, Jinnah too espoused a view of representation as a descriptive activity and sought to subject Congress to the criteria which official ideology had validated. In a context where this ideology had tended also to undervalue the significance of popular consent and political mandates as necessary bases for representation, the League knew that Congress's representative credentials could be made to seem less adequate than they really were.

The second set of assumptions was grounded in the notion of representation as a trust whose delegation to non-Muslims negated the very purpose for which the 'community of believers' was deemed to have been created, that is, to ensure that Muslims lived their lives in obedience

---

[66] Jawaharlal Nehru to M.A. Jinnah, 13 December 1939 in Jamil-ud-din Ahmad (ed.), *Historic Documents of the Muslim Freedom Movement* (Lahore, Publishers United, 1970), p. 363.

[67] B.C. Parekh, 'India: A Case Study in the Ideology of Representation', *Seventh World Congress of the International Political Science Association, 1967*, Brussels, 1967, pp. 11–12.

to God's law. Such representation was derived essentially from a vision of society as a division between Muslims and non-Muslims, as well as from a belief in the inherent superiority of Muslims over non-Muslims. Although it is true that a sizeable body of 'nationalist' Muslims continued to believe that they could, in fact, be represented by a predominantly non-Muslim organisation like Congress *and* continue to practise their faith as they understood it,[68] the League's stance against Congress revived crucial issues of substance that had dominated Indo-Muslim thinking on representation since the late nineteenth century. Of these, the most important concerned the question of Muslim power. The idea of separate Muslim representation had, admittedly, evolved in part as a pragmatic response to ensure that those who had once exercised power would continue to participate in a restructured political hierarchy. At the same time, it is also clear that separate Muslim representation expressed the pre-eminent claims of a tradition whose followers believed their destiny to lie in the pursuit, through political means, of an order subject ultimately to Divine rules. It might reasonably be argued therefore, that while the League's endeavour to deny Congress the right to represent Indian Muslims was indisputably a bid to consolidate its quest for power, it was also an authentic manifestation of a doctrine that held Muslim domination to be the indispensable condition of a universal society.

Pakistan in the making, 1940–1947

The notion of parity then, to the extent that it rested upon a view of the political community as an extension of religious fellowship and upon the established dichotomy of Muslim and non-Muslim, may be seen to be deeply rooted in a Muslim political tradition. Its assumptions were to shape much of the conduct of the League's politics in the 1940s, in particular its demand for a political order subject exclusively to Muslim control and equal in status to a non-Muslim federation. This is not to say that the League, or indeed Jinnah, believed, or consciously engaged, in the politics of religion. On the contrary, Jalal assures us that the sheer complexity of managing an unruly band of Muslim satraps in the provinces while keeping an eye out for the wiles of Congress and the mandarins in Government House, left Jinnah and his party little time to

---

[68] The issue was, however, rather more complex as far as the 'nationalist' *'ulamā'* were concerned, for they rejected Jinnah's vision of a separate Muslim state precisely on the grounds that it envisaged a secular order where non-Muslims would be allowed representation in government. Peter Hardy, *Partners in Freedom*, p. 39.

ponder their indebtedness to the values of a religious tradition. This may well be true; but it is important to recognise that the claims Jinnah and the League were intent on making were actually, and perhaps could only be, grounded in the political assumptions of a faith whose authority among its followers was undiminished. To acknowledge this may, in the final analysis, be the only means of imparting to the emergence of Pakistan 'the quality of conscious and spiritual determination which its magnitude deserved'.[69]

The outbreak of the Second World War in September 1939 was a decisive moment in the evolution of Muslim politics in India. The resignation of Congress ministries in the provinces in protest against Britain's decision to engage India in a War without first consulting her elected representatives, precipitated a crisis which left the government bereft of the support of a majority. It turned, perhaps naturally, to the only other organisation which pretended, against overwhelming odds, to have an all-India following. The League, for its part, was unlikely to have rebuffed the government's overtures. It, and particularly Jinnah, knew that the party's chances of re-establishing its representative credentials might ultimately have to depend upon obtaining government recognition. Devoid of an electoral mandate and with only a tenuous hold over Muslims in the majority provinces, the League sought deliverance in colonial definitions which equated representation with recognition, and such recognition, itself, as the reward for political support. In a resolution passed by its Working Committee shortly after the onset of hostilities, the League offered to co-operate with the government on the understanding that it was 'the only organisation that can speak on behalf of Muslim India'.[70]

Armed with the fragile support of a minority, the Government of India sought to restore the function of representation as pre-eminently a mode of consultation reminiscent of the advisory bodies of the late nineteenth century. The stress was once more upon representatives as 'sounding boards'; upon Indians who 'stood', rather than 'acted' for others; upon a 'range', instead of a 'consensus' of interests; and upon the value of 'equal representation'.[71] The contradictions of pursuing such a

---

[69] Kenneth Cragg, *Counsels in Contemporary Islam* (Edinburgh University Press, 1965), p. 28.

[70] Resolution of the Working Committee of the All India Muslim League on the War Crisis, 17–18 September 1939 in Gwyer and Appadorai (eds.), *Speeches and Documents* II, p. 488.

[71] Linlithgow to Zetland, 21 December 1939, *Zetland Collection*, MSS EUR E 609 (18). See also Linlithgow's Declaration of 'War Aims' in Marquess of Linlithgow, *Speeches and Statements, 1936–1943* (Simla, Government of India Press, 1945), pp. 209–10.

policy in the context of the early 1940s were obvious to those less vulnerable to this nostalgia for the heyday of empire. As Lord Zetland, the Secretary of State, harshly emphasised, the Government of India's practice of impartiality was all very well so long as it did not interrupt the course of reforms which Britain herself had initiated.[72]

However, if British officials were tempted by the possibility of devaluing, at least for the time being, the notion of representation as a substantive political activity, they had clearly misjudged their capacity to do so. In February 1940, Jinnah reminded the Viceroy, Lord Linlithgow, of the terms of his party's support and stressed that the kind of representation it envisaged for itself extended beyond 'the region of consultation and counsel'.[73] Jinnah was categorical: negotiations between the government and Indian parties could no longer be conducted like some traditional *durbār*. The League was not an adjunct of officialdom, nor did it 'stand' tamely for Indian Muslims. It was not content merely to be taken 'into confidence'; what it sought was nothing less than 'the authority and the control of the Governments, central and provincial'.[74] Indeed, it assumed that 'Muslim representation must be equal to that of the Hindus if Congress comes in [to an Executive Council]', or else Muslims should have 'the majority of additional members'.[75] In short, the only kind of representation acceptable to Jinnah was one that enabled his party to *act* on behalf of a Muslim 'nation' entitled to 'real power' and 'perfect equality' with the majority.[76]

By the summer of 1940, it was becoming increasingly clear that officials were prepared to concede to the League the quality of representation that it demanded. It recognised the League's constituent status and ruled out 'a system of government whose authority [was] directly denied by large and powerful elements in India's national life',[77] namely 'the great Muslim community'.[78] Whilst Britain was per-

---

[72] Zetland to Linlithgow, 4 February 1940, *Zetland Collection*, MSS. EUR. E 609 (11).
[73] M.A. Jinnah to Linlithgow, 23 February 1940 in S.S. Pirzada (ed.), *Quaid-i-Azam Jinnah's Correspondence* (Karachi, Guild Publishing House, 1966), p. 373.
[74] Resolution of the Working Committee of the All India Muslim League on the War Crisis, 17–18 September 1939 in Gwyer and Appadorai (eds.), *Speeches and Documents* II, p. 488. See also M.A. Jinnah's tentative proposals for co-operation with the government, 1 July 1940, *ibid.*, pp. 502–3.
[75] M.A. Jinnah to Laithwaite, 1 July 1940, note on his discussions with the Viceroy on 27 June 1940 in S.S. Pirzada (ed.), *Quaid-i-Azam Jinnah's Correspondence*, p. 383.
[76] Jinnah's speech to the Muslim University Union, Aligarh, 6 March 1940, in Jamil-ud-din Ahmad (ed.), *Speeches and Writings of Mr. Jinnah*, I, pp. 138, 139.
[77] Linlithgow's statement on the expansion of the Governor-General's Executive Council and the establishment of an advisory War Council, 8 August 1940 in Gwyer and Appadorai (eds.), *Speeches and Documents*, II, p. 505.

suaded that the League would not accept Hindu domination, it was left to Jinnah to explain why. A 'democratic parliamentary system of government', he maintained, was antithetical to Muslims because Islam 'does not advocate a democracy which would allow the majority of non-Muslims to decide the fate of the Muslims ... [or] in which non-Muslims merely by a numerical majority would rule and dominate us'.[79]

To grasp Jinnah's point is to grasp the very essence of the demand for parity. For it points to concerns which lay well beyond the political struggle between Congress and League which have so held the attention of historians of modern India. It suggests that while the notion of parity may have evolved as a political response to the prospects of responsible government and majority rule, its significance lay in its relation to Muslim political thinking. The dichotomy of Muslim and non-Muslim as two separate political categories; the idea that non-Muslims, notwithstanding their diversity, could legitimately be treated as a 'whole' that was antithetical to Muslims, and the belief that the loss of Muslim power was inconsistent with the Muslims' quest for a more humane, universal society, were steadily to emerge as intrinsic elements in the formulation of parity.

The duality between Muslims and non-Muslims in the context of India owed much to the notion that India's different religious communities were all eventually variations of a non-Muslim ethic, namely, Hinduism. Jinnah accepted this premise and allowed it to dictate his 'politics of parity'. His view was that a more accurate 'description of India' would be that 'two-thirds of its inhabitants profess Hinduism *in one form or another* as their religion', while 'over seventy seven millions are followers of Islam...'[80] (my italics) The assumption that the multiplicity of India's religious communities shared a common world-view and by definition common politics that were distinct from Muslims, was to lead Jinnah later to insist upon the parity of Muslims in relation to all other non-Muslim groups as a condition for a constitutional settlement.

However, there was another more profound consideration that underlay the demand for parity. This was the assumption that by enabling Muslims to exercise power as the equals of a non-Muslim majority, a more humane society would ensue. Jinnah shared this

[78] See L.S. Amery's speech to the House of Commons, 14 August 1940, *Hansard's Parliamentary Debates* (Commons) (1940), volume 364, columns, 872–3.
[79] Jinnah's speech to the Muslim University Union, 6 March 1940 in Jamil-ud-din Ahmad (ed.), *Speeches and Writings*, I, pp. 139–40.
[80] M.A. Jinnah, 'Constitutional Maladies of India', 19 January 1940 in *ibid.*, I, p 116.

assumption and regarded it as the most compelling moral ground for parity. It was a measure which he believed would ensure that society did not degenerate into barbarism; for the alternative, that is to say, Hindu domination, would introduce the unacceptable vertical divisions of caste.[81] Power wielded by Muslims in equal part could, in his view, ultimately prove to be the only real guarantee of a democratic society predicated upon 'the equality and brotherhood of man'.[82]

Between 1940 and 1946, it became increasingly clear that the League's demand for parity with Congress actually signified the parity of Muslims and non-Muslims. Although each form of parity had quite distinct implications for the evolution of a free political society in India, they were bound by the internal logic of a Muslim political tradition. The League's understanding of parity presupposed the notion of communal representation, that is to say, the representation of religious communities by members of these communities. It assumed that as an avowedly Muslim organisation the League, not Congress, was properly representative of Indian Muslims. By the same token, Congress as a predominantly Hindu organisation would act on behalf of Hindus. It followed then that inter-party parity would ensure the parity of Hindus and Muslims. However, the League also insisted that to the extent that Congress assumed the representation of non-Muslim interests, parity necessarily implied the equality of Muslims and non-Muslims. It was this fundamental duality between Muslims and non-Muslims which the League's vision of parity sought to endorse.

The manner in which these ideas permeated the League's understanding of parity may be more closely discerned through the play of constitutional negotiations which preceded the partition of India in 1947. In August 1940, the Viceroy, Lord Linlithgow, submitted an 'Offer' which sought formally to restore the participation of Indian parties in government through an enlarged Executive Council.[83] Although the 'August Offer' did not suggest that such a Council would form the nucleus of a responsible government, Jinnah was determined that parity must form the basis of any body to which the League would henceforth be party. In July, he had told the Viceroy that a proposed Executive Council must recognise parity between League and Congress as the representative of Muslims and Hindus respectively. While Jinnah was implicitly prepared to concede that Congress represented a variety

---

[81] *Ibid.*, pp. 116–17.
[82] M.A. Jinnah's presidential address to the All India Muslim League, 24 April 1943, in S.S. Pirzada (ed.), *Foundations of Pakistan*, II, p. 415.
[83] Linlithgow's statement on the expansion of the Governor-General's Executive Council, 8 August 1940, in Gwyer and Appadorai (eds.), *Speeches and Documents*, II, pp. 504–5.

of non-Muslim communities, he was concerned primarily to ensure that the League alone represented Muslims at the all-India level.[84] This, as Jalal has shown, made eminent political sense for a party whose only real chance of power at the centre lay precisely in its recognition as 'the sole spokesman' for Indian Muslims. But the League's political sense, as Jalal herself demonstrates, was not always backed by political force, as the crisis over the National Defence Council in 1941, for example, was to bring home so brutally.[85] How then did Jinnah and the League establish their claims among Indian Muslims? They did so by directing their politics on the basis of assumptions which formed part of a tradition which they, like those they sought to represent, accepted as authoritative. When Jinnah asserted that the League was the exclusive representative of Indian Muslims, he took for granted that Muslim representation was a Muslim prerogative; when he acknowledged Congress's larger non-Muslim constituency in opposition to his party's limited claim to a Muslim electorate, he was merely postulating the necessary duality of Muslims and non-Muslims.

The League's insistence upon its exclusive right to represent Muslims as a necessary condition of parity was rejected by Linlithgow as 'constitutionally impossible'.[86] However, his 'Offer' clearly accepted, at least in theory, the possibility of a Muslim veto exercised through the League upon any future constitution that it deemed to be inadmissible.[87] Congress, for its part, rejected any suggestion of parity as altogether unjustified. Its Working Committee rejected the Viceroy's 'Offer' as a cynical attempt to grant an unwarranted degree of control to minorities while refusing to transfer full responsibility to India's elected representative. There was no question of statutory parity between Congress and League and certainly none to concentrate the power to nominate Muslims in the hands of the League.[88] The Viceroy's unwillingness to categorically endorse the League's understanding of parity, and Congress's unqualified rejection, ensured that the League turned down any proposal for its immediate participation in a restructured Executive Council.[89]

---

[84] M.A. Jinnah's tentative proposals for co-operation with the government, 1 July 1940, in *ibid.*, p. 502.

[85] Jalal, *The Sole Spokesman*, pp. 67–9.

[86] Linlithgow to Jinnah, 6 July 1940 in S.S. Pirzada (ed.), *Quaid-i-Azam*, p. 387.

[87] The Viceroy wrote '... my statement [the August 'Offer'], clearly safeguarded the Muslim position in relation to future constitutional development ...', *ibid.*, p. 390.

[88] See Resolution of the All India Congress Committee, 15–16 September 1940, in Gwyer and Appadorai (eds.), *Speeches and Documents*, II, pp. 505–6.

[89] See Resolution of the Working Committee of the All India Muslim League, 28 September 1940, *Indian Annual Register*, 1940, II (Calcutta, The Annual Register Office), p. 251.

Later Jinnah explained his party's dissatisfaction with the 'Offer' as stemming from the 'offer's' short-sighted vision of the basis of power and authority.[90] Echoing a common, yet fundamental, refrain of Muslim political thinking, he cast doubt on the validity of 'number[s]' as an adequate criterion for representation and responsibility. Like many of his fellow Muslims who had sought to distinguish the process of *ijmāʿ* from the rules of a Western democratic consensus by stressing its relation to Divine law, Jinnah too seemed conscious of the norms of a 'just' constitution that could not be reduced to a mere 'counting of heads'.[91] Although Jinnah may not, as Taylor suggests, have believed that the merits of such a constitution derived either from its sacrosanct nature or its expression through a 'learned elite', he is likely to have seen it as 'essentially in keeping with the rational foundations of a modern legal system'.[92]

The arrival of the Cripps Mission in March 1942 revived the issue of parity and its relationship to territorially defined Muslim centres of political power in India. In March 1940, the League's suggestive 'Pakistan Resolution' had shown how a Muslim 'nation' implied in the notion of parity might evolve towards a territorial consolidation of power. Although much has been made of whether or not Jinnah himself intended Muslim 'nationhood' to result in independent Muslim 'statehood',[93] there is no mistaking the new twist which sought to formalise India's constitutional impasse as an 'international' problem free from considerations of size and number.

The question which confronted Britain most immediately however, was how best to 'aid India in the realisation of full self-government'

[90] M.A. Jinnah's address to the Muslim University Union, Aligarh, 2 November 1941 in Jamil-ud-din Ahmad (ed.), *Speeches and Writings*, I, p. 310.
[91] *Ibid.*
[92] David Taylor, 'Jinnah's Political Apprenticeship, 1906–1924' in A.H. Dani (ed.), *World Scholars on Quaid-i-Azam Mohammad Ali Jinnah* (Islamabad, Quaid-i-Azam University, 1979), pp. 105–6.
[93] The thrust of Jalal's argument lies precisely in the claim that Jinnah sought neither partition nor Pakistan, but a share of power in an all-India centre. Jalal, *The Sole Spokesman*. Others, like R.J. Moore, are less sure and suggest that although Jinnah did, in fact, accept 'different constitutional forms' that ran counter to independent statehood to independent statehood, most notably the Cabinet Mission Plan of 1946, 'the essence of the Pakistan demand – the right to a territorial asylum, to the self-determination of a Muslim nation in the north-western and eastern regions of India – was never compromised'. In short, he believes, that there is no real basis to support 'speculation that the Pakistan demand was Jinnah's bargaining counter for power in a united India, or that the Partition hoisted him with his own petard'. R.J. Moore, 'Jinnah and the Pakistan Demand', *Modern Asian Studies*, 17, 4 (1983), p. 561. See also Stanley Wolpert, *Jinnah of Pakistan* (New York, Oxford University Press, 1984) for a view that comes closer to Moore's than to Jalal's interpretation.

without seriously endangering her War effort against the Japanese. Churchill had emphasised that his government would no longer allow a minority 'to impose an indefinite veto upon the wishes of the majority'.[94] At the same time, he, like many of his colleagues, was aware that Britain's successful resistance to Japanese Fascism might have to depend, for the time being, upon paying more attention to parties like the League which were prepared to co-operate with the government of India. The Draft Declaration submitted by the Cripps Mission shortly after its arrival embodied these dilemmas. While it endorsed India's right to frame a constitution after the War through an independent constituent assembly, it recognised, at least in principle, a minority's right to opt out of any constitutional arrangement.[95] More importantly perhaps, in what can only be construed as a concession to the League, it undertook to establish the principle of parity by accepting that any constitution framed by a minority would enjoy the 'same full status as the Indian Union'.[96] However, what the Mission gave with one hand it threatened to take away with the other. For the parity to which it referred did not so much postulate a seceding *nation* as a seceding province or provinces.

Although Congress was visibly appalled at this espousal of the principle of secession,[97] it is clear that what the Mission hoped to demonstrate was that parity did not necessarily postulate a separate Muslim homeland. Its provision enabling provinces to opt out of an Indian federation made a mockery of the League's demand that Muslim majority provinces in the north-west and east should be 'grouped' to form the constitutional bases of Muslim control and parity at the centre.[98] However, the Mission's secession clause appeared to conceal a more fundamental end: to test the very assumptions of parity, that is to say, the presence of a Muslim 'nation'. For it aimed quite clearly to appeal to Muslim bosses in the large majority provinces of Punjab and Bengal to reassert their independence and possibly undermine the very basis of the League's claim to speak on behalf of a politically united 'nation'.

---

[94] See Winston Churchill's speech to the House of Commons, 11 March 1942, *Hansard's Parliamentary Debates* (Commons) (1942), volume 378, column 1069.
[95] See the Commission's Draft Declaration for discussion with Indian leaders in Gwyer and Appadorai (eds.), *Speeches and Documents*, II, pp. 520–1.
[96] *Ibid.*, p. 520.
[97] Resolution of the Working Committee of the All India National Congress, 2 April 1942, *ibid.*, p. 525.
[98] Resolution I passed by the All India Muslim League, 23 March 1940, in Pirzada (ed.), *Foundations of Pakistan*, II, p. 341.

The dangers implicit in the Declaration were obvious to Jinnah. In a guarded appraisal of the Mission's proposals which he accepted as a 'veiled recognition' of 'the principle of Pakistan', he berated its preoccupation with territorial autonomy.[99] The real issue, he maintained, was 'the right of national self-determination' not the 'territorial entity of the provinces'[100] – an assertion for which he was to pay dearly in 1947 following the partition of Bengal and the Punjab. Jinnah knew that whatever form parity was subsequently to assume, whether it was effective veto power at the centre or a separate Muslim federation, nothing was possible without the constitutional recognition of 'the entity and integrity of the Muslim nation'.[101] For a man not widely known to champion the cause of separate electorates, Jinnah even seized upon the Mission's proposals to scrap the system, for fear, no doubt, that it might have reopened the question about the special status of Muslims in India.[102]

However, the dilemmas that the Mission posed for Jinnah and the League by conceding the thrust of the Lahore resolution, namely territorial autonomy, at the price of testing its spirit, that is, Muslim 'nationhood', were never wholly exposed. For this there was Congress to thank.[103] From the start its leaders, most notably Jawaharlal Nehru, tended to focus upon what appeared to them to be the Mission's bizarre scheme to 'balkanize' the subcontinent. At the same time there was also a growing feeling among some members of Congress like C. Rajagopala-chari, the leader of the Madras Congress Legislature Party, that some concession, in principle, might have to be made to the League in the interests of forming a national government.[104] It is also possible, although this is more difficult to establish, that the emergence at about this time of Soviet theories of 'nationalities' propounded by Muslims like Maulānā 'Ubaidullāh Sindhī working within Congress, were beginning to exercise some influence.[105] Although Sindhī's political

[99] Jinnah's presidential address to the All India Muslim League, 3 April 1942, *ibid.*, II, p. 388. See also the Resolution passed by the League's Working Committee on 2 April 1942 in which it acknowledged that the Mission's offer had recognised 'the possibility of Pakistan ... by implication by providing for the establishment of two or more independent Unions'. Gwyer and Appadorai (eds.), *Speeches and Documents*, pp. 526–8.

[100] Pirzada (ed.), *Foundations of Pakistan*, p. 388.

[101] *Ibid.*

[102] *Ibid.*, p. 387.

[103] Jalal, *The Sole Spokesman*, p. 80.

[104] Z.H. Zaidi, 'Aspects of the Development of Muslim League Policy, 1937–1947', in Philips and Wainwright (eds.), *The Partition of India*, pp. 265–6.

[105] Aziz Ahmad, *Islamic Modernism*, pp. 195–201; Qureshi, *Ulema in Politics*, pp. 312–18.

following within Congress was minimal, his views are likely to have reflected the spread of a 'progressive-minded' appreciation of India as 'a confederation of multi-national states, each a linguistic and cultural unit'.[106]

Aware no doubt of these prevailing trends, Congress chose therefore in its initial response to the Mission's proposals to concede that it could not 'think in terms of compelling the people of any territorial unit to remain in an Indian Union against their declared and established will ...'.[107] Despite this, however, it underlined its fundamental commitment to a 'co-operative national life' and refused to endorse the principle of national self-determination for minorities. Congress's willingness to compromise on an issue that was unquestionably central to its political identity, as well as to its ideology, was not enough however to ensure the success of the Mission's proposals. For at heart lay the question of the scope of the National Government which the Mission had come to negotiate. While Congress argued that it could not accept any proposal for a government that did not also have the right to manage its own defence, Churchill was determined to withhold any effective transfer of the war-time Defence portfolio.[108] Dominated by the debate over defence without which it seemed there could be no National Government, parity tended to assume only peripheral importance. It was obvious, however, as the Congress president, Maulānā Āzād, was to make clear to Stafford Cripps, that his party would not be bound by any *a priori* agreement on 'minority participation' in a future National Government.[109]

It would be interesting to speculate on what might have happened had Congress agreed to forego its stand on defence. Would the League have been obliged to accept the Mission's offer, or would it have been unwilling to expose the idea of a Muslim 'nation' to a degree of critical scrutiny that it may not have withstood? It is difficult to tell. What is certain is that by rejecting the Mission's terms for a National Government, Congress unwittingly let slip the only real opportunity to test the

[106] Aziz Ahmad, *Islamic Modernism*, p. 201.
[107] Resolution passed by the Working Committee of Indian National Congress, 2 April 1942, in Gwyer and Appadorai (eds.), *Speeches and Documents*, p. 525.
[108] Churchill's reluctance was shaped partly by a profound anti-Congress animus and partly by a stubborn refusal to contemplate complete British withdrawal from India after the War. R.J. Moore, *Churchill, Cripps and India, 1939–45* (Oxford, Clarendon Press, 1979) pp. 134–5.
[109] Maulana Abul Kalam Āzād to Stafford Cripps, 11 April 1942, in Gwyer and Appadorai (eds.), *Speeches and Documents*, II, p. 535.

political validity of the ideas which sustained the quest for Muslim power in India.

The intensity of the War during 1943 and 1944 left little time for Britain to pursue the Cripps proposals any further. As the war dragged slowly to an end towards the summer of 1945, there were fresh moves to resuscitate plans for an Interim Government that would function until the transfer of full responsible government to India. In June, the British government announced its intention to resume negotiations with a view to obtaining a constitutional settlement that would be acceptable to all parties. Although it would not yet consider Congress's demand for an immediate transfer of power to the majority, it was keen to be seen to be initiating 'some step forward'.[110] It recommended, therefore, a series of proposals to reorganise the Viceroy's Executive Council with a view to securing a 'balanced representation of the main communities, including equal proportions of Moslems and Caste Hindus'.[111] This novel approach was guaranteed to restore the importance of parity as the very nub of the constitutional debate. It is likely, however, that officials themselves had hoped that this solution would resolve, rather than confound, the issue. For while it met the League's demand for Hindu–Muslim parity, it aspired also to establish majority rule by providing for the separate representation of Scheduled Caste Hindus.

Armed with His Majesty's Government's new set of proposals, the Viceroy, Lord Wavell, set about the task of convening a meeting of the leaders of the main Indian parties. While Jinnah gave no hint of what he expected to achieve at the proposed Conference in Simla, set for the last week in June, Gandhi's cable to the Viceroy on the eve of the Conference was clearly designed to intimate Congress's position on the new offer and, in particular, its stand on parity. It suggested that the party was likely to be distinctly conciliatory on the question of parity between Congress and League although it would resist the idea of statutory parity between Caste Hindus and Muslims on the grounds that it would institutionalise religious divisions.[112] At the same time, Gandhi emphasised that Congress would also be especially bound to oppose any representation that attempted to restrict its identity to the role of spokesman for Caste Hindus. Congress, Gandhi maintained, was a political organisation that could not, constitutionally, be made subject to the rules of communal politics.[113]

[110] L.S. Amery's statement to the House of Commons, 14 June 1945, *ibid.*, II, pp. 557–60.
[111] *Ibid.*, p. 559.
[112] Gandhi to Wavell, 17 June 1945, *The Indian Annual Register*, 1945, I (Calcutta, The Annual Register Office), p. 245.
[113] 'The fixity of parity between Caste Hindus and Muslims as an unchangeable religious

The gist of Gandhi's communication to the Viceroy was formalised in a set of instructions issued by Congress to its delegates attending the Simla Conference.[114] Congress accepted the new proposals on parity on the understanding that they were purely temporary and would not constitute the principles of a constitutional settlement. Whilst Congress was willing, for the time being, to compromise on communal parity between Muslims and Caste Hindus, it was clearly determined to resist any party's exclusive claim to a part of the Indian electorate. Parity, it emphasised, 'did not mean that all Muslim members of the National Government will be nominated by the Muslim League'.[115] It is clear that what was involved here was an issue whose implications could have extended well beyond questions relating directly to Congress's identity as a political organisation, for it concerned the very viability of a free electoral system, and possibly, the future of India as some form of recognisable democracy. However, this was the language of European liberalism predicated upon notions of a common political society and a common 'good', neither of which was familiar to Muslim political discourse and neither of which acceptable to Jinnah at Simla.

To understand how Jinnah made the extraordinary claim for parity between Muslims and *all* other Indian communities which so decisively wrecked the Conference, is to acknowledge his debt to Muslim modes of thinking. In his first public assessment of the difficulties which confronted his party in Simla, Jinnah dismissed the proposal for parity between Caste Hindus and Muslims on the Executive Council as an illusion.[116] He maintained that the inclusion of other, smaller communities, including Sikhs and members of the Scheduled Castes, would actually reduce Muslims to 'a minority of one-third'.[117] The outcome would 'be such as to enable the Congress invariably to command a majority'.[118] Given that the nomination of neither Scheduled Castes nor Sikhs (to say nothing of the two British members) was expected to rest with Congress, whose quota was theoretically restricted to Caste Hindus, Jinnah's conclusion appeared self-evident on the basis of one assumption alone: all non-Muslims shared a common ethos that was recognisably distinct

---

division will', he maintained, 'become officially stereotyped on the eve of independence. Personally, I can never subscribe to it, nor the Congress if I know its mind'. *Ibid.*, p. 254.
[114] See Instructions issued by the Working Committee of the Indian National Congress to its representatives attending the Simla Conference, 21–22 June 1945, *ibid.*, p. 224.
[115] *Ibid.*
[116] See Jinnah's statement to the Press on Wavell proposals, 29 June 1945, in Jamil-ud-din Ahmad (ed.), *Speeches and Writings*, II, pp. 175–80.
[117] *Ibid.*, p. 177.
[118] *Ibid.*

from, and antithetical to, that of Muslims. Although Jinnah acknowledged 'the social tyranny and economic oppression in Hindu society' which set both Scheduled Castes and Sikhs apart, he was nevertheless persuaded that they all shared a common political ideal.[119] This, he believed, was their commitment to a united India. Jinnah was probably right but not, as one might expect, because of his 'liberal' understanding of the voluntary basis of political coalitions, but because he believed that Scheduled Castes, Sikhs and Christians *must* share the same goals as 'ethnically and culturally they are very closely knitted to Hindu society'.[120] The underlying premise was unquestionably that of an 'organic' non-Muslim 'community' poised to counter the legitimate claims of Indian Muslims. Ultimately it mattered little whether Muslims and non-Muslims could conceivably be treated as coherent, collective 'wholes', what was important was that all politics should be conducted as if they were.

The single most important fact that confronted the Cabinet Mission sent by the new Labour government in March 1946 was the League's established position as the authoritative representative of the Muslims of India. In all-India elections held between 1945 and 1946, the party was returned with a decisive majority of Muslim seats at both the central and provincial levels.[121] For the advocates of parity, the political uncertainties of the early 1940s seemed well on their way out. Jinnah was categorical; he told a League legislators' convention, 'you have shown to the world that we are a united nation, and that we mean business'.[122] To discern the precise nature of that business was the task of Britain's new delegation to her troubled colony.

In his statement to the Commons in February 1946, the new Prime Minister Clement Attlee trod a familiar path when he stressed that although his government was 'mindful of the rights of minorities ... we cannot allow a minority to place a veto on the advance of the majority'.[123] The inherent dilemmas of pursuing such a policy in the context of India were once more to become apparent. As before, the right of the minority was to be defined as no less than the right to separate 'nationhood', while the claims of the majority hinged upon the

---

[119] *Ibid.*
[120] See Jinnah's statement at a press conference, 14 July 1945, *ibid.*, p. 187.
[121] Sayeed, *The Formative Phase*, p. 135.
[122] See Jinnah's address to the League Legislators' Convention, 7 April 1946, in Pirzada (ed.), *Foundations of Pakistan*, II, p. 510.
[123] Clement Attlee's speech in the House of Commons, 17 March 1946, *Hansard's Parliamentary Debates* (Commons) (1946), volume 420, columns 1421–2.

very notion of a 'united India'. In April 1946, the League renewed its call for the recognition of Hindus and Muslims as 'two distinct major nations' entitled to 'two separate constitution making bodies... set up by the people of Pakistan and Hindustan'.[124] Congress, on the other hand, was clearly determined to obtain a constituent assembly that would be a sovereign body empowered to establish, independently, the future relations between a Union centre and the provinces.

The question of parity which dominated earlier negotiations now assumed a more complex, and yet, clearly defined, focus. For while in the context of war-time India the issue tended, necessarily, to be confined to the composition of an Interim Government without real responsibility, it now promised to impinge upon the entire constitutional structure of India as a self-governing polity. At the same time, however, while in the past the balance between Congress and League in an Interim Government was sometimes disturbed by the representation of smaller parties, the consolidation of groups of provinces broadly designated 'Pakistan' and 'Hindustan' now helped to restore the simple duality of Muslims and non-Muslims.

In its attempt to accept the principle of parity *and* preserve the structure of a federated India, the Cabinet Mission drew up for discussion a constitutional scheme based on two groups of provinces, 'the one of the predominantly Hindu Provinces and the other of the predominantly Muslim provinces'.[125] Although the Mission refrained from defining their precise status in relation to one another, their parity was implied by the provision that the Legislature and the Executive of the Union would consist of 'equal proportions from the Muslim majority Provinces and from the Hindu majority provinces'.[126] At the Tripartite Conference held in Simla in May 1946, attended by members from Congress, League and Cabinet Mission, it was clear that the main sticking point between the two major Indian parties was the question of parity.[127] While the League insisted upon the consolidation of Muslim majority provinces in the north-west and east to act as a single

[124] See the 'Delhi Resolution' passed by the League Legislators' Convention, 9 April 1946, in, Pirzada (ed.), *Foundations of Pakistan*, II, pp. 512–3.
[125] Lord Pethick Lawrence to Maulana Abul Kalam Azad and M.A. Jinnah, 27 April 1946 in Gwyer and Appadorai (eds.), *Speeches and Documents*, II, p. 572.
[126] See suggested points of agreement between the Congress and the Muslim League put forward by the Cabinet Mission Plan, 8 May 1946, *Papers Relating to the Cabinet Mission Plan to India, 1946* (Delhi, Manager of Publications), p. 15.
[127] Archbold Percival Wavell, *Wavell: The Viceroy's Journal*, Penderel Moon (ed.) (London, Oxford University Press, 1973), pp. 257–67.

constitutional entity equal in status to the body of Hindu provinces,[128] Congress was bent on resisting any plan to organise groups of provinces and 'was entirely opposed to parity of representation as between groups of Provinces in the Union Executive or Legislature'.[129]

Having failed to arrive at an agreement between Congress and League, the Cabinet Mission then decided to submit a revised set of proposals which signified a radical departure away from the League's own position. The Mission's May 16 plan rejected the consolidation of a single Muslim entity and did not recommend sovereignty for the group of provinces, designated as 'Pakistan' by the League, on the grounds that it would unjustly include sizeable Hindu minorities in the Punjab and Bengal. It proposed therefore a confederal structure for India consisting of three tiers – two predominantly Muslim groups of provinces in the north-west and east, including the whole of the Punjab and Bengal respectively, and one predominantly Hindu group. In addition, the Mission provided for the right of any group to opt out of the confederation after an initial period of ten years, although it clearly intended to inhibit any easy recourse to secession by the Muslim groups by allowing individual provinces within groups also to withdraw once the process of constitution making was complete.[130]

In his response to the new scheme, Jinnah singled out for particular attention the Cabinet Mission's decision to 'negative (sic) the Muslim demand for the establishment of a complete Sovereign State of Pakistan'.[131] The 'crux' of his party's demand, namely 'that the six Muslim Provinces should be grouped together as Pakistan Group and the remaining as Hindustan Group' had, he implied, been undermined by dividing Pakistan into two.[132] Above all, he claimed, 'parity of representation between the Pakistan Group and the Hindustan Group' had decisively been set aside in favour of other, highly unsatisfactory, safeguards.[133] Whilst Jinnah had clearly perceived that the Mission's Plan for a constitutional arrangement diverged sharply from his party's formal claim for a separate Muslim federation equal in status to a

[128] See 'Terms of the Offer made by the Muslim League as the basis of agreement', 12 May 1946; in Gwyer and Appadorai (eds.), *Speeches and Documents*, II, pp. 573–4.
[129] Note by Congress on the terms offered by the Muslim League, 12 May 1946, *ibid.*, pp. 575–7. See also 'Terms offered by Congress as a basis for agreement, 12 May 1946', *ibid.*, pp. 574–5.
[130] Statement by the Cabinet Mission of India and the Viceroy, 16 May 1946, *ibid.*, pp. 577–84.
[131] Jinnah's statement on the Cabinet Mission Plan, 23 May 1946, in Jamil-ud-din Ahmad (ed.), *Speeches and Writings*, II, p. 292.
[132] *Ibid.*, pp. 291–2.
[133] *Ibid.*, p. 295.

predominantly Hindu federation, he nevertheless recommended its acceptance. Although his decision to accept the Plan as it stood has been seen as the final and most conclusive proof of Jinnah's commitment to a united India[134] there are some important considerations to be borne in mind when assessing the real significance of his gesture.

Although Jinnah appears to have made a heroic compromise in order to avert partition, it was far from obvious that either he or the League would contribute to the evolution of a common political society in India. For when Jinnah persuaded his Working Committee to accept a plan that denied Indian Muslims parity of status in the form of a sovereign Pakistan, he did so on the understanding that the principle of parity between Congress and League would not only be firmly established as a principle of governmental organisation, but that it would rest categorically upon the League's exclusive right to speak on behalf of Indian Muslims.[135] In a meeting with the Viceroy shortly before his party's formal acceptance of the League's offer, Jinnah had been assured that the ratio of Congress to League in a proposed Interim Government would be 5:5 with two additional portfolios reserved for other minorities, drawn from the Sikh and Christian communities.[136] What was significant about this new formula for parity was that it effectively, if not formally, allowed the League to monopolise Muslim representation. For with a 5:5 ratio, Congress could not afford to nominate a Muslim member on its quota, whatever the dictates of its political ideology, without reducing Hindus to a minority. For the first time the League actually had within its grasp what had eluded it from the beginning – parity with Congress and the exclusive right to represent Indian Muslims. The power that this bestowed upon the League was not to be under emphasised, nor indeed, were its implications for an independent Muslim political order in the subcontinent. It was left to Jinnah to spell it out. 'Let me tell you', he warned his Council, 'that Muslim India will not rest content until we have established full, complete and sovereign Pakistan... It is a big struggle and continued struggle. The first struggle was to get the representative character of the League accepted. That struggle... had started and... had [been] won'.[137]

---

[134] Jalal, *The Sole Spokesman*, chapter 5.
[135] Jinnah to Wavell, 8 June 1946, in. S.S. Pirzada (ed.), *Quaid-i-Azam Jinnah's Correspondence*, pp. 321–2.
[136] *Ibid.*
[137] See Jinnah's speech to the Council of the Muslim League, 5 June 1946, *Indian Annual Register*, 1946, I (Calcutta, The Annual Register Office), p. 181.

However, the significance of Jinnah's acceptance of the Mission's plan must be assessed in other ways as well. The critical question here is not whether Jinnah himself chose finally to display the 'inwardness' of his strategy, namely to preserve the unity of India, but whether or not the dominant trends in Indo-Muslim political thinking since the late nineteenth century *could* have sustained his personal stance in 1946. For the clamour for an Islamic state, however diverse its meaning, had tapped a chord of profound nostalgia for the days of Muslim supremacy in India as well as revived a much more serious intellectual preoccupation with the 'Islamic' dispensation of power. Jinnah may well have denounced the quest for a theocratic state,[138] nor was he out of step with an established modernist tradition on the subcontinent; but his promise of Muslim power is likely to have signified for many Muslims the only real opportunity in modern times to consciously fashion a society in keeping with the ends they believed God devised for Man. From the *sajjadā nashīns* of rural Punjab,[139] to the *sharīf* urban literati of Upper India, Jinnah's strategy was bound by the vision of a community with the political means to regulate its life in keeping with the traditions of its faith.[140]

The League's willingness to proceed with the Cabinet Mission Plan did not however culminate in the success of the Plan or indeed the unity of India. Congress had already expressed its anxieties about the Mission's proposals for a regrouping of Indian provinces, but it categorically rejected any arrangement based on parity of representation in the Interim Government, let alone one predicated upon the League's exclusive right to nominate Muslims.[141] A final, feeble attempt by the Mission to save its Plan by abandoning parity but leaving intact the League's sole right to represent Indian Muslims, met with little enthusiasm.[142]

---

[138] See Jinnah's concluding address to the League Legislators' Convention, 9 April 1946, in S.S. Pirzada (ed.), *Foundations of Pakistan*, II, p. 523.

[139] David Gilmartin, 'Religious Leadership and the Pakistan Movement in the Punjab', *Modern Asian Studies*, 13, 3 (1979), p. 509.

[140] Raja of Mahmudabad, 'Some Memories', in Philips and Wainwright (eds.), *The Partition of India*, p. 388. Others, like Khalid bin Sayeed, have recognised, more explicitly than in their earlier studies, Jinnah's appeal as stemming from a promise of political power 'which the Qur'an had promised to [Muslims] and which their forbears had wielded in India'. Khalid bin Sayeed, 'Jinnah and his Political Strategy', *ibid.*, p. 293.

[141] See Resolution passed by the Working Committee of the Indian National Congress, 24 May 1946, in Gwyer and Appadorai (eds.), *Speeches and Documents*, II, pp. 591–3; Maulana Abul Kalam Azad to Lord Wavell, 13, 14, 16 June 1946, *ibid.*, pp. 597, 598–9, 600; and Wavell, *The Viceroy's Journal*, pp. 283–305.

[142] Statement by the Cabinet Delegation and the Viceroy on the Formation of an Interim Government, 16 June 1946 in *Papers Relating to the Cabinet Mission*, pp. 43–4.

The failure of the Cabinet Mission Plan signalled the end of a process which demonstrated, perhaps more than anything else, the force of radically different assumptions grounded deep in Muslim tradition about the organisation of society and the proper focus of men's allegiance. These called into question the basis of political groupings, and probed the significance of the political community as an extension of men's religious faith. However, their greatest significance lay perhaps in the Muslim endeavour to restructure a political and electoral system whose sources lay in an order that was extraneous to human society.

Conclusion

The decline of Muslim power and the consolidation of British rule, far from resulting in massive Muslim resignation, led to renewed and vigorous efforts to restore the dignity of Islam and the political fortunes of its adherents. Whatever the differences that characterised the approaches of those predominantly *sharīf* Muslims engaged in this enterprise – whether 'reformist' like Deoband, or 'liberal' like Aligarh – they were bound by their conviction that salvation lay in a return to the fundamentals of the faith.[1] What these fundamentals implied for the modes of accommodation and resistance to Western intrusion, both intellectual and political, were, in each case, quite distinct. Deoband remained unshaken in its opposition to British rule; while Aligarh, certainly until the end of the first decade of this century, clearly preferred co-operation.

However, more important even than their political strategies and intellectual orientations were their attitudes to the relationship of Islam with its community of believers. The reformist *'ulamā'* who were allied for the most part, although by no means wholly, with the seminary at Deoband tended to regard the Western threat primarily as an onslaught against Islam as a religious and cultural entity. Their concern was to safeguard Islam; for they believed that so long as the faith was intact the community itself was immune to disintegration. For them, the integrity of the faith was to be ensured not so much by means of overt political action, although its importance was recognised, but by a process of cultural resistance sustained by elaborate rules governing individual behaviour and forms of devotional practice drawn from codes of Islamic law and education.[2]

---

[1] The most comprehensive, if not authoritative, studies on Deoband and Aligarh at the present time are those of Metcalf, *Islamic Revival In British India: Deoband, 1860–1900* (Princeton University Press, 1982) and Lelyveld, *Aligarh's First Generation: Muslim Solidarity in British India* (Princeton University Press, 1978). Both however would doubtless acknowledge their debt to earlier studies including Ziya ul Hasan Faruqi, *The Deoband School and the Demand for Pakistan* (Bombay, Asia Publishing House, 1963), Margaret Case, 'The Aligarh Era: Muslim Politics in North India, 1860–1910', unpublished Ph.D. dissertation, University of Chicago, 1970 and M.S. Jain, *The Aligarh Movement: Its Origin and Development, 1858–1906* (Agra, Sri Ram Mehra, 1965).

[2] Metcalf, *Islamic Revival*, chapter IV. This is not to suggest, however, that the

228

The concern to protect Islam as a cultural entity did little, however, to displace its vision as a polity or its promise of power which many Muslims believed, although unlikely to be 'Islamically' wielded, ought at least to be wielded by Muslims. It was this vision that the early founders of the Aligarh movement and its political heirs found so compelling.[3] For them, the import of the British presence lay unquestionably in its political consequences as the power that had threatened and subsequently vanquished Muslim rule in India. The problem that confronted them and the growing numbers of Muslims who responded to their call, was how best to restore the pre-eminence of their community in the newly established hierarchy of power.

Differently from the reformist *'ulamā'*, they came to believe that the survival of Islam in India depended ultimately upon its regeneration as a political community rather than upon its defence as a mere cultural ideal.[4] What they stressed was not communal withdrawal and the intensification of religious faith but the consolidation of a distinct Muslim identity shaped by the forces of modern, Western education and intelligible to their new imperial masters.

Contrasting counsels made for contrasting practices. There were those, like Maulānā Abū'l Kalām Āzād and the *'ulamā'* of the Jam'īyyat al-'Ulamā'-i-Hind, who endorsed the politics of composite nationalism on the grounds that the protection of Indian Islam as a social and cultural ideal did not depend upon the creation of a separate

'reformist' *'ulamā'* were altogether oblivious of the political dimensions of their battle against the West. As Metcalf herself observes, 'a return to textual norms' offered an opportunity 'for active mastery and effort in one sphere of an individual's life... it was not, one might note, understood to be devoid of political implications. The Deobandis, much like Gandhi later, believed that if individual lives were properly ordered, the community's life would be transformed as well', pp. 253–4. These considerations were to become much more explicit with the creation of the Jam'īyyat al-'Ulamā'-i-Hind in 1919 through which many Deobandis hoped 'to implement their strictly Islamic ideals in the Muslim community by actively participating in the political struggle.' Anne-Marie Schimmel, *Islam in the Indian Subcontinent* (Leiden-Koln, E.J. Brill, 1980), p. 218.

[3] Of the vision of the 'educated townsmen' – or the Muslim *ashrāf* – to whom Sayyid Ahmad principally appealed, Marshall Hodgson has written, 'Their Islam, diluted by some generations of liberalism, had come to be more a matter of communal allegiance than of cosmic awe. Yet Islam, however debased, remained all the religion they had; to restore at least a nucleus of the Mughal-Islamic culture of full political power became a sacred cause.' Marshall Hodgson, *The Venture of Islam: Conscience and History in a World Civilization. Volume III* (University of Chicago Press, 1974), p. 353.

[4] '...Aligarh has summoned up in both friend and foe an image of Muslim participation – as Muslims – in India's new political institutions. A large part of Aligarh's significance, its meaning, lies in this image and in the imaginations of those who created it, quite aside from any assessment of how influential they were in the society at large'. Lelyveld, *Aligarh's First Generation*, p. 346.

230 Community and consensus in Islam

Muslim state.[5] There were others, deeply influenced by the vision of the poet, Muhammad Iqbāl, who held steadfastly to the view that the temporal destiny of Islam in India (and elsewhere) was bound inextricably to its relationship with power within a recognisable Muslim political order.[6] Yet others, who went by the name of 'nationalist Muslims' in Congress, were committed to a more secular understanding of Islam as part of men's subjective, rather than political, orientations. For them, there were good reasons, historically, to believe that the association between Muslims and democratic politics had been both fragile and problematic, and that the future for a more 'progressive' Islam lay in the secular vision propounded by Congress.[7]

These tensions were not, however, symptomatic of fundamental discontinuities in beliefs or values. For however diverse their political choices, these Muslims, 'reformist' or 'modernist', 'nationalist' or 'separatist', practising or not, shared a common consciousness – a consciousness shaped not only by a specifically Indo-Muslim Mughal tradition but also by a faith which stressed a community bound in service to some higher end. If it is the case that Muslims in India tended increasingly to regard their community as a 'cultural nation' rather than as the extension of some universal *umma*,[8] it did little to erode the profound sense of the distinctiveness of being Muslim. There was, across the political spectrum, an unmistakable awareness of the ideal of Muslim brotherhood; a belief in the superiority of Muslim culture and a recognition of the belief that Muslims ought to live under Muslim governments.

One may ask what these assumptions actually meant in the colonial context of the late nineteenth and early twentieth centuries, and how, in fact, did they interact with official prescriptions of Indian society?

The predominant image of India, constructed from the anthropological endeavours of British officials like Herbert Hope Risley, consisted in the view that Indian society was primarily a conglomeration of disparate

---

[5] Peter Hardy, *Partners in Freedom and True Muslims: The Political Thought of some Muslim Scholars in British India, 1912–1947* (Lund, Scandinavian Institute of Asian Studies, 1971), pp. 21—36; Aziz Ahmad, *Islamic Modernism in India and Pakistan, 1857–1964* (London, Oxford University Press, 1967), pp. 175–94.

[6] Schimmel, *Islam*, pp. 223–33; Aziz Ahmad, *Islamic Modernism*, pp. 156–64 and Kenneth Cragg, *Counsels in Contemporary Islam* (Edinburgh University Press, 1965), pp. 59–66.

[7] See, for example, V.N. Datta and B.E. Cleghorn (eds.), *A Nationalist Muslim and Indian Politics: Being the Selected Correspondence of the late Syed Mahmud* (Delhi, Macmillan, 1974) and Mushirul Hasan (ed.), *Muslims and the Congress: select correspondence of Dr. M.A. Ansari, 1912–1935* (New Delhi, Manohar, 1979).

[8] Hardy, *Partners in Freedom*, p. 42.

communities, races and tribes.[9] The wider political implications of this image were to manifest themselves in the belief that an individual's political affiliations counted for little except as the reflections of his communal, racial and tribal identity. Armed with this repertory of sociological assumptions about India, colonial officials were persuaded that their principal task lay in the steady development of a system that would emphasise the representation of corporate social entities, rather than of individuals.[10]

Official thinking was also noticeably influenced by contemporary debates on representation in Britain. Whig[11] and Utilitarian theories of representation[12] found their way imperceptibly into the morass of colonial policy then being devised for India. Their emphasis upon the legitimacy of corporate representation and their view of representative institutions as instruments of political equilibrium left a lasting imprint upon colonial formulae for separate communal representation and parity.

Much of the appeal of colonial Muslim claims lay precisely in their congruence with ideas of representation that were then current in Britain. The denial of Congress's representative mandate predicated on the idea of an Indian 'nation', which was to form the cornerstone of Muslim separatism, sounded a familiar note. Since the last decades of the nineteenth century, parliamentary reform in Britain had come

[9] See his massive study Herbert Hope Risley, *The People of India* (London, W. Thacker, 1908), especially Chapters 2, 5 and 8. See also Dietmar Rothermund, 'Emancipation or re-integration: The Politics of Gopal Krishna Gokhale and Herbert Hope Risley' in D.A. Low (ed.), *Soundings in Modern South Asian History* (London, Weidenfeld and Nicolson, 1968), pp. 131–58. See also Lucy Carroll, 'Colonial Perceptions of Indian Society and the Emergence of Caste(s) Associations', *Journal of Asian Studies*, 37, 2 (1978), pp. 233–49 and Bernard Cohn, 'Recruitment of Elites in India under British Rule'. Paper presented to the Conference on Modern South Asian Studies at the University of Cambridge, 5–9 July 1968.

[10] S.T. Chakravarty, 'The Evolution of Representative Government in India 1884–1909, with reference to Central and Provincial Legislative Councils', unpublished Ph.D. dissertation, University of London, 1954 and J.L. Hill, 'Congress and Representative Institutions in the United Provinces, 1886–1901', unpublished Ph.D. dissertation, Duke University, 1966.

[11] R.J. Moore, 'The Twilight of the Whigs and the Reform of the Indian Councils, 1886–1892', *Historical Journal*, 10, 4 (1967), pp. 400–14 and R.J. Moore, *Liberalism and Indian Politics, 1872–1922* (London, Edward Arnold, 1966).

[12] On Utilitarian notions of political representation see Hannah Pitkin, *The Concept of Representation* (Berkeley, University of California Press, 1972), pp. 198–207. See also Dennis Thompson, *John Stuart Mill and Representative Government* (Princeton University Press, 1976); Joseph Hamburger, *Intellectuals in Politics: John Stuart Mill and the Philosophic Radicals* (New Haven, Yale University Press, 1965) and Samuel Beer, 'The Representation of Interests in British Government: Historical Background', *American Political Science Review*, 51, 3 (1957), pp. 613–50.

increasingly to feel the influence of political Utilitarianism.[13] The gist of the Utilitarian argument lay in the contention that the credibility of a 'national' institution depended upon the actual presence of those classes and groups it claimed to represent. Colonial officials pursued the spirit of this argument by attempting to ensure that Congress's nationalist pretensions did not obscure the problem of Muslim representation nor conceal the real absence of such representation.

These ideological parameters of colonial policy were not however, independent of the political exigencies of the time. Of these, the threat of a more articulate and better organised Congress party was of paramount importance. Nervous colonial officials recognised in Muslim claims powerful arguments with which to cripple the developing relationship between Congress's predominantly Hindu leadership and a potential Muslim constituency. This is not to say that there obtained a perfect symmetry between Muslim claims and the imperatives of colonial policy. The thorny question of Hindu–Muslim parity and later, the Muslim League's claim to act as the exclusive representative of Muslims in India, were instances of the growing rupture between Indo-Muslim and colonial views on representation. Admittedly, official policy on Indian representation, at least since the 1860s, had always envisaged some form of parity or mutual equality between existing social groups. The preference for 'balanced' representation, consisting of evenly poised social entities which would act as 'sounding boards' of native opinion, signified a trend that was to become an established part of official thinking on Indian representation.[14]

However, the prospect of imminent British withdrawal from India in the 1940s made clear that this notion of parity which had served the ends of colonial domination, was profoundly incompatible with the idea of a politically responsible Indian democracy. By refusing to concede parity on the basis of the League's exclusive claim to represent Indian Muslims, officials did not so much endorse the kind of majority rule then being sought by Congress, as acknowledge the premise that a free electorate was an indispensable condition of a free political society.

A focus upon colonial policy might suggest, not without some reason, that Muslim attitudes to representation; the emergence of Muslim separatism and, indeed, the creation of Pakistan, were all decisively shaped by the direction of such policy.[15] It might even be argued that

---

[13] David Cresap Moore, *The Politics of Deference: a Study of the Mid-Nineteenth Century English Political System* (Hassocks, Sussex, The Harvester Press, 1976).
[14] Hill, 'Congress and Representative Institutions'.
[15] Peter Hardy, *The Muslims of British India* (Cambridge University Press, 1972), chapters V and VI and Francis Robinson, *Separatism among Indian Muslims: The Politics of the United Provinces' Muslims, 1860–1923* (Cambridge University Press, 1974) pp. 98–105, 345–54.

Conclusion 233

without an official policy which encouraged Muslims to organise politically as Muslims, there might well have been no 'Muslim' representation to speak of.[16] This is true. At the same time, this study shows that the elements that sustained the politics of Muslim representation were also grounded deep in a tradition the sources of which were believed to lie in divine revelation. It was this tradition that imparted to Muslims in India the body of assumptions concerning the pivotal role of the religious community, its exclusive claim to individual allegiance, the nature of political consensus and the organisation of power in society.

By the 1880s, the growing concern among some Muslims about the trend of liberal reform in India forced a public debate on the merits of Western representation. While the thrust of Muslim opposition was more ostensibly concerned with the political disadvantages that such representation would bring to bear upon Muslims in India, it rested upon a more profound critique of the ends of Western representation. This questioned the theory of individual representation and denied that men's political commitments were independent of their religious faith. It rejected the justice of arithmetical democracy and called for the restoration of moral superiority as a condition of men's claim to power.

While much of the opposition to Western representation tended to stem from groups of Muslims politically at odds with Congress, Muslim assumptions about the nature of the Islamic community, its relationship to non-Muslims and its proximity to power, were more widely espoused than is commonly acknowledged. There is very little to suggest, for example, that the 'reformist' and 'nationalist' *'ulamā'* who shared Congress's commitment to political independence, also espoused its vision of a secular India, or indeed, its notion of a political society with no relation to the 'fixed' quantities of men's religious affiliations. We now know that many tended, on the contrary, to endorse a degree of 'jurisprudential apartheid',[17] which stressed a system of parallel laws, Muslim and non-Muslim, against a more general 'secular' law extending to all Indians.[18]

In 1883, Sir Sayyid Ahmad Khān provided the first coherent statement of Indo-Muslim attitudes to representation.[19] He argued that

---

[16] See also Carroll, 'Colonial Perceptions' and Anil Seal, 'Imperialism and Nationalism in India', *Modern Asian Studies* 7, 3 (1973), pp. 321–47.
[17] Hardy, *Partners in Freedom*, p. 34.
[18] *Ibid.*, pp. 31–6. See also Yohannan Friedmann, 'The attitude of the Jam'iyyat-i-'Ulamā'-i-Hind to the Indian National Movement and the Establishment of Pakistan' in Gabriel Baer (ed.), *The 'Ulamā' in Modern History* (Jerusalem, Asian and African Studies, Israeli Oriental Society, VII, 1971), pp. 157–83.
[19] His concerns about the application of 'western' representative institutions to India are more fully discussed in chapter 3.

the introduction of 'western' elective representation would contribute substantially to Hindu tyranny. He asserted that an individual's political preferences were governed by his religious affiliations, and that Hindus, as the largest religious group, would tend always to be politically dominant. He emphasised that arithmetical democracy which granted one-man one-vote, was all the more objectionable as it failed to take into account the special claims of groups, like Indian Muslims, whose historical and political significance was not reflected in their numbers.

The intensity with which politically active, primarily urban, Muslims pursued the debate along these lines has been well documented.[20] What has received much less attention, is just how much the outlook of these Muslims owed to the norms of a *sharīf* culture grounded in Mughal tradition, and to the assumptions of their religious faith. The preoccupations of Muslims, like Sir Sayyid Ahmad Khān, Nawāb Mohsin-ul-Mulk, Sayyid Hussain Bilgrāmī, Sayyid Amīr 'Alī, Shiblī No'mānī, Maulānās Muhammad 'Alī and Abū'l Kalām Āzād, reflect their debt to the values of their Mughal heritage and to 'Islamically' derived modes of thinking. For these men, their faith informed not only their individual conduct, but their larger, collective quest to restore their community to its 'charismatic' status.

That Muslim discourse on representation was shaped as much by these considerations as by the 'interests' of Muslims as a political minority, was particularly manifest in the issue of separate Muslim electorates. Historians have argued that the demand for separate electorates was prompted primarily by the fear that elections on the basis of mixed territorial constituencies would be politically ruinous to Muslims in India.[21] This is true. However, the demand for separate Muslim electorates, and Muslim communal representation more generally, embodied not only a concern to ensure 'Islamic outcomes'[22] by obtaining Muslim representatives for Muslim constituencies, but also an

---

[20] In particular by Lelyveld, *Aligarh's First Generation*; Hafeez Malik, *Sir Sayyid Ahmad Khan and Muslim Modernization in India and Pakistan* (New York, Columbia University Press, 1980); Shan Mohammad, *Successors of Sir Syed Ahmad Khan: Their Role in the Growth of Muslim Political Consciousness in India* (Delhi, Idarah-i-Adabiyat-i-Delhi, 1981) and S.M. Ikram, *Modern Muslim India and the Birth of Pakistan* (Lahore, Shaikh Muhammad Ashraf, 1970).

[21] See the comprehensive studies on the demand for separate Muslim electorates by S.R. Wasti, *Lord Minto and the Indian Nationalist Movement* (Oxford, Clarendon Press, 1964) and Matiur Rahman, *From Consultation to Confrontation: A Study of the Muslim League in British Indian Politics, 1906–1912* (London, Luzac and Company, 1970). See also Shafique Ali Khan, 'Separate Electorates as the Genesis of Pakistan' in A.H. Dani (ed.), *Quaid-i-Azam and Pakistan* (Islamabad, Quaid-i-Azam University, 1981), pp. 139–64.

[22] Hardy, *Partners in Freedom*, p. 19.

appreciation, grounded in Mughal values, of the worth of social status and high birth as the bases of representation.

The Muslims who led the Simla Deputation in October 1906 were admittedly concerned to secure a degree of representation for their community which, they felt, was more in keeping with its historical and political importance. At the same time, they were also deeply preoccupied with the restoration of Muslim power. Although some historians have tended to believe that Akbar's inter-confessional culture had done much to erode the Indian Muslim's image of his community as the locus of power, the appeal of an Islamic political order was no less compelling at the turn of the century than in the heyday of Muslim expansion.[23] To understand the profound unwillingness of Indian Muslims to envisage a role for their community outside the framework of power, is to understand the significance of 'weightage' and parity.

The emergence of the Muslim League in December 1906, and its subsequent evolution as an organisation which claimed to speak exclusively for Indian Muslims, is most commonly perceived as evidence of a Muslim 'national consciousness'.[24] What this study has sought to establish is that the League's political development as an authoritative Muslim body was also sustained by Muslim ideas of political consensus and legitimacy. These ideas stressed notions of consensus that were more substantive than procedural, and that tended to assume that Muslims were given more to defer than to differ.[25] This understanding of consensus contributed significantly to the idea that a unitary Muslim political organisation was axiomatic. What is noteworthy, therefore, is not merely that the League succeeded in consolidating its claim to embody an Indo-Muslim political consensus but that it did so

---

[23] Among the better studies that deal with the resilience of this vision in the face of the more universalistic culture favoured by the Mughal emperors after Akbar see, I.H. Qureshi, *The Muslim Community of the Indo-Pakistan Sub-Continent* (The Hague, E.J. Brill, 1962); Peter Hardy, 'Islam in Medieval India' in William de Bary (ed.), *Sources of Indian Tradition, Volume I* (New York, Columbia University Press, 1964), pp. 429–54 and Hodgson, *op. cit.*, III, pp. 60–86.

[24] The League and the growth of separatist politics in India were not of course the only catalysts of Muslim 'national' consciousness. Equally important was the phenomenon of pan-Islamism which assumed the form of the Indian *khilāfat* movement in the early 1920s. Minault has shown how this movement, far from being at odds with Muslim 'nationalism', actually promoted it by postulating a common identity based on religion and by enabling 'an astute set of political leaders to mobilize Indian Muslims as a political constituency'. Minault, *The Khilafat Movement: Religious Symbolism and Political Mobilization in India* (New York, Columbia University Press, 1982) p. 3. For another discussion of how the pan-Islamic Movement succeeded, paradoxically, in consolidating a Muslim separatist identity in India see Ali Ashraf, 'Khilafat Movement: A Factor in Muslim Separatism' in Mushirul Hasan (ed.), *Communal and Pan-Islamic Trends in Colonial India* (Delhi, Manohar, 1981), pp. 66–84.

[25] Hardy, *Partners in Freedom*, p. 12.

by drawing upon established interpretations of the ideal conduct of a Muslim community.

The notion that Muslim representation was a 'trust', delegated exclusively to Muslims, was critical to the political consolidation of the League as the authoritative spokesman for Muslims in India. This understanding of political legitimacy has been a characteristic premise of Muslim political thinking. At its heart lies the notion that 'Muslim-ness' is an elementary condition of legitimate political power. It is this that has constituted for Muslims over the ages the ultimate test of representative status and political legitimacy.[26] What the League and its Muslim followers sought to establish, therefore, was not only that Congress did not represent the vast majority of Muslims in India, but that as a non-Muslim body, it *could not*, represent a Muslim consensus. The constitutional dilemmas that confronted Indian Muslims in the 1940s led to a more explicit definition of their assumptions concerning the organisation of representative institutions and the distribution of power in society. The League objected to a federal centre based on majority rule and demanded instead statutory parity between Muslims and non-Muslims, with itself as exclusive spokesman for Muslim 'interests'. That the League's demands were guided by a palpable urge to share power as equals with Congress is not in question.

However, there was more at stake here than power for power's sake. The dictates of their faith have led Muslims, more often than not, to presuppose the division of society into Muslims and non-Muslims. Political institutions are deemed to conform to society's essentially dichotomous, communal character. They exist not so much to generate the fluid political alignments familiar to democratic political theory as to endorse the diverse ends professed by rigidly defined religious groups. For the League, as for the mass of its Muslim followers, the indiscriminate patterns of 'arithmetical' democracy threatened this idea of a world divided into 'Muslim' and 'non-Muslim'. Nor did their vision encompass the notion of a common law outside of Muslim principles that would transcend the distinct codes that shaped the conduct of those who inhabited that world.[27]

---

[26] See E.I.J. Rosenthal, *Political Thought in Medieval Islam* (Cambridge University Press, 1958) and Ann K.S. Lambton, *State and Government in Medieval Islam: an introduction to the study of Islamic political theory: the jurists* (Oxford University Press, 1981).

[27] A question dealt with in greater detail, although primarily in relation to Muslim personal law, in Tahir Mahmood, *Muslim Personal Law: Role of the State in the Subcontinent* (New Delhi, Vikas Publishing House, 1977).

BIBLIOGRAPHY

List of primary sources and works cited

Sources in Urdu

'Abdu'l Halīm Siddīquī, Maulānā, *Jam'īyyat al-'Ulamā'-i Hind kī chand ahm khidmāt-i millī kā mukhtsar tazkira* (Delhi, Jam'īyyat al-'Ulamā'-i Hind, 194).

'Abdu'l Rahmān, Sayyid Subāhuddīn, 'Shiblī No'mānī', *Nuqūsh, Shakhsīyāt Number* (Lahore), volume 2, January 1956, pp. 18–25.

Āsī, Mumtāz 'Alī, *Maulānā Maudūdī aur Jamā'at-i Islāmī: ek Jāeza* (Lahore, Maktaba'-i Jadid, 1964).

Āzād, Abū'l Kalām, Maulānā, *Mazāmīn-i al-Balāgh*, Mahmūd ul Hasan Siddiquī (ed.), (Lahore, 'Ainah'-i 'Adab, 1981).

Khutbāt-i Āzād Mālik Ram (ed.) (Delhi, Sahitya Academy, 1974).

Mas'ala-i khilāfat wa Jazīra-i 'Arab (Lahore, Central Khilafat Cāmītī, 1920).

'Azīz Mirza, Muhammad, *Muslim Pālītiks* (Lucknow, All India Muslim League, 1910).

Batālvī, Āshiq Husain, *Iqbāl kē Ākhrī dō sāl* (Lahore, Iqbāl Academī, 1969), reprint.

Bihārī, Sulaiman Ashraf, Maulānā, *Al-Balāgh: Musalmānon kē tanazzul kē asbāb aur khilāfat-i usmānīya kē tārikhī wāqēyāt* (Aligarh, Matba'-i Ahmadi, 192-).

Dehlavī, 'Ināyetullah, 'Sir Sayyid Ahmad Khān', *Nuqūsh, Shakhsīyāt Number* (Lahore), January 1956, pp. 559—62.

Hālī, Altāf Husain, Maulānā, *Nuqūsh, Makātīb Number* (Lahore), volume 1, number 65, November 1957, pp. 137–48.

Hayāt-i Jāwed (Lahore, Ishrat Publishing House, 1965).

'Ibrāhīm, Muhammad, Maulānā, *Quam aur mazhab* (Amritsar, Munshī 'Abdu'l Rahman Shauq, 1911).

Kashmīrī, Shōrish, 'Zafar 'Alī Khān', *Nuqūsh, Shakhsīyāt Number* (Lahore), volume 1, January 1956, pp. 596–603.

Kidwaī, Jalīl, 'Maulānā Hasrat Mohānī', *Nuqūsh, Shakhsīyāt Number*, Lahore, volume 1, January 1956, pp. 168–79.

Madanī, Husain Ahmad, *Muttahida' Qaumīyyat aur Islām* (Delhi, 1938–39?).

Naqsh-i Hayāt, 2 volumes (Delhi, 1953).

Mehr, Ghulām Rasūl, 'Maulānā Abū'l Kalam Āzād', *Nuqūsh, Shaksīyāt Number* (Lahore), volume 1, January 1956, pp. 235–41.

237

238 Community and consensus in Islam

Muhammad 'Alī, Maulānā, *Nuqūsh, Makātīb Number* (Lahore), volume 1, number 65, November 1957, pp. 335–66.

Mohānī Hasrat, Maulānā, *Khutba'-i Sadārat* (Lucknow, Muhammad 'Isma'īl Mushtāq, 1925).

Mohsin-ul-Mulk, Nawāb, *Nuqūsh, Makātīb Number* (Lahore), volume 1, number 65, November 1957.

Sarwar, Muhammad, *Maulānā Ubaidullah Sindhī* (Lahore, 1943).

Sauhadravī, 'Ināyetullah Nasīm, *Zafar 'Alī Khān aur un ke 'ahd* (Lahore, Islāmī Publishing House, 1982).

Sayyid Ahmad Khan, *Asbāb-i Baghawāt-i Hind* (Lahore, Munshi Fazluddin, n.d.).

   Maktūbāt-i-Sir Sayyid Ahmad Khān, volume 1, Shaikh Muhammad Isma'īl Panīpatī (ed.) (Lahore, Majlis-i taraqqī-i 'adab, 1976).

   Nuqūsh, Makātīb Number (Lahore), volume 1, number 65, November 1957, pp. 112–30.

   'Khilāfat aur Khalīfa', *Mazhabī wa Islāmī Mazāmīn* (Lahore, Majlis-i-Tariqqī-i-'Adab, 1962), pp. 164–8.

Shaukat, 'Alī, Maulānā, *Nuqūsh, Makātīb Number* (Lahore), volume 1, number 65, November 1957, pp. 367—70.

Shiblī No'mānī, Maulānā, *Rasa'īl-i Shiblī* (Amritsar, Vakil Trading Company, 1911).

   'Musalmānon kī pālītical karwat', *Maqalāt-i Shiblī*, volume 8 (Azamgarh, Ma'aref Press, 1938), pp. 148–81.

Sources in English

(a) *Unpublished private papers* (all at the India Office Library in London)

Dufferin Papers, MSS EUR F 130
Harcourt Butler Papers, MSS EUR F 116
John Morley Papers, MSS EUR D 573
Lansdowne Papers, MSS EUR D 558
Linlithgow Collection, MSS EUR F 125
Zetland Collection, MSS EUR E 609

(b) *India Office Library official records*

Indian Constitutional Reforms and Muhammedans. Papers presented to Parliament. L/PJ/6.

Rahmat Ali Papers. L/P&J/8/689.

Private Office Records. L/PO/48, L/PO/49.

Proceedings (Home) Public, volumes 8150, 8151.

Public Letters from India, 1888, volume 9.

Selections from Native Newspapers – NWP. & United Provinces, 1906, 1909, L/R/5/81 and L/R/5/84.

(c) *Parliamentary papers*

1883 Cmd. 3353, *Resolution of the Government of India, Department of Finance and Commerce, 30 September 1881.*
1883 Volume LI, *Extension of Local Self-Government in India.*
1908 Cmd. 4426, *Proposals of the Government of India and Despatches of the Secretary of State.*
1908 Cmd. 4435 & 4436, *Replies of the Local Governments to Proposals of the Government of India.*
1918 Cmd. 9109, *Report on Indian Constitutional Reforms* (Montagu-Chelmsford Reforms).
1918 Cmd. 9178, *Addresses Presented in India to his Excellency, the Viceroy and the Rt. Honourable, the Secretary of State for India* (House of Commons Papers, 1918, volume 18).
1932 Cmd. 4147, *Communal Decision.*
1937 Cmd. 5589, *Return Showing the Results of Elections in India, 1937.*

(d) *Parliamentary debates* (Hansard's)

Year Volume
1833 19 *(Commons)*
1861 163 *(Commons)*
1883 227 *(Lords)*
1890 342 *(Lords)*
1892 3 *(Lords)*
1906 161 *(Lords)*
1908 198 *(Lords)*
1909 3 *(Commons)*
1940 364 *(Commons)*
1942 378 *(Commons)*
1946 420 *(Commons)*

(e) *Other Government publications*

Proceedings of the Legislative Council of the Governor General of India (Calcutta, 1893).
Papers Relating to the Cabinet Mission to India 1946 (Delhi, Manager of Publications, 1946).
Indian Annual Register, 1940; 1945; 1946, Vol. I (Calcutta, The Annual Register Office).

(f) *Published party records, political statements and constitutional documents*

Aligarh, *Aligarh Movement: The Basic Documents, 1864–1898*, volume 3, Shan Mohammad (ed.) (Meerut, Meenakshi Prakashan, 1978).
All India Muslim Conference, *The All India Muslim Conference, 1928–1935: A*

Documentary Record, K.K. Aziz (ed.) (Karachi, National Publishing House, 1972).

All India Muslim League, *Foundations of Pakistan: Documents of the All India Muslim League, 1906–1947*, volumes I and II, Syed Sharif-ud-din-Pirzada (ed.) (Karachi, National Publishing House, n.d. & 1970).

Report of the Enquiry Committee appointed by the Council of the All India Muslim League to enquire into Muslim grievances in Congress Provinces, 15 November 1938 (Pirpur Report) (Delhi, 1938).

Report of the Enquiry Committee appointed by the Working Committee of the Bihar Provincial Muslim League to enquire into some grievances of Muslims in Bihar, 1938–1939 (Sharif Report) (Patna, 1938).

Banerjea, S., *Speeches of Babu Surendernath Banerjea, 1876–1880*, volume I, R.C. Palit (ed.) (Calcutta, S.K. Lahiri, 1880).

Bilgrami, Syed Husain (Sayyid Husain), Nawab Imadul-Mulk Bahadur, *Speeches, Addresses and Poems* (Hyderabad, Government Central Press, 1925).

Central National Mahommedan Association, *Rules and Objects of the Central National Mahommedan Association and its Branch Associations with the Quinquennial and Annual Reports and Lists of Members (1885)*.

Gokhale, Gopal Krishna, *Speeches and Writings of Gopal Krishna Gokhale*, volume 2, D.G. Karve and D.V. Ambedkar (eds.) (London, Asia Publishing House, 1966).

Indian Constitution, *Indian Constitutional Documents*, volume 1, Durga Das Basu (ed.) (Calcutta, S.C. Sarkar, 1969).

Speeches and Documents on the Indian Constitution, 1921–1947, volumes I and II, M. Gwyer and A. Appadorai (eds.) (London, Oxford University Press, 1957).

Indian National Congress, *Proceedings of the First Indian National Congress held in Bombay on the 28th, 29th and 30th December, 1885* (Bombay, Indian National Congress, 1886).

Congress Presidential Addresses, volume 2 (Madras Natesan, n.d.).

Iqbal, Muhammad, *Speeches, Writings and Statements of Iqbal*, Latif Ahmad Sherwani (ed.) (Lahore, Iqbal Academy, 1977).

Jinnah, Muhammad Ali, *Speeches and Writings of Mr. Jinnah*, volumes I and II, Jamil-ud-din Ahmad (ed.) (lahore, Shaikh Muhammad Ashraf, 1960, 1964).

Linlithgow, Marquess of, *Speeches and Statements, 1936–1943* (Simla, Government of India Press, 1945).

Muhammad Ali, Maulana, *Mohamed Ali in Indian Politics: Select Writings*, volume I and II, Mushirul Hasan (ed.) (New Delhi, Atlantic Publishers, 1982, 1983).

National Liberal Club, *The Awakening of India* (G.K. Gokhale's address to the National Liberal Club, 15 November, 1905) (London, Political Committee of the National Liberal Club, 1905), listed under India Office Library Tracts, Pol. 993.

Pakistan, *Pakistan Resolution to Pakistan, 1940–1947: A Selection of Documents*

presenting the Case for Pakistan, L.A. Sherwani (ed.) (Karachi, National Publishing House, 1969).
Historic Documents of the Muslim Freedom Movement, Jamil-ud-din Ahmad (ed.) (Lahore, Publishers United, 1970).
Sayyid Ahmad Khan, *Writings and Speeches of Sir Syed Ahmad Khan*, Shan Mohammad (ed.) (Bombay, Nachiketa Publications, 1972).

(g) *Memoirs, essays and select correspondence*

Aga Khan, *The Memoirs of the Aga Khan: World Enough and Time* (London, Cassell, 1954).
    India in Transition: A Study in Political Evolution (London, Philip Lee Warner, 1918).
Ameer Ali, Syed (Sayyid Amir Ali), *The Spirit of Islam: A History of the Evolution and Ideals of Islam* (London, Christopher's, 1961).
    Ameer Ali: His Life and Work (a single volume in 2 parts), K.K. Aziz (ed.) (Lahore, Publishers United, 1966).
    On Islamic History and Culture, S.R. Wasti (ed.) (Lahore, People's Publishing House, 1968).
Blunt, W.S., *India Under Ripon: A Private Diary* (London, T. Fisher Unwin, 1909).
Chiragh Ali, *The Proposed Political, Legal and Social Reforms in the Ottoman Empire and Other Mohammedan States* (Bombay, 1883).
Chirol, Sir Valentine, *Indian Unrest* (London, Macmillan, 1910).
Dilke, Sir Charles, *Greater Britain* (London, Macmillan, 1868).
Duchesne, A.E., 'The Indian Mohammedans and the Reforms', *Empire Review,* 17, 100 (1909), pp. 254–63.
Faruki, Kemal, *Islamic Constitution* (Karachi, Khokrapur Gateway Publication, 1952).
Fazl-i-Husain, *Letters of Fazl-i-Husain*, Waheed Ahmad (ed.) (Lahore, Research Society of Pakistan, 1976).
Frere, Bartle, *The Means of Ascertaining Public Opinion in India* (London, John Murray, 1871).
Hakim, Khalifa Abdul, *Islamic Ideology: The Fundamental Beliefs and Principles of Islam and their Application to Practical Life* (Lahore, The Institute of Islamic Culture, 1965).
Iqbal, Muhammad, *The Reconstruction of Religious Thought in Islam* (London, Oxford University Press, 1934).
    Rumuz-i-Bekhudi, The Mysteries of Selflessness, R.A. Nicolson (trans.) (London, J. Murray, 1953).
    Letters of Iqbal, Bashir Ahmad Dar (ed.) (Lahore, Iqbāl Academy, 1978).
Jinnah, Muhammad Ali, *The Pakistan Issue: being the Correspondence between S.A. Latif and M.A. Jinnah on the one hand, and between him and Maulana A.K. Azad, Dr. Rajendra Prasad and Pandit J. Nehru on the other and connected papers on the subject of Pakistan* (Lahore, Shaikh Muhammad Ashraf, 1943).

Quaid-i-Azam Jinnah's Correspondence, S.S. Pirzada (ed.) (Karachi, Guild Publishing House, 1966).

Lawrence, Sir Henry, *Essays: Military and Political Written in India*, volume I (London, W.H. Allen, 1859).

Maine, H.S., *Popular Government* (London, John Murray, 1885).

The Effects of Observation of India on Modern European Thought (London, John Murray, 1875).

Maududi, Abul Ala, *The Islamic Law and Constitution* (Lahore, Islamic Publications, 1967).

The Nature and Contents of Islamic Constitution, Khurshid Ahmad (ed.) (Karachi, Jammat-i-Islami Publications, n.d.).

Muhammad Ali, Maulana, *My Life: A Fragment*, Afzal Iqbal (ed.) (Lahore, Shaikh Muhammad Ashraf, 1966).

Parwez, Ghulam Ahmad, *Islam: A Challenge to Religion* (Lahore, Idara-i-Tule-e-Islam, 1968).

Rahmat Ali, Chaudhri, *The Millat and the Mission* (Cambridge, Pakasia Literature, 1942).

Pakistan: The Fatherland of the Pak Nation (Cambridge, Pakasia Literature, 1947).

Risley, H.H., *The People of India* (London, Thacker, Spink and Co., 1908).

Sayyid Mahmud, *A Nationalist Muslim and Indian Politics: Being the Selected Correspondence of the Late Syed Mahmud*, V.N. Datta and B.E. Cleghorn (eds.) (Delhi, Macmillan, 1974).

Stephen, J.F., 'Foundations of Government in India', *Nineteenth Century*, 39 (1883), pp. 451–568.

Wavell, Archbold Percival, *Wavell: the Viceroy's Journal*, Penderel Moon (ed.) (London, Oxford University Press, 1973).

(h) *Newspapers*

Aligarh Institute Gazette (Aligarh)
Civil and Military Gazette (Lahore)
Pioneer (Allahabad)
The Times (London)

Select list of secondary works cited
(For details of other secondary sources see footnotes)

Ahmad, Aziz, *Studies in Islamic Culture in the Indian Environment* (Oxford, Clarendon Press, 1964).

Islamic Modernism in India and Pakistan, 1857–1964 (London, Oxford University Press, 1967).

An Intellectual History of Islam in India (Edinburgh University Press 1969).

Ahmad, Imtiaz, 'The *Ashraf-Ajlaf* Distinction in Muslim Social Structure in

India', *Indian Economic and Social History Review*, 3, September 1966, pp. 268-78.

(ed.), *Caste and Social Stratification Among the Muslims* (Delhi, Manohar, 1973).

(ed.), *Family, Marriage and Kinship Among Muslims in India* (Delhi, Manohar, 1976).

(ed.), *Ritual and Religion Among Muslims in India* (Delhi, Manohar, 1981).

Modernization and Social Change Among Muslims in India (Delhi, Manohar, 1983).

Ahmed, Rafiuddin, *The Bengal Muslims 1871-1906: A Quest for Identity* (Delhi, Oxford University Press, 1981).

Arnold, T.W., *The Caliphate*, reissued with a conclusion by Sylvia Hiam (London, Routledge and Kegan Paul, 1965).

Asad, Muhammad, *The Principles of State and Government in Islam* (Los Angeles, University of California Press, 1961).

Baljon, J.M.S., *The Reforms and Religious Ideas of Sir Sayyid Ahmad Khan* (Leiden, E.J. Brill, 1949).

Brass, Paul, *Language, Religion and Politics in North India* (Cambridge University Press, 1974).

Carré, Olivier (ed.), *L'Islam et l'Etat dans le Monde d'Aujourdhui* (Paris, Presses Universitaires de France, 1982).

Case, Margaret, 'The Aligarh Era: Muslim Politics in North India, 1860-1910', unpublished Ph.D. dissertation, University of Chicago, 1970.

Chakravarty, S.T., 'The Evolution of Representative Government in India 1884-1909, with reference to Central and Provincial Legislative Councils', unpublished Ph.D. dissertation, University of London, 1954.

Coupland, Reginald, *The Indian Problem, 1883-1935* (London, Oxford University Press, 1942).

Indian Politics, 1936-1942. Report on the Constitutional Problem in India, volume 2 (London, Oxford University Press, 1943).

Cragg, Kenneth, *Counsels in Contemporary Islam* (Edinburgh University Press, 1965).

Cross, Cecil, *The Development of Self-Government in India, 1858-1914* (Chicago University Press, 1922).

Das, M.N., *India Under Morley and Minto: Politics Behind Revolution, Repression and Reform* (London, George Allen and Unwin, 1964).

Esposito, John (ed.), *Voices of Resurgent Islam* (Oxford University Press, 1983).

Faruqi, Zia ul Hasan, *The Deoband School and the Demand for Pakistan* (Bombay, Asia Publishing House, 1963).

Gallagher, John, *et al.* (eds.), *Locality, Province and Nation: Essays on Indian Politics, 1870-1947* (Cambridge University Press, 1973).

Garaudy, Roger, *Promesses de l'Islam* (Paris, Editions du Seuil, 1981).

Gardet, Louis, *La Cité Musulmane: Vie Sociale et Politique* (Paris, Librarie Philosophique J. Vrin, 1961).

Gökalp, Ziya, *Turkish Nationalism and Western Civilization: Selected Essays by*

Ziya Gokalp, Niyazi Berkes (ed., & trans.) (London, George Allen and Unwin, 1959).

Goldziher, Ignaz, *Le Dogme et la Loi de l'Islam* (Paris, Edition Geuthner, 1920).

Gopal, S., *British Policy in India, 1858–1905* (Cambridge University Press, 1965).

— *The Viceroyalty of Lord Ripon, 1880–1884* (London, Oxford University Press, 1953).

Gordon, Leonard, *Bengal: The Nationalist Movement, 1876–1940* (New York, Columbia University Press, 1974).

Graham, G.F.I., *The Life and Work of Syed Ahmad Khan, K.C.S.I.* (London, Hodder and Stoughton, 1909).

Grewal, J.S., *Muslim Rule in India: The Assessments of British Historians* (Calcutta, Oxford University Press, 1970).

Haq, Mushirul, *Muslim Politics in India, 1857–1947* (Meerut, Meenakshi Pradashaw, 1970).

Hardy, Peter, *Partners in Freedom and True Muslims. The Political Thought of Some Muslim Scholars in British India, 1912–1947* (Lund, Scandinavian Institute of Asian Studies, 1971).

— *The Muslims of British India* (Cambridge University Press, 1972).

Hasan, Mushirul, *Nationalism and Communal Politics in India, 1916–1928* (Delhi, Manohar, 1979).

— *Mohamed Ali: Ideology and Politics* (Delhi, Manohar, 1981).

Hill, J.L., 'Congress and Representative Institutions in the United Provinces, 1886–1901', unpublished Ph.D. dissertation, Duke University, 1966.

Hodgson, Marshall, *The Venture of Islam: Conscience and History in a World Civilization,* volumes 1–3 (Chicago University Press, 1974).

Hourani, A.H., *Arabic Thought in the Liberal Age: 1798–1939* (London, Oxford University Press, 1962).

Hourani, G.F., 'The Basis of Authority of Consensus in Sunnite Islam', *Studia Islamica,* 21 (1964), pp. 13–60.

Ikram, S.M., *Modern Muslim India and the Birth of Pakistan* (Lahore, Shaikh Muhammad Asraf, 1970).

Iqbal, Afzal, *The Life and Times of Mohamed Ali* (Lahore, Institute of Islamic Culture, 1974).

Islam, *Encyclopaedia of Islam,* III (Leiden, E.J. Brill, 1971).

Jain, M.S., *The Aligarh Movement: Its Origin and Development, 1858–1906* (Agra, Sri Ram Mehra, 1965).

Jalal, A., *The Sole Spokesman: Jinnah, the Muslim League and the Demand for Pakistan* (Cambridge University Press, 1985).

Kaura, Uma, *Muslims and Indian Nationalism: The Emergence of the Demand for India's Partition, 1928–1940* (Delhi, South Asia Books, 1977).

Keddie, Nikki (ed.), *Scholars, Saints and Sufis: Muslim Religious Institutions since 1500* (Berkeley, California, University of California Press, 1972).

Koss, Stephen, *John Morley at the India Office, 1905–1910* (New Haven, Yale University Press, 1969).

Laoust, Henri, *Les Schismes dans l'Islam* (Paris, Payot, 1965).

Lelyveld, David, *Aligarh's First Generation: Muslim Solidarity in British India* (Princeton University Press, 1978).

Majumdar, S.S., *History of Indian Social and Political Ideas: From Ram Mohun to Dayananda* (Calcutta, Bookland Private, 1967).

Malik, Hafeez, *Moslem Nationalism in India and Pakistan* (Washington, Public Affairs Press, 1963).

  Sir Sayyid Ahmad Khan and Muslim Modernization in India and Pakistan (New York, Columbia University Press, 1980).

McDonough, Sheila, *The Authority of the Past: A Study of Three Muslim Modernists* (Chambersburg, Pennsylvania, American Academy of Religion, 1970).

Mehrotra, S.R., *The Emergence of the Indian National Congress* (New York, Barnes and Noble, 1971).

Metcalf, Barbara D., *Islamic Revival in British India: Deoband, 1860–1900* (Princeton University Press, 1982).

Metcalf, Thomas R., *The Aftermath of the Revolt* (Princeton University Press, 1965).

Minault, Gail, *The Khilafat Movement: Religious Symbolism and Political Mobilization in India* (New York, Columbia University Press, 1982).

Mill, J.S., *Considerations on Representative Government* (Chicago, Henry Regnery, 1962).

Mohammad, Shan, *Successors of Sir Syed Ahmad Khan: Their Role in the Growth of Muslim Political Consciousness in India* (Delhi, Idarah-i-Adabiyat-i-Delhi, 1981).

Moore, David C., *The Politics of Deference: A Study of the Mid-Nineteenth Century English Political System* (Hassocks, Sussex, The Harvester Press, 1976).

Moore, R.J., *Liberalism and Indian Politics, 1872–1922* (London, Edward Arnold, (1966).

  Sir Charles Wood's Indian Policy (Manchester University Press, 1966).

  The Crisis of Indian Unity, 1917–1940 (Oxford, Clarendon Press, 1974).

  Churchill, Cripps and India, 1939–1945 (Oxford, Clarendon Press, 1979).

Mujeeb, Muhammad, *The Indian Muslims* (London, George Allen and Unwin, 1967).

Naim, C.M. (ed.), *Iqbal, Jinnah and Pakistan* (Delhi, Jinnah Publishing House, 1982).

Nizami, Khaliq Ahmad, *Some Aspects of Religion and Politics in India during the Thirteenth Century* (Bombay, Asia Publishing House, 1961).

Page, David, *Prelude to Partition: The Indian Muslims and the Imperial System of Control, 1920–1932* (Delhi, Oxford University Press, 1982).

Philips, C.H. and Wainwright, M.D. (eds.), *The Partition of India: Policies and Perspectives, 1935–1947* (London, George Allen and Unwin, 1970).

Pitkin, Hanna, *The Concept of Representation* (Berkeley, University of California Press, 1972).

Qureshi, I.H., *The Muslim Community of the Indo-Pakistan Subcontinent* (The Hague, E.J. Brill, 1962).

The Struggle for Pakistan (University of Karachi Publications, 1965).
Ulema in Politics: A Study Relating to the Political Activities of the Ulema in the South Asian Sub-Continent from 1556 to 1947 (Karachi, Ma'aref, 1972).
Rahman, Fazlur, Islam (University of Chicago Press, 1979).
Rahman, Matiur, From Consultation to Confrontation: A Study of the Muslim League in British Indian Politics, 1906-1912 (London, Luzac, 1970).
Rida, Rashid, Le Califat dans la Doctrine de Rasīd Ridā, Henri Laoust (trans.) (Beirut, L'Institut Franças de Damas, 1938).
Rizvi, S.A.A., A History of Sufism in India: From Sixteenth Century to Modern Century, volume 2 (Delhi, Munshiram Manoharlal, 1983).
Robinson, Francis, Separatism Among Indian Muslims: The Politics of the United Provinces' Muslims, 1860-1923 (Cambridge University Press, 1974).
'Islam and Muslim Separatism', in David Taylor and Malcolm Yapp (eds.), Political Identity in South Asia (London, School of Oriental and African Studies, 1979), pp. 78-112.
'Islam and Muslim Society in South Asia', Contributions to Indian Sociology (n.s.), 17, 2 (1983), pp. 185-203.
Rodinson, M., Mohammed (Middlesex, Penguin, 1983).
Roff, William (ed.), Islam and the Political Economy of Meaning: Comparative Studies of Muslim Discourse (London, Croom Helm, 1987).
Rosenthal, E.I.J., Political Thought in Medieval Islam (Cambridge University Press, 1958).
Rosenthal, Franz, The Muslim Concept of Freedom (Leiden, E.J. Brill, 1960).
Sadiq, Muhammad, A History of Urdu Literature (Delhi, Oxford University Press, 1984, second edition).
Saiyid, M.H., Mohammad Ali Jinnah: A Political Study (Lahore, Shaikh Muhammad Ashraf, 1962).
Sayeed, Khalid bin, Pakistan: The Formative Phase, 1857-1948 (London, Oxford University Press, 1968).
Schacht, Joseph, An Introduction to Islamic Law (Oxford, Clarendon Press, 1964).
Schimmel, Anne-Marie, Gabriel's Wings (Leiden, E.J. Brill, 1963).
Islam in the Indian Subcontinent (Leiden-Koln, E.J. Brill, 1980).
Seal, Anil, The Emergence of Indian Nationalism (Cambridge University Press, 1971).
Skinner, Quentin, 'Some Problems in the Analysis of Political Thought and Action', Political Theory, 2, 3 (1974), pp. 277-303.
Voll, John O., Islam: Continuity and Change in the Modern World (Boulder, Colorado, Westview Press, 1982).
Wasti, S.R., Lord Minto and the Indian Nationalist Movement (Oxford, Clarendon Press, 1964).
Watt, Montgomery, Muhammad at Mecca (Oxford, Clarendon Press, 1953).
Muhammad at Medina (Oxford, Clarendon Press, 1956).
Islamic Political Thought (Edinburgh University Press, 1980).

Wolpert, Stanley, *Jinnah of Pakistan* (New York, Oxford University Press, 1984).

    Morley and India, 1906–1910 (Berkeley & Los Angeles, University of California Press, 1967).

Zaidi, Z.H., 'The Partition of Bengal and its Annulment, 1902–1911', unpublished Ph.D. thesis, University of London, 1964.

Zakaria, Rafiq, *Rise of Muslims in Indian Politics: An Analysis of Developments from 1885 to 1906* (Bombay, Somaiya Publications, 1970).

INDEX

'Abduh Muhammad, 28; on *ijmā'*, 32–3
al-Afghānī, Jamāl al Dīn, 17, 29
Āgā Khān, 123, 126, 128, 134, 159, 186;
  on communal representation, 145, 152;
  participation in the Muslim League,
  164; resignation from the League, 168;
  participation in Round Table
  Conference, 186, 188–9
ahl adh dhimmī, 37; *see also dhimmī*
ahl al kitāb, 39
Ahmad, Aziz, 1, 29, 31, 33, 34, 84; on
  ijmā', 35–6; on Sayyid Ahmad Khān
  and Caliphate, 177–8; *Islamic Culture
  in the India Environment*, 35
Ahmad, Imtiaz, 1
Ahmed, Rafiuddin, 1, 82
Aitchison, Charles, 59
ajlāf, 4n
Ajmal Khan, Hakīm, 147, 183
Akbar (Mughal emperor), 104, 153, 235
'Alī, the fourth Caliph, 177; caliphate of,
  179
'Alī, Chaudhri Rahmat, *see* Rahmat 'Alī,
  Chaudhri
'Alī, Chirāgh, *see* Chirāgh 'Alī
'Alī Imām, Sayyid, 149, 151; and
  campaign for separate electorates, 147–
  8; Mughal ancestry of, 153
'Alī, Sayyid Amīr, *see* Amīr 'Alī, Sayyid
Aligarh, 104, 105, 228, 229; and Muslim
  political organisation, 134; influence on
  Muslim League, 160; orientations of
  movement based in, 181
All India Khilafat Committee, 174, 175,
  183
All India Muslim Conference, 187–8.
All India Muslim League, 5, 6;
  foundation of, 125, 135, 235;
  dominance of Aligarh Muslims in, 160,
  165; loyalist politics of, 165–6; and
  separate Muslim ￫lectorates, 146–8;
  London branch of, 147; Deccan
  Provincial League, 152; and self-
  government, 167; and Lucknow Pact,
  169–70, 184; and provincial Muslim

politics, 161, ￫72, 173, 174, 184–5, 197;
  and notions of representation, 164–5,
  209–10, 236; and *khilāfat* movement,
  175–6, 184; thinking on *khilāfat*, 176,
  180; and Nehru Report, 187; and
  parity, 195, 212, 214, 215; and elections
  of 1937, 196–7; pact with Unionist
  Party, 199; coalition with Krishak-
  Praja Party, 199; and schemes for
  Muslim homeland, 206–7; demand for
  Pakistan, 216, 218, 223; and
  resignation of Congress ministries,
  211–12; and 'August Offer', 214–15;
  terms of entry into Executive Council,
  215; and Cripps Mission, 216–18; and
  elections of 1946, 222; position at
  Tripartite Conference, 223–4 and
  Cabinet Mission, 223–5
amīr, 16
amīrates, 99
amīr-i-Hind, 182
Amīr 'Alī, Sayyid, 32, 83, 87, 96, 98, 102,
  105, 196, 111, 118, 121, 133, 134, 149,
  151, 152, 154, 159, 166, 180, 181, 182;
  on *ijmā'*, 34, 100–1, 147, 163, 192; on
  Muslim representation, 88, 92; on
  Indian self-government, 89; as
  representative of Mughal culture, 95–6,
  234; on political consultation, 100; on
  elective representation, 103–4; on
  Western representation, 114; on foreign
  ancestry of Indian Muslims, 116; and
  campaign for separate electorates, 147–
  9; on Indian Councils Act of 1910,
  153; resignation from Muslim League,
  168; on *khilāfat* and pan-Islamism,
  178–9; on Islamic solidarity, 190–1;
  The Spirit of Islam, 182
Ampthill, Lord Arthur, 159
Animists, 140
Anjuman-i-Himāyat-i-Islām, 144
Anjuman-i-Islāmī, 83, 85, 86; on political
  consultation, 101
Ansārī, M.A., 168, 183
Anstey, Chisolm, 67

248

78, 88, 120; foundation of, 59, 67, 133, 208–9; demand for Western representation, 67, 73; Muslim opposition to, 77, 109, 110, 119; Muslims in, 105–6, 144; official attitudes to, 127–8; on self-government, 122, 167; and Lucknow Pact, 161, 169–70; and Nehru Report, 187–8; elections of 1937, 194, 198; resignation of provincial ministries, 211; on parity, 215; and Cripps Mission, 217–19; on proposals for Interim Government, 220–1; and Cabinet Mission Plan, 224, 226; secular vision of, 21, 230

Iqbāl, Muhammad, 11, 12, 16, 22, 26, 28, 30, 154, 179, 205, 206, 230; on *ijmā'*, 31, 163; on Islamic universalism, 46–7, 202, 205; and modernist thinking, 181; on communal representation, 121, 142, 145; on Western democracy, 192; on Turkish Caliphate, 180–1; on pan-Islamism, 181; on role of *'ulamā'* in *khilāfat* movement, 181; on Islamic solidarity, 190; on Muslim League, 192; on Muslim consensus, 193; on Muslim nationhood, 195, 198, 200–2, 203–5; on European nationalism, 201, 204; *Reconstruction of Religious Thought in Islam*, 182; *Rumūz-ī-Bekhudī*, 142

Irwin, Lord Edward, 189

Islam, 2, 4, 8, 11, 12, 38, 45, 46, 48; folk, 191; 'high', 4n; in history, 14; expansion of, 15; the state in, 8, 28, 42, 44, 226; the community in, 13–23; consensus in, 23–37; co-existence in, 39–40; communal solidarity in, 17–18; individual rights in, 18–19; Shiblī on superiority of, 41; Hālī on superiority of, 117–18; universalism in, 21, 46–7; and nationalism, 22; Iqbāl and Madanī on nationalism and, 201–4; Indian, 1, 2, 14, 15, 16, 17, 33, 228–30

Islamia College, 144

'Islamisation', 82

Ismaʿīl Khān, Hājī Muhammad, Nawab, on Western representation, 109, 132, 133

jāhilīyya, 17

Jalal, Ayesha, 3, 5, 6, 210, 215

Jallianwala Bagh, 173

Jamʿīyyat al-'ulamā'-i-Hind, 48, 182, 229; on autonomous Muslim order in India, 143; as political organisation of

the *'ulamā'*, 174, 175; on composite nationalism, 229

Jawnpūrī, Karamat 'Alī, Maulvi, 86, 100

Jews, 14; and medieval political theory, 23; resistance to Muhammad, 38; relationship to early Muslims, 40

jihād (also *jehad*), 8, 148, 144, 158

Jinnah, Muhammad 'Alī, *see also* Quā'id-e-A'zam, 5, 6, 7, 8, 171, 200, 207, 210, 211, 213; on Muslim democratic consensus, 163–4, 193, 216; and Lucknow Pact, 170; on role of the *'ulamā'* in *khilāfat* movement, 182; and Simon Commission, 186; and Nehru Report, 187; agreement with Unionists and Prajaists, 199; on League's representative standing, 192; on Congress's representative standing, 208, 215; on Muslim nationhood, 194, 198; and reorganisation of the League, 196–7; and notions of representation, 209; on League's entry into Executive Council, 212; on democracy, 213; on Hindu-Muslim dichotomy, 213, 222; on parity, 212–13; and 'August Offer', 214–15, 216; and Cripps Mission, 218; on proposals for Interim Government, 221, 225; on Pakistan, 224–5; acceptance of Cabinet Mission Plan, 225–6

jizya, 39; Shiblī on, 42

al-Jizya (Shiblī), 42

Judaism, 16, 46

Kanpur, issue of mosque in, 167

Kayasths, 70, 89

Khabardar, 152

Khāksārs, 206

Khān, 'Abdu'l Ghaffar Khān, *see* Ghaffar Khān, Khan 'Abdu'l

Khān, Hakīm Ajmal, *see* Ajmal Khān

Khān, Liāquat 'Alī, *see* Liāquat 'Alī Khan

Khān, Muhammad Ismaʿīl, Nawab, *see* Ismaʿīl Khān, Muhammad, Nawab

Khan, Naushād 'Alī, Raja, *see* Naushad 'Alī Khān, Raja

Khān, Sayyid Ahmad, *see* Sayyid Ahmad Khān

Khān, Shafaʿāt Ahmad, *see* Shafaʿāt Ahmad Khān

Khān, Sikander Hayāt, *see* Sikander Hayāt Khān

Khilafat Committee, *see* All India Khilafat Committee

Khudā'ī Khidmatgārs, 197
Kimberley, Lord John, 64
Kitchlew, Saifuddin, 183
Krishak Praja Party, 197; coalition with
Muslim League, 199

Labour Party (British), 6; in government,
222
Latīf, 'Abdu'l, Nawab, 85, 87, 96, 98; on
Muslim representation, 86, 92;
familiarity with Mughal culture, 95
Lansdowne, Lord Henry, 71, 72
Laoust, Henri, 30
Lawrence, Henry, 52
Lelyveld, David, 82, 93, 94, 106, 114, 115
Liāquat 'Alī Khān, 47
Liberal Party (British), 50, 59, 65, 102,
121, 122; in government, 52, 58, 80,
119, 124
Linlithgow, Lord Victor, 212, 214, 215
Lucknow, 82, 108
Lucknow Pact, 161, 169–70, 172, 184,
185; Jinnah on, 170, Muslim
opposition to, 170–1
Lyall, Alfred, 64; on Indian society, 68;
on Indian representation, 157; *The
Rise and Expansion of British Dominion
in India*, 68

Macaulay, Thomas, 52
Mackenzie, Alexander, 60
Madanī, Husain Ahmad, Maulānā, on
Muslim nationalism, 202–3
Madras, 50; government of, 63
Mahmood, Tahir, 48
Mahmudabad, Raja of, 159, 164
Mahomedan Literary Society, 85; on
representation, 86, 87, 88, 104; on
partition of Bengal, 127–8
Mahmūd, Sayyid, *see* Sayyid Mahmūd
Maine, Henry, 68, 69
al-Manar, 30, 32
Mashriqī, 'Inayetullāh, 205, 206
Maudūdī, Abū'l A'lā, Maulānā, 28; on
non-Muslims, 43–4; *Islamic Law and
Constitution*, 43
al-Māwardī, 23
Mazdaism, 40
Mecca, 14; Meccans, 38
Medina, 14, 38
Metcalf, Barbara, 1, 81, 93, 118
Mill, James, 68
Mill, John Stuart, 54, 55, 56, 57, 61, 103;
on Indian society, 156
millat (also *millet*), 41, 46, 142, 205; Iqbāl
on, 204; Madanī on, 203; Rahmat 'Alī

on, 206
'Mirrors of Princes', 97
Minault, Gail, 1, 175
Minto, Lord Gilbert, 166; on partition of
Bengal, 128, 135; on 'political
importance' of Muslims, 149–50; on
Simla Deputation, 164; on the Muslim
League, 164
Mohammedan Anglo-Oriental College,
105; *see also* Muslim University
Mohānī, Hasrat, Maulānā, 183; on
Muslim nationhood, 200
Mohsin-ul-Mulk, Nawab, 121, 122,
126, 134, 179; on Caliphate, 178; as
representative of Mughal culture, 234
'Mongol-Mughal', *see* Mughal
Montagu, Lord Edwin, 172, 174
Montagu-Chelmsford Reforms, *see*
Report on Indian Constitutional
Reforms
Morley, Lord John, 124, 152, 156–7, 158;
budget speech of 1906, 121, 122; on
joint electoral college, 148, 157
Mughal ('Mongol-Mughal'), 95, 96, 106,
115, 230, 234; values in Simla
Memorial, 140, 153; political culture, 9,
79, 93, 98; political structures, 106;
traditions of government, 93, 94
Muhammad, the Prophet, 10, 13, 14, 15,
20, 29, 38, 39, 40, 46, 101, 117, 177
Muhammad 'Alī, Maulānā, 134, 147, 154,
168, 183, 234; on separate electorates,
142, 144–5; on defence of the
Caliphate, 179–80; on pan-Islamism,
180
Mujeeb, Muhammad, 1
mujtahid, 32
mullah, 82
Munro, Thomas, 52
Muslim, 'folk theology', 2; political
tradition, 6, 10–48, 96–101, 141–9,
162–4, 209–10; 'political importance'
of, 133–4; representation, see
Representation; separatism, 3, 4, 5, 7,
8, 21, 30, 125–6, 141–54; 'nationlists',
105, 106, 166, 230; nationhood, 30, 194,
198, 200–7; *see also* Islam
Muslims, in India, foreign ancestry of, 79,
115–16; in the Middle East, 21; in
Bengal, 76, 82, 85, 86, 89, 127–8, 130,
133, 160, 186; in Bihar, 76, 87, 89, 133;
in Bombay, 76; in North Western
Provinces, 76, 89; in United Provinces,
130; in North West Frontier Province,
197
Muslim Educational Conference, 135

CAMBRIDGE SOUTH ASIAN STUDIES

These monographs are published by the Syndics of Cambridge University Press in association with the Cambridge University Centre for South Asian Studies. The following books have been published in this series: